COMPUTER PERIPHERALS
THAT YOU CAN BUILD
2ND EDITION
DR. GORDON W. WOLFE

TAB TAB BOOKS Inc.
Blue Ridge Summit, PA 17214

SECOND EDITION
FIRST PRINTING

Library of Congress Cataloging in Publication Data

Wolfe, Gordon W.
Computer peripherals that you can build.

Bibliography: p.
Includes index.
1. Computer input-output equipment—Amateurs'
manuals. I. Title.
TK9969.W64 1986   621.398′4   86-6005
ISBN 0-8306-0749-8
ISBN 0-8306-2749-9 (pbk.)

Contents

Introduction to the Second Edition

Nothing is constant except change. I started working with computers when a high-power mainframe computer was an IBM 1620, with 4K of memory and a megabyte of disk, with no terminals and no timesharing. A lot has changed in twenty years.

The changes in the four and a half years since the first edition of this book was written are just as profound. At that time, the hottest-selling computers on the market were the Apple II and the TRS-80 model 1. There was a rumor that IBM, DEC, and XEROX were going to come out with personal computers and take over the whole market. The TIMEX/SINCLAIR computer has just been introduced, and its price of $100.00 showed that it threatened to be a major force in the industry.

IBM, DEC, and XEROX did indeed come out with personal computers, but only IBM, trading on its name and making some wise marketing decisions, became a major market force. Apple still manufactures the Apple II in many forms and has introduced the Macintosh, which has become the second largest selling computer, after the IBM-PC, on the market. Tandy no longer manufactures the model 1, and has dropped models II and III as well. The model 4 is still manufactured, and the color computer and the PC-clones, the 1000 and 2000, are doing very well. COMPAQ and LEADING EDGE are major market forces with their IBM-compatibles. Essentially, the personal computer market has settled down into three groups: IBM and its look-alikes, Apple, and the others.

This book is being updated with a new edition for just these reasons: the state of the art of personal computers has changed so much that much of the original book was obsolete. Material on the TRS-80 model 1 has been removed, as well as material for the Commodore PET. I have not been able to confirm that there are any manufacturers of S-100 computers still in business at this time, nor any board manufacturers, so all references to S-100 machines have been dropped. There are at least two manufacturers of SS-50 computers, as well as a magazine devoted to those machines (*6800 Micro Journal*), so that type of machine has been retained. Discussion of Apple computers has been expanded to include the Macintosh, while Commodore's references have been changed from the PET to the C-64. The Tandy computers covered in this edition will be the Color Computer, the model 4, and the PC-lookalike, the model 2000. Naturally, the IBM-PC, as well as the XT and AT, and plug-compatibles such as COMPAQ and LEADING EDGE, are covered in detail.

Additional peripherals are being added as well. There is considerable interest in the use of a mouse or a trackball, so discussions of those have been included. I have also included a description of methods of construction of a bar-code reader. There is a short discussion of running serial peripherals from parallel ports, and vice-versa. Lastly, there is a description of the method to add a second or third disk drive to your system at a much reduced cost. Several errors in the first edition have been corrected as well.

One final comment must be made: An author receives a goodly volume of mail about his work. Unlike most authors, I try to answer most of mine. However, by far the majority of the mail I received from the first edition was of the form, "How do I interface peripheral X to computer Y?" One real example was from a gentleman who wanted me to supply him with complete wiring diagrams and assembly listings to connect an Olivetti 791 typewriter to a Sinclair 1000 computer to be used as a letter quality printer. I must confess that I am not an expert, nor do I keep complete schematics around the house of every computer ever made, nor do I know how to program in assembler for more than two computers. I took this request to a friend of mine who is a professional electronics technician and asked him what he would charge to do that connection. He said that, after purchasing the complete schematics for both machines, the hardware part could be done in about 50 hours (at a cost of $25.00 per hour). Total price about $1500.00, with no guarantees that it would work. Note that this does not include programming. As a result, I regret that I will be unable to respond to requests of this type. Also, even my own computer needs have changed with the times. My SWTP 6800, mentioned in the first edition, has been donated to charity, and I'm coming home to an Apple Macintosh after working hard on an IBM mainframe all day.

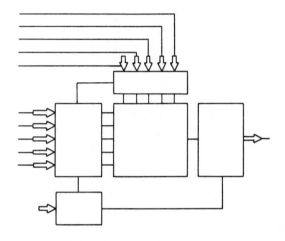

Chapter 1

What Is a Microcomputer?

In 1973, a remarkable thing happened. It is entirely possible that future generations may look back to that date and say, "Modern history begins here." In 1973, the Intel Corporation came out with a new device called a *microprocessor.* This was a large-scale-integration (LSI) integrated circuit (an electronics package containing many thousands of individual components) that was designed to be a *programmable logic device.* Intel called their new marvel the 8008.

Until then, builders of electronic equipment had spent thousands of man-hours designing circuits for the equipment. In the 1930s this involved high-voltage power supplies and hundreds of vacuum tubes. With the invention of the transistor in 1956, designers were able to do away with both high voltage and tubes and go to lower power and smaller packages.

Soon designers found that they were spending a lot of time designing and redesigning the same circuits over and over again for the same purposes. They found that several transistors could be made from the same crystal of silicon and kept on the same package: The *integrated circuit* was born! Soon, an integrated circuit held an entire circuit such as a *gate,* building block of logic design. Gates could then be strung together to form logic devices and create a whole device to do a specific task.

As the task requirements got more and more difficult, designers once more found that they were again and again putting the same configuration of gates together in the same patterns in order to do the same types of jobs. Manufacturers countered by putting more transistors on a chip so that patterns of gates could exist on a single integrated circuit. Thus began medium-scale integration (MSI). For example, why build a clock out of individual gates, flip-flops, and counters—why not build a clock all on one chip?

Large-scale integration, with even more components on a chip, saw the advent of whole chips being designed to do specific jobs, such as counters, clocks, digital voltmeters, memory circuits, television display generators, and the like.

Some bright person at Intel got the idea that, because it's expensive to create a different integrated circuit for each and every new task that comes along, why not make an integrated circuit that can be made to do anything if only you set it up right. It wasn't enough to have a set of output pins on the chip to configure it for various tasks. What you really needed was to have the chips read a set of instructions and perform a set of tasks based on what those instructions said to do. This is the microprocessor.

Everyone started jumping on the bandwagon. Designers worldwide began to see how they could build devices using a microprocessor as the central element. Many other manufacturers began selling their own versions of the microprocessor. At this writing, Intel has all but dropped the 8008, concentrating on the 8080, and has just released the 8086 and 8085. Zilog developed the Z-80, which used the same set of instructions as the 8080, but was faster, easier to use, and had a wider variety of instructions. Motorola brought out the 6800 family of microprocessors and also marketed the 6502. RCA manufactures the 1802. There are several others as well.

More recently, later generations of processors have begun to concentrate on the wider parallel-processing ranges: The Motorola 6809 is a processor that has 8-bit data lines and 8-bit registers, but has a set of registers that can handle 16-bit data all at once. The Intel 8088 processor used in the IBM-PC also has 8-bit data lines, but all its registers are 16- or 20-bit registers. The newest generation of microprocessor chips, such as the Motorola 68000 and the Intel 80186 all have 16-bit data lines, and 32-bit registers, and the 68020 and 80286 are 32-bit by 32-bit chips, just like many mainframe processors.

Microprocessors started showing up everywhere. One automatic manufacturer began installing microprocessors in its cars to monitor fuel/air mixtures, among other things.

Two unforeseen things happened to change the course of electronic history. Surprisingly, both led to the same final conclusion. The first was that manufacturers of electronic devices were delighted to find that product-design times went from thousands of hours to only a few dozen hours. At the same time they were horrified to discover that their technicians and engineers were still spending thousands of hours on product development—only this time they were spending all the time trying to *program* the device to do what they wanted! Many of the technicians had never done any programming before and were trying to figure out programming methods while designing the product. The answer to this was, of course, to develop the *microprocessor trainer*, a small microprocessor with some memory and readouts upon which the technician could learn the programming language of the microprocessor.

The second development was even more significant as far as you are concerned. The MITS company of Albuquerque, New Mexico, which had been a manufacturer of teaching and scientific instruments, developed a product called the AL-TAIR. It was designed to be a small, home-built computer programmable in machine language only and readable only by a set of lights on the front panel. This might have gone by the wayside were it not for two facts: First, it was expandable. Inside the case there were slots for adding more components, such as memory and *peripheral interfaces.* Second, and more important, the computer kit was described in *Popular Electronics.* This magazine appeals to the home electronics hobbyist. MITS was overwhelmed by the large number of letters and phone calls asking for information about the computer and placing orders for it.

MITS had used the microprocessor as the central processing unit in a computer, thereby inventing the *microcomputer.* It became a small device which had the computing power (if not the size and total storage capabilities) of a large IBM mainframe computer. Suddenly everyone wanted one. People who had been hounding surplus dealers for scrapped PDP-8s were now able to build and own their own computer. Hobbyists discovered microprocessor trainers, which were, in effect, small computers themselves. The age was born.

BUS-TYPE COMPUTERS

The ALTAIR computer was significant, not only because it was the first computer for public use, but also because it was a *bus-type* computer. It has a number of plugboard slots on a *motherboard,* which takes signals from one plug-in circuit board to another plug-in circuit board. The lines of conductor that travel along the motherboard from one board to another are called *bus lines.* The idea of a bus is significant because it allows the computer to be expandable. As your needs change, you can change the computer by simply adding more circuit cards to the plug-in slots. The original ALTAIR came with a motherboard and power supply, a front panel for data input by switches and data output by flashing lights, a plug-in card containing a microprocessor and some support circuitry to make it work as a computer, and a plug-in card with a very small amount of memory (128 bytes). It used an 8080 processor.

Two other bus-type computers were developed within a year. One was the IMSAI, which used the same bus structure as the ALTAIR (and the same processor) but was specifically designed to be expandable. The power supply was huge compared to the ALTAIR's, so more boards could be plugged in. Also, it had more slots available for future use. The important advantage was that it was designed to be *compatible* with the ALTAIR. IMSAI boards would fit in the ALTAIR, and vice versa. Programs for one would run on the other. This was the birth of the S-100 bus.

The other bus-type computer marketed at the same time as the IMSAI was developed by Southwest Technical Products Corporation (SWTP) of San Antonio, Texas. It broke with tradition and used the Motorola 6800 processor. It developed a whole *new* bus structure, completely different from the 100-line S-100 bus of the 8080. Since it had only 50 lines, it was deemed the SS-50. SWTP captured a large part of the microcomputer market by offering more memory (about 16 times as much as the ALTAIR), doing away with programming switches and lights on the front panel, and putting into permanent memory a *monitor* which would allow input to the computer and printout via a teletypewriter or video terminal. In addition, they began selling their programs for ridiculously low prices. ($5.00 for a BASIC interpreter), and that

their computer sold for less than either the AL-TAIR or IMSAI, and the race was on! Several other manufacturers, caught by SWTP's low prices, began manufacturing plug-in boards for this bus or offering programs for this computer.

As an aside, it is interesting to note that at this writing, there are hundreds of S-100 and SS-50 bus manufacturers marketing circuit boards, but AL-TAIR and IMSAI are no longer manufactured, while SWTP is still going strong. The reasons have to do more with business management than the quality or desirability of the products, though.

SINGLE-BOARD COMPUTERS

While the bus-type computers were very versatile, a minimum system to begin computing was quite expensive, more than $1,000 in 1977. Many people thought that they should be able to get into personal computing for a lot less than that. Many of them turned to microprocessor trainers. Still others began manufacturing a minimum computer system on a single circuit board. IMSAI manufactured one for a short time. RCA got into this market with the COSMAC ELF. It was the KIM-1 computer, and more importantly, the Apple computer that essentially captured this market.

(We are speaking here of the original Apple I computer, which was a single-board computer, and not the more famous Apple II. The Apple I had 1K of on-board memory and a video interface, but the user was required to supply the power supply, keyboard, and cassette player.)

The KIM and the Apple were self-contained. There was no fancy (expensive) case with blinking lights, just a processor, some memory (usually 1024 bytes), a monitor, and a hexadecimal keyboard and display. The Apple had its own video-display circuitry to be hooked up to a TV set for readout and a connector for a keyboard. Both could be connected to a small cassette recorder for permanent storage of programs. The total price was somewhere around $650.00.

The savings was substantial, but there was one drawback: they were not easily expandable. The bus was still there, but it took some work to be able to use it.

DESKTOP COMPUTERS

In 1978, another step forward was taken for the home user of computers. Until this time, the home computer had required some knowledge of computer systems or electronics on the part of the user. Single-board computers frequently had to have power supplies constructed and added. The boards for the plug-in computers had to be addressed and configured.

Then the Tandy Corporation did what others had been planning for some time—they marketed the desktop computer. For the first time, no knowledge of computer systems or electronics was required of the user. There was nothing to assemble or wire: Just take it out of the box, plug it in, and turn it on. Tandy was selling the TRS-80, a Z-80 processor-based home microcomputer. It was destined to outsell all other computer manufacturers *combined.* Not only was the hardware insignificant to the user in that he didn't have to do anything but type on the keyboard, but the days of programming it in machine language were also gone. The TRS-80 had its own built-in BASIC interpreter, which was available for the user from the minute the computer was turned on.

Other manufacturers soon followed suit. Commodore put out the PET, which used a 6502 processor, and Apple came out with the Apple II. Instead of a single-board computer, it was now a fully self-contained desktop unit, with all the features of the TRS-80 (and then some). Furthermore, there was provision for expansion of the computer with a peripheral bus in the back! In all cases, the user did his programming in BASIC, graphics (drawing of pictures on the screen) were available, there was instant cassette storage, and provision had been made for some peripherals—such as disk drives, printers, and telephone connections—to be added later. The *expansion port* became the key to more capability of the computer. In fact, what the expansion port really is, is the computer's bus brought out to a connector so that more "boards" may be plugged into it.

Then a thing happened which legitimized the microcomputer as a professional business tool: The giant among all computer companies, IBM, entered the personal computer market with its "Personal Computer," or simply PC. It offered a 16-bit processor; that is, it could process 16 bits of information at a time. The computers discussed above could only process 8 bits of information at a time. While IBM was not the first to offer a 16-bit computer (the Radio Shack Color Computer was the first widely-sold machine to do so, but Tandy never exploited this fact in its advertisements, for some reason). The fact that the giant had taken the initiative to do so spurred a new "war" in the personal computer power and speed game. For the first time, memory sizes over 64K became commonplace. Probably the most important happening in this development of personal computers was the fact that IBM gave its blessing to the personal computer and brought all of its marketing, financial, and repair network skill to bear on the sale and support of its machines. Other major manufacturers of mainframes, such as DEC and Sperry, also brought out personal computers.

Another important aspect of the arrival of major personal computers was that, with large memory sizes, the *Disk Operating System* became an integral feature of the computer. Instead of operating from cassette tapes, virtually all programs operated from disk. Coupled with the larger memory size, this meant programs could be more complex, performing more sophisticated functions.

In 1984, Apple Computer Corporation brought the Macintosh computer to the personal computer market. This computer was the successor to its "Lisa," which never sold well, probably due to its high price. The Macintosh was a 32-bit machine, surpassing in raw computing power all previous machines. The important aspect of the Macintosh will probably be seen by historians to be its unique "user interface," which does not require the user to learn any complex command syntax or lists of commands. Apple boasts that half of the owners of the Macintosh have never opened the users manual. Its use should be completely intuitive.

This book shows you how to tie into that expansion port in your desktop computer, or into the bus of your bus-type computer, and add additional capabilities to your computer.

COMPARISONS TO LARGER COMPUTERS

There is really very little difference between the microcomputer and its larger cousins, the minicomputer and the standard mainframe. The differences are only two: physical size and word size.

Until about ten years ago, a "computer" was a behemoth manufactured by IBM, or Honeywell, or Control Data Corporation. A computer filled up a room and took a large staff of experts to run. The popular idea of a computer was several large racks full of blinking lights and spinning tape drives. The minicomputer of ten years ago did little to change that concept beyond shrinking the size of the machine to the size of a refrigerator. Microcomputers today tend to be about the size of a television set or a sewing machine. Prices are commensurate with size.

Until a few years ago, it was easy to differentiate between microcomputers, minicomputers, and mainframe computers. A micro used an 8-bit *data word* (how many "bits" the computer could process simultaneously), a mini used a 16-bit word, and a mainframe used a 32-bit word. We have already seen above that the Macintosh has a 32-bit data word. Does that make it a mainframe computer? Hardly.

It is difficult to pin down the exact difference between these three basic types of computers. Especially when the field is confused by terms such as "supermini" and "supercomputer." (Example: the CRAY-2 is reputed to be able to process a 64-bit word 100 *billion* times a second! Cray Research Corporation markets a "supercomputer.") The IBM 4361 processes a 64-bit word at 1.5 million instructions per second, and is sold as a "supermini," but is probably really a medium-sized mainframe.

For the benefit of those who are dying of curiosity, this author will do his best to find a definition of the difference between a micro, a mini, and a mainframe: A microcomputer uses a microprocessor, will usually fit on a desktop, and (with a few exceptions) is a single-user, single-task machine. That is, one user can operate it at a time, and can only do one thing at a time. A minicomputer is usually floor-standing, always has at least a 16-bit word (superminis at least 32), can support multiple users, and uses the processor for most of the I/O work along a single (or double) output bus. Each user can do one task at a time. The mainframe always has a 32- or 64-bit word, is floor-standing, allows the user to handle multiple tasks simultaneously, can support many users at a time, and distributes its processing and I/O tasks among several "slave" processors, called either "channels" or "control units" or "coprocessors" depending on their function. Whereas a mini may have one or two output "busses," the mainframe may have multiple (as many as 16) output "channels" to direct data to disk drives, tape drives, terminals, printers, and so on.

A *bit* is a single on-off state in a computer. Eight bits together form a *byte* (note: four bits together are a *nybble*). A byte is a convenient size to process because it can represent a binary number from 0 to 255, any one of 128 letters or characters, or one of 256 data instructions. Note that a minicomputer processes two bytes at a time; a mainframe processes four, and a micro, only one. It is said that a micro has a one-byte *word,* a mini has a two-byte word, and a mainframe has a four-byte word. (Chapter 2 discusses bits, bytes, and words further.)

Some people say that the real difference between a microcomputer and the others is that a microcomputer uses a microprocessor as the central processing unit. This is not necessarily so. The Digital Equipment Corporation PDP-11 minicomputer uses a 16-bit microprocessor called the LSI-11. There are several other 16-bit microprocessors on the market.

Physical size is no guarantee that the computer is a mini or a micro, either. *All* computers have the capability of adding more memory or more peripheral equipment. (That's what this book is all about.) A microcomputer can interface with a 9-channel magnetic tape drive just as easily as a mainframe can. Hard disk drives are already common on many microcomputers. Basically, a general rule that the microcomputer enthusiast should not forget is *a microcomputer can do anything any larger computer can do.* It may take it a little more time, but it can be done, subject only to sufficient memory and the operator's willingness to interface more equipment to it. Most peripherals that will work with a mainframe will also work with a micro (with the right interfacing).

STRUCTURE OF MICROCOMPUTERS

All computers (including microcomputers) have the same basic internal structure. They all have a processing unit (in this case the microprocessor), memory for both permanent and temporary storage of data or instructions, and a means of sending data to or receiving it from some other device. (It has to get the data from some place and do something with it when it's done.) Figure 1-1 is a general illustration of a computer.

The central portion of the microcomputer is the microprocessor, which acts as a central processing unit. It requires a source of power and clock pulses (which in effect tell it when to execute the next instruction). As far as the computer as a whole is concerned, it acts by itself as a *bus driver*. Connected to the bus driven by the CPU are the various memory locations and input/output registers. These supply data to the bus, store data from the bus, or take data from the bus and deliver it to an outside device, called a *peripheral*. It is the delivery of information to and from these peripherals via the data bus that we are concerned with in this book.

Every microcomputer has three busses. They generally run side-by-side, so we can talk about the "computer's bus," but it is in reality three different busses. The first of these is the *data bus*. In a microprocessor system this is usually eight lines, sixteen, or thirty-two that can carry data in either direction, either from the microprocessor to the addressed device, or from the device to the microprocessor. Some busses, such as the S-100 bus, have two single direction data busses. This increases the complexity of the system slightly, as you will need bus drivers for each of the busses and

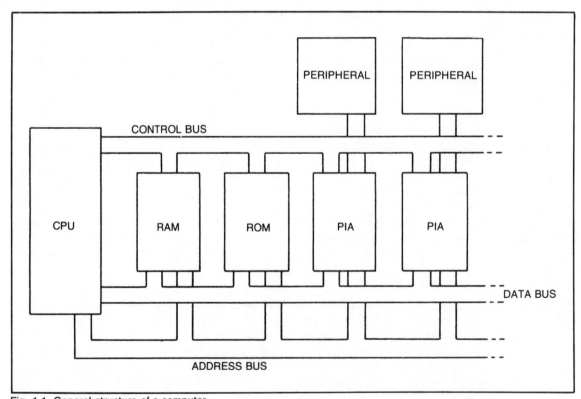

Fig. 1-1. General structure of a computer.

logical systems to tell when each of the busses needs to be used. In most systems, there exists only a single bidirectional data bus of eight lines, with only one "transmitter" and one "receiver" active on the bus at a time. (More is given in Chapter 2 in the discussion on three-state buffers and bus logic.)

The second of the busses is the *address bus.* Most microprocessors use a sixteen-line address bus, although some use only an eight-line bus. Still others use eight lines as a data bus sometimes, and the same eight lines as part of the address bus. The Motorola 6809 does this. Since each of the address-bus lines can be in either a high ($+5$ V) or a low (0 V) state at any time, there are 2^{16} possible combinations of high-and-low on the address bus. This means that 65,536 possible *addresses,* or memory locations, may be accessed by the processor. Each memory location is a spot that contains, can take, or can supply eight data bits to or from the data bus. This is the *memory* of the computer. It will be very useful to you if you have a *memory map* of your computer. This tells you where in memory (at what values of the address bus) your readable memory and input/output devices are. It will be indispensable for interfacing to peripheral devices. (See Chapter 2 on address decoding for more on memory maps.)

There are some that use a 20-line bus, others that use a 24-line bus. The Motorola 68020 shares 32 lines of its address bus with 32 lines of its data bus. With 16 address lines, you can address 65,536 bytes of memory; with 20 you can address over a million. 32 bits gives you the capability to directly address more than 2 *billion* bytes of memory! (Certainly more than you could afford at today's prices—but we were saying that about 64K of memory only eight years ago.)

An interesting little "trick" that has been used to expand addressability in many computers is the use of the Dynamic Address Translator, or DAT. This is just a memory manager circuit that adds an additional four or eight lines to the address bus. It takes up a few bytes of memory in each "bank" of 64K, and software writes into it the "address" of the "bank" that it wants to access. You can have

16 lines of "actual" address (64K), with a byte or two controlling four more (16 times 64K, or 16 "banks" of 64K, for a full megabyte!). Even the addition of one line doubles your memory capability. This trick is used on several popular machines whose processors do not have the direct addressing capability, but whose manufacturers wanted to expand the memory size of their machine.

The third bus may be the most important of the three. It is the *control bus.* It essentially tells the other busses how and when to work. The control bus is usually 10 to 12 lines (although it may be many more, as in the S-100 bus) which tell the external components on the bus what the microprocessor wants from them. Types of signals will vary from one microprocessor to the next, but generally there will be signals such as the system clock, ground line, power lines, signals to tell the memory locations that a memory address is being looked for, signals to tell the memory whether the present operation is a read or a write operation, interrupt-request lines, requests for the processor to halt for a DMA (*direct memory access*) operation by a peripheral, confirmation by the processor that it's okay to go ahead with DMA, a signal to reset the whole system, and the like. Some busses use a line to let the memory location know that the present operation is an input/output operation, while others will use separate lines to inform the memory of read and write operations. Still others, such as the SS-50 bus, keep the serial-data-rate clock signals on the bus. Most will have at least two separate interrupt lines, maskable and non-maskable, while others will have interrupt-priority vectors. The whole thing can get quite complicated. If you are going to be interfacing to the bus, you really need to know what all those bus lines do and what their signals mean.

THE CENTRAL PROCESSING UNIT

The central processing unit has come to mean the microprocessor itself. That is, it means the LSI integrated circuit that performs the logical and arithmetic functions. However, it is actually more than that. It also includes the bus driver/buffers, the system clock, the reset functions, and the like.

A microprocessor cannot function by itself; it needs some *support hardware*, just as it needs a certain minimum amount of memory to perform basic tasks.

First, though, what is a microprocessor and how does it work? Broadly, it is a programmable logic device that can obtain and execute instructions. That is, the function or logical operation that the device accomplishes may be altered by supplying additional data at its inputs. By the execution of these instructions, the microprocessor can cause the rest of the microcomputer to do the following:

1. It can input and output data in digital form. The data can be numbers, characters, or control codes. This data can be exchanged between and among the microprocessor and several peripheral devices, such as memory, printers, video displays, paper tape readers, disk memories, cassette tapes, and laboratory instruments.

2. It contains an arithmetic logic unit (ALU) which can perform arithmetic or logical operations such as add, subtract, compare, store, shift the data, perform logical AND, perform logical OR, take the complement of.

3. It can take any data from its interior and send it to a specific memory location, where it may be stored or sent to a peripheral device.

4. It is programmable; that is, it can have its function changed externally by allowing the memory to contain different instructions. Data and instructions may be arranged in any order, in contrast to a programmable calculator, in which data goes into data registers and instructions go into instruction registers.

You might ask how does a microprocessor work? It is not strictly necessary to know how it works to be able to use it, just as it is not necessary to know how a television set works to be able to watch the news. Perhaps it might be instructive to give a general description of the interior:

Figure 1-2 gives a block diagram on the interior of the Motorola 6800 processor. Notice that the insides seem to be filled with *registers*. A register is a place for temporary storage of data. All a microprocessor does is move data from one register to another or modify the data existing in a register.

As an example of how a processor works, let's take the following three instructions of 6800 code and work through them step-by-step to see what is really happening in the microprocessor.

B6 01 07	LDA A $0107	Load register A with the contents of the memory location whose address is 0107 (hexadecimal).
8B 06	ADD A #$06	Add 6 to what is in A.
08	INX	Increment the index register by 1.
B7 00	STA A 0,X	Store register A in the memory location given by the value in the index register.

The way the processor will do it is this:

LDAA $0107   Increment the program counter. Put the value of the program counter into the Address register. Send a "read memory" request, and get the information from the data register. Increment the program counter. Put the value of the program counter into the address register. Put out a "read memory" request, and get the information from the data register. Put the two bytes of data just received into the address register. Send a "read memory" request, and get the data from the data register. Put the data from the data register into accumulator A.

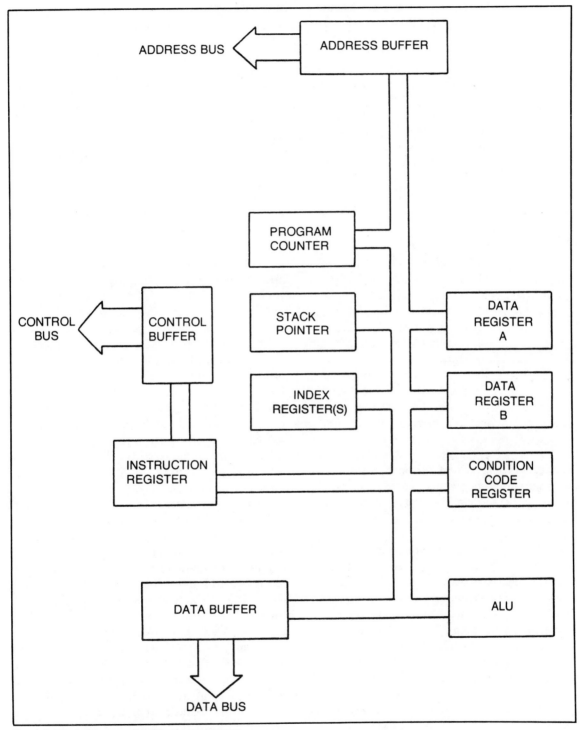

Fig. 1-2. Block diagram of 6800 microprocessor.

Increment the program counter and get the next instruction from memory.

ADDA #$06   Increment the program counter. Place the contents of the program counter into the address register. Send a "read memory" request and wait for data from the data register. Add the contents of the data register to the A register. Increment the program counter and get the next instruction.

INX   Add one to the index register. Increment the program counter and get the next instruction.

STAA 0,X   Place the index register into the address register. Place register A into the data register. Increment the program counter. Send a "write data" request. Increment the program counter and get the next instruction.

The act of getting the next instruction involves placing the program counter onto the address register, sending a "read data" request, getting the data from the data register, and placing it in the instruction register.

All this seems like an awful lot of work, but it only takes 17 machine cycles, which is about 17 microseconds. Note that all that is happening is the data is being moved around from one register to another or is being modified while in a register. It is the control-bus signals that tell the rest of the computer what to do. The address register is connected to the address bus, and the data register is connected to the data bus.

Please note also, that a location in memory may contain either data or instructions. The machine can execute an instruction to get an instruction from a specific location in memory, and that instruction may tell it to work on some data at another memory address. The data itself may consist of a number in any of several formats. It may be a character in any of several formats which may, for example, be part of a letter that is being written on the computer keyboard (to be printed later on a typewriter), or it may be some condition code that is meaningful only in the context of the particular program being run at the time (such as, if this location contains a one, print the results on the printer, if it is zero, put the results on the video display).

I mentioned above that the address and data registers were connected directly to the address and data busses. When a read or write is commanded from the CPU, that is meant to state that "an address is on the address line—look at it, and if you are the address in question, read (or write) data from (to) the data bus." The problem with most microprocessors is that they are usually rather low-power devices. These low-power devices have to interface to many chips, sometimes dozens or scores, that read the information on them. This process is called *fanout*. Microprocessors are capable of delivering what is called "one TTL load," which is a way of saying that they can interface to one TTL integrated circuit without affecting either the voltage or current characteristics of the output. Once you try to interface the microprocessor to several chips, which are all likely to be TTL integrated circuits, you have trouble.

That is why there are special integrated circuits called *bus drivers* that take the "one TTL load" for the microprocessor and increase the capability of its bus lines. Some of these integrated circuits are capable of driving a total of 30 TTL loads, or of having 30 TTL integrated circuits "listening in" on the bus. If you need more than 30, just space the drivers down the bus every so often. For address-bus lines, the bus drivers need to work only in one direction. The microprocessor tells, via the address bus, what address is to be accessed. For data-bus lines, depending on the type of bus, you may need bidirectional drivers, that is, drivers which will send information either to or from the processor.

MEMORY

The very concept of the data processor, which executes one instruction after another, assumes that the instructions and the data upon which to work are stored in a place that the processor can get to easily. Earlier I talked about the continuous fetch and execute cycle. The CPU is continually fetching instructions and then executing them on data, both of which are brought in from external memory. This important concept of the CPU relying on memory cannot be overstressed. The CPU is a very important and powerful part of a microcomputer, but it cannot work without memory. The CPU needs to be told what to do, when to do it, and what to do it with. The arrangement of instructions in the memory is the *software,* or the computer program.The instructions or data are entered into memory, not by the CPU, but by the computer programmer. The CPU can only interpret and carry out these instructions and act upon the data in memory. The CPU does *not* contain the instructions or data, but only looks for them in memory.

How does the computer know what part of the memory to look for its instructions in? The arrangements of highs and lows on the address bus, as well as control signals that tell the computer that the CPU is looking for a specific memory location, tells the computer memory that a fetch or write cycle is being processed. Each individual memory location asks itself, "is it me?"—"is it me?"—"is it me?" Only the one that corresponds to the same patterns of highs and lows can answer, "YES!—It's me!" and will either place its contents on the data bus, or change its contents to correspond to what is on the data bus. The "Is it me"—"yes, It's me" cycle is *memory address decoding*, and the whole process is called a *memory read/write cycle.*

Note that with 16 data lines, there are 2^{16} possible memory locations, or 65,536 possible data bytes in memory. Each group of 1024 (2^{10}) is called a K of memory (K is electronic shorthand for 1000, and 1024 is close) so a microprocessor is capable of 64K possible memory addresses by direct addressing from the processor. Also note that any data location may be accessed independent of what data location was accessed before it, so the process is

called *random-access-memory* (RAM).

When computers were first built, memory was a series of mechanical relays. My first experience with computers was on an aging Bendix G-15, which used about 10,000 12AX7 vacuum tubes for the processor and a rotating drum of magnetic material for all of 2K of memory. To a 15-year-old boy in 1963, it was glorious!

A decade ago, computer memory meant one thing: magnetic core. Memory was stored in magnetic fields on little doughnut-shaped beads. It was advantageous because when the power was turned off, the magnetism didn't go away, so the program and data were still there when the power came back on. But it was expensive, as each bead had to be strung onto four wires by hand.

As semiconductor technology advanced, memory became available in silicon chips, first as small 256-bit chips, then upward until today when 64K chips are common. Today, only the largest and oldest of computers are still using core memory. There are two basic types of semiconductor memory, RAM and ROM (*read-only memory*).

Figure 1-3 shows the internal structure of the 2102 memory chip, which is arranged as a 1K array of single data bits. Eight of these circuits are required to make up 1K of memory, one for each data bit. Essentially the working is as follows: There are ten address lines, which correspond to the least significant of the sixteen address lines of the address bus. There is also a *chip enable* input, which is activated whenever the accompanying circuitry detects that the most significant six of the sixteen address lines of the bus correspond to the correct address for that chip, and that the "access memory" control-line is active. Only when *all* of these conditions have been met will the chip respond to a read or write command. The read/write line tells the chip what operation to perform—read from or write to the data bus.

Such a discussion is important because most peripherals are treated the same as a memory address in memory with interfacing chips requiring similar signals, decoding, and structure: "Activate the data bus when the address lines have this pattern and when the control bus has this pattern."

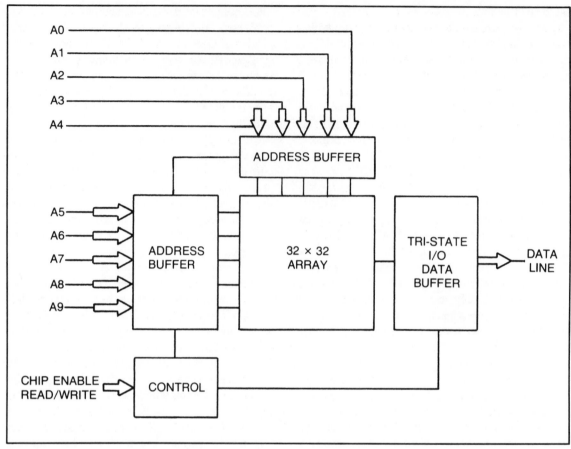

Fig. 1-3. Internal structure of 2102 RAM chip.

The 2102 is rather obsolete, now, but it is still a mainstay of many computer systems. It is an example of the type of memory which has come to be called RAM (for random-access memory) as opposed to ROM (for read-only memory). Actually, RAM is a misnomer—both RAM and ROM can be accessed randomly. RAM should be called read-write memory because it can be read from or written to by the processor. But RWM is hard to say, where the acronym RAM is easy.

There are two types of RAM, static and dynamic. Since this is a manual on computer interfacing, we need not go into detail about the two types. Suffice it to say that dynamic memory must be *refreshed* by continually accessing it, whereas static memory does not—once that data is in there, it stays until it is changed or the power goes off.

Needless to say, static memory is more expensive than dynamic.

In the early years of personal computing, dynamic memory was not well understood by design people, and had problems with "forgetting" what it had stored. Manufacturers advertised that their machine had only static memory in it. Nowadays, engineers have dynamic memory refresh techniques down to a fine science, and since more memory cells can be put on a chip with dynamic memory than static memory, it has become the standard of the industry. Fortunately for us, most interfacing chips to peripherals act more like static memory. This makes the interfacing job a whole lot easier, because refresh circuits tend to be complicated.

The important thing to remember about RAM is that it is read/write memory. That is, you can either read from it or write to it, to use it for temporary working storage of data or programs. Often times a manufacturer will push his product by telling you in his advertisements that it has 64K of memory, or 512K of memory. This is the amount of memory that is available for you to put programs or data into. But you must be careful, because they don't tell you that even though your computer has 128K of memory, 78K of that is used for the operating system, and another 40K is used for the word processor program, leaving only 10K for your own work. The more sophisticated the program, the more memory it is going to take up in your machine.

Another problem with RAM is that it is *volatile,* meaning that the memory will forget everything in it when the power is turned off. You may have spent hours putting in a program that takes up 8K of memory, only to have your efforts wiped out when you hit the off switch. (This is one of the reasons for mass storage, like cassettes or disk. Once the program is in, save it, and you don't have to enter it again.)

Early microcomputers, such as the ALTAIR, had a "front panel," an array of switches and lights that connected directly to the bus. The lights showed the current value on the address bus, for example. You could enter data to memory directly through the switches without going through the microprocessor. This was a big advantage at the time, because early microcomputers did not have a keyboard or video display. You had to buy an expensive interface and a terminal to be able to communicate with the computer. Even then, in order to tell the computer that there *was* an interface it could use, you had to spend time keying in, through the switches, a "loader" program to tell the computer to read a paper tape to get a program called a *monitor,* which told the computer how to communicate with the terminal. The whole start-up procedure could take twenty minutes or more.

How much more convenient it would be if only the monitor program was already inside the computer in non-volatile memory, so that it would be there, up and running, as soon as the power came on. Note that in today's desktop computers, the machine is ready to use BASIC as soon as the power comes on.

The solution is to replace part of the RAM with a different kind of random-access memory, called read-only memory, or ROM. ROM never forgets what's in it, even with loss of power. In fact, it won't change its contents, even if you ask it to with a write command! It is *read-only.* There are several types, including mask-programmed, or field-programmed. Most computers have a *reset vector,* so that whenever the "reset" button is pushed, the computer goes to a certain address and executes the instruction found there. It is easy to arrange it so that the reset vector is addressed whenever the power comes on, and that the reset vector points to the beginning of the monitor program so that the monitor program comes up with the power. *Any* program can be used as a monitor or can be accessed through reset.

The only problem with ROM is that, once it's in the machine, you can't change the contents. With mask-programmed ROM, if you want to change the program, you throw the ROM chip away and order a new one from the manufacturer, one programmed to your specifications. With others, you may have to re-program the chip using a machine called a programmer. A machine for erasing and programming the types of ROMs which lend themselves to erasing and reprogramming can cost hundreds of dollars.

Mask-programmed ROM is a memory chip whose storage cells are designed by the manufacturer to permanently store a 1 or a 0 by selectively building 1 or 0 generating cells into the array at predefined memory locations. Once built, it cannot be changed. Mask-programmed ROMs are very reliable, permanent, and (in large quantities) cheap. Since the set-up charge can run a thousand dollars or more, they are not practical for single-use applications.

ROMs that can be programmed by the user are available as well. One type is the PROM, or *programmable read-only memory.* In this type, small strings of metal are set up inside the chip, which correspond to a "1" at the outputs. By the application of a high voltage at the "program" input, while accessing a particular address, the small string of metal can be made to melt like a fuse blowing and become a "0." At a future date, if you find the program is wrong or out of date, you can always change a "1" to a "0," but never a "0" to a "1." In the latter case, the PROM must be thrown away, and a new one programmed. PROMs are quite inexpensive and need little circuitry to program them or to read them—they work just like a RAM chip. Their only drawback is that not many memory cells can be placed on a chip. The typical size is 64 bytes of 8-bit words. It takes a lot of PROM chips to make 4K of memory.

Most popular among microcomputers is the EPROM. This is an *erasable-programmable read-only memory*. The user can erase and re-program the read-only memory as required. Instead of fusible links, programming places a charge at the gate of a field-effect transistor, which will then either conduct or not depending on the charge, resulting in either a "0" or a "1." The memory chip may be erased by exposure to strong ultraviolet light. The charge will stay on the gate until erased or until it leaks off, which can take as long as ten years. The programming circuitry is rather complex, requiring accurate timing and high voltages. These chips are popular because they *can* be altered, and because they are rather high density. The obsolete 1702A holds 256 8-bit bytes, and the popular 2708 will hold 1024 8-bit bytes. EPROMs are available that will hold 4K of memory in one chip. Their major drawbacks are that they are rather expensive— about $2.00 per 256 bytes—and that exposure to strong sunlight or a sunlamp will erase them. Also, the programmer tends to be expensive.

There are several other types just entering the market, such as the Electrically Alterable Read-only Memory, which can be erased by an "erase" signal, and the magnetic bubble memory, which retains its information (like ROM) with power off but can be written to like RAM.

ROMs, like RAMS, have addressing inputs, data outputs, and chip-select inputs, so they can be used just like static RAM. Just remember—any location that contains ROM cannot contain RAM for your programs. This is usually not a problem, because most programs only use about 16K of memory, while there is 64K of space available.

I mentioned cassette storage and disks above.

It is impractical to store all the programs that one could conceivably use in RAM all at once. In the first place, they wouldn't fit! Editors, Assemblers, BASIC interpreters, Compilers, word processors, and *disk-operating-systems* (DOS) all take up a certain amount of memory. Early DOS systems took 4K to 8K each. The Macintosh FINDER DOS version 4.1 takes up 47K. The driver for the Imagewriter printer in the Mac takes 25K. The word editor program MACWRITE v. 4.5 takes 102K! This is a lot of memory usage in a machine whose smallest version is only 128K. The author recalls the time he wrote a complete cassette-based text editor in only 470 bytes, less than 1/2 a K!

Then, the programs or data they work on take even more. Since usually only one systems program and one data set or user program is required at a time, it is convenient to store the unused programs someplace else until they are needed. This is called *mass storage* and is usually much slower to access than RAM or ROM. While a program may take 16K in RAM, the computer sees the mass storage device as only a few bytes of memory, because it is continually writing information into one address and telling another address where to put it. Examples of mass storage devices are cassette storage, disk drives, and magnetic tape. These are *serial* devices in that only one data byte at a time can be written or read, and they must be written or read in a specific order.

Mass storage devices are, actually, peripherals. Data is read to and from them just like any other peripheral. They are slow but only take up a few bytes of memory space.

Because RAM, ROM, and peripherals all act like memory locations, it is important to know what memory addresses correspond to each of the blocks of RAM and ROM, and where the peripheral addresses can be so as not to interfere with RAM and ROM. This is the importance of the memory map.

PERIPHERALS

A peripheral is any device that is controlled by the CPU, receives data from the CPU, or sends data to the CPU, and is not RAM or ROM. One example of a peripheral is mass storage. Other examples are printers, keyboards, terminals, graphics display, plotters, joysticks, controllers, music and sound generators, speech-recognition circuits, voltage-measuring devices. There are many, many, more.

Each peripheral does not connect directly to the data and address busses. It requires an *interface* circuit. Depending on the type of peripheral to be interfaced, and the type of data it will be processing, this interface circuit can be as simple as a single integrated circuit, or quite complicated. Whole books have been written about interfacing of computers, and a few are listed in the Bibliography.

Microcomputer interfacing, a whole art in itself, has traditionally been the art of designing complex boards of logic maintaining the data transfer and synchronization signals necessary for the processor to communicate with an external device. Large-scale-integration of circuits on single chips has resulted in making the interfacer's job much easier. A complete interface board, today, is shrunk to only a few LSI chips and some support circuitry.

There are three basic ways of interfacing a peripheral to a computer. Only one of these ways treats the peripheral interface as a memory location.

The first of these is *memory-mapped input/output* (I/O). In this method, the interface circuit is treated as a location in addressable memory, and the device is accessed just as if it were a RAM location. Memory-type instructions, such as STORE and LOAD, are used to send data to the peripheral, or to read data from it. In addition, besides the data input and output registers in the peripheral interface, there are usually memory locations reserved for control registers, which can turn the peripheral on or off or let the computer know that the peripheral is not ready yet for a data transfer.

The advantage of memory-mapped I/O is that the same powerful instructions that are used with memory can be used for data transfers. There are usually many more memory instructions than there are input/output instructions. Furthermore, arithmetic and logical operations can be performed directly on the peripheral-interface data registers,

without having to shift the information into the CPU registers first. The disadvantage is that, for every memory location used as an I/O port, there is one less memory location that can be used for RAM or ROM. Thus, if all 65,536 addresses are needed for RAM or ROM, memory-mapped I/O should not be used. Clearly, this will be the case only rarely in a microcomputer system. Also, memory-mapped instructions may take longer to execute than I/O instructions because of the need for extra address bytes in the instructions, or because of extra software needed to perform the operation.

In *I/O-mapped input/output,* the processor sends signals indicating that the present cycle is for input or output only, and not for memory. Two special control-bus lines are provided for this purpose—for I/O read and for I/O write. When I/O mapping is used, only the lowest-significant eight address lines are used, since most computers will not need very many I/O ports. In effect, this gives you 65,536 memory locations *and* 256 I/O ports. But since it requires two additional control pins on the microprocessor chip, the technique is generally not used, except with systems that are compatible with the 8080 or Z-80 processors. The 6800 and 6502 processors do not have these special control pins, nor do they have the special I/O instructions that go with them, so I/O mapping cannot be used with these processors. Note that with I/O mapped output, the most significant eight lines of the address bus are simply not used.

The last type of peripheral interfacing to be discussed is *direct memory access,* or DMA. With DMA, the processor has nothing to do with the data transfer sequence at all. The peripheral sends a HALT command to the processor, and the processor completes the current instruction and then cuts itself loose electrically from the data, address, and control busses. The peripheral then has free access to the bus and can store its information directly into memory without having to go through the processor. This type of peripheral data exchange is the fastest and most sophisticated of all the data transfer types. However, the peripheral has to know exactly where in memory to store its data. In the case of a single data byte, the peripheral could be set up to always send the data to a specific location in memory. If the peripheral has several data bytes to send to memory, then somehow the peripheral must know that "this one goes here, the next one goes in the next slot, and so on . . ." This procedure requires a rather complex set of logic. Fortunately there exist special integrated circuits for this task called *DMA controllers*. There are, in effect, special-purpose microprocessors built especially for this task. They can be quite expensive.

In this work, I do not use DMA data transfer because of its complexity and expense. I'll stay with memory-mapped I/O until we get to the IBM-PC, which uses I/O mapped output.

SOFTWARE

Software is the "programming" of the computer, as opposed to the hardware, which is the electronics. To program a computer, or to create its software, the programmer creates a set of very precise instructions in a form that the machine can understand.

In everyday life most people give imprecise instructions. We tend to assume that the other person has enough sense to be able to interpret the instructions to do the job correctly. We assume that we know what the other person means when we ask them "set the table for dinner." Many, if not most, disagreements between people are caused by conflicts over the understanding of such instructions. Imagine what confusion would result if you had a visitor for dinner who was from another culture where plates and utensils are not used, and you asked him to help out by setting the table! He might not even know what you meant by "table."

On the other hand, a good way to irritate someone is to follow his instructions literally and precisely, doing no more or no less than specifically instructed. At some of the military academies, there is a course given in "order writing." The student is presented with a problem in which he has to generate a set of orders for someone else to do a specific job. At the next class meeting, those orders are read out loud. If there is any way in which those

orders can be misinterpreted, the student fails that assignment.

With computers, the problem is even more acute. Computers are so incredibly stupid that you not only have to tell them *exactly* what to do, but you have to also define each of the things you want them to do it with and tell them the *exact* series of steps it will take to do it. In order to "set the table," you have to:

Define what is meant by "table."
Define what is meant by "set."
Define what is meant by "plate."
Define what is meant by "silverware."
Tell the computer where the table is.
Tell the computer where the plates and silverware are.
Tell the computer where to place the plates and silverware on the table.
Tell the computer exactly what series of motions is necessary to get the silverware and plates from storage to the table.
Tell the computer to perform those sets of motions.
Tell the computer to get out of the way when it's done.

A person programming a computer must not only think of everything so that the computer will know what he means, but he must also see that there are contingency plans in case anything goes wrong. Lastly, he has to talk to the computer in *its* language.

With peripherals, a computer has to know exactly what to do with the data it gets from or sends to the peripheral. It may be enough just to put the information in the memory register, or you may need "handshake" lines to tell the peripheral that data is present. Also, the peripheral may have a "busy" line to say "don't send me any data yet— I'm still working on the last batch." The computer must know exactly what to do in each of these cases. Such a program to handle the input or output of data to or from a peripheral is called a *peripheral handler routine*.

High-level languages, like BASIC, have statements like "OUT(25,34)" which means output the number 34 to port number 25, or "PRINT #7, X" which means output the number given by the symbol "X" to port number seven. Within the BASIC Compiler somewhere, there is an output handler routine in machine language which takes care of it. If you put a new port into your computer to handle new input or output devices, that device *has* to have a handler.

A handler can be a simple program or a very complicated one. Generally speaking, there is a tradeoff between the electronic complexity of the peripheral device and the simplicity of the peripheral handler. The more electronics there is in the peripheral, usually, the simpler the handler program. Also, the faster you want the device to run, the *less* software it should use—software execution takes time.

Two examples come immediately to mind: The first is a comparison between an ASCII video terminal and an IBM Selectric typewriter terminal in correspondence code. Most microcomputers use the ASCII coding for letters and characters. A handler for an ASCII-coded terminal which is full-duplex (communicates both ways simultaneously) will take about 30 bytes of memory with a good asynchronous interface chip. Selectric uses a different coding system which essentially tells the typewriter which set of mechanical levers to push. Add to that the fact that the typewriter is coded in half-duplex (only sends one direction at a time) and you have to keep track of which direction is being used at the time and switch it if necessary. A Selectric terminal can have a handler 400 or more bytes long.

The second example is that of a converter to change voltages to digital numbers (see Chapter 5). One form of this uses a counter to count the amount of time it takes for a steadily increasing signal to match the input signal. You can build in a hardware counter and just read the counter when you are done, or you can have the computer do the counting for you. The second way takes more computer time than the first, while the first uses more electronics.

You have to speak the language of a computer, too. For peripheral handlers, this means machine language. I/O instructions *must* be couched in terms of sending the data in this register to the I/O register located at this address (or to the I/O port with this number). Nothing but machine language will do for a good job on this. It is possible to use the PRINT or INPUT or OUT statements in BASIC, but they may not work for a port that was not sold with the machine, so you will have to go into the BASIC interpreter and *modify* the interpreter with a new handler. If your BASIC is located in ROM, this modification is not possible. It is possible to use the PEEK and POKE statements of BASIC, but these are about a thousand times slower than machine language. The best bet is to get a good assembler/editor, and write the handling instructions assembly language, and have the assembler translate it to machine language. If you use an editor/assembler, you can easily make modifications to it later for other needs. An assembler will take care of keeping track of branch addresses, as well.

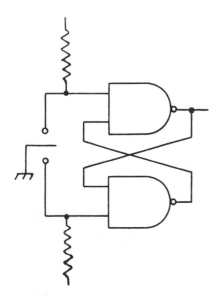

Chapter 2

Conventions and Definitions

By digital electronics, I refer to circuits in which there are only two possible *states* of that circuit possible at any point. For example, a transistor may be in full conduction (saturation) or in a totally non-conductive (cutoff) state but may not be in between, except while it is changing rapidly from one to another. By sending this current through a resistor, we can speak instead of the *voltage* at a given point as being either *high* or *low*. These two states can represent any number of a variety of "bits" of information. The following are only a small sample.

One bit of a number
One bit of a character
Whether a switch is opened or closed
Whether some analog level is above or below some limit
Whether some event has happened
Whether or not some action should be taken.

The HIGH and LOW states represent the TRUE and FALSE states of Boolean logic. The problem is that they may not represent them respectively.

The purpose of this chapter is to define what is *true* and what is *false* in the Boolean sense when we are speaking about voltages at a point.

Figure 2-1 illustrates the four possible states of logic in defining signals. We are allowed to select the "ground" of a voltage signal anywhere we so desire. When working with NPN transistors, we usually take the negative terminal of the battery to be the ground and consider that the positive terminal of the battery is, for example, +9 volts above ground. We could just as easily have taken the positive terminal to be the ground and said that the negative terminal was −9 volts below ground! The circuit doesn't care where ground is, so long as there is a difference of 9 volts between its battery terminals.

There is a tendency to refer to anything that is at ground potential to be in the "off" state, and to refer to anything different from ground to be in the "on" state. But which ground? Does it matter? The answer is a most emphatic "Yes!" It *does* matter. Not only that, but we could just as easily have said that the "on" state was when the signal was

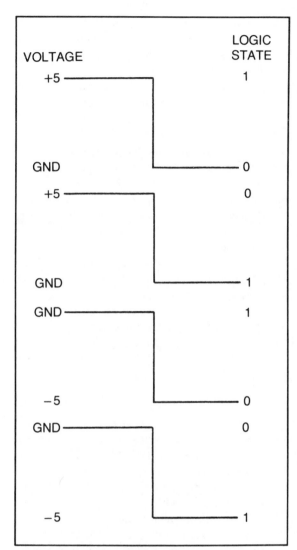

VOLTAGE		LOGIC STATE
+5		1
GND		0
+5		0
GND		1
GND		1
−5		0
GND		0
−5		1

Fig. 2-1. The four possible logic states.

at ground (whatever that is. . .) and the "off" state is when the signal is different from ground. These are the four possible definitions of logic states.

I will use the so-called *positive logic* approach. This definition is the one that has been adopted by most manufacturers of integrated circuits for digital use. Simply put, we define ground to be the negative terminal of the battery or power supply and the positive to be higher in voltage than the negative. The "on" state will be defined to be whenever the point at which the voltage is mea-

sured is above ground significantly, and the "off" state to be whenever the voltage measured is at or near ground. As shown below, the "on" state will be referred to as the HIGH state, or the "1" state (for convenience with binary number representation later), and the "off" state will be referred to as the LOW state, or the "0" state.

Logic States

+5 V	on	HIGH	1
ground	off	LOW	0

All these terms have exactly the same meaning and will be used interchangeably.

Note that we have defined +5 volts as high. Most digital logic integrated circuits work on a 5 volt supply. It should be noted however, that some CMOS circuits require a 12-volt supply, and in this case +12V will be considered to be HIGH.

Unfortunately, we're still not done defining what "on" and "off" mean. Look closely at Fig. 2-2. We said above that a circuit's state could represent whether a switch is open or closed. In Fig. 2-2, when the switch is closed, the output of the circuit is at ground, or LOW. So a LOW signal means that "the switch is closed." When the switch is open, the output is no longer connected to ground, but to +5V through a "pull-up" resistor. (If the

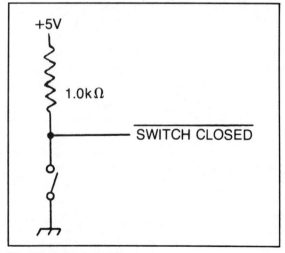

Fig. 2-2. Active-low logic.

current to the output is small, there is little voltage drop across the resistor, so the output will be HIGH.) With the switch open, the output is HIGH. So, therefore, HIGH at the output means "the switch is open." We say that the signal is "active low," or that "switch closed" means LOW. We write this as $\overline{\text{SWITCH CLOSED}}$, with the bar over the information meaning that the information is true when the signal is LOW.

A digital circuit must "know," by both programming and wiring, what each state of each wire means. You, the builder of the circuit and the programmer of the computer, must make sure that all your signals and programming are consistent with what you think they mean.

A word about voltage levels of logic: in TTL logic (the most common kind) a HIGH does not necessarily mean +5V. In fact, due to the internal construction of TTL devices, HIGH means any voltage greater than 3.4 volts, and LOW means any voltage less than 0.8 volts. With CMOS circuits, LOW is any voltage less than 2.5 volts above ground, and HIGH is any voltage greater than 2.5 volts (assuming 5-volt supplies, of course.)

I have been using the terms "bit" and "byte" for the whole of this book so far, and have yet to really define them. The word *bit* is short for "binary digit." It stands for a number expressed in the least-significant place-value place in the base-2 number system. More simply put, a bit is a single place within a system that contains information which may be either HIGH or LOW. A bit may be part of a larger number, or it may have significance all by itself. But it is *one* digit.

A *byte* is a grouping of eight bits. The bits in a byte will always be taken together as a unit. They may be separated to form parts of other bytes, but they are really a unit. Digital electronics uses an eight-bit byte because it takes at least seven bits to describe a character of the alphabet, with all the numbers, special symbols, and upper- and lowercase letters. Seven bits will give you 2^7, or 128 possible combinations of ON and OFF. The eighth bit is frequently used for "parity," which is an error checking method, or it may be used to mean special graphics symbols. In addition, it takes at least four bits to describe any of the integers be-

tween one and ten, so in the BCD (binary-coded decimal) code, a byte can be two decimal numbers (more on this later in the chapter). Each four-bit unit is called a *nybble*.

A microprocessor is called a *parallel processor*, which means it can process eight bits, or a whole byte, all at once. There are eight data lines into and out of the microprocessor, just for this purpose. Many calculators use one-bit processing; that is, they only process one bit at a time. A microprocessor is said to have a "word size" of one byte. Minicomputers have a two-byte word, and mainframes usually have a four-byte word. Remember, some microprocessors can process 16, 20, 24, or 32 bits simultaneously.

A byte can be used to represent a number. Since there are 256 possible combinations of 1s and 0s within eight bits, and since one of those combinations is all 0s, any integer between 0 and 255 can be represented by one byte. Consider the following byte:

$$1\ 0\ 0\ 1\ 0\ 1\ 1\ 1$$

How do we know what number this represents? In our modern decimal system, we read numbers with a *place-value*, so that the number farthest to the left is the highest power of ten. We could read the above number from left to right, with left being the most significant (highest value), or we could read it from right to left, with right being the most significant. We will follow the same convention as is used with decimal numbers, and read from left to right, with the leftmost digit being the largest part of the number. We will call the leftmost digit, or bit, the *most significant bit* (msb), and the rightmost bit the *least significant bit* (lsb). We call the lsb the D0 bit, and the msb the D7 bit, as follows:

1	0	0	1	0	1	1	1
D7	D6	D5	D4	D3	D2	D1	D0
msb							lsb

We will then say, as will be shown later in this chapter, that this number represents the decimal number 151 as read from left to right, and not the number 233 read from right to left.

DIGITAL GATES

Microcomputer interfacing has traditionally been the art of designing complex boards of logic, maintaining and managing the data transfers and the synchronization signals necessary for the processor to communicate with the external devices. Multiple-board implementations of interfacing are now generally obsolete. The new market created by microprocessors has caused manufacturers to provide the required interface components. Most interfaces have shrunk to only a few chips, with one or more of those chips being LSI.

Before attempting to design microcomputer interfaces and systems, it is wise to become familiar with the components available. What could be more disheartening than spending a week designing a special interface circuit, only to find that a simple one-chip interface would have done the job?

Some degree of experience and background in digital circuits and integrated devices is required. It is assumed that you have a familiarity with the basic concepts of digital circuitry and logic.

A discussion of logic gates as used in digital circuits is included here for three reasons: as a review; in order to state explicitly the signs and conventions being used; and as a handy reference to the interfacer.

Even though most interfacing circuitry is contained in the LSI chips that are available, the variety of signals that the user is likely to encounter in a particular application make it impossible to have one interface chip that will respond precisely to those signals, whatever those signals may be. It will usually be necessary to condition the signals from the bus or the device so as to make them compatible with the interfacing chip being used.

This conditioning is done by various digital *gates*. A gate is nothing more than a device which presents one of two states to the output depending on the arrangement of states at the input(s). Most of the larger integrated circuits are nothing more than a collection of gates which have been combined to achieve a particular purpose. In most cases, we can think of a device as working like a gate, or as working like a flip-flop. It works like a

gate if the output responds to the inputs immediately, and like a flip-flop if it requires the action of some *clocking pulse* in order to make the output respond to the inputs.

There are seven basic types of gates: the AND, OR, NAND, NOR, EXCLUSIVE OR, EXCLUSIVE NOR, and INVERT gates.

The AND gate is the best place to start. The logical symbol for an AND gate, as well as its *truth table* is shown in Fig. 2-3. Let's start with the upper symbol, which is the "active high" representation. With two inputs, there are four possible ways we can have the inputs. Input A can be a 1 or a 0, and input B can be a 1 or a 0. Thus, we can have AB = 00, AB = 01, AB = 10, or AB = 11, four possible states. These are summarized on the left-hand side of the truth table. The right-hand side of the truth table shows what the output will be for each of the possible values of the inputs. Notice that the output will be a 1 *only* if *both* the inputs are 1s. Another way of saying this would be "The output is a 1 if A is a 1 *and* B is a 1." This is *active-high* logic. We ask what is the combination of 1s at the input to give a 1 at the output. If that question has an answer that prominently features the word "and," then the gate is an active-high AND gate.

AND gates can have more than just two inputs, but the more inputs you have, the more possible combinations of those inputs you can have. The number of combinations goes up exponentially.

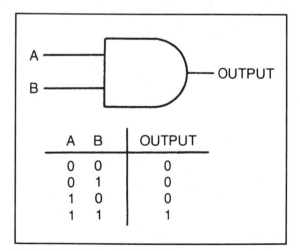

A	B	OUTPUT
0	0	0
0	1	0
1	0	0
1	1	1

Fig. 2-3. AND gate and truth table.

With two inputs, you have 2^2 combinations, or 4, with three inputs, there are 2^3, or eight combinations. The 7430 integrated circuit contains an AND gate with *eight* inputs. In this case, there would be 2^8, or 256 possible combinations of the arrangements of 1s and 0s at the inputs. While this may seem to make the truth table enormous, it doesn't matter, really, because we know that an AND gate will only have a 1 at the output when *all* the inputs are 1s. If any one of the inputs is a 0, then the output will be a 0. We will discuss the other representation in Fig. 2-3 in a moment.

For now, let's move on to the OR gate, symbolized in Fig. 2-4, along with its truth table. As with any gate, two inputs means four possible combinations of inputs, since each input can be only in one state. With this gate, there seem to be a veritable profusion of 1s in the output. Indeed, there is only one state for which the output is a 0. That state is when both inputs are 0s. If either of the inputs happens to be a 1, then the output is a 1. We can state this as, "The output is a 1 if input A is a 1 *or* if input B is a 1." Since the word "or" appears prominently in the statement, we call this gate an OR gate.

The logic of the EXCLUSIVE OR gate, or XOR as it is sometimes abbreviated, is only subtly different from the OR gate. The symbol and the truth table are given in Fig. 2-5. When we say in English, "this *or* that," we are also implying this *and* that is also acceptable. Our English representation of the truth table for the OR gate should really read, "The output is a 1 if input A is a 1 or input B is a 1 or if *both* are 1s." In logic classes in mathematics or philosophy departments, this condition is sometimes referred to as the inclusive-OR logic. What if we wanted to say, "The output is a 1 if input A is a 1 or input B is a 1, *but not both!*" Then we would be using exclusive-or logic. Note that, in the truth table, the output is a 1 if the combination is 10 or 01, but is 0 if the combination is 00 or 11.

As an aside, there is another gate which really isn't thought of as a "real gate," so we will not include it as part of our seven. It is the *BUFFER*, or *driver*. The symbol and truth table are shown in Fig. 2-6. Note that the output is exactly equal to the input. If the input is a 1, so is the output, and vice-versa. These gates are used to supply additional current in order to drive many devices at once. The symbol for a buffer is just a little triangle that means "current amplifier."

The reason we bring up the buffer at all, is that, with the addition of a little circle to the output, we get the inverting gate or INVERTER, as it is commonly called. The little circle means "take whatever you find at this point and change it to the other state." Since, with a buffer, the input becomes the

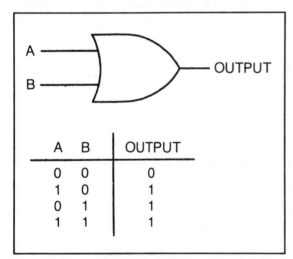

Fig. 2-4. OR gate and truth table.

A	B	OUTPUT
0	0	0
1	0	1
0	1	1
1	1	1

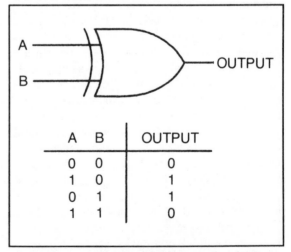

Fig. 2-5. EXCLUSIVE OR or XOR gate and truth table.

A	B	OUTPUT
0	0	0
1	0	1
0	1	1
1	1	0

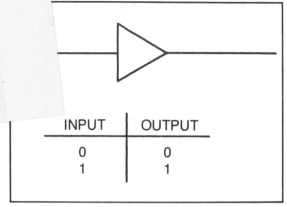

INPUT	OUTPUT
0	0
1	1

Fig. 2-6. Buffer.

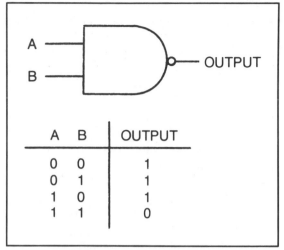

A	B	OUTPUT
0	0	1
0	1	1
1	0	1
1	1	0

Fig. 2-8. NAND gate.

output, with an INVERTER, the output becomes the *complement* of the input, or its opposite state. The symbol and truth table are shown in Fig. 2-7.

With an inverter at hand, we can now add the inversion process to each of the other three gates. The inversion process is sometimes called the NOT process, so an inverter hung onto the end of an AND gate would be a NOT-AND gate, or NAND for short.

The NAND gate (Fig. 2-8) is an extremely useful and powerful gate, as we shall see. Looking closely at the truth table, note that we simply take an AND gate, and everywhere in the output we see a 0 we replace it with a 1, and everywhere we see a 1 we replace it with a 0, to get the truth table of the NAND gate. It is not surprising that the symbol for a NAND gate is just the symbol for an AND

gate with a little inverter symbol on it.

By inverting the outputs of the OR and XOR gates, in a similar manner, we get the NOR (Fig. 2-9) and the EXCLUSIVE NOR or XNOR (Fig. 2-10) gates.

These gates are extremely useful. It is not physically possible to give an exhaustive list of the possible uses of the various gates, either singly or in combination. It *is* possible to give an example of their use. In Fig. 2-11, we see a set of signals as might be applied to an AND gate. Input A is a series of pulses such as might come from a clock

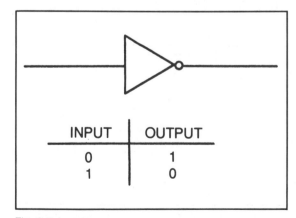

INPUT	OUTPUT
0	1
1	0

Fig. 2-7. Inverter.

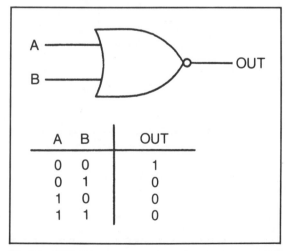

A	B	OUT
0	0	1
0	1	0
1	0	0
1	1	0

Fig. 2-9. NOR gate.

23

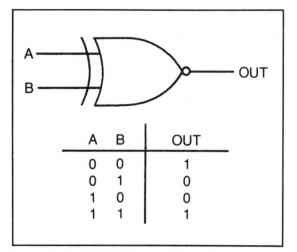

A	B	OUT
0	0	1
0	1	0
1	0	0
1	1	1

Fig. 2-10. EXCLUSIVE NOR or XNOR gate.

generator. We can call input B the "gating pulse." The net result is that clock pulses from input A only reach the output when input B is in a HIGH or 1 state. When this occurs, the output is a 1 if input A is a 1, and is a 0 when input A is a 0. If input

B is a 0, then it doesn't matter what the state of input A is, the output will be a 0. We can say that input B allows input A to pass through the gate whenever input B is HIGH.

Thus far, we have spoken only of active-high logic. That is, we have been concerned about what combination of 1s at the input causes a 1 at the output. We could ask the question the other way around. What combination of 0s at the input results in a 0 at the output? When we ask about 0s, we are asking about *active-low* situations. We presume that the state we are interested in is the 0 state, not the 1 state. Going back to the AND gate of Fig. 2-3, we see the following truth table:

A	B	OUTPUT
0	0	0
0	1	0
1	0	0
1	1	1

We could re-arrange the table to look like this:

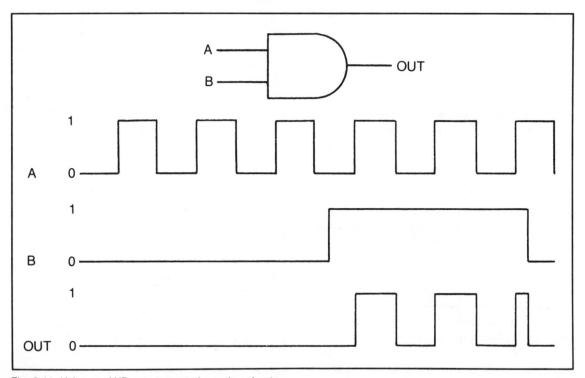

Fig. 2-11. Using an AND gate to control a series of pulses.

A	B	OUTPUT
1	1	1
1	0	0
0	1	0
0	0	0

Before, we were interested in 1s. Suppose that we are now interested in 0s, instead. The above looks like a truth table for an OR gate, where all the 1s have been replaced by 0s and all the 0s have been replaced by 1s in both the inputs and the outputs. In fact, if we take an OR gate, and put inverters on all the inputs, then a 0 at the input will be changed to a 1 before it gets into the OR gate. Any 1 at an OR gate input becomes a 1 at the output. If we put *another* inverter at the output, the output becomes a 0. To summarize, with inverters on all inputs and outputs, any 0 at an input will give a 0 at the output. Another way of putting it is "The output will be a 0 if A is a 0 or B is a 0."

What we are really saying here is that an AND gate for active-high logic is exactly the same as an OR gate in active-low logic. We can draw the symbol for an AND gate either as an AND gate, or as an OR gate with inverters on all the inputs and outputs. We will use the convention that whenever the inputs to a gate are active-high, the ordinary symbol will be used. Whenever the inputs are active-low, the symbol with the inverters on the inputs will be used. If an AND gate for active-high is an OR gate for active-low, what is an OR gate in active-low? Why, it's an AND gate, of course. With an OR gate, the only way you can get a 0 at the outputs is if both inputs are 0s. This is just another way of saying AND with active-low logic. Again, you can replace the symbols for an OR gate with the symbol for an AND gate, with inverters on all inputs and outputs.

Consider, now, the inverter. An inverter just changes 1s to 0s and 0s to 1s. It doesn't matter if the signal is active-high or active-low.

Recall that whenever a signal is active-low, the mnemonic for that signal is written with a bar over it. Therefore, the truth table for the AND gate (active-high) can be written like this:

A	B	A AND B
0	0	0
0	1	0
1	0	0
1	1	1

or like this:

$\overline{A}$	$\overline{B}$	$\overline{A \text{ OR } B}$
1	1	1
1	0	1
0	1	1
0	0	0

The bar can also be read as "the opposite of." This is why we put inverters on all the gate inputs, to invert it to active-high logic.

A NAND gate in active-high logic becomes a NOR gate in active-low logic, and vice-versa. An EXCLUSIVE OR gate becomes an EXCLUSIVE NOR, and vice-versa.

Some people will insist that an active-low output must always be connected to an active-low input and an active-high output must always be connected to an active-high input. If you need to change one to another, just use the inverter. Sometimes it is difficult to tell what is active-high and what is active-low. Even worse, what do you do when one input of a gate is active-high and the other is active-low? As far as is possible, however, without sacrificing readability of the circuit diagrams, we will attempt to follow this convention.

When conditioning a set of signals, we often end up using a set of gates which could easily be simplified to one or two gates. Examples of several of these are given in Fig. 2-12. In the first example, four NAND gates are grouped together. A close examination of the truth table for this grouping shows that the four NAND gates could easily be replaced by a single XOR gate. In the second example, the three OR gates, each with two inputs, are replaced by a single OR gate with four inputs. In the third, both inputs of a NAND gate are connected together, and the result has the same truth table as an INVERTER. The point of this discussion is that, not only can you simplify your designs

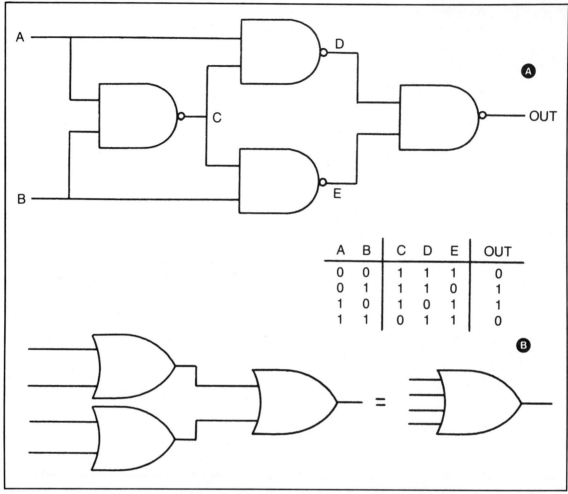

A	B	C	D	E	OUT
0	0	1	1	1	0
0	1	1	1	0	1
1	0	1	0	1	1
1	1	0	1	1	0

Fig. 2-12. (A) XOR gate made from NAND gates; (B) 4-input OR made from 2-input OR gates.

with fewer gates, but if you don't happen to have exactly the right gate, they can often be made up from other gates that you do have. The NAND gate-INVERTER is a good example: Suppose you were to have a circuit that required two NAND gates and one INVERTER. Instead of leaving unused two of the NAND gates in an integrated circuit that contains four, and bringing in another integrated circuit with six INVERTERs, and only using one of those and leaving the others unused, why not change one of the unused NAND gates into an IN-VERTER and keep the total parts count down? It's cheaper and simpler in the long run. Indeed, the use of a NAND gate as an INVERTER is one of

the most common substitutions in electronics.

Any of the eight gates we have discussed can be constructed using only NAND gates, or only NOR gates. We can see directly from Fig. 2-11 that an XOR gate can be made from four NAND gates. It takes five NOR gates to make an XOR gate equivalent. Putting these gates together out of NANDs and NORs is a good exercise in learning how to use gates.

In addition to gates, we have flip-flops and latches. Flip-flops and latches (which are different forms of the same thing) differ from gates in two basic ways. First, a flip-flop requires a clocking pulse to actuate it. This clocking pulse may be con-

26

tained in a gate transition, or it may be required separately. Second, the flip-flop or latch will maintain the state of the output, *even after the input data is gone*, until it is reset by another data input.

The simplest kind of flip-flop is the RS flip-flop, shown in several forms in Fig. 2-13. Its simplest arrangement consists of two cross-connected NOR gates. To follow the logic, if the S (for *set*) input goes high, the $\overline{Q}$ output goes low, forcing the Q output high. The high state on the Q output is fed back into the first NOR gate, keeping $\overline{Q}$ low and Q high and maintaining the state of the outputs, even if S goes low again. Any further change of S will not affect the states of the two complimentary outputs Q and $\overline{Q}$. (Note that Q and $\overline{Q}$ are always opposite to each other. That's why they have the same symbol, but with one inverted.) The *only* way to return the two outputs to the other state is by letting the R (for *Reset*) input go high. Since the circuit is symmetrical, the same arguments apply. Now the states of the outputs are immune to any further change in the value of R until the S input goes high again. This is the reason this circuit is called a latch. The output Q is set to a 1 by a high value on the S input, and is reset to a 0 by a 1 on the R input. A different version of the same flip-flop with active-low inputs and active-high outputs can be made from NAND gates, as shown.

RS flip-flops are used whenever you want to set a signal (flag) that a pulse has occurred on a line, no matter how short that pulse may be. It is a good indicator (event register) to show that an event has occurred.

RS flip-flops are also used in *switch debouncing*. The problem with many mechanical switches and relays is that when the contacts are just closed or just opened, the contacts may "bounce" several times and give you several rapid pulses in a row. The bounce period may last several milliseconds. Bounce may not be a problem in your particular circuit, but if you are using a switch as an input to a counter, where you are counting the number of pulses, the bounce can be disastrous, because each pulse will be counted. Figure 2-14 shows a switch debouncing circuit using an RS flip-flop.

By the addition of two more gates, the RS flip-

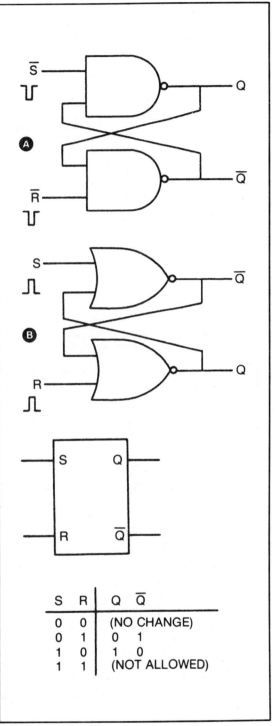

S	R	Q	$\overline{Q}$
0	0	(NO CHANGE)	
0	1	0	1
1	0	1	0
1	1	(NOT ALLOWED)	

Fig. 2-13. RS flip-flops.

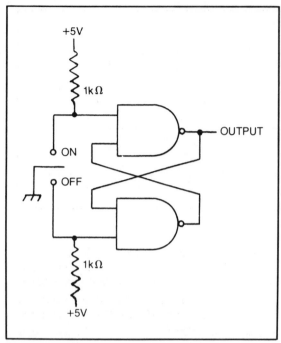

Fig. 2-14. Debouncing of a mechanical switch.

flop can be turned into the JK flip-flop (Fig. 2-15). In this device, the J and K inputs function the same as the R and S inputs but will not change until the clock or *trigger* input, T, goes high. However, there now is more capability. We can allow both J and K to be low, and nothing will happen to the outputs for any change of the trigger input. The output is latched again. Before, with the RS flip-flop, the R and S inputs were not allowed to be both high at the same time. By feeding part of the output back into the input in a cross-connect, we now achieve a situation where if both J and K are high, the action of the outputs with the input AND gates causes a "routing" of the input pulse to the proper secondary gate of the RS flip-flop, and the states of the outputs will change with every clock pulse. In this configuration, the flip-flop becomes a *divide-by-two* counter. By comparing the frequencies of the input and output pulse trains, we see that the output changes state with every input pulse, so that the output pulses are twice as long and twice as far apart (Fig. 2-16).

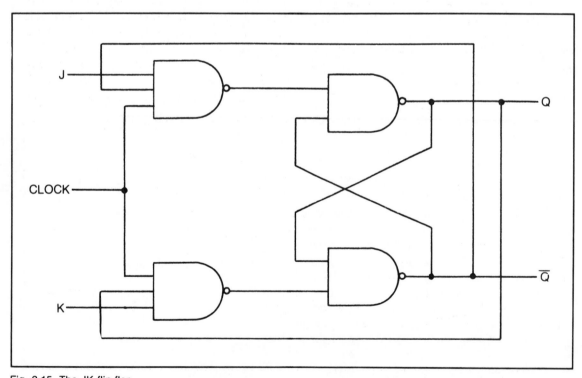

Fig. 2-15. The JK flip-flop.

28

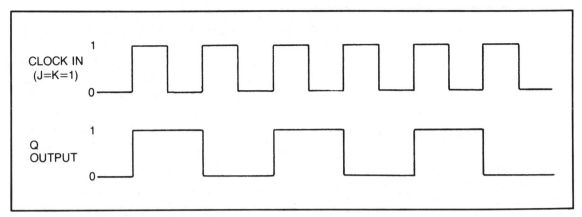

Fig. 2-16. Using a flip-flop to divide by two.

Lastly, another slight modification to the RS flip-flop is shown in Fig. 2-17. Here an inverter is used to ensure that the R and S inputs of the flip-flop are exactly opposite to each other. This variation of the flip-flop is known as the *D-type flip-flop*. It has only one input, or data line, in addition to the clock. This input data will be duplicated at the output whenever a proper trigger pulse is seen. This is the true latch. Place data at the input, supply a latching pulse to the trigger, and whatever data was present at the input during the latching pulse will remain at the Q output, no matter what happens to the D input from there on, so long as there is no other latching pulse. Want to change it? Just put

in new data and send another latching pulse.

Figure 2-18 shows the various gates with their symbols for both active-high and active-low logic. All use positive logic. In addition, there is a list of the gates available as TTL or CMOS integrated circuits, with the number of inputs per gate and devices per package.

A word about outputs on these gates. These are three basic types of outputs: the TTL totem-pole output, the open-collector output, and the CMOS output. Each has distinct advantages. Figure 2-19 shows examples of the output stages of each. For most TTL applications, the totem-pole output is just fine. One transistor or the other is conducting

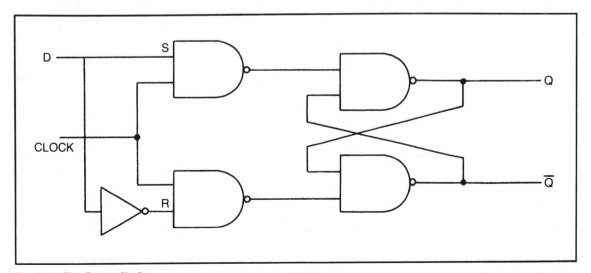

Fig. 2-17. The D-type flip-flop.

29

Gate	Symbol	Active-Low Symbol	Inputs	No. per Chip	TTL	CMOS
AND	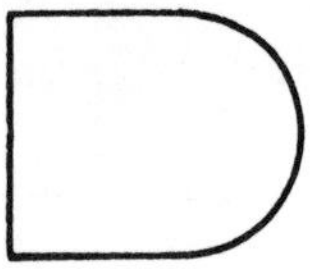	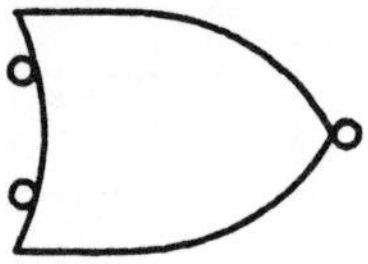	2 3 4	4 3 2	7408 7411 7421	4081 4073 4082
NAND	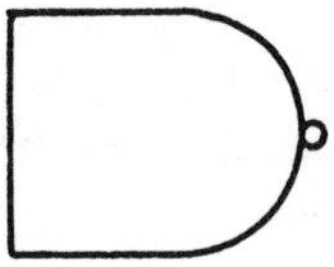	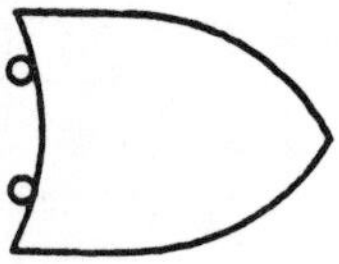	2 3 4 8	4 3 2 1	7400 7410 7420 7430	4011 4023 4012 4068
OR	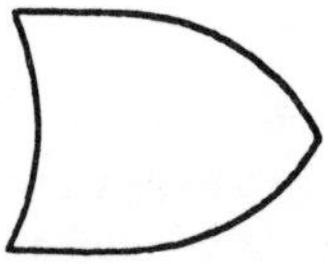	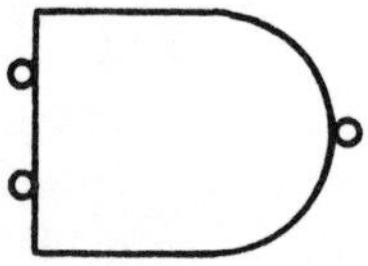	2 3 4	4 3 2	7432	4071 4075 4072
NOR	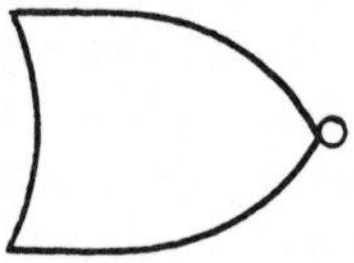	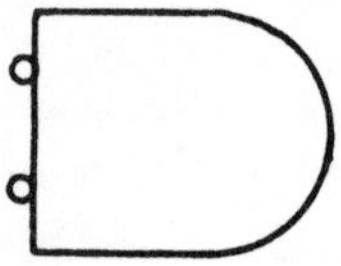	2 3 4 8	4 3 2 1	7402 7427 7425	4001 4025 4002 4078
XOR	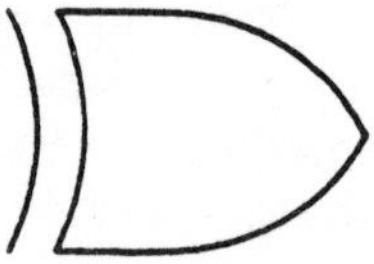	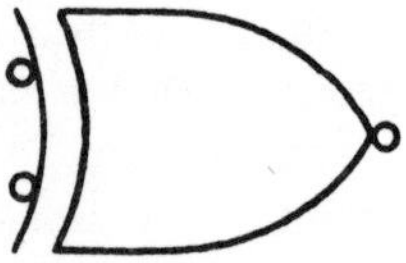	2	4	7486	4070
XNOR	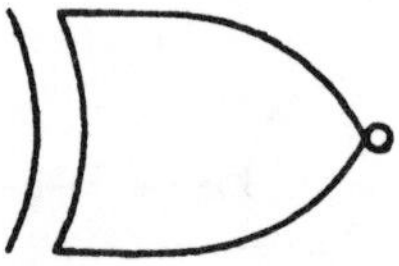	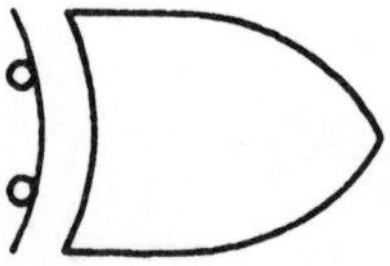	2	4	74266	4077
BUFFER	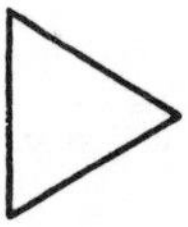	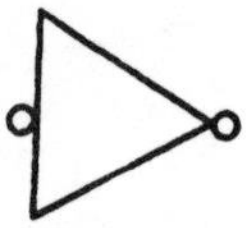	1	6	74365	4050
INVERTER	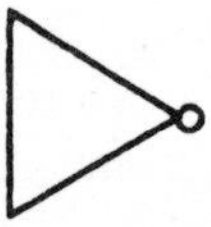	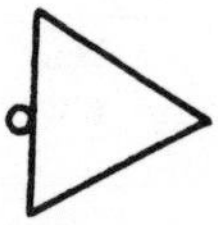	1	6	7404	4049

Fig. 2-18. Symbols of the various types of gates and chips.

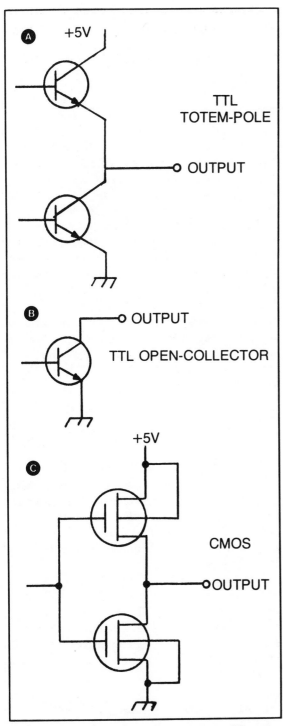

+5V

TTL
TOTEM-POLE

TTL OPEN-COLLECTOR

C

+5V

CMOS

○OUTPUT

Fig. 2-19. Output stages of TTL totem-pole, TTL open-collector, and CMOS chips.

at a given time, so that the output is essentially connected either to the power-supply rails or to ground through a transistor. The output impedance is quite low. The only difficulties with this type of output stage are that, because of the voltage drops across the transistors, the output doesn't get below about 0.4 volts for a 0, or above about 4 volts for a 1. Also, the output stage is quite limited in the amount of current it can source or sink (provide or consume).

The open-collector output solves most of these problems. The user provides a collector resistor to the supply voltage, and the output can go all the way to the supply value, and almost all the way to ground. Higher currents and higher voltages can be used on this output stage, so it may be used for interfacing to higher voltages or for a fanout expander. The disadvantage is that the user must supply additional parts to the circuit.

CMOS interfaces quite well to both CMOS and TTL; that is, the output of a CMOS circuit will drive either TTL or CMOS inputs. TTL, will, of course, drive TTL circuits may not be able to drive CMOS circuits. CMOS may be running on 12 volts instead of 5 like TTL, or the CMOS gate may not recognize the 0.4 volt low output of a TTL gate as "low." It is always best to interface TTL to CMOS with an open-collector gate.

BINARY NUMBER SYSTEMS AND OTHER SHORTCUTS

Why do we use 1 and 0 for the high and low representations of the two states of digital logic? The answer lies in the way we represent numbers.

All numbering systems are really a form of counting. When we want to know how many objects there are, say in a certain place, we count them:

1 2 3 4 5 6 7 8 9 10 11. . .

Ask yourself this question: Why did we suddenly go from single-digit numbers to two-digit numbers? Here we can find an answer in the place-value system we all learned about in grade school. The farther to the left a digit is in a number, the more significant that number is. In the number 12, the

1 means a bigger part of the number than the 2, even though the 2 is a bigger number by itself than the 1. When we say "12," we are actually saying $1 \times 10 + 2$. The one is said to be in the "tens" place, and the 2 in the "ones" place. We can write the number 3284 like this:

$$3 \times 1000 + 2 \times 100 + 8 \times 10 + 4 = 3284.$$

Notice that each of the multipliers increases by one zero the farther we go to the left. This same number could also be written like this:

$$3 \times 10^3 + 2 \times 10^2 + 8 \times 10^1 + 4 \times 10^0 = 3284$$

Recall here that $10^0 = 1$. In short, the farther you go to the left, the higher the power of ten you use.

Then, the next question is, why do we use ten as the multiplier?

Good question.

We probably use ten because there are ten fingers on our hands, and early cultures learned to count by using their fingers. (An aside: The biblical expression "forty days and forty nights" actually translates from the Aramaic as "more days and nights than can be counted on all fingers and toes twice." It simply means "an uncountable number of days and nights." As we will see, for those of us who use computers, it might be easier if we were to have four or eight fingers on each hand.

Suppose the numbers eight and nine didn't exist—that we didn't have any concept for them as a single digit, any more than we have a concept of the number 12 as a single digit. Then we would count like this:

$$1\ 2\ 3\ 4\ 5\ 6\ 7\ 10\ 11\ 12\ 13. . .$$

Ten becomes the place where we run out of numbers and have to start over in the next column. But now, that column doesn't mean 10^1, it means 8^1. This is the base-8 number system, or the *octal* number system, as opposed to the base-10 number system, or the *decimal* number system. The number 3274 in each system is expressed as follows:

$$3 \times 10^3 + 2 \times 10^2 + 7 \times 10^1$$
$$+ 4 \times 10^0 = 3274_{10}$$
$$3 \times 8^3 + 2 \times 8^2 + 7 \times 8^1$$
$$+ 4 \times 8^0 = 3274_8 =$$
$$1724_{10}.$$

The *subscript*, which is always in decimal, gives the *base* of the counting system.

Note that the decimal system has ten digits available for its use, including the "place holder," or zero: 123456789-0, whereas the octal system has only eight, including zero: 1234567-0. We can envision systems of base 6, where you count up to five and then start the next column, or base 9, where you count up to eight and start the next column. But why restrict ourselves to number bases less than or equal to ten? As long as we invent special symbols to take the place of the double-digit numbers above nine, we can use bases as high as we want. Suppose, for example, that we were interested in the base-16 number system. Then, using the first six letters of the alphabet to represent the decimal numbers 10, 11, 12, 13, 14, and 15, we would count like this:

$$1\ 2\ 3\ 4\ 5\ 6\ 7\ 8\ 9\ \text{A}\quad \text{B}\quad \text{C}\quad \text{D}\quad \text{E}\quad \text{F}\quad 10. . .$$
$$(10)\ (11)\ (12)\ (13)\ (14)\ (15)\ (16)$$

Notice we don't get to the number 10_{16} until we get to the number 16_{10}. Base-16 is *hexadecimal*.

You may ask, "Why would anyone in his right mind use any number system other than ten? It's worked all right for me up to now!" Believe it or not, we use these other number systems because, when dealing with computers, they make our understanding of what's going on easier.

To see exactly what is meant here, consider the base-2 number system. The only numbers that are allowed are the 0 and the 1 (sound familiar?). Instead of using a "2," we go immediately to the 2s place and write 10. Counting in this system would go like

1	10	11	100	101	110	111	1000	1001
1	2	3	4	5	6	7	8	9

The number 10110111 in base 2 translates to base 10 as follows:

$$1 \times 2^7 + 0 \times 2^6 + 1 \times 2^5 + 1 \times 2^4 + 0 \times 2^3 + 1 \times 2^2 + 1 \times 2^1 + 1 \times 2^0 = 183_{10}$$

The advantage of base 2 should be obvious. Since a digital circuit can have only two states, represented by a 0 or a 1, and since base 2 can only have two numbers, a 0 or a 1, we can electronically represent numbers in base 2 by series of high and low bits. An eight-bit byte can represent any number in base 2 from 00000000 to 11111111, or 0 to 255 in base 10. Larger sets of bits can, of course, represent larger numbers. Sixteen bits can represent integers from 0 to $65,535_{10}$.

So why all the excitement about base-8 and base-16? Octal and hexadecimal happen to be shorthand notations for base-2, or *binary*, as it is called. Consider the above number in binary:

$$1\ 0\ 1\ 1\ 0\ 1\ 1\ 1_2$$

If we group the digits in groups of three, starting from the right and moving to the left, and then translate each of those groups into its octal equivalent, we get:

$$\begin{array}{ccc} 10 & 110 & 111 \\ 2 & 6 & 7 \end{array}$$
$$= 267_8$$

The binary number 10110111_2 is exactly equal to the octal number 267_8. Suppose further that, instead of making groups of three, we make groups of four, like this:

$$\begin{array}{cc} 1011 & 0111 \\ B & 7 \end{array}$$
$$= B7_6$$

This should be apparent just from the fact that three binary digits can represent the numbers from 0 to 7, just as the digits in octal do, and four binary digits can represent the numbers from 0 to 15_{10}, just as hexadecimal does.

All in all, we can say that:

$$10110111_2 = 267_8 = 183_{10} = B7_{16}$$

It's all the same number, just different ways of writing it.

Since we will work so much with binary numbers in the remainder of this text, rather than write out all those digits, we will do what the computer companies have been doing for decades—we will use one of the shorthand notations, octal or hexadecimal. Octal is used primarily by Digital Equipment Corporation, and by companies who use their software, like Heath. Most companies in the large mainframe business, and the greater majority of microcomputer manufacturers and suppliers, use hexadecimal, so we will too.

If you see a number written as B7H, that means the number B7 is hexadecimal. The Motorola company uses the symbolism $B7 for the number $B7_{16}$. This does not mean that the chip costs B7 dollars; it is a notation that the number to follow is hexadecimal.

At this point, other books would spend a lot of time describing how to do conversions from one number system to another, and how to do arithmetic in these various number systems. For what the ultimate purpose of this book is—building interfaces and connecting them to peripherals that we have built or purchased, we really don't need to know how to do this. We are more concerned with the bit-by-bit arrangement of data bits, for which hexadecimal (Hex for short) is quite adequate. We will do very little arithmetic, mostly just adding or subtracting from some register. Conversion from one number base to another should not be necessary, unless you intend to do your programming exclusively in BASIC, which only works with decimal. If you need additional assistance, please consult some of the fine books listed in the Bibliography.

There are still two other representations of binary that we need to examine before we can leave this topic. These are binary coded decimal and ASCII.

Arithmetic processors in higher-level languages, such as BASIC or FORTRAN or PASCAL, will do their arithmetic in one of two ways: If the arithmetic is limited to integers, and the range of integers itself is limited to plus or minus 32,767 ($2^{15} - 1$), then chances are the language interpreter does the arithmetic in straight binary. However, if the language uses what is called *floating-point* arithmetic and can handle any number (not just integers) from $+/- 1 \times 10^{-99}$ to $+/- 9.9999999 \times 10^{99}$, with several digits of precision, then chances are the arithmetic is done with *binary coded decimal* (BCD). With BCD, the number is sort of half binary and half decimal.

Decimal uses the numbers from 0 to 9. In order to represent the numbers from 0 to 9 in binary, four bits are required. Three bits will only give you up to seven. As in hexadecimal, we group the bits into groups of four, but instead of allowing each group of four to increase all the way to fifteen, then incrementing the fifth bit, we only allow it to go to 9 before incrementing the fifth bit. Like this:

7	0000 0111
8	0000 1000
9	0000 1001
10	0001 0000
11	0001 0001

In this way, a byte of eight bits can represent two decimal numbers with a place-value system much like that of other systems. BCD arithmetic is much slower than binary arithmetic on a computer, but it is really the only way to represent numbers other than integers. Note the special significance the groups of four bits have now—that's why they've been given the special name of "nybbles"—two nybbles make a byte!

Motorola thinks that the BCD arithmetic is so important that they've included a special instruction specially for it in the microprocessors they manufacture. On the 6800 series, it's DAA (Decimal Adjust Accumulator), or, "Take the binary number in the A-register and turn it into a BCD number."

The other version of binary coding that is used extensively on microprocessors is the American Standard Code for Information Interchange, or AS-CII (pronounced AS-key) for short. As we have said

earlier, numbers are not the only things that can be stored in memory in a computer. Besides instructions, there are alphabetic and numeric characters. In order to send a letter or number to a printer or terminal, you must send the proper *code* for that letter or number, so that the printer or terminal will recognize it.

Several years ago, a number of experts got together to formulate a code for the transmission of character data from one machine to a peripheral. Until that time, the codes used had been IBM's EBCD code, and the Baudot code used in Teletype® machines. Both of these were all-capitals codes (no lowercase letters) and required extensive use of the shift mechanism to exchange between numbers and punctuation characters. The experts determined that any code used for the transmission of character data should include both upper- and lowercase letters, numbers, all punctuation symbols, and some *control codes* for the purpose of turning devices on and off, ringing bells, returning the carriage, skipping to the next line, shifting, and special codes to denote the beginning and ends of data records and transmissions. In order to do all of these, 128 separate codes were required. Since this is exactly 2^7, they added an eighth bit, in addition to the seven bits whose combinations were needed to express the characters, for error checking. This eighth bit is called *parity*, and is simply equal to the number of 1s in the other seven bits. If there were three 1s in the other seven, there were an odd number, and the parity was said to be *odd*, and assigned a value of 1. Four bits equal to 1 gave an even number, for *even* parity, for a parity bit value of 0.

The ASCII code, as this code came to be called, is listed in Table 2-1. You might expect that the number 4 would be, for example, the binary number 4. This is not the case. A number is its binary number plus the hexadecimal number $30 (48 decimal). Remember, we are using *characters* here, not numbers. A lowercase letter is the same as an uppercase letter, with the sixth bit set equal to a 1. All control characters have bits five and six set equal to zero. Parity is generally not used with most microcomputers.

A special word about two ASCII characters,

Table 2-1. The ASCII Code. (Continued on Page 36.)

Character	Binary	Hexadecimal	Decimal	
NUL	0000000	00	00	Null
SOH	0000001	01	01	Start of Heading
STX	0000010	02	02	Start of Text
ETX	0000011	03	03	End of Text
EOT	0000100	04	04	End of Transmission
ENQ	0000101	05	05	Enquiry
ACK	0000110	06	06	Acknowledge
BEL	0000111	07	07	Bell
BS	0001000	08	08	Backspace
HT	0001001	09	09	Horizontal Tab
LF	0001010	0A	10	Line Feed
VT	0001011	0B	11	Vertical Tab
FF	0001100	0C	12	Form Feed
CR	0001101	0D	13	Carriage Return
SO	0001110	0E	14	Shift Out
SI	0001111	0F	15	Shift In
DLE	0010000	10	16	Data Link Escape
DC1	0010001	11	17	Device Control 1
DC2	0010010	12	18	Device Control 2
DC3	0010011	13	19	Device Control 3
DC4	0010100	14	20	Device Control 4
NAK	0010101	15	21	Negative Acknowledge
SYN	0010110	16	22	Synchronous Idle
ETB	0010111	17	23	End of Block
CAN	0011000	18	24	Cancel
EM	0011001	19	25	End of Medium
SUB	0011010	1A	26	Substitute
ESC	0011011	1B	27	Escape (or ALTMODE)
FS	0011100	1C	28	File Separator
GS	0011101	1D	29	Group Separator
RS	0011110	1E	30	Record Separator
US	0011111	1F	31	Unit Separator
(space)	0100000	20	32	Space
!	0100001	21	33	
"	0100010	22	34	
#	0100011	23	35	
$	0100100	24	36	
%	0100101	25	37	
&	0100110	26	38	
'	0100111	27	39	
(	0101000	28	40	
)	0101001	29	41	
*	0101010	2A	42	
+	0101011	2B	43	
,	0101100	2C	44	
-	0101101	2D	45	
.	0101110	2E	46	
/	0101111	2F	47	
0	0110000	30	48	
1	0110001	31	49	
2	0110010	32	50	
3	0110011	33	51	
4	0110100	34	52	
5	0110101	35	53	
6	0110110	36	54	
7	0110111	37	55	
8	0111000	38	56	
9	0111001	39	57	
:	0111010	3A	58	
;	0111011	3B	59	
<	0111100	3C	60	
=	0111101	3D	61	
>	0111110	3E	62	
?	0111111	3F	63	
@	1000000	40	64	
A	1000001	41	65	
B	1000010	42	66	
C	1000011	43	67	
D	1000100	44	68	

Character	Binary	Hexadecimal	Decimal	
E	1000101	45	69	
F	1000110	46	70	
G	1000111	47	71	
H	1001000	48	72	
I	1001001	49	73	
J	1001010	4A	74	
K	1001011	4B	75	
L	1001100	4C	76	
M	1001101	4D	77	
N	1001110	4E	78	
O	1001111	4F	79	
P	1010000	50	80	
Q	1010001	51	81	
R	1010010	52	82	
S	1010011	53	83	
T	1010100	54	84	
U	1010101	55	85	
V	1010110	56	86	
W	1010111	57	87	
X	1011000	58	88	
Y	1011001	59	89	
Z	1011010	5A	90	
	1011011	5B	91	
	1011100	5C	92	
	1011101	5D	93	
	1011110	5E	94	
	1011111	5F	95	
—	1100000	60	96	
a	1100001	61	97	
b	1100010	62	98	
c	1100011	63	99	
d	1100100	64	100	
e	1100101	65	101	
f	1100110	66	102	
g	1100111	67	103	
h	1101000	68	104	
i	1101001	69	105	
j	1101010	6A	106	
k	1101011	6B	107	
l	1101100	6C	108	
m	1101101	6D	109	
n	1101110	6E	110	
o	1101111	6F	111	
p	1110000	70	112	
q	1110001	71	113	
r	1110010	72	114	
s	1110011	73	115	
t	1110100	74	116	
u	1110101	75	117	
v	1110110	76	118	
w	1110111	77	119	
x	1111000	78	120	
y	1111001	79	121	
z	1111010	7A	122	
	1111011	7B	123	
	1111100	7C	124	
	1111101	7D	125	
	1111110	7E	126	
DEL	1111111	7F	127	Delete

$00 or NUL, and $7F, or RUBOUT. NUL is all zeroes, and is used either for denoting the end of a character string, or as a "do nothing" character. The RUBOUT is all ones (unless no parity is used, in which case the seventh bit is a zero) and is a "do nothing" character.

Serial data transmission (Chapter 3) is always preceded by a "start bit" of 0. If, for some reason, a "glitch" appears on the data lines when no data is present, the receiver will treat the "glitch" as a start bit with all ones after it. If we just have the receiver ignore all RUBOUTs that it receives, we don't have to worry about these "glitches."

Unfortunately, ASCII doesn't provide for subscripts, superscripts, exponents, Greek letters, or many mathematical symbols. It is indeed unfortunate that there aren't characters for pi, mu, omega, and the degree symbol, since these crop up frequently in technical writing. Also missing are the 1/2 and 1/4 fractions commonly found on typewriters.

DATA BUSSES

As we stated in Chapter 1, the microprocessor communicates with memory and peripherals by using the various busses. We have the address bus, the data bus, and the control bus. The control lines of the control bus let us know what is happening on the other two busses. The address bus tells us what particular location in memory is being accessed, and the data bus carries the information to or from the microprocessor. We will discuss the address bus in greater detail when we cover address decoding in the last section of this chapter.

The data bus may be a unidirectional bus, or it may be a bidirectional bus. If it is unidirectional, as in the S-100 systems, there must be eight data lines for "data in," or data sent to the microprocessor, and eight more data lines for "data out," or data sent from the microprocessor to memory or peripherals. This is the common convention for data signals: data *in* to the processor, *out* to the memory. With a bidirectional bus, data can flow in either direction along the bus. There must be a control line to tell the peripherals which direction the data is flowing. In addition, only one memory device may "talk" at a time. The read/write line serves the function of telling the memory which direction the data is to flow, and the address lines tell the memory/peripheral devices which one is to be the "talker" or "listener." Unless there is a DMA transfer, the microprocessor can be either one: during a write cycle, the processor is the talker; during a read cycle, it is the listener.

I have said before that a digital device can have only two possible states—the 1 state, corresponding to +5V, and the 0 state, corresponding to 0 V. Yet I've just stated that only one memory device may "talk" at a given time. If the device can only be a 1 or a 0, it would seem that all devices that are connected to the data bus will be "talking" either 1s or 0s.

How do we separate a true data signal from all this cacophony? There would be little problem if—I say *if*—there were only the processor and the one particular memory/peripheral device being talked to on the bus at a given time. Then there would be no question as to where the data was coming from or where it was going. What we really need is a way to electrically disconnect a device from the bus when it is not being directly used.

Fortunately for us, it is possible to electrically disconnect a sending device from the bus. We don't have to worry about listening devices too much, because a listening device can be designed so that its *input impedance* is very high. The input impedance is the ratio of its input voltage to input current, and is a measure of the amount of current that is needed to drive the input of the device. If the input impedance is high, the amount of current needed to drive it is very low. If the input impedance is high enough, a sending device can provide power to many input devices with no adverse effects on the signal. The *output impedance* of a device, however, needs to be low so that it can drive a lot of devices.

For sending devices, however, its output impedance needs to be low only when it is talking to another device. If it were high when it was not "busy," then it would effectively be disconnected from the data bus.

Electrical engineers came up with the *three-state output*. The name is misleading: it is not digital logic with three voltage levels. It's just an ordinary logic gate, with an additional input called an *enable* input. When activated, this input, and it may be active-high or active-low depending on the particular integrated circuit, will allow the outputs to be in the low-impedance state and will give either a 1 or a 0 at the output. When disabled, the output will be in a high-impedance state and can supply very little current. The terms 0 and 1 become meaningless—the output is essentially disconnected from the bus line.

There are several types of data chips designed

especially for three-state logic. Special chips exist which are just buffers or inverters with an enable input for three-state output. In addition, most LSI chips these days have three-state outputs on them. Certainly all memory chips do, as well as most special-purpose interface chips.

Three-state logic chips have another advantage, as well. Because of their very low output impedance, they can supply quite large amounts of current and can be used as *bus drivers*.

Most microprocessors and other MOS LSI integrated circuits are constructed with large numbers (10,000 or more) transistors on a single chip. The only real problem to putting large numbers of transistors onto a single chip is the amount of power they consume. Most of this power shows up as heat, and the dissipation of this heat is one of the greatest problems in integrated-circuit design. The use of MOSFETs in integrated circuits has reduced the heat output by reducing the current requirements of the individual transistors. The only problem is that the transistors on the chip cannot supply very large currents to other chips.

LSI integrated circuits are generally constructed to be able to drive one *TTL load*. This is the amount of current, voltage, and power required to drive the inputs of a standard TTL integrated circuit. Anything that drives one TTL input must be capable of providing 40 microamperes in the 1, or +5V, state, and sinking (absorbing) up to 1.5 milliamperes in the 0, or ground state. In parallel with the input, from the input to ground, is an effective capacitance of about 30 picofarads. This is one TTL load. By comparison, a three-state input in the disabled (high-impedance) state draws about 2 microamperes.

Address-bus inputs cannot be placed in the three-state disabled mode. Otherwise, how would they know when to work? These inputs must be "listening" all the time. Since only the processor talks, this is no problem, other than the fact that the processor can only drive one TTL load, while there may be ten or twenty logic cards or logic devices on the address bus listening to the output of the address register of the CPU. The solution is to use buffers on the address bus lines out of the CPU. The one-TTL-load output can drive the address lines through the TTL buffers, since they represent only one TTL load, and the buffers can drive up to 20 TTL loads on the bus. Some buffers will drive 30 or more loads.

By using three-state buffers in each direction, and with proper read/write/decode/enable circuitry, the data busses can be used in either direction. The input lines are three-stated when the output lines are enabled. Figure 2-20 is an example of this type of procedure. When the ENABLE line is in the low state, signal flow through the system in either direction is blocked, because both buffers are in the high-impedance state. With the ENABLE line in the high state, the buffer that is in the high-impedance state is governed by the DIRECTION input. A high level on this line means data input, and a low level means data output.

We can put data out to an interface chip over the data lines, but what happens if the interfaced peripheral doesn't read it right away? In the next cycle, there will be different data on the lines. Does this mean that the peripheral must read it right away, before it changes? Not at all. Most interface chips have a *latch* in them. If they don't, we can add one. This simply means that every data output line has on its output D-type flip-flop which is clocked when the data is sent to it. In this way, the

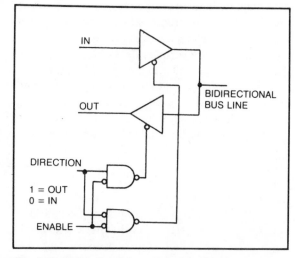

Fig. 2-20. Bidirectional three-state bus driver.

latches will hold on to the information until it is specifically changed by another write cycle.

Enough of definitions and general theory about busses for now. Let's take a look at some of the busses that are actually being used in computers on the market today. (Things change very rapidly in the microcomputer field, and this information will probably be obsolete in five years.)

At about the same time that the MITS AL-TAIR with an 8080 processor and S-100 bus hit the market, another computer with a different bus was introduced. This was the Southwest Technical Products (SWTP) machine with a 6800 process and the SS-50 bus. This main bus is shown in Fig. 2-21, and its lines are summarized in Table 2-2. The SS-50 bus has 50 lines which are quite wide. Since the computer runs at a lower clock speed, cross-talk is significantly reduced. The bus is more or less standardized, as well, so that boards from one manufacturer work well with boards from another manufacturer. Of the 50 lines, there are the usual eight data lines and 16 address lines, and eight lines that are used only for power and ground. There is even a line that isn't used at all except to make sure the board is seated properly. The bus is loosely designed around the pin-out signals of the 6800 microprocessor. However, some manufacturers have designed SS-50 boards with other microprocessors as the CPU. Most of the other signals are control signals, with the exception of five serial data-rate signals. The SS-50 bus is extremely easy to use for interfacing because relative few control lines are needed. Also, there are quite a few manufacturers who support this bus—dozens, in fact. SWTP has branched out from the hobbyist to the educational market, and is using the 6809 processor. Some of the more successful computer manufacturers on the SS-50 bus are GIMIX and Smoke Signal Broadcasting.

The SS-50 bus is two different busses. The above describes the so-called "main bus," but the motherboard generally has an "output bus" at the rear specifically for the connection of peripherals to the computer. This output bus, since it has only 30 lines, is sometimes referred to as the SS-30 bus. The only real difference between the two is that

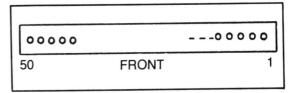

Fig. 2-21. The SS-50 bus pin location.

most of the address decoding has been done (all but the least significant two of the address lines), and the number of control lines has been reduced. Figure 2-22 and Table 2-3 show the bus. Each location on the SS-30 bus corresponds to four addresses. This is just right for the 6820 PIA interface chip (for which the bus was designed). Eight slots on the SS-30 bus take up a total of 32 addresses. Memory and mass-storage controllers are situated on the SS-50 bus, while single-chip interfaces for peripherals reside on the SS-30.

In going to the 6809 processor, SWTP has made a slight change in the SS-50 bus that can make some boards incompatible with the new bus. Memory and peripherals are generally not affected under certain conditions. The 6809 has an additional interrupt input called FIRQ. This line has been added, the $\theta 1$ system clock line has been deleted since almost no boards use it anyway, and the serial data-rate lines have been deleted. Lines are introduced to support *extended addressing*, where electronic tricks are used to extend the range of addresses that the processor may control from 16 address lines to 20, with only 16 address lines on the processor. Unless your system requires extended addressing, an FIRQ interrupt, or serial data rates, there will likely be little difference in your system whether you use the SS-50 bus, or the new SS-50C bus. When in doubt, consult the manufacturer of your machine.

The Apple II microcomputer does not have a full-feature bus as on SS-50 models. This computer is essentially a one-card microcomputer with the keyboard, video generator, memory, and processor built into the case as part of the single board, so it really doesn't need such a bus. There is, however, a row of eight 50-pin connectors at the rear on the main board for connection to peripherals. A

Table 2-2. SS-50 Bus Lines (SWTP 6800).

Line No.	Symbol	Function
1	$\overline{D0}$	Data line 0
2	$\overline{D1}$	Data line 1
3	$\overline{D2}$	Data line 2
4	$\overline{D3}$	Data line 3
5	$\overline{D4}$	Data line 4
6	$\overline{D5}$	Data line 5
7	$\overline{D6}$	Data line 6
8	$\overline{D7}$	Data line 7
9	A15	Address line 15
10	A14	Address line 14
11	A13	Address line 13
12	A12	Address line 12
13	A10	Address line 10
14	A9	Address line 9
15	A8	Address line 8
16	A7	Address line 7
17	A6	Address line 6
18	A5	Address line 5
19	A4	Address line 4
20	A3	Address line 3
21	A2	Address line 2
22	A1	Address line 1
23	A0	Address line 0
25-27	GND	System ground
28-30	+8V	System unregulated 8V power
31	−12V	−12 to −15 volts @ 1A
32	+12V	+12 to +15 volts @ 1A
33	INDEX	Board seating (no electrical connection)
34	MRST	Manual reset
35	NMI	Non-maskable interrupt request
36	IRQ	Maskable interrupt request
37	UD2	User defined
38	UD1	User defined
39	02	Phase 2 system clock
40	VMA	Valid memory address present
41	R/W	Read cycle if high, write cycle if low
42	RST	System reset
43	BA	CPU acknowledges DMA request
44	01	Phase 1 system clock
45	HALT	DMA request to CPU
46	110	110 baud ×16 clock
47	150	150 baud ×16 clock
48	300	300 baud ×16 clock
49	600	600 baud ×16 clock
50	1200	1200 baud ×16 clock

diagram of these connectors, and their functions, are given in Fig. 2-23 and Table 2-4. Printers, disk drives, and various other peripherals can be interfaced to the Apple II by using these connectors. There are several ways this can be done. All 16 address lines and all eight data lines are present on the output bus, so the output bus can be used for the addition of any memory-related device. In addition, each slot has its own "port number," given by N, where N goes from 0 to 7. Decoding of the most significant 8 address lines is done on the main board, and the I/O SELECT line will go low when address lines corresponding to $CNXX are accessed. For slot number three, the I/O SELECT line

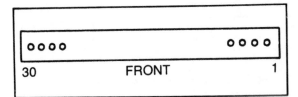

Fig. 2-22. The SS-30 output bus pin location.

Table 2-3. The SS-30 Bus (Memory-Mapped I/O Bus to SS-30).

Line No.	Symbol	Function
1	UD3	User defined
2	UD4	User defined
3	−12	−12V to −15V unregulated
4	+12	+12V to +15V unregulated
5, 6	GND	System ground
7	INDEX	Board seating—no connection
8	NMI	Non-maskable interrupt request
9	IRQ	Maskable interrupt request
10	RSO	Register select—same as A0
11	RS1	Register select—same as A1
12	D0	Data line 0
13	D1	Data line 1
14	D2	Data line 2
15	D3	Data line 3
16	D4	Data line 4
17	D5	Data line 5
18	D6	Data line 6
19	D7	Data line 7
20	02	Phase 2 clock
21	R/$\overline{W}$	Read cycle if high, write cycle if low
22, 23	+8V	+8V unregulated power
24	1200	1200 baud X16 clock
25	600	600 baud X16 clock
26	300	300 baud X16 clock
27	150	150 baud X16 clock
28	110	110 baud X16 clock
29	RESET	System reset
30	SELECT	Board select

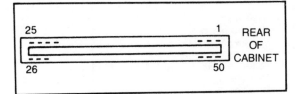

Fig. 2-23. The Apple expansion bus.

will go low when any address from \$C300 through \$C3FF is accessed. Each slot used in this manner occupies 256 consecutive addresses. A full 2K of memory can be accessed in any of the data slots by using the I/O STROBE line, which goes low whenever address lines \$C800 through \$C8FF are accessed.

The Apple II supports daisy-chain priority encoding for both interrupts and DMA. The way it works is as follows: A DMA request or INTERRUPT REQUEST is generated by one of the peripherals. Then the highest-priority device gets the INT IN or DMA IN signal. If it did not generate the interrupt or DMA request, its INT OUT or

Table 2-4. Apple Bus Peripheral Connector.

Line No.	Symbol	Function
1	I/O SELECT	Board select-low when CNXX addressed, where N=slot no.
2	A0	Address line 0
3	A1	Address line 1
4	A2	Address line 2
5	A3	Address line 3
6	A4	Address line 4
7	A5	Address line 5
8	A6	Address line 6
9	A7	Address line 7
10	A8	Address line 8
11	A9	Address line 9
12	A10	Address line 10
13	A11	Address line 11
14	A12	Address line 12
15	A13	Address line 13
16	A14	Address line 14
17	A15	Address line 15
18	R/W̄	High for read, low for write
19	no connection	
20	I/O STROBE	Low during 02 if memory locations C800-CFFF accessed
21	RDY	Forces CPU to wait state
22	DMA	DMA request
23	INT OUT	Interrupt priority daisy chain
24	DMA OUT	DMA priority daisy chain output
25	+5V	+5V power supply
26	GND	System ground
27	DMA IN	DMA priority daisy chain input
28	INT IN	Interrupt priority daisy chain
29	NMI	Non-maskable interrupt request
30	IRQ	Interrupt request
31	RESET	System reset
32	INH	Inhibit all internal ROMs
33	−12V	−12V power supply
34	−5V	−5V power supply
35	no connection	
36	7M	7 MHz system clock
37	Q3	
38	01	System phase 1 clock
39	USER	User defined
40	00	System phase 0 clock
41	DEVICE SELECT	Low if one of 16 peripheral addresses assigned to slot accessed
42	D7	Data line 7
43	D6	Data line 6
44	D5	Data line 5
45	D4	Data line 4
46	D3	Data line 3
47	D2	Data line 2
48	D1	Data line 1
49	D0	Data line 0
50	+12V	+12V power supply

DMA OUT line sends the request on to the IN input of the next highest priority. It is all done with hardware and is very, very fast.

Lastly, the Apple II can supply small amounts of power to the peripherals through the +5, -5, +12, and -12 volt lines. This power will be just sufficient to run the interface cards. In large peripherals that require significant amounts of current, it is best to use a separate power supply.

MACINTOSH

The Macintosh computer constitutes a revolution in the way personal computing is done. It comes with 128K, 512K, or now 1024K of internal memory, and one or two disk drives, with a "hard" disk available as an optional extra. The internal processor is the Motorola 68000, which is a 32-bit parallel processor pushing data over 16-bit data lines.

For the Macintosh computer, interfacing is quite limited, especially with the 128 and 512K versions of the computer. The bus is not readily available to the user without opening the case and tracing the circuit lines directly off the PC board. For this reason, there is no way that a parallel device can be run directly off the Macintosh.

There are two serial ports, the printer port and the modem port, which are for all practical purposes identical. These are routed to two DB-9 connectors on the back (two DIN-8 connectors on the Macintosh Plus). See Fig. 2-24. These connectors are RS-422 serial connectors, and can be run at speeds up to 9600 baud without handshaking, and up to 57600 baud with handshaking.

See the next chapter for a discussion on RS-422 and how it relates to RS-232 serial communications. You can use some of the circuits there to translate RS-422 to RS-232 and back, and to translate it to "pseudoparallel" data transmission.

The Macintosh is programmed differently from any other computer discussed in this book. Most computers are "program-driven." That is, the program is written so that it does what you tell it to do from the keyboard, and keeps doing it until it asks you for more information from the keyboard. The Macintosh is "event-driven." That is, most

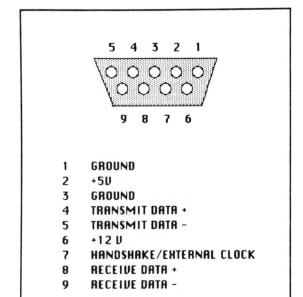

1	GROUND
2	+5U
3	GROUND
4	TRANSMIT DATA +
5	TRANSMIT DATA -
6	+12 U
7	HANDSHAKE/EXTERNAL CLOCK
8	RECEIVE DATA +
9	RECEIVE DATA -

Fig. 2-24. Macintosh RS-422 serial output connector.

programs are written to go through a loop searching for "events," such as the mouse button being down, a new disk in the drive, an input from the keyboard, and the like. When it finds one of these events, it takes the appropriate action on it, depending on several factors, such as the position of the mouse pointer. For this reason, the Macintosh is more difficult to program than other computers. It is not possible here to give a complete description of how to interface hardware to the serial ports of the Macintosh. Those who have the expertise to try this type of interfacing are encouraged to obtain a copy of *Inside Macintosh*, from Addison-Wesley Publishing. Volume II, pages 245-259 gives information on the software drivers, and Volume III, pages 22-25 gives information on the hardware interface inside the Macintosh itself. The serial ports can also be driven through one of the terminal emulation software packages on the market. *Macterminal* and *Red Ryder* are two of the best, and you can get *Freeterm* for free if you are a member of the Micronetworked Apple Users Group (MAUG) on COMPUSERVE.

Just before the second edition went to press, Apple introduced the Macintosh Plus, a one-megabyte version of the Macintosh, with an extra output port on the rear called the SCSI port. This port is intended for expansion of the Macintosh with additional devices. At this time, there is little, if anything, available as an explanation of how this port is to be interfaced with other devices. What little is available says that the SCSI port can be attached to as many as 7 other devices. The port is similar to the IEEE-488 standard, except that it is serial instead of parallel. The transfer rate is reputed to be in excess of 320,000 bits per second.

TANDY COLOR COMPUTER

The Color Computer from Tandy Radio Shack is probably one of the most underrated computers on the market. The Motorola 6809 processor has 16-bit capability in its internal registers using an 8-bit data bus, and a simple hardware modification to the printed circuit board allows use of the full 64K of memory, instead of the 32K it comes with. It can work with the OS-9 disk operating system which gives a set of powerful disk commands, as well as access to a library of OS-9 software. Tandy has done a great disservice to this little machine by selling it primarily as a games computer.

There are two primary methods of interface to the Tandy TRS-80 Color Computer, or "COCO" as it is usually called informally. The first is through the printer port. This port is a DIN-4 connector on the back of the machine which is, in actuality, an RS-232 serial port. It is configured by firmware to run at 600 baud, but can be changed by software to run at a variety of different speeds. A diagram of the port connector is shown in Fig. 2-25. The transmit data, receive data, and ground lines are readily apparent. In addition, pin 1 is an interrupt line, which causes an interrupt to the system if it goes low. This last can be useful if you have a peripheral that needs to cause an interrupt. This line is connected to the CA1 input line of an internal PIA at address $FF21. The RS-232 inputs and outputs are "software UART's," as described elsewhere in this book. The RS-232 output comes from line PA1 of a PIA at address $FF20, and the input line is connected to line PBO of a PIA at $FF22. All three lines go through level-shifters to convert TTL to RS-232 and back.

The other method of interfacing to the COCO is to go through the ROM slot on the side of the computer. This is the slot where ROM cartridges are placed for games and programs. There are also a variety of peripherals, such as additional RS-232

Fig. 2-25. 4-pin DIN connector, RS-232 port of Color Computer.

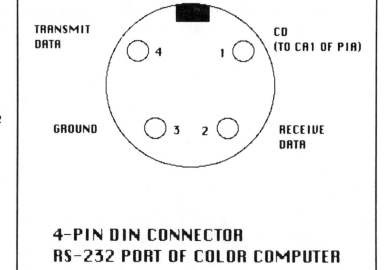

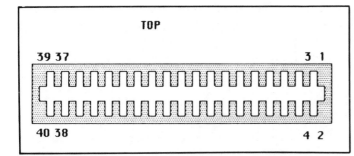

TOP

39 37   3 1

40 38   4 2

Fig. 2-26. Color Computer ROM cartridge slot connector.

ports and disk drives that come directly off the ROM slot. In essence, the ROM slot is an expansion port that takes the bus signals of the 6809 processor chip and makes them available to other equipment. A diagram of the COCO ROM slot is shown in Fig. 2-26, and the function of each of the

Table 2-5. Tandy Color Computer Cartridge Port Pins.

Pin	Signal	Decription
1	– 12 Vdc	
2	+ 14 Vdc	
3	HALT	Low halts CPU
4	NMI	Active low, Non-Maskable Interrupt
5	RESET	Active Low, Power on or Reset
6	E	Clock
7	Q	Clock
8	CART	Cartridge Sense
9	+ 5 Vdc	
10	D0	Data Bus
11	D1	Data Bus
12	D2	Data Bus
13	D3	Data Bus
14	D4	Data Bus
15	D5	Data Bus
16	D6	Data Bus
17	D7	Data Bus
18	R/W	Read/Write, low for write
19	A0	Address Bus
20	A1	Address Bus
21	A2	Address Bus
22	A3	Address Bus
23	A4	Address Bus
24	A5	Address Bus
25	A6	Address Bus
26	A7	Address Bus
27	A8	Address Bus
28	A9	Address Bus
29	A10	Address Bus
30	A11	Address Bus
31	A12	Address Bus
32	CTS	Low when addresses COOO-DFFF active
33	GND	Signal ground
34	GND	Signal ground
35	SND	External Sound, enables sound to TV audio
36	SCS	Low when addresses FF40-FF5F active
37	A13	Address Bus
38	A14	Address Bus
39	A15	Address Bus
40	SLENB	Low disables internal address decoding

pins is shown in Table 2-5. The COCO ROM slot is a card-edge connector designed to interface with a 40-pin double-sided PC edge connector.

TRS-80 MODEL 4

The TRS-80 model 4 from Tandy has proven to be a very popular computer. It is a totally self-contained machine, with 64K or 128K of memory, up to two disk drives, and built-in BASIC and Disk Operating System, and has an 80-column upper/lowercase display and graphics. It is one of the most powerful 8-bit parallel processing machines on the market, and there is a wide selection of software available for it. It uses an 8-bit data bus.

Without actually taking the model 4 apart and disconnecting some of the internal data lines, interfacing to the model 4 is limited. There are only two output connectors on the model 4 accessible from the outside of the machine.

The first port is a standard RS-232 serial port. It is reached through the DB-25 connector on the bottom of the machine. This port is made for connection to a modem or a serial printer, but it can be used for almost any serial device using standard RS-232.

The other output port is slightly less standard. This is the port that is actually intended for connection to a parallel printer. It is a parallel output port using the Centronics standard of parallel output, but does not use the Centronics connector. Instead, there is a PC card edge at the bottom of the computer. A diagram of the pins is shown in Fig. 2-27, and a table of the function of the pins is given in Table 2-6. Notice that there is no ACK signal, which is standard for Centronics parallel. Instead, it relies upon the BUSY signal for parallel handshaking. If it were not for the connector, this would be straight Centronics parallel. Radio Shack sells a cable which converts the card-edge connector to a Centronics connector, or you can make one of your own for a lot less with the information given here.

Using these two ports, it is possible to interface parallel or serial devices to the Model 4 without much difficulty.

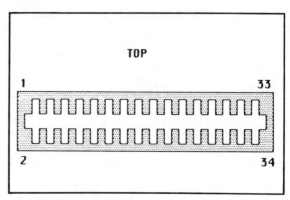

Fig. 2-27. TRS-80 Model 4 parallel printer port connector.

TRS-80 MODEL 1000

The Tandy model 1000 is a popular computer that is very similar to the IBM-PC. It will run the IBM software unchanged in most cases. The place where it differs is in the hardware.

The model 1000 has three expansion slots much like those on the IBM-PC, except that PC cards will not fit into the slots with the cover on. The connections to the slots are electrically identical to those of the PC, but the case of the model 1000 has a "lower profile" than the PC, and the expansion cards sold by Tandy are necessarily shorter in height. If you would be willing to run the 1000 without a cover or front panel, PC cards would probably work just fine. For those who have an interest in interfacing to the 1000 through the expansion slots, consult the section on the IBM-PC.

The Model 1000 also has a built-in parallel port, which is marked as the "printer" port. This is a card-edge connector on the rear of the case. This connector is identical to the parallel port on the Model 4, discussed above.

TRS-80 MODELS 1200 AND 3000

Tandy sells the TRS-80 models 1200 and 3000 as "clones" of the IBM-PC XT and IBM-PC AT, respectively. Most IBM software created for the IBM personal computer will run unmodified on these models. In addition, Tandy has configured these machines so that Tandy expansion boards may be used in the IBM-PC and most IBM-PC ex-

Pin	Line	Function
1		NC
2	GND	Logic ground
3	PD0	Data line 0
4	GND	Logic Ground
5	PD1	Data line 1
6	GND	Logic ground
7	PD2	Data line 2
8	GND	Logic ground
9	PD3	Data line 3
10	GND	Logic ground
11	PD4	Data line 4
12	GND	Logic ground
13	PD5	Data line 5
14	GND	Logic ground
15	PD6	Data line 6
16	GND	Logic ground
17	PD7	Data line 7
18	GND	Logic ground
19		not used
20	GND	Logic Ground
21	BUSY	high when printer busy
22	GND	Logic Ground
23	PAPER	Printer sets this when out of paper
24	GND	Logic Ground
25	UNIT SEL	Select device
26		not used
27	GND	Logic Ground
28	FAULT	Problem with printer (active low)
29		not used
30		not used
31		no connection
32		not used
33		no connection
34	GND	Logic ground

Table 2-6. Tandy Model 4 Printer Port Lines.

pansion boards will fit into these models. For further information about interfacing to one of these models, consult the section on interfacing to the IBM Personal Computer.

THE IBM PERSONAL COMPUTER, PC-XT, AND PC-AT

When any new technology is sufficiently advanced to become profitable, major corporations begin to move into the market. The personal computer market was started by companies like MITS and SWTP, defined as a consumer product by companies like Tandy and Apple, and has come into its own as a major market force through the efforts of IBM. International Business Machines, as of this writing, has almost 70% of the world market in mainframe computers, and because of its excellent reputation in that field, has come to capture the largest percentage of the personal computer market. Indeed, its reputation is so excellent that people will buy an IBM personal computer without even comparison shopping, simply because of the IBM name. For this reason, and for the quality of its product, the IBM personal computer is, at this writing, the standard against which personal computers are measured.

The IBM-PC is a physically large machine, with up to 640K of memory, serial and parallel output ports, up to two floppy disk drives, and one high-speed "hard" disk drive. The internal processor is an 8088 16-bit parallel processor, with 8-bit data bus lines.

There are several methods of interface to the IBM-PC. Up to two parallel ports can be plugged into the expansion slots, as well as up to two serial RS-232 ports. Custom interfaces can also be connected to the internal expansion slots.

A diagram of the card connector for the expansion slots is shown in Fig. 2-28. Table 2-7 gives the function of each of the pins in the slot. The PC has twenty address lines, and can directly address a full megabyte of data, although internal system addresses reserve the upper 400K of memory, so that only the lower 640K is actually usable by RAM.

COMMODORE 64

The Commodore 64 is an extremely popular little machine. It is a very powerful computer, with a whole set of peripherals available, and retails for a very reasonable price. It uses the Motorola 6510 processor, which is similar to the 6502 processor of its predecessors, the PET and VIC. This is an 8-bit parallel processor with an 8-bit data path. It can address a full 64K of memory. The Commodore 128 is very similar, with a few differences, the major one being that it can address 128K of memory.

The C-64 has three connectors on the back which are suitable for connection of peripherals. One is the so-called "serial port." Rather than being a true RS-232 serial port, it is actually a port which is similar to the IEEE-488 bus. Multiple devices can be attached to this port, so each device has to have a way of identifying itself to the C-64 as a unique device, so they don't get each other's signals mixed up. In the IEEE-488 bus, each device has a "talk address" and a "listen address." This method is similar to that used on the C-64, except that the IEEE-488 is a parallel bus, and the C-64 serial port is a serial bus, with only one data line.

There is also another port called the "user

port." It is basically an 8-bit parallel port, with a few extra control lines. It also uses the "Attention" line of the serial bus above. With proper software to control the status lines, and a little re-wiring to a Centronics connector, it could be used as a standard parallel port.

The interface we are interested in is the "ex-

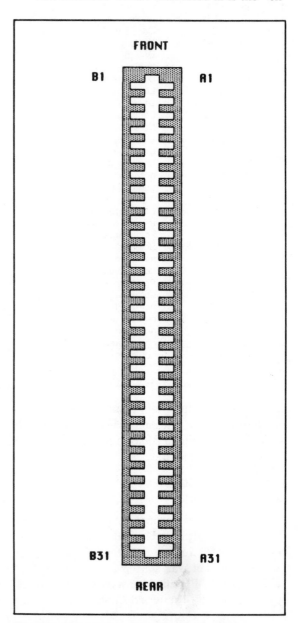

Fig. 2-28. IBM internal expansion slot connector.

Table 2-7. IBM-PC Expansion Slot Pin and Signal Definitions.

PIN	SIGNAL	DEFINITION
A1	I/O CH CK	Active low, reports error on I/O channel
A2	D0	Data
A3	D1	Data
A4	D2	Data
A5	D3	Data
A6	D4	Data
A7	D5	Data
A8	D6	Data
A9	D7	Data
A10	I/O CH RDY	I/O Channel ready, for slow memory or I/O
A11	AEN	Address enable, DMA cycle in progress
A12	A19	Address
A13	A18	Address
A14	A17	Address
A15	A16	Address
A16	A15	Address
A17	A14	Address
A18	A13	Address
A19	A12	Address
A20	A11	Address
A21	A10	Address
A22	A9	Address
A23	A8	Address
A24	A7	Address
A25	A6	Address
A26	A5	Address
A27	A4	Address
A28	A3	Address
A29	A2	Address
A30	A1	Address
A31	A0	Address
B1	GND	Signal ground
B2	RESET DRV	High during system power-up
B3	+5 Vdc	
B4	IRQ2	Interrupt request 2
B5	−5 Vdc	
B6	DRQ2	DMA request 2
B7	−12 Vdc	
B8		(not used)
B9	+12 Vdc	
B10	GND	Signal ground
B11	MEMW	Active low. Write data into memory.
B12	MEMR	Active low. Read data from memory
B13	IOW	Active low. Write to I/O port on addr bus
B14	IOR	Active low. Read from I/O port.
B15	DACK3	DMA access acknowledge 3
B16	DRQ3	DMA request 3
B17	DACK1	DMA access acknowledge 1
B18	DRQ1	DMA request 1
B19	DACK0	DMA access acknowledge 0
B20	CLK	4.77 MHz clock, synchronized to memory read cycle
B21	IRQ7	Interrupt request 7
B22	IRQ6	Interrupt request 6
B23	IRQ5	Interrupt request 5
B24	IRQ4	Interrupt request 4
B25	IRQ3	Interrupt request 3
B26	DACK2	DMA access acknowledge 2
B27	T/C	Terminal count. Blocks DMA transfer.
B28	ALE	Address Latch Enable. Address bus is valid.
B29	+5 Vdc	
B30	OSC	14.318 MHz signal, 50% duty cycle
B31	GND	Signal ground

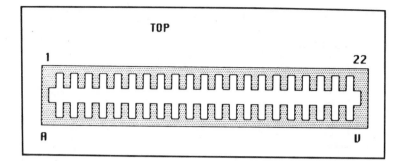

TOP

1   22

A   U

Fig. 2-29. Commodore C-64 expansion port connector.

pansion port." Like the Color Computer, this is just a connector which brings the various bus lines of the 6510 processor out to where they can be reached. Figure 2-29 gives the structure of the connector to this port, and Table 2-8 is a table of the functions of each of these lines.

COMPAQ, LEADING EDGE, KAYPRO-PC, AND OTHER IBM-COMPATIBLES

These computers are sold for the "plug-compatible" market. That is, they are sold as "clones" of the IBM-PC, with one or more special advantages, such as higher speed. Virtually all sell for lower prices than the PC, which is their main calling card. Most IBM software created for the IBM personal computer will run unmodified on these models. In addition, the manufacturers have configured these machines so that most IBM-PC expansion boards will fit into these models. For further information about interfacing to one of these models, consult the section on interfacing to the IBM Personal Computer.

ADDRESS DECODING

All the addresses that can be used, whether in I/O-mapped interfacing or in memory-mapped interfacing, are contained on the address bus. There are 65,536 possible memory-mapped addresses, and 256 possible I/O-mapped ports. In order to be able to use these addresses and ports, we must be able to decode the address bus so that one port or interface location is used and no other.

We need to develop some circuits that will tell us when the correct address is being used. The only difference between memory-mapped I/O decoding

and I/O-mapped decoding is that in memory-mapped I/O, all 16 address lines must be tested to make sure that the correct address is being used, while in I/O-mapped decoding, only the least significant eight bits of the address bus must be tested. To be sure, different control-bus signals will be used for each.

Address decoding is essentially performing the AND function on a number of data bits on the address bus. If we were going to use the hexadecimal location $8004 for an interface chip for an output port, we look at what $8004 means:

$$\$8004 = 1000\ 0000\ 0000\ 0100_2$$

When we decode this address, we want to have a signal inactive when these particular patterns of 1s and 0s are *not* on the address bus, and active when this particular pattern of 1s and 0s *is* present on the address bus. We are really saying that "we want the output to be active when A15 is a 1 *and* A14 is a 0 *and* A13 is a 0 *and* A12 is a 0 *and* . . . ."

It would seem logical that the use of an AND gate would give us the proper decoding of the address. (By the way, most address-decode signals are active-low. That is, we want the signal that says we have the proper address to be low when, in fact, we do have the proper address, and high otherwise.) The problem with this type of decoding is that the inputs can be either high or low, and we want an AND when there is a certain pattern of 1s and 0s present. Also, there is no 16-input AND gate available for sale. The 7430 integrated circuit is an eight-input NAND gate, and since we want active-low anyway, it can serve for eight bits at a time. To get the proper patterns of 1s and 0s, all we need to do

PIN	SIGNAL	USAGE
1	GND	Signal ground
2	+5 V	
3	+5 V	
4	IRQ	Active low; interrupt request to processor
5	R/W	Read/Write. Write is low.
6	DOTCLK	8.18 MHz dot scan cycle
7	I/01	Active low; low for addresses DEOO to DEFF
8	GAME	Active low; input to address manager
9	EXROM	Active low; input to address manager
10	I/O2	Active low; low for addresses DFOO to DFFF
11	ROML	Active low; output from address manager
12	BA	Bus Available: Valid data on bus
13	DMA	Active; disconnect processor from bus
14	CD7	Data bit 7
15	CD6	Data bit 6
16	CD5	Data bit 5
17	CD4	Data bit 4
18	CD3	Data bit 3
19	CD2	Data bit 2
20	CD1	Data bit 1
21	CD0	Data bit 0
22	GND	Signal ground
A	GND	Signal ground
B	ROMH	Output from address manager
C	RESET	Active low; reset system
D	MNI	Active Low; non-maskable interrupt
E	02	System clock
F	A15	Address line 15
G	A14	Address line 14
H	A13	Address line 13
I	A12	Address line 12
J	A11	Address line 11
K	A10	Address line 10
L	A9	Address line 9
M	A8	Address line 8
N	A7	Address line 7
O	A6	Address line 6
P	A5	Address line 5
Q	A4	Address line 4
R	A3	Address line 3
S	A2	Address line 2
T	A1	Address line 1
U	A0	Address line 0
V	GND	Signal ground

Table 2-8. C-64 Expansion Port.

is to INVERT all the desired 0s to 1s, so that the input to the NAND gate will all be 1s when the correct address appears. For two NAND gates, we must perform an active-low AND on the outputs of the eight-bit NANDs to get an active-low SELECT signal.

The complete circuit to decode the address $F7F8 is given in Fig. 2-30. The hexadecimal number $F7F8 is 1111 0111 1111 1000_2. We want 0s to appear on address lines A11, and A0, A1, and A2. These lines are inverted so that a 0 appears as a 1 at the input of the gate. The lower part of the diagram shows the single-gate decoding of the hexadecimal number 9 out of four address bits.

This type of decoder is good if you want to decode one address and have only that address or

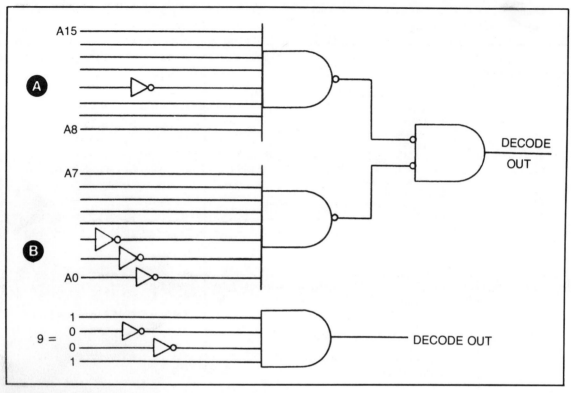

Fig. 2-30. (A) NAND gate decoding; (B) A 4-bit decoder for the number 9.

range of addresses on the card. When you have several devices on the same card, it is not necessary to have a separate decoder for each. The major disadvantage of the decoder is that it requires a lot of separate chips and a considerable amount of wiring. Also, once the wiring is set up, it is difficult to change it without rewiring the circuit. In addition, it responds only to one address.

As you might expect, there are special decoder chips made especially for the purpose of address decoding. These are chips like the 74LS138 three-line to eight-line decoder, and the 74154 four-line to sixteen-line decoder. Recall that there are eight possible addresses spanned by the least-significant three address lines, and sixteen addresses by four lines. These decoders drop an output line to zero corresponding to the address inputs. For example, the 74LS138 has three address lines and eight output lines, numbered 0 through 7. When the address inputs are the binary number 3, then output line 3

goes low, and no others. Both the '138 and the '154 have enable inputs as well (they are not three-state), so they ignore any address at the inputs when the enable input is inactive, and no outputs will go low.

Figure 2-31 shows how a 74154 might be used as a primary memory decoder for a memory board. The 2114 static memory is organized as 1K by 4 bits, so it only takes two 2114 chips to make 1K of memory. Each 2114 has an enable input that enables the chip and releases the outputs from the three-state. To make a bank of 16K of memory using 2114s, the top two address lines are decoded to the proper bank area using a 74LS138, and the particular chip is enabled by the output of the 74154 corresponding to that pair of chips. With 16 outputs, 16 pairs of chips can be accessed, for a total of 16K of memory. Note that the decode for the most significant two address bits is used as an enable for the next four. The 2114s have their own internal decoders for the least significant ten address bits. If the board were larger, we could use another 74154 to be enabled by another output of the 74LS138, and 32 more 2114s, to get another 16K of memory. There are several uses of this type of memory decoding. First of all, note that in Fig. 2-32, we can use a 74LS138 to decode three address bits, and then select, by wiring to the particular output, what the decoded address will be. This is called *jumper address assignment*. We could replace the jumper by a series of switches, as in a *dipswitch*, which has eight SPST switches in a package that fits an integrated-circuit socket. By letting just one of the switches be on, and all the others open, we can select the address decoding for the device. In this way, the address decoding is easily changeable, without extensive rewiring.

This type of memory decoding is widely used. The SS-30 bus, the Apple II output bus, all use this type of decoding, and the active-low output is called the SELECT line on the bus. All the output ports are therefore in consecutive order according to the output of the decoder chip.

For decoding which can be easily and rapidly changed by means of switches, the 7485 four-bit comparator is hard to beat. It examines four bits each of two inputs, designated "*a*" and "*b*," and issues an output that tells their relationship. The three possible outputs are *a* equals *b,a* is less than *b*, and *a* is greater than *b*. The *a* equals *b* output is used as a device-selector line. The *a* inputs are connected to a bank of four bits of the address bus, and the *b* inputs are connected to a set of switches

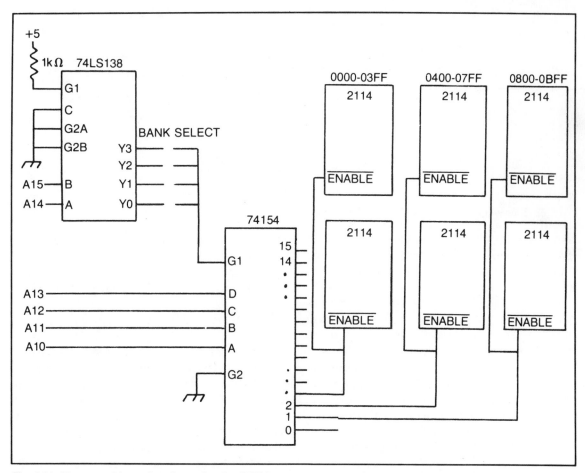

Fig. 2-31. Memory address decoding using the 74154.

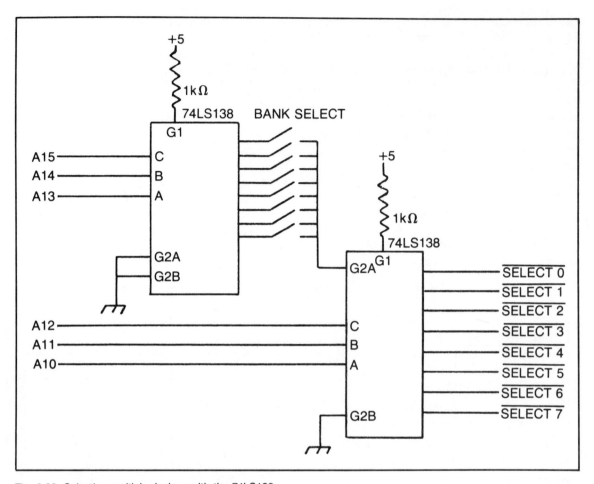

Fig. 2-32. Selecting multiple devices with the 74LS138.

that can be set to either 0 or 1, as shown in Fig. 2-33. The address desired can be selected by setting the switches, or the address can be hard-wired by connecting the *b* inputs to ground, or to the power supply through a 10000-ohm resistor. The only time the *a = b* line will be high will be when the address present at the *a* inputs is the same as the address programmed into the *b* inputs.

As was shown in Fig. 2-31, these decoder chips can be cascaded to give a full decoding of all 16 addresses, or as many chips as needed can be cascaded together to decode as many addresses as necessary. You usually will find that the more significant digits will have to be decoded for some SELECT or ENABLE line, while two, or four, or ten of the least significant lines will remain undecoded

except internally by the memory or interface chip itself. This will be necessary because the memory chip or interface chip contains more than one register and must have several addresses it can respond to.

Lastly, if you have lots of memory space to waste, you don't have to decode *all* of the address lines, but you may use partial-address decoding. For example, if you have an interface at $8000 and will be putting nothing into the whole block of addresses from $8000 to $8FFF, it will only be necessary to decode the $8. For example, if you are using a 6820 peripheral-interface adapter, which needs four addresses on the bus, and want to put it from $8000 to $8003, and will use nothing else all the way up to $8FFF, you need only supply the A0 and A1

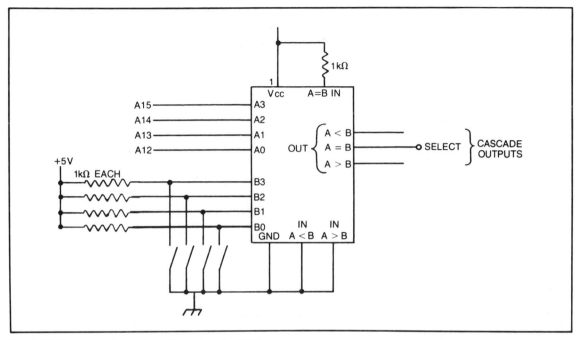

Fig. 2-33. Memory address decoding using the 7485.

lines to the 6820, and decode A12 through A15 to be an $8. The other addresses don't matter. The register which is at $8000 will respond to $8000, and to $8004, $8008, $800C, $8010, . . . all the way to $8FFC. The other combinations from the address lines A3 through A11 will not be decoded, so all combinations of those lines are allowed. Many manufacturers save money on development costs by using partial-address decoding in this manner.

It has been mentioned before that a *memory map* is a necessity for the interfacing task. This is because you will not want to place an interface at a memory location where there already exists RAM, ROM, or another peripheral. If you did so, the data lines would overlap and the data sent to the processor would be confused. To put in an interface, you must place it where nothing else exists at the time.

A memory map is a diagram, or at least a listing of where everything is in memory, what it is used for, and where the blanks are. The sample memory map in Fig. 2-34 shows that there is RAM from $0000 through $7FFF, an interface at $8004 through $8007, more RAM from $A000 through

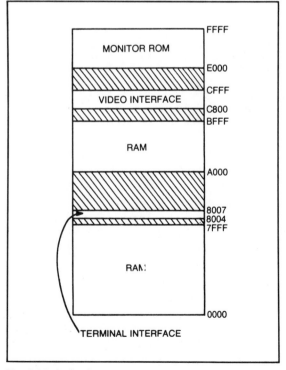

Fig. 2-34. A simple memory map.

$BFFF, a video interface from $C800 through $CFFF, and a ROM monitor from $E000 through $FFFF. There is plenty of empty space in the system to add additional interfaces.

Before you add any interfaces to your system, be sure you have a memory map, know what areas to avoid, and where you can expand your RAM and interfaces in the future.

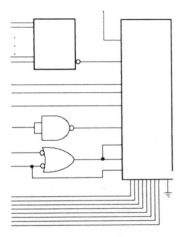

Chapter 3

Interfacing

The process of connecting a peripheral to a computer is called interfacing, which can be a formidable task. There is address decoding to worry about, as well as gating of the control signals and three-state buffers.

So far, we have only thought about the types of signals on the computer side of the interface. Standards do exist for the signals on the peripheral side of the interface, as well. Let's spend a little time discussing the nature of these signals.

PARALLEL INTERFACE STANDARDS

The title of this section is really a misnomer, because *standards* for parallel interfacing do not exist. There are probably as many ways of interfacing a peripheral through parallel lines as there are manufacturers that make those peripherals. Some common patterns do exist, however, and there is one pattern —the *Centronics parallel* method—which is used by a great many manufacturers and has been more or less accepted as a de facto standard.

Parallel input/output is the communications method which sends all eight bits of the data word to the peripheral (or receives them from the peripheral) all at once. Each data bit requires one wire, or data line, from the interface to the peripheral. There must also be a ground line for reference, for a total of nine lines. In addition, there may be one or more control lines from the interface to the peripheral for the purpose of informing the peripheral or computer that data is present on the lines, and another to acknowledge that the data has been accepted. These latter are not necessary in many cases, but are indispensable for high-speed communications. These extra lines are called the control-bits, or *handshaking*, lines.

Again, the convention for the direction of the data is that if the information flows from the peripheral to the computer, it is said to be an input process, while if data flows from the computer to the peripheral, it is an output process.

Data lines are usually not inverted, so that a + 5 volt signal on the data line represents a 1, and a grounded line is a 0. All data lines are active-high.

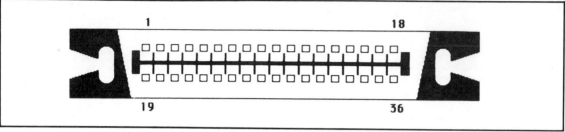

Fig. 3-1. Centronics parallel connector.

Handshaking in the Centronics system is fairly simple, using only two (or three, sometimes) extra wires in the bundle of wires connecting peripheral to computer. There are eight data lines, a ground line, and two handshaking lines, the STROBE and BUSY lines. The STROBE line is normally high, and goes low momentarily when the sending device puts data onto the data lines. The BUSY line is normally low, and is set high by the receiving device while it is "busy" processing the data. When it is finished, it takes the BUSY line low, indicating to the sending device that it is ready to receive another STROBE pulse.

An alternate, and perhaps more commonly used form of this handshaking method is to send the short STROBE pulse as above, and then for the receiving device to send a short, active-low AC-KNOWLEDGE pulse back to the sender when the receiver has finished with the data.

In most printers with a parallel input, both methods are available. Check your user manual for the printer you own. EPSON and IBM parallel printers mostly have both types in the connector.

Since readers may have parallel equipment that they want to interface to a computer, or may wish to connect some of the devices described in this book to a computer's parallel port, the Centronics parallel connector itself is shown in Fig. 3-1, with the number of all data lines indicated. There are 36 possible lines, many of which are not used in most applications. The function of the most commonly used lines is indicated in Table 3-1. In most cases, it will be necessary to connect ground only to pin 16. Some applications will also require that pin 17, the chassis ground, be connected. A very few applications will not want to use a common ground, but will want grounds for all the data lines individually. Pin 19 is the ground for STROBE,

Table 3-1. Centronics Parallel Data Lines.

PIN	NAME	FUNCTION
1	STROBE	Active low. Signal that valid data is on lines.
2	D1	Data line 1
3	D2	Data line 2
4	D3	Data line 3
5	D4	Data line 4
6	D5	Data line 5
7	D6	Data line 6
8	D7	Data line 7
9	D8	Data line 8
10	ACK	Active low. Data received, ready for more data
11	BUSY	High indicates device cannot receive data
16,17	GND	Chassis and logic ground

Lines 19 through 27 may also need to be tied to ground.

while pins 20 through 27 are the grounds for data lines D1-D8, respectively. Pins 28 and 29 are the grounds for ACKNOWLEDGE and BUSY. In a few instances, you may have to connect all of these pins to logic ground.

In either case, the purpose of the handshaking is to inform the device sending the data that the receiving device has accepted and processed the data and to let the receiving device know that the data on the lines right now is new data, not old data.

Centronics corporation manufacturers printers. Although computers could conceivably send data to a printer several thousand times a second, there is a maximum rate at which a printer can print. Depending on the type of printer, this maximum rate can vary from ten to a few hundred characters a second. It is certainly obvious that the computer can send faster than the printer can put ink to paper. The printer has to have a way to tell the computer, "I'm still busy with the last one—don't send anything else yet." The problem is especially acute when the carriage return is processed. Some printers take a full second to move the carriage return to the opposite side of the page. The computer has to know not to send any more characters until the carriage return has been executed.

It isn't always necessary to use full handshaking, or for that matter, it may not be necessary to use handshaking at all. If a parallel port is connected just to a series of switches whose value can be either a 0 or a 1 (called *sense switches*), all you are interested in doing is reading the status of the switches at that moment; no handshaking is required. Also, in the case of a keyboard, the computer can process the input from a keyboard much faster than the fingers of the operator can type the information. The computer simply accepts the information, processes it, and waits for the next READY pulse; again, no handshaking is required.

In short, an ACK pulse is only required if the receiving device is slower than the sending device. A READY signal is only required if an ACK signal is needed, you want to make sure that the data you are reading is new, significant data, even though the data may be the same as it was a few instants ago.

Parallel data communications is one-directional only. For two-way communications, two separate parallel lines are needed. Also, parallel communications are only satisfactory over short distances—a few meters at most. At greater distances than this, the mutual capacitance of the lines causes crosstalk between the lines. Also, if the data lines have to be routed through an area where there is a lot of electronic or high-voltage electrical equipment, the data lines can pick up stray voltages from their surroundings.

SERIAL INTERFACE STANDARDS

For longer distances, many of the above problems with parallel interfacing can be solved with *serial data transfer*. Centronics parallel requires at least eleven conductors for a data transfer. Such cable is expensive—a dollar will buy a few feet at most. For distances of hundreds of yards or more, the price would be prohibitive. The connectors on either end are expensive as well.

If one is not interested in the maximum possible data transfer rate, or if the receiving device is slow anyway, serial data transfer offers a solution.

Serial transmission has, however, standardized on a type of connector for RS-232 transmission. This is the DB-25 connector, shown in Fig. 3-2, and the most commonly used pins of this connector are shown in Table 3-2. Pins 1 and 7 are ground, and are frequently tied together. The data itself is put over lines 2 and 3. Be sure that the input of one device is connected to the output of another, and vice-versa. (Sometimes these two lines are reversed when connecting to a modem.) The Request to Send (RTS) and Clear to Send (CTS) are handshaking lines, active high. Lastly, Data Set Ready (DSR) and Data Terminal Ready (DTR) are indicators (active high) that the terminal or data set (modem) to which the particular piece of equipment is connected is turned on and ready to process data. In the *asynchronous* mode, only one data line and one ground line are needed to send data from the sending device to the receiving device. Only three wires are needed for full two-way communications. Some terminals require additional wires to make sure that

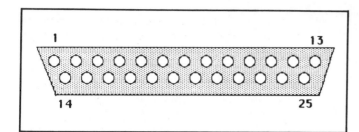

Fig. 3-2. DB-25 connector for RS-232 serial data transmission.

the data-rate clocking is correct, or to make sure that the receiving device is turned on and ready to work. Some manufacturers use this line to actually turn the machine on.

Since there is only one data line in each direction, the sending of eight bits of data requires that the information be time-multiplexed. That is, that different bits are sent out at different times. Serial communications works like this: A data bit is placed on the line. After a specified length of time, the next data bit of the byte is placed on the line, and another specified time length is waited. This process is continued until all data bits have been sent. The usual standard is that you send the least-significant bit first, then the second, ending up with the most-significant bit.

One method of doing this is to use synchronous serial communications in which a clock line is in parallel with the data and ground lines. The rising edge of the clock pulse indicates that a bit is being sent. The transmit and receive shift registers depend on this clock line to stay in synchronization. If the shift registers get even one clock period out of synch, then data is transmitted incorrectly. Also, a synchronous system must either be transmitting data all the time, or have special codes (the ASCII control codes form the basis for these control codes) to indicate the start and stop of a transmission.

A very common form of serial-data communication (much more common than synchronous) eliminates the need for a clock line or start and stop control codes. This form is called *asynchronous serial-data* communication. Asynchronous communication relies on the fact that two clocks of approximately the same frequency will remain fairly well synchronized over a short period of time. Instead of having a clock line along with the data lines, both transmitter and receiver have their own clocks running at the same frequency, or close enough as makes no difference over the space of time needed to send one byte.

Instead of having start-transmission and stop-transmission control codes, data may arrive at any time. The receiver knows that it is to start processing input data into its shift register by the receipt of a *start bit*, which is always a "0." Then eight data bits are sent in succession, and the series of data is finished off with either one or two *stop bits*, which are always "1." Some systems, such as those using slow Teletype® machines need two stop bits, while most video display terminals need only one.

The most commonly used form of serial-data transmission is the *RS-232* standard. This standard was developed for communications between computers and data terminals where the data lines have to go through areas where there is a lot of stray electrical noise, such as from the plant office to a foreman's office through a machine shop. It is extremely resistant to noise. The standard defines a "0" to be any voltage between +3 and +18 volts. A "1" is any voltage between -3 and -18 volts. The region between -3 and +3 volts is considered to be "no signal." Figure 3-3 shows how a data bit

Table 3-2. RS-232 DB-25 Data Lines.

PIN	NAME	FUNCTION
1	GND	Chassis ground
2	TD	Transmitted data
3	RD	Received data
4	RTS	Request to send
5	CTS	Clear to send
6	DSR	Data set (modem) ready
7	GND	Signal ground
20	DTR	Data terminal ready

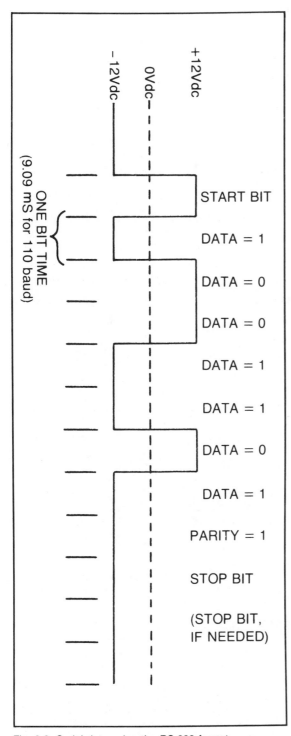

+12Vdc

0Vdc

−12Vdc

ONE BIT TIME
(9.09 mS for 110 baud)

START BIT

DATA = 1

DATA = 0

DATA = 0

DATA = 1

DATA = 1

DATA = 0

DATA = 1

PARITY = 1

STOP BIT

(STOP BIT,
IF NEEDED)

Fig. 3-3. Serial data using the RS-232 format.

would appear in RS-232. The data line is normally held at − 12 volts. The receiver ignores anything that happens on this data line until a "0" is received—that is until the data line rises to *at least* + 3 volts. Furthermore, the "0" must stay on the line for at least one-half of one full bit time to be valid. After this start bit is received, the receiver begins to process the remaining bits in order, until eight have been received. Then, one or two stop bits of "1" *must* follow the data, or the receiver will decide that the data received was in error, and flag it to be a possible error. This last is called a *receiver framing error*. If parity is used, the eighth bit just before the stop bit(s) will be the parity.

In addition to the data and ground lines, some RS-232 receivers need additional lines to carry information about the status of the terminal or the computer, such as RTS (request to send) and DSR (data set ready) and CTS (clear to send). Others are used only when connected to a *modem* (modulator/demodulator) for telephone communications.

Serial communications require very complex circuitry to handle the shifting-in and shifting-out of data bits from a time-multiplexed line. The RS-232 standard, especially, has found wide application, and for this reason, a number of special-purpose integrated circuits have been developed especially for use in asynchronous serial-data communication. Among these are the Asynchronous Communications Interface Adapter (ACIA) and the Universal Asynchronous Receiver Transmitter (UART). These integrated circuits will be discussed along with their applications later in this chapter.

There are even circuits that will translate the 1 and 0 of TTL logic levels (active-high) to RS-232 levels. These circuits are quite simple, and a few are shown in Fig. 3-4. These circuits are essentially inverters which operate from RS-232 power-supply levels and TTL power-supply levels, and convert one to the other. It can be done with a single transistor, with common operational amplifiers, or with the special-purpose integrated circuits available, such as the MC1488 and MC1489 RS-232-to-TTL drivers. Use of these latter will guarantee proper output impedances.

Very similar to RS-232 is the 20 mA TTY loop.

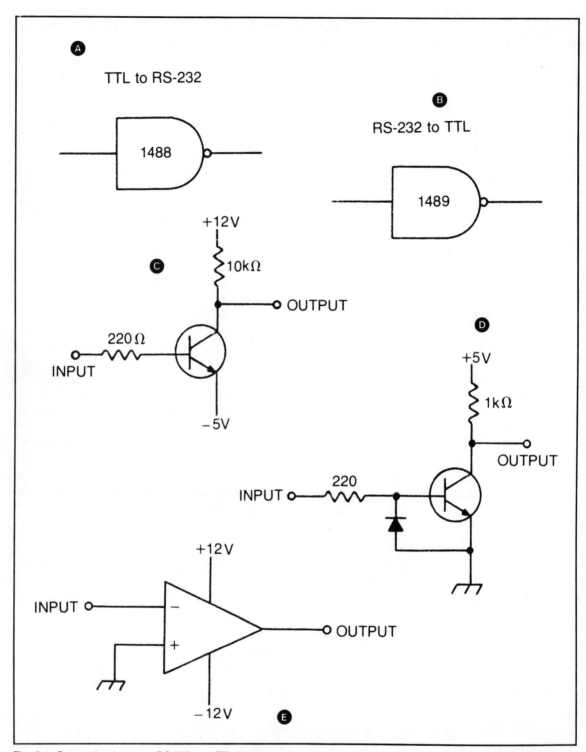

Fig. 3-4. Conversion between RS-232 and TTL levels.

Again, start and stop bits are used, with separate lines for data in and data out. In this case two stop bits are used. The major difference is that in RS-232, the voltage levels are important, while in TTY loop, the current levels are the determining factor as to whether a bit is a 0 or a 1. Here, a "0" is a current of 20 milliamperes in the loop, and a "1" is no current. The 20-milliampere current is used to drive a set of solenoids which actuate the printing mechanism, or is created by the closing of a switch so that current may flow.

Conversion from RS-232 to TTY loop or back is quite simple. A method of doing so is illustrated in Fig. 3-5, as is the means of connection of such signals to the ASR-33 Teletype® machine which is manufactured by the Teledyne corporation. This terminal is among the most popular used by the hobbyist because it combines printer, terminal, and mass-storage device (in the form of a paper tape reader and punch) all in one inexpensive package.

We have not yet answered the question, "How fast are the data bits sent over a serial line?" The answer is just about any speed you would like to send them. The limiting factor will be, of course, the maximum data rate capability of either the receiver or the transmitter, whichever is slower. Usually, a microcomputer can send very fast, and it is the receiving device that limits the data rate.

The rate at which data is sent over the serial-data lines is called the *baud rate*. The baud num-

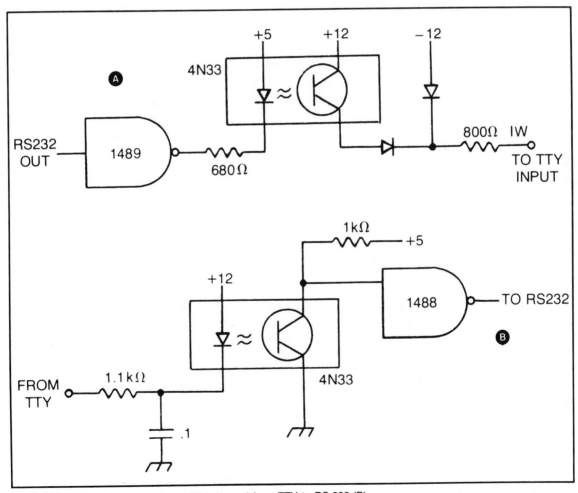

Fig. 3-5. Conversion from RS-232 to TTY (A), and from TTY to RS-232 (B).

63

ber is, for all practical purposes, the number of bits, including start, stop, and parity bits, that are sent every second. This isn't the exact definition of the baud rate, but it will do for our purposes. One start bit, one stop bit, and eight data bits totals ten bits. A rate of 300 baud would be 30 × 10 data bits per second, or 30 characters per second. One of the most common data rates used with peripheral devices is 300 baud. Fast video terminals can run 1200 baud or faster. Some printers can go to 9600 baud, and there are devices that run ten times faster yet.

The ASR-33 Teletype® uses 110 baud. This is 10 characters per second, not 11 as you might expect, because the ASR-33 requires two stop bits, not one, and 11 bits must be sent for one character.

There are three ways to generate a data clock to send serial data. The obvious way is to use a data clock that changes with the data being sent. No problem with this in transmitting, but one cannot guarantee that the data will arrive on the rising edge of the receiver's data clock. For this purpose, most data rate clocks run at a multiple of the data rate. The most frequently used values are 16 times the data rate, and 64 times the data rate, called × 16 and × 64 data clocks. Both ends of the system have to agree *exactly* on what the bit rate is and what clock rate is to be used to run it. With microcomputers, the most common data rate is 300 baud, with a × 16 clock. The × 16 clock allows the received data to be received even if not directly on a rising clock pulse, but very close to it. The 1200-baud data rate is the fastest that can be handled by the telephone company without the use of specially dedicated lines or expensive modems. The fastest baud rates—9600 and above—generally use a synchronous data transmission. With 110 baud, a bit time is 9.09 milliseconds. That is, the start bit lasts 9.09 milliseconds, and each successive bit lasts 9.09 milliseconds.

To sum up, the way a serial asynchronous data receiver works is this: When the serial input line to the receiver goes to + 12 Vdc for the first time, indicating that a start bit has been received, the receiver counts eight clock pulses to locate the cen-

ter of the start bit. The sampling point is then taken as every sixteenth clock pulse from that point on. This will eliminate any confusion as to what the value of the data bit is on a rising or falling edge. Note that for a start bit to be valid, it must stay in the + 12V position for at least 8 clock pulses, which is done to reject noise on the serial input line. When all eight bits have been received, the receiver still has to check to see that a stop bit of the proper length is present.

The asynchronous method depends on accurate × 16 clocks. For accuracy, the clock of the transmitter and the clock of the receiver must not differ in frequency more than about one percent. Figure 3-6 shows four ways that a baud-rate clock can be constructed. We will need such a clock generator later in this chapter.

The least expensive way (and one of the simplest) to build a bit-rate clock is to use a 555 timer chip wired for astable operation, as shown in Fig. 3-6A. The resistor, R_b, is a potentiometer, and should be one of the ten-turn types to allow for precise adjustment of the data rate. The frequency of the clock is given by the simple formula:

$$f = 1.5 \times [C \times (R_a + R_b)] - 1$$

Where the frequency is in Hertz, and the values of the capacitance and resistance are in farads and ohms, respectively. It is fairly easy to choose values of the resistances and capacitance that will produce the particular frequency desired. Ideally, R_a should be about 20 percent larger than R_b, so that the frequency may be adjusted by 20 percent either side of the desired value, to allow for variations in the values of the components. An oscilloscope will give you a readout to within 10 percent. To get within 1 percent, a frequency counter is needed. These can often be borrowed from a local high school, college, or ham-radio operator. Two data-rate clocks can be tuned to each other (but not necessarily to the exact data rate required) by the method of Lissajous figures on an oscilloscope.

The 555 circuit works well but must be fine-tuned with help of a frequency counter, and the frequency will tend to drift slightly with heating or aging of the components. If different bit rates are required, it is necessary to change the component values. For really precise data rate clocks, a crystal-controlled oscillator is needed. Crystals can hold a frequency to well within 0.001 percent for a good-quality crystal. Even inexpensive crystals are good to within 0.005 percent.

Since a baud-rate $\times 16$ clock is such a common circuit to use, it is only natural that there should exist integrated circuits that will produce the required waveform. The Motorola MC14411P bit-rate generator is a CMOS LSI circuit that contains a crystal oscillator and a set of frequency dividers that will allow the user to select any commonly used data rate from 75 baud to 921.6 kilobaud. Output rates are available for $\times 1$, $\times 8$, $\times 16$, and $\times 64$ serial-data transmitter/receivers. The circuit that uses this chip, and the connections to be made, are shown in Fig. 3-6B. For example, for a 300 baud $\times 16$ clock (4800 Hz) RSA is set to 0, RSB is set to a 1, and the output is taken from output F9 (pin 7). The only connections that need to be made to this chip are the power and ground, rate select, output, and the crystal itself. Because of its versatility (to change baud rates, just switch to another pin output on the chip) the use of the MC14411P is preferred over any of the other methods.

The use of the MC14411P is easy and elegant. The only problem is that the MC14411P is rather expensive and generally sells for between $12.00 and $20.00 *each*. The crystal is also about $5.00. Since the frequency of the crystal is 1.8432 MHz, only a crystal specially cut for this chip will do.

To save money, at the expense of a lot of wiring, a baud-rate generator may be made from TTL integrated circuits, as shown in Fig. 3-6C. This generator uses only three integrated circuits, and the 2-MHz clock line available on many busses. The circuit is a presettable counter loaded with the "negative" (two's complement) of the divisor required to divide the 2-MHz signal down to the desired bit rate. When the carry output of the last counter goes high, it generates an output pulse and reloads the divisor back into the counter. The divisor is set into a set of switches, S0 to S11. For a bit rate of 300 baud, which requires a clock rate

of 4800 Hz, we divide 2 million by 4800 to get 417. To find the two's complement, invert the data bits (turn all 0's to 1's and all 1's to 0's) and add one. Like this:

$$
\begin{aligned}
417_{10} \quad &= 0100\ 0001\ 0111_2 \\
&= 1011\ 1110\ 1000\ \text{inverted} \\
&= 1011\ 1110\ 1001\ \text{inverted, add one.}
\end{aligned}
$$

Set the switches to this binary sequence (least significant bit is switch S0) and the output of the divider will be exactly 4800 Hz.

If your computer does not have a 2-MHz clock, it is fairly easy to construct one using a 2-MHz crystal. Also, note that the setting switches S0 through S11 can be replaced by the Q output of a latch, such as the 7475, and the D inputs of the latch connected to a parallel output port, so that the data rate could be selectable under software control.

Still a fourth method of generating baud-rate clocks is shown in Fig. 3-6D. The 2-MHz and 1.8432-MHz crystals can be expensive. There is a crystal around which you can probably buy used at a TV repair shop for a dollar or so. In most color TV sets, there is a color-burst oscillator which runs at 3.579545 MHz. By building an oscillator and using a divider similar to that used above you can get crystal-stable baud-rate clocks accurate to 2 percent or better. Again, the baud rate is selectable by use of jumpers or a switch to the correct divider output.

Lastly, notice the part of the circuit using the three 7404 inverters and the crystal. If you need a clock oscillator for Fig. 3-6C, use the part of this circuit with the crystal, but substitute a 2-MHz crystal for it.

A word should be said here about serial handshaking. Some serial networks use READY TO SEND, CLEAR TO SEND, and REQUEST TO SEND data lines in parallel with the serial data. Decoding circuitry is needed to make sure that the transmitter is ready to send and that the receiver is capable of accepting the data. The Motorola 6850 ACIA has output/input pins especially for these functions.

Also, some equipment being used runs in the

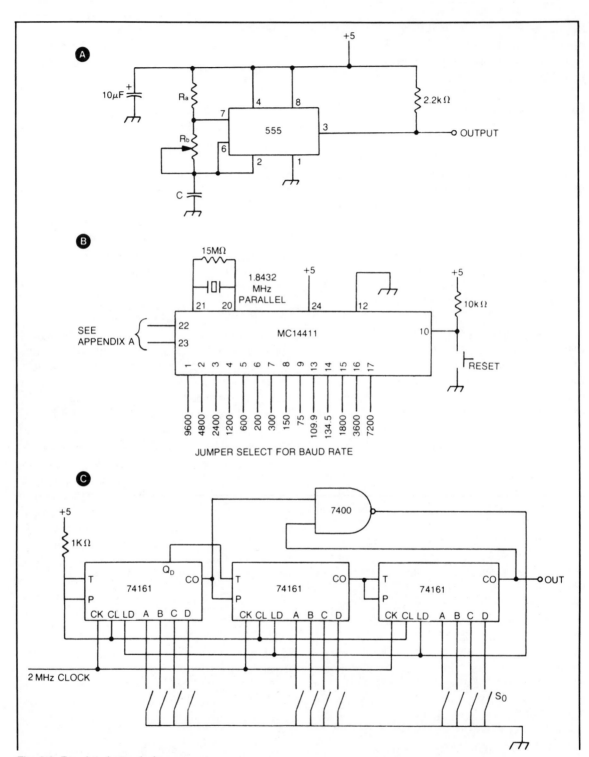

Fig. 3-6. Four baud-rate clocks.

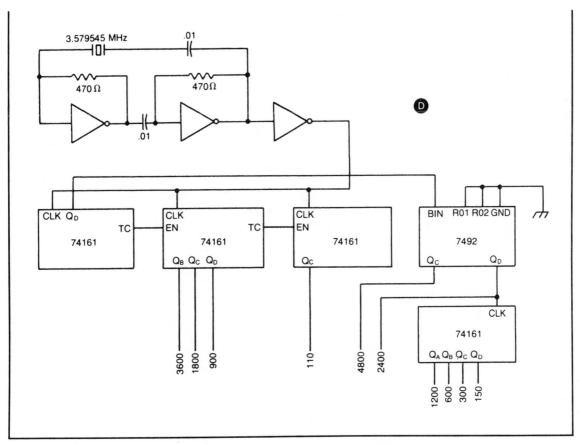

half-duplex mode (device cannot receive while transmitting, and vice-versa) as opposed to the *full-duplex* mode, in which data can flow in either direction at the same time. Most two-way peripherals are full-duplex. Some IBM equipment, notably the Selectric type data terminals are half-duplex. A special character needs to be sent from the computer to the peripheral to tell the peripheral that transmitting is over—the computer is ready to receive, and the terminal can start transmitting now. On the IBM Selectric, this is an EOT character ($04) from the computer, or a carriage return ($0D) from the keyboard. Check the manual or manufacturer of your machine to determine if it is full- or half-duplex, and what the handshaking characters are if it is half-duplex.

The most common use of serial data transmission is between a terminal and a computer. Some terminals do not "print" the transmitted character on the screen when a character is entered from the keyboard to be transmitted to the computer. Others have the provision for turning the print off, so that the computer can send the received character back to the terminal and print it on the screen, so that the operator may confirm that the computer received the correct character. In either case, it is necessary to have the computer *echo* back the received character. This can be done very easily as part of the data receive handler—just add a few lines of program to tell the computer to send the character it just received.

RS-422—AN ALTERNATIVE SERIAL SPECIFICATION

RS-232 is not the only specification for serial data transmission, although it is by far the most widely used. In large mainframes, RS-449 is becoming more and more popular. For small machines, RS-422 is an acceptable alternative which provides many benefits.

RS-232 has one transmit line and one receive line which depend on voltage levels with respect to some ground line. This scheme effectively limits the transmission distance between two RS-232 devices to about 100 meters at 300 baud, and less at higher speeds. For longer transmission distances, or higher speeds, RS-422 provides a "cleaner" signal, with less data errors.

Instead of having one transmit and one receive line, RS-422 has two of each. Instead of having a ground line for reference for the data lines, it has a reference line for each of the transmit and receive lines. These are called TD+ and TD−, and RD+ and RD−. Instead of sensing the absolute voltages, it senses the *difference in voltage* between the two lines in a pair. It is not important to RS-442 what the voltage on a line is, merely which of the two lines is higher in voltage.

The Macintosh 512 and Macintosh 128 both use RS-422 for communication to their modem and printer. It is the *only* input or output option on these machines.

Figure 3-7 shows how TTL serial levels can be converted to RS-442, and vice-versa. There is, of course, a chip created especially for this task, just as there is for conversion from TTL serial to RS-232.

RS-442 can be interfaced almost directly with RS-232 by means of a little "trick." If we leave the TD+ line unconnected, and connect the TD-line to the RS-232 transmit data line, and if we ground the RD+ line and connect the RD− line to the RS-232 receive data line, we are essentially converting RS-422 to RS-423, which can be "understood" by RS-232 transmitters and receivers. This procedure is illustrated in Fig. 3-8.

It is even possible to convert RS-422 to parallel using the trick above to convert to RS-232, then converting the RS-232 using a UART, as we shall see later in this chapter.

DATA INPUT METHODS

We have been assuming all along that the computer can read a word from the input interface any time it wants to. That's true, and very nice to have, but how does the computer know that there's anything at the interface that's worth reading?

In some situations, you may want the computer to read data from the interface at equally spaced time intervals. In others, we can conceive of possibilities where the computer is ready to read the data, but the peripheral isn't ready to send it yet. One example would be an analog-to-digital converter that gets a "send-data" command from the computer, and then has to spend a few milliseconds converting a voltage to a series of digital bits before it can send the digital bits to the computer. If the input is latched, and if the conversion time for the converter is well known, we can just wait a few cycles in a *wait loop* for the converter to be done.

But consider the problem of input from a keyboard, such as that on a Teletype® or video terminal. You don't want characters to get lost, and it's impossible to type so that a character is sent with precise regularity in time. Most computers have an "active-response" role with their keyboard. That is, the program will ask a question of the user via the terminal, and the user is expected to provide an answer. What if the user doesn't know the answer? What if he has to go look it up? How does the computer know that the user is entering his answer *now*?

We now introduce the methods required for basic I/O interfacing. We need to manage data transfers. There are three basic methods of *data input scheduling:* they are called *programmed I/O* or *polling, interrupt,* and *Direct Memory Access.*

Most input interfaces have, in addition to the *input register* which can be read by the computer, a *status register* which is set or reset by a number of data-control lines, or by the start bit on a serial-data line. Is is this status register which can be used to tell the computer that data is available. The analogy has been made, in the case of submitting eight bits of data to a computer, of telling a moving company to pick up some goods, but not tell the company where or when to pick them up. Even if you know the address of the input-data register (analogous to the house address), the truck still has to

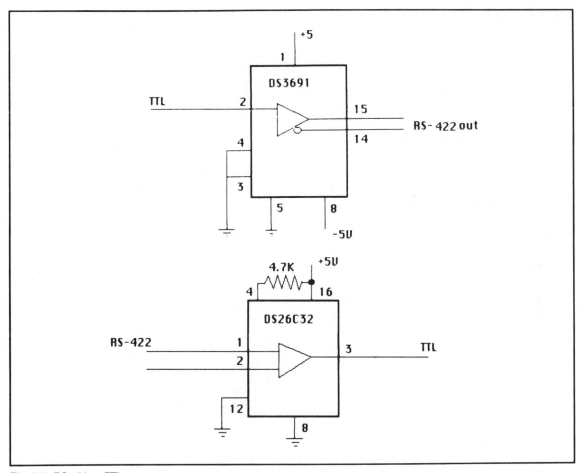

Fig. 3-7. RS-422 to TTL converter.

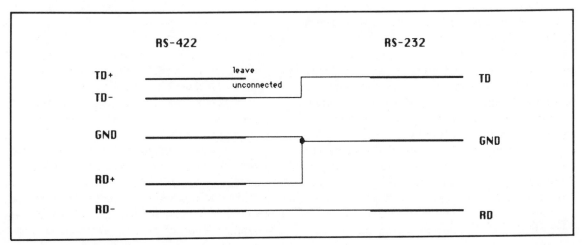

Fig. 3-8. RS-422 conversion to RS-232.

know what day of the week to show up. Too early, and the people aren't ready to move. Too late, and someone else is living there.

In this example the keyboard entry, the basic method for determining if an I/O operation is needed is through the use of *flags*. A flag is a single data bit (which may be part of a byte, as in part of a status register) which, when set, indicates that a condition has occurred that requires the attention of the processor.

If the flag is continually checked, it is said to be *polled*, and the procedure for continually checking it is called polling. Imagine a conversation between the computer and the status register of a peripheral interface that goes something like this:

> *Computer:* "Do you have data for me?"
> *Status Register:* "No."
> *Computer:* "Do you have data for me?"
> *Status Register:* "No."
> *Computer:* "Do you have data for me?"
> *Status Register:* "No."
>
> .
>
> .
>
> *Computer:* "Do you have data for me?"
> *Status Register:* "Yes."

(At this point, the computer runs off to perform the service routine to get the data from the input register and to reset the status register for more data.)

This is called a *polling loop*, and a flowchart of a sample polling loop is shown in Fig. 3-9.

The program continually loops through a series of tests to determining if input (or output) should be performed. Note that this method is especially effective when there are several devices that might want to send data to the computer. The computer can poll the status register of each of the input interfaces in turn, until it finds one that is in need of attention. The computer can even poll them in order of their priority, or importance, to make sure that a high-priority device gets checked right away.

In an ACIA, the status register flag is set upon the receipt of a valid start bit. With parallel entry, one of the handshaking control lines is used to set

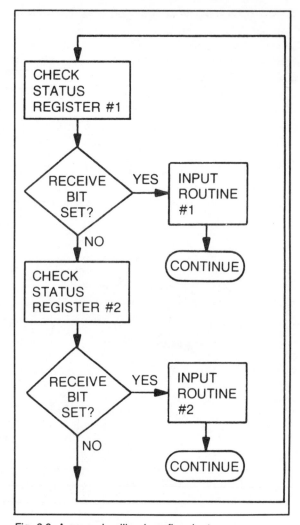

Fig. 3-9. A general polling loop flowchart.

the status register flag. Using the example of the keyboard above, the act of pressing one of the keys or the keyboard will generate a "keypressed" strobe on a parallel-data line, which can either be used directly to set the status flag, or the whole data byte can be converted to serial using the "keypressed" strobe to initiate the serial conversion.

Polling is the most common and simplest method of I/O control. It requires no special hardware and all input-output transfers are controlled by the program.

The major advantage of polled I/O is its hardware simplicity. The major disadvantage is the amount of processing time it takes. Constantly watching the device status flags is very consuming of the processor's time—it is said to take a lot of *overhead*. Leaving the polling loop for even a short period of time may cause data to be missed. While the processor is continually checking and rechecking the status flags, it cannot do anything else.

Although the polling method will suffice for most peripherals, it has the serious drawback that it cannot "announce" that some action needs to be taken. It has to wait to be "asked" by the CPU whether or not that action *should* be taken. The CPU may be busy on some other task, such as running through an arithmetic calculation in BASIC. Devices such as disk drives or analog-to-digital converters that need quick action may not be processed in time to keep from losing their data to the next data byte in the stream. What is needed is a mechanism to allow a peripheral to interrupt the normal processing of the CPU when something needs to be done, so that the CPU can check the status register and find out what needs doing *now*.

Interrupts are provided for on every microprocessor available on the market. Yet they are the most misunderstood and feared aspect of microprocessor science. Say "interrupt" to most microcomputer owners, and if they know the word at all, chances are nine out of ten that the response will be "too complicated." While it is true that a mistake in interrupt programming can destroy a program already resident in the computer, the interrupt process is quite simple and can result in vast savings of processor time.

On every microprocessor, and with every data bus, there is at least one INTerrupt line. This line is generally an active-low line so that the "wired-OR" technique can be used. That is, the line is generally held high through a pull-up resistor, and all the interrupt outputs of all the peripheral interfaces are tied to it. These outputs are open-collector type of outputs. If any one of the transistors of the open-collector outputs conducts, the interrupt line is brought low. This will generate an interrupt sequence in the processor.

The interrupt sequence varies from one processor to another, but the general series of events is as follows: The processor finishes the instruction that it is working on, and then tests to see if the interrupt is *masked*. A masked interrupt means that an internal flag is set in the CPU which, when set, causes the CPU to ignore all interrupts. Some CPU's have *non-maskable* interrupt lines separate from the regular lines. Others have only maskable interrupt lines, while some do not have the masking feature at all. Check with your computer manufacturer. If the interrupt is not masked, the CPU begins to store all of its internal registers into a specially set-aside region of memory called the *stack*, which functions as a last-in, first-out temporary storage.

When the CPU is finished stacking the registers, then it may begin the interrupt process. This process frequently begins by polling all the interfaces to see which one caused the interrupt. Fortunately, the polling process need only be done once. The appropriate routine is executed, and the CPU can then retrieve all its registers off the stack and resume right where it left off. An example flowchart of the general interrupt process is shown in Fig. 3-10.

It doesn't matter where the interrupt routine is situated in memory. It is, after all, just another part of the program with the exception that the last instruction must be a "return from interrupt" command. So long as no part of memory that is used by the regular program is changed (unless by design), there will be no conflicts with the interrupt program and the regular program. Indeed, if the interrupt program doesn't use any temporary memory storage other than the program itself and the CPU registers and stack, it is called *reentrant*, which means that another interrupt can occur while the first one is being processed.

Along these lines, there is an internal register in the CPU called the *stack pointer,* which points to the next available location of the stack. In many systems that don't use their interrupt capability, the stack pointer is used as a temporary register. When using interrupts, the stack must be kept "clean,"

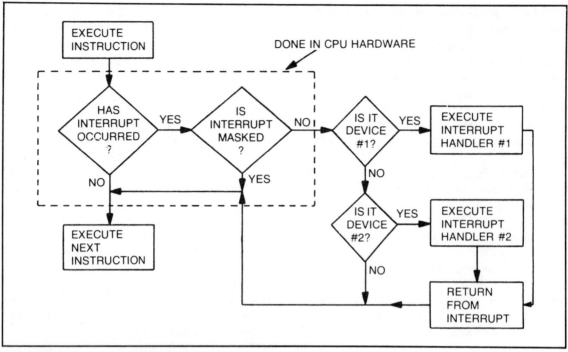

Fig. 3-10. The interrupt process flowchart.

that is, the stack pointer must *always* point to the next location on the stack, and not be used for any other purpose. If you decide to use interrupts and find you have trouble, especially when using programs others have written, check to see that the stack pointer is "clean."

There is another way of using interrupts which requires considerably more hardware than usual. An *Interrupt Priority Encoder*, such as the Intel 8214 or the Motorola 6828 can be placed on the address lines. The 8214 can accept up to eight simultaneous interrupts of different priority, and choose the one (hardwired) highest priority, and actually change the data on the address lines so that the next instruction executed will be the address of the interrupt service routine. Since it is unlikely that the users of this book will be using multilevel priority interrupts from lots of devices, the details of the hardware will be left to other books.

A word should be said about "daisy-chain" priority controlling, see Fig. 3-11. In some systems there is an "interrupt in" line and an "interrupt-out" line, such as that found in the Apple II bus.

Upon receipt of an interrupt request along the IRQ line, the CPU sends a "interrupt out" pulse down the INT OUT line. The first device to receive should have the highest priority. If it is not the device which caused the interrupt, then *its* INT OUT line sends a pulse to the INT IN line of the interface with the next highest priority. The device that caused the interrupt pulls the data line called INTP low. This information gets passed back through the "daisy chain" of interfaces to the CPU, and the CPU can service the interrupt through the daisy chain. Only the device electrically closest to the CPU that has interrupted will answer the interrupt query. This sets up a "serial priority" chain with devices closest to the CPU getting serviced first. An important point, though: when removing a card from the bus, be sure to jumper the interrupt-in and interrupt-out lines so that the query can be passed on through.

Special consideration should be given to the console-terminal interface. The terminal should always be able to gain access to the CPU to change its operation; otherwise, the terminal, and *you*, the user, may be locked out of your own program!

The 6800 family of processors has a special instruction called "Wait For Interrupt." With this instruction, all registers are saved, and the CPU halts until an interrupt is received. This single instruction takes the place of the entire polling loop with polled I/O.

In summary, the interrupt method of input-output is used to save time on the CPU. The device that is sending a data byte to the CPU causes an "interrupt," which causes the processor to halt what it's doing and service the device by getting the data and clearing the status register. Then the processor picks up where it left off.

The third method of input/output is called Di-rect Memory Access (DMA). It requires a lot of hardware support, but very little programming.

There are situations in which data must be moved very rapidly to or from a peripheral device. Examples would be very fast disk drives or tape drives for which a whole block of data must be moved to or from memory rapidly, or a multichannel pulse-height analysis system making a transfer of its internal memory to computer memory.

Interrupt processing might be too slow for these types of processes. Even with a 2-MHz system clock, a typical instruction might take as long as three microseconds to execute. A 15-instruction transfer loop would then take 45 microseconds to complete, for a maximum data transfer rate of 22

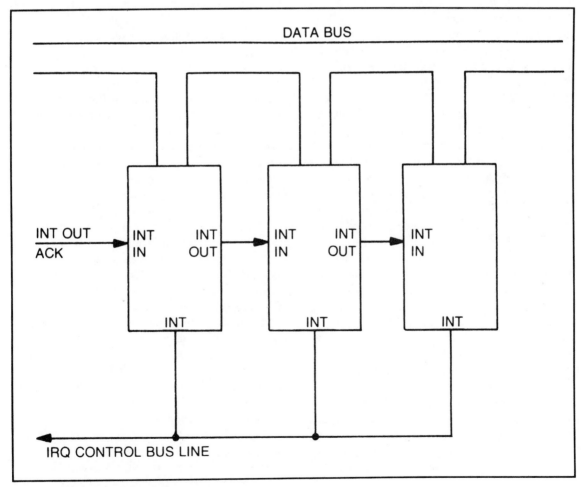

Fig. 3-11. Daisy-chained interrupts.

kilobytes per second. This may seem fast, but most disk drives have a capability nearly ten times this!

Additionally, while the transfer of a block of data is being done, the CPU can't do anything else, as it is totally dedicated to the transfer process. A typical block is 256 bytes, which would take about 15 milliseconds to transfer under a normal "read and store" instruction loop. A DMA transfer could do the same in about 15 microseconds, saving almost 99 percent of the processor's time.

The purpose of the third type of information input, DMA, or Direct Memory Access, is to save processor time. The important thing is that no programming is involved. The data is moved from the peripheral to the data bus without the intervention of the processor.

A complete discussion of the methods of DMA transfer, including sample hardware, is entirely beyond the scope of this book. But a brief discussion of the processes and philosophy involved can be instructive in understanding how the data and address busses work.

Most microprocessors have DMA capability. There will be a control line called HOLD or HALT or BUS REQUEST which is actually a DMA request line. Upon receipt of a signal on this line, the processor completes the current instruction, and sets all of its address, data, and most of its control lines into the three-state (high-impedance) mode. Another control line, called something like HOLD ACKNOWLEDGE or BUS AVAILABLE, is held low as a signal to the DMA controller that the microprocessor is now disconnected from the bus, and that the controller can now send data directly to the bus. The DMA controller must then send out data *and* address information so that information can be stored in the correct memory locations. When it is finished, the controller removes the signal from the DMA request line, and the processor continues.

An alternative way of doing DMA is to use *cycle-stealing*. That is, to use the address and data busses at times when the processor is not using them, in much the same way that many dynamic memory-refresh circuits work. This way does not interfere with the processor's functioning, but is considerably slower. Maximum DMA transfer rates are usually in the neighborhood of a million bytes per second.

There is always a tradeoff in any computer between hardware and software. The more software you use, generally the less complicated the hardware must be. Since DMA uses no software, the associated hardware must be very complex. The DMA controller must be able, not only of transferring the data from its own memory, but also of knowing where in the computer's memory to place it. This latter function is usually accomplished by having a counter connected to the address bus lines through a three-state buffer, and initializing the counter in some previous processor instruction. All this hardware is contained inside a chip (or series of chips) called a DMA controller. Modern DMA controllers are, essentially, dedicated microprocessors themselves. Since DMA controllers do not sell in the same quantities as microprocessors, they tend to be much more expensive than a microprocessor chip. In some instances, it may be cheaper to use a second microprocessor specifically for the purpose of DMA transfer than to invest in a DMA controller. Situations such as the one described above are called *multiprocessing*, where more than one microprocessor shares the same bus. One processor can be dedicated to arithmetic operations, another to I/O transfers, and a third can be the "main" processor. It happens more often than you might think, although in most cases, the secondary processors are specially dedicated to their task, and built for them. Examples would be the Western Electric 1771 Disk-Controller chip, or a special arithmetic processor.

In any data input sequence, you will want to make sure that the data your processor has received is correct data. Most microcomputers just leave it to faith that the data that is presented to the processor is correct. There are ways of telling if the information received is faulty, and even ways of correcting it if wrong.

Over short data lines, error detection is not much of a problem. Only when the lines are long, or pass through an electrically noisy area, is there a chance for the lines to pick up false information.

A part failure, or a noise spike can easily cause a 0 to become a 1 or a 1 to become a 0. Computers depend on their information being 100 percent accurate (the old saying goes—"garbage in-garbage out"), and a whole set of schemes has been developed for the purpose of detecting errors.

The most common form of error detection used in microcomputers is *parity*. It is used with single bytes of data, either serial or parallel transmission. The parity of a byte is just the sum of the numbers of 1s in the byte. If the sum is an even number, the parity is even and is assigned a value of 0; if the sum is an odd number, the parity is odd, and is assigned the value of 1.

The 74180 and 74LS280 are integrated circuits used to generate or to check the parity of a byte. The LS280 is a nine-bit checker/generator, whereas the 180 is an eight-bit checker generator. With the LS280, used for parallel transmission the full eight bits are put into the chip, and a parity line is generated, which is sent with the eight bits of data and the control lines. At the receiving end, the eight bits *and* the parity are put into another LS280. A signal will be produced if the parity of the received data is the same as the received parity line. If it is not, the received will reject the data, and ask for a re-transmission.

The 74180 is used when transmitting ASCII characters, which are only seven bits in length. The eighth bit is generally used for parity.

Several of the serial-to-parallel conversion chips, such as the AY-5-1013 by General Instruments, have built-in parity generators and checkers, so that the seven data bits are followed by an eighth parity bit, if desired.

It might be noted as well that some computers, such as the Digital Equipment Corporation PDP-15, have a nine-bit byte especially for the purpose of carrying the parity along. The PDP-15 has a 36-bit word, organized as four nine-bit bytes.

The major problem with the single-byte parity system is that it is designed to detect single errors in a byte. If one bit changes from a 0 to a 1, the number of 1s changes, and so does the parity. But if two 0s change to 1s, then the number of 1s is increased by an even number, and the parity does not

change. The same can be said for two 1s changing to 0s. Furthermore, if a 1 and a 0 change places, then the parity still will not change.

Eight-bit plus parity requires either an additional data line for parallel transmission, or longer transmission times for serial data transmission. The use of parity also makes the hardware slightly more complex.

It might not be that we want to know that a single byte of data is in error. We may only want to know if an entire block of data has been received correctly. The method of *checksum error detection*, also known as "cyclic redundancy checking," is often used to determine the correctness of a data block. It can be done entirely with software, with no additional hardware needed.

The method is very simple. Let each eight-bit byte (whether it be a number, a character, or an instruction that is being transmitted) be a binary integer. Then simply add all these integers together as they are being transmitted. The problem is that the sum for a realistic sized block of data will grow to be so large that the sum will require two or more bytes of data to contain it. But this is no problem: let the sum overflow—the eight-bit sum will contain the least significant eight bits of the sum anyway, and if there is any change in any byte of data, it will show up first in the least significant digits of the sum.

When the block has been transmitted, take the complement of the sum, and send it as the last data byte. (You have to know just how many bytes are being sent to do this.) This last byte is the checksum byte.

The receiver, when collecting the data bytes, will also be summing up the bytes, without regard for overflow, into one eight-bit byte. When the last byte arrives, it simply adds the checksum byte to its own sum (the checksum is complemented, remember), and should end up with exactly zero for a total sum if the block of data is correct. If it is not, then the sum will be different from zero by the error of one or more bytes. The receiver can then throw out that block of data, and ask for a re-transmission.

Checksums are most frequently used with

mass-storage devices such as cassette tape or disk drives or in transfer of files over telephone lines, such as with the use of the XMODEM protocol. The data is transmitted by the computer with a checksum at the end, and the whole block is stored on magnetic medium just as it is transmitted. Upon readback, the computer becomes the receiver, and uses the checksum to determine that the block has been read correctly. In the case of a disk drive, the computer can re-read the data block to try for the correct data again. Tape cannot be re-wound, of course.

As an example of the use of a checksum, let's examine the XMODEM protocol format. This is a protocol developed by Ward Christensen for his original Computer Bulletin Board Service for CP/M computer systems. It was originally used as a method to upload and download files to and from the "host" computer to a computer which had dialed in over the telephone lines. In this way, it could be used as a method of exchanging data and programs. The XMODEM protocol has become a *de facto* file transfer standard for small computers.

Data is stored on computer disk and diskettes in *sectors*. Originally, the size of a sector on a 5-1/4 inch diskette was 128 bytes. Even now, this sector size is unchanged, or is some integer multiple of this amount. It is logical, then, to send files over telephone lines in blocks of 128 bytes. Even the IBM mainframe 3780 protocol uses the 128-byte block.

In XMODEM, the blocks are numbered by each computer in sequential numeric order, starting with block 1. The receiving computer sends an ASCII NAK (Negative Acknowledge) character (hex 15, Control-U) to tell the sending computer to begin sending data. The sending computer will do nothing until it receives the NAK. The sending computer sends the data prefaced by an ASCII SOH (Start of Heading) character (hex 01, Control-A), then sends the number of the block to be sent, followed by the two-s complement of the block number. Then all 128 bytes of data are sent, followed by the checksum of the data block. If the receiving computer gets all the data, and the block number and checksum indicate that the data is cor-

rect, it sends the ACK code (04 hex, Control-D) to the sending computer to tell it "All's well on this end, send the next block." The process continues until the *sending* computer sends an EOT character (Also 04 hex, Control-D) instead of an SOH. Notice that the number of data bytes is fixed to 128 in the data block, plus 4 for the header, block numbers, and checksum, for a total of 132. We always know when to stop looking for more data bytes in a block.

The two's complement of a number is created by taking all the 1's in a number and changing them to 0's, and all the 0's and changing them to 1's, then adding 1 to the result. It is the binary equivalent of the negative of a binary number. Notice that the SOH character, plus the block number, plus the two's complement of the block number *must* add up to zero, exactly. For example, take transmission of block 1:

$$\text{SOH} \quad + \quad 1 \quad + \quad (\text{2's complement of 1})$$
$$01 \quad + \quad 01 \quad + \quad \text{FE} \quad = \quad 100$$

which, when you take the two least significant digits, is 00 hexadecimal. If we then add the data bytes themselves, one at a time, and then add the checksum (which is the complement of the sum of the data bytes), we should get, again, exactly zero, and we can store the data block on disk or wherever.

If we do *not* get exactly zero, then an error in transmission has occurred. The error could have been caused by faulty data reading, faulty equipment, or noise in the telephone lines. If this is the case, then the receiving computer sends a NAK character again to signal the sending computer that it should send the same data block again. Notice that the receiving computer can tell which data block has been sent just by looking at the block number.

If the sending computer does not receive an ACK or a NAK within 10 seconds after sending the data block (possibly because noise obscured the ACK or NAK), it assumes the transmission failed, and sends the same block again. The receiver doesn't care, it just records the same block again and stores it in the proper place.

If the receiving computer doesn't get any data at all in 10 seconds, it sends a NAK again and again every 10 seconds until it does get data, or an EOT, or a command to cancel the transmission effort. Either end can cancel the transmission between any block by sending a CAN character (18 hex, Control-X).

The use of XMODEM protocol can have many uses. Most of the On-line data services, such as the Source, Compuserve, Delphi, and Dow Jones have file transfer capability using XMODEM. Some of these have interest or user groups for most of the major computer types on the market, and have libraries of programs and data which are free for the cost of the computer time to download them to your computer. See Fig. 3-12.

It is even possible in some instances to recover lost data. If parity and checksum are both being used, and only one parity error is detected, the checksum can be used to reconstruct the erroneous byte. There are many other methods of error correction that can be used, as well, such as the Hamming Code, which intersperses parity bits with data. Error-correcting codes are a bit wasteful and very slow.

A UNIVERSAL PARALLEL INTERFACE FOR ALL BUSSES

Now we come to the nitty gritty. How to build an interface for a peripheral that will connect to *your* computer, so you can build all the wonderful cir-cuits in the next few chapters of this book. We'll start with a parallel interface first, and then show you how to convert it over to a serial interface.

It is assumed that you have read and understand the section on address decoding in Chapter 2. That information will be used extensively here. Indeed, the interfaces to be designed will have only a section which will be a large box with the words "address decoder" on it, which contains the circuitry for decoding addresses. Decode *only* the address lines indicated on the diagram. The others will have additional purposes.

Every bus is different. That means simply that we will need a different interface for every single bus. We will develop examples of a universal interface for the following busses. The SS-50 and SS-30 buses, that Apple-II bus, the bus for the IBM-PC and all compatible machines, the Tandy Color Computer, the Tandy 1000, and the Commodore C-64. It simply isn't possible to show an interface for all the busses of all the microcomputers and minicomputers on the market today, and especially not for all those that have been manufactured in the last five years. We will just show examples for the most commonly used busses, and if your computer does not use one of those, we will endeavor to give enough information so that if you can find the bus in your computer and can decipher the control signals and their polarities, you can use the information to build your own universal interface.

The most difficult decision to make is, "how should the interface be constructed?" There are a number of ways that it can be done. We could build

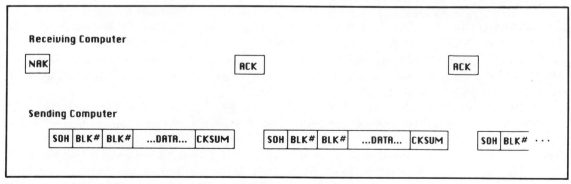

Fig. 3-12. XMODEM data protocol for transmission of files over phone lines.

a number of data latches around a three-state buffer. Or, we can use one of the many interface chips available on the market. Since the latter course does not require us to re-invent the wheel, and since the price of the interface chips is generally reasonable, we will choose the latter course.

The next question is, "which one?" Here the decision is not easy. There are dozens available on the market, each more or less as good as the next. Two of these chips, however, find themselves in wider use than the others: The Intel 8255 Programmable Peripheral Interface (PPI), and the Motorola 6820/6821 Peripheral Interface Adapter (PIA). The 6821 is an improvement over the 6820, and is a pin-for-pin replacement for it. Both chips have three-state data buffers for connection to the data bus, and both can carry two eight-bit bytes in either direction, with handshaking lines. The 8255 was designed for use with the 8080 processor, while the 6820 was designed for use with the 6800. This doesn't matter, though, because either interface chip can be used with any processor. Each major manufacturer of microprocessors has its own version of a programmable interface chip. Their function is essentially similar; only the details of connecting it to the bus and programming it are different.

Figure 3-13 shows a block diagram of the 8255. This interface chip occupies four addresses on the address bus, selected by address lines A0 and A1. Three of these addresses correspond to three I/O buffers, called A, B, and C. The fourth address accesses the control register which does various things. Buffers A, B, and C may be individually programmed to act on input or output *as a byte*, but not as individual bits.

The 6820 is shown in Fig. 3-14 in block diagram form. Again, there are two data registers that can be input or output registers to the peripherals. Also, there are four addresses the 6820 can respond to. Only this time, these four addresses connect to six registers: two each of data, control, and data direction. For the two output/input registers, each bit can be individually programmed to be an input or an output. Furthermore there are two handshaking lines with each I/O buffer that can be controlled

through the control register.

The 6820 and the 8255 are nearly identical in function and in price. We could develop interfaces for all the busses using both of these fine chips, but that would require a lot of space, not to mention a different set of programming for each interface for each use, nearly doubling the size of the remainder of this book. The decision of which chip to use must depend on the fine differences between them.

The 6820 is slightly more difficult to program and has four fewer output lines than the 8255. This is offset by the fact that the 6820 has interrupt capability; each bit of either side is individually programmable to be an input or an output and (most important for our purposes) is, on the CPU side of the chip, *pin compatible* with the 6850 ACIA for serial communications. The 8255 has no serial counterpart. For these reasons, we will choose the 6820/6821 PIA as the mainstay of our universal parallel interface.

Both the 8255 and the 6820 have control registers and will therefore need to be *initialized* by the computer before they can be used. Let's take a closer look at the 6820.

The 6820 is a one-chip I/O port in which all communications to or from peripherals are done through registers internal to the chip itself. Each of the registers acts just like a memory location, and may be read from or written to just like memory. Two pins are provided on the chip called RS0 and RS1. These are register-select pins and will be connected to address lines A0 and A1. There are three chip-select pins, whose function is to disconnect the 6820 from the data bus (three-state) whenever they are not active. These chip-select pins should be connected to the address decode circuitry for address bits A2 through A15. The RESET line, when pulled low, will reset all internal registers to 0.

The PIA has two sides—the A side and the B side. Each side functions as an independent input or output port, with handshaking. To select the A side for any purpose, RS1 should be a 0. To select the B side for any purpose, the register select RS1 should be a 1. Each side of the PIA consists of three

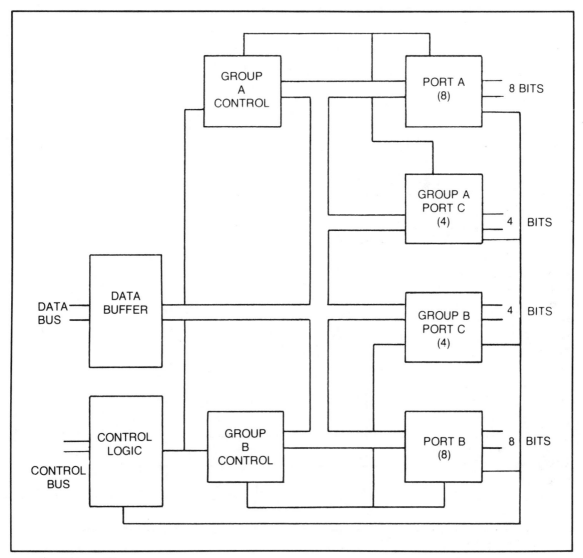

Fig. 3-13. The 8255 PPI chip architecture.

registers; a data register, a control register, and a data-direction register. These three registers occupy two (total) locations in memory. The control register occupies one of these two memory locations, and the data direction and data registers share the other memory location. Which of these two registers is selected when the memory location is accessed depends on the state of bit 2 of the control register.

The selection of the registers is summarized in Table 3-3. For example, if the PIA is addressed to occupy addresses $801C to $801F, the address $801C is either the data-direction or data-buffer register of side A, $801D is the A-side control register, $801E is the B-side data-direction or buffer, register, and $801F is the B-side control register.

To use the PIA, the registers must first be initialized. The initialization begins by setting the data direction registers. To do this, first access the control registers and clear them, setting all bits to

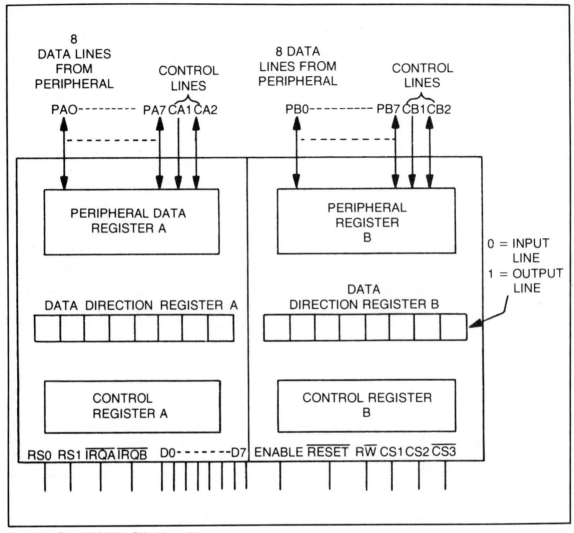

Fig. 3-14. The 6820/6821 PIA chip architecture.

Table 3-3. Selection of PIA Registers in the 6820 PIA.

RS1 = 0 selects port A register
RS1 = 1 selects port B register
RS0 = 1 selects either A or B control register (depending on RS1)
RS0 = 0 selects either data direction register or data register for side A or B (depending on state of bit 2 of control register and RS1)

RS1	RS0	CRA(2)	CRB(2)	Register
0	0	0	X	Data direction register A
0	0	1	X	Data register A
0	1	X	X	Control register A
1	0	X	0	Data direction register B
1	0	X	1	Data register B
1	1	X	X	Control register B

zero. Actually, only bit 2 of each register needs to be cleared, but it is usually easier to clear the whole register. With bit 2 cleared, any access to the data register actually accesses the data direction register. For any bit of the side to be an output, the data-direction register's same bit must be a 1. For it to be an input, the data-direction bit must be a 0. For example, if we want bit 4 of side B to be an output, and bit 5 to be an input, bits 4 and 5 of the side-B data-direction register must be 1 and 0 respectively. The directions of any of the bits (all sixteen of them) may be mixed and matched indiscriminately or even changed in the middle of a program, so long as the associated hardware is capable of handling the data direction indicated. The general scheme is for one side of the PIA to be an output and the other to be an input. Side A is usually chosen to be the input and side B the output, as shown in Fig. 3-15.

After the initialization of the data-direction register, each of the control registers needs to be initialized for use. First of all, bit 2 (see Fig. 3-16) has to be returned to a 1 so that the data-buffer register can be accessed instead of the data-direction register.

The rest of the bits in the control register have to do with the use of the handshaking lines. There are two handshaking lines associated with each side of the PIA, CA1 and CA2 for the A side, and CB1 and CB2 for the B side. CA1 and CB1 are input-only lines, while CB2 and CA2 may be programmed for either input or output. They may be used as additional data lines, as their status is readable on input from the control register and controllable as

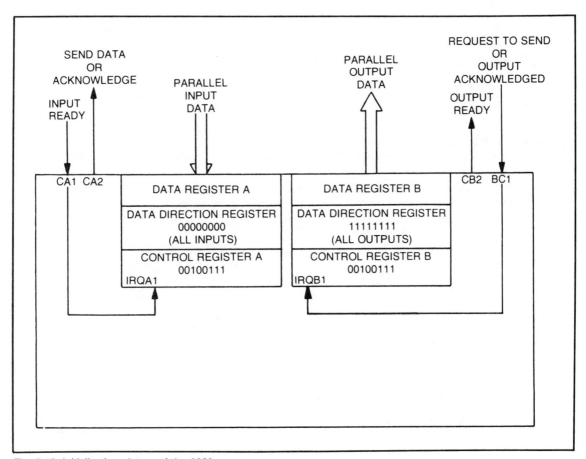

Fig. 3-15. Initialization picture of the 6820.

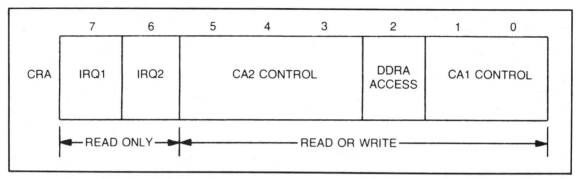

	7	6	5	4	3	2	1	0
CRA	IRQ1	IRQ2	CA2 CONTROL			DDRA ACCESS	CA1 CONTROL	

◄—READ ONLY—► ◄————————— READ OR WRITE —————————►

Fig. 3-16. The control register of the 6820.

outputs from the control register. They may be used in the traditional handshake modes, or even as hardware interrupt lines. The function and status of these lines is directly readable from the control register. The programming of these control lines is somewhat difficult to understand because they are so versatile, and this difficulty has given the 6820 somewhat of a reputation as a "hard" chip to work with. Let's take it one step at a time, following Table 3-4.

Lines CA1 and CB1 are input-only lines. They are controlled by the first two bits of their respective control registers, bits 0 and 1. These lines are sensitive to *transitions* of the voltage on them—from a 0 to a 1 or a 1 to a 0. If the right transition occurs

(controlled by bit 1), then bit 7 is set to a 1. The only way bit 7 can be set to a 0 is to read the control register for that side. In order to respond to a 1 → 0 transition (from high to low), bit 1 must be a 0. Bit 7 will respond *only* when line CA1 (or CB1 for the B side) goes from high to low. Going from low to high won't affect it, nor will being in a 0 or a 1 state; only the transition. Conversely, to set bit 7 on a low-to-high (0-1) transition, bit 1 must be a 1.

You can see that, in order to use CA1 as an auxiliary input, some creative programming is needed. Bit 7 must be set to a 0 by reading the control register, then the CA1 line must be set to the value of 0 and programmed for a low-to-high transition. If CA1 ever becomes a 1, then so does bit 7.

Table 3-4. Controlling Actions of Peripheral-Control Lines CA1 and CB1.

Bit 0: If 0, prevents processor interrupt through IRQA or IRQB
If 1, allows processor to be interrupted
Bit 1: If 0, sets bit 7 = 1 if 1-0 transition on line CA1 or CB1
(depending on which side of PIA is used)
If 1, sets bit 7 = 1 on 0-1 transition of CA1 or CB1 (depending on which side of PIA is used)

CA1 or CB1 Transition	Bit 1 CRA or CRB	Bit 0 CRA or CRB	IRQA1 or IRQB1 Transition	Processor Status
1-0	0	0	0-1	not interrupted
1-0	0	1	0-1	interrupted
0-1	1	0	0-1	not interrupted
0-1	1	1	0-1	interrupted

NOTE: All information about CA1 is controlled by control register CRA, and flag IRQA1 will be affected, and interrupt will occur via IRQA. All information about CB1 is controlled by control register CRB, and flag IRQB1 will be affected, and interrupts will occur via IRQB.

Bit 0 of the control register decides what the PIA will do with the information in bit 7. The PIA has two interrupt lines which connect to the interrupt lines of the processor. These lines are normally high. If the interrupt lines IRQA and IRQB (A-side and B-side interrupts) are connected to the interrupt line on the control bus, then the PIA may cause the processor to be interrupted depending on the state of bit 0. If bit 0 is a 0, the PIA simply notes the status of CA1 in bit 7, and nothing else is done with it. If, however, bit 0 is a 1, upon the change of bit 7 from a 0 to a 1 the PIA will cause the interrupt line to go low for one clock cycle, interrupting the processor. If side A's control-register bit 7 has been forced high, then IRQA will do the interrupting, and similar for side B.

The lines CA2 and CB2 may be programmed to act either as inputs or as outputs. The status of bit 5 of the appropriate control register determines whether the lines are inputs or outputs. If bit 5 is a 0, the line is an input much the same as CA1 or CB1; if bit 5 is a 1, the line is an output in one of several modes.

Using, for example, CA2 as an input with bit 5 of control register A as a 0. The line acts identically to CA1, being controlled by bits 3 and 4, just the way CA1 is controlled bits 1 and 2. Instead of a transition affecting bit 7, now the transition affects bit 6 of the control register. As before, if bit 4 is a 1, bit 6 will be set on a $0 \rightarrow 1$ transition of CA2, and if bit 4 is a 0, bit 6 will be set on a $1 \rightarrow 0$ transition. If bit 3 is set, the setting of bit 6 will cause the processor to be interrupted and will not cause such an interruption if bit 3 is not set.

Using CA2 or CB2 as an output requires a detailed knowledge of just how the PIA works. With bit 5 set to a 1, there are four combinations of 1s and 0s for bits 3 and 4.

With bits 3 and 4 both 0 in side A, this side of the PIA enters what is called the "handshake mode." CA1 and CA2 work together in this mode. CA2 starts out normally high, and drops low when *any* data is written to the data register of side A. It does this automatically, with no further need to access the control register. CA2 will stay low until CA1 makes the proper transition required by bit

1 of the control register and bit 7 is set. Then CA2 returns to the high state. The reason that is called the "handshake" mode should be obvious. Line CA2 tells the peripheral that output data is present by going low when the data is placed in the data register. It remains low until the peripheral has sent a signal back over CA1 telling the computer that the data has been accepted, and sets bit 7 to inform the processor (which, we presume, has been polling bit 7, or waiting for an interrupt). Then that side of the PIA is ready to present more data.

When bit 4 is a 0 and bit 3 is a 1 in the output mode, CA2 will send out a short "pulse" of about one clock period. Again, this is automatic. When the A-side data register is written to, CA2 will go from high to low. The next time the ENABLE input of the 6820 goes high, CA2 also goes high. Since the ENABLE line is generally tied to the system clock, this transition should occur on the next rising edge of the clock. CA1 is not affected.

If bits 4 and 3 are 1 and 0 respectively when configured as an output, CA2 will always be low. This is the best way to use CA2 as an output if you want the output to be low. In this way, line CA2 becomes just another data line.

With both bits 3 and 4 set to 1, line CA2 becomes a data line that is always high. Again, line CA2 is now just another output line.

Anything said above for line CA2 is also applicable for line CB2 by accessing the B-side control register instead of the A-side control register. See Table 3-5.

Last, we have the data input/output registers. If side A is configured by the data-direction register to be an input, then any data that is placed on the pins PA0 through PA7 will appear in the data register and can be read directly by the computer the same as any other memory location. If side B is configured to be an output, then any piece of data that is placed in the B-side data register immediately appears on the output pins PB0-PB7 as the appropriate voltages. It is "written to" just the same as any other memory location. Notice that what happens to the data, input or output, from the data registers, does not depend on what is happening with the control lines. Those control lines are

Table 3-5. CA2 and CB2 Use.

Bit 5 of control register set to 0: Line is an input.
If Bit 5 of the control register is cleared, the respective C2 line is designated as an input. The input works the same as CA1 or CB1, and bits 3 and 4 are programmed the same as bits 1 and 0. The only difference is that bit 6 responds to the input instead of bit 7.

Bit 5 of control register set to 1: Line is an output.
Bits 5, 4, 3 = 100 (Handshake Mode)
Bits 5, 4, 3 = 101 (Pulse Mode)
Bits 5, 4, 3 = 110 C2 is always high after these bits are set to 110.
Bits 5, 4, 3 = 111 C2 is always low after these bits are set to 111.

---

there for handshaking, as additional inputs or outputs, or for interrupting the processor. The data will flow out over the lines or into the register no matter what happens to the handshaking, so long as the hardware and software are compatible.

Once you get over the complexity of the control register, the 6820 PIA is extremely easy to interface with a computer and completely versatile to almost any parallel application you might have.

The only word of caution about the 6820: it is a CMOS device, and the output buffers can drive only one TTL load. It would be wise to add additional TTL buffers to the inputs and outputs both to prevent static damage to the chip and to be able to drive more than one additional chip, if necessary.

Our simple universal parallel interface, then, consists of the 6820 PIA and the associated circuitry needed to drive it from the respective busses. All we really need there is the appropriate signal conditioning of the control lines of the bus and address decoding of the chip. Let's see how the interface will look, then, for the various busses of our study (see Fig. 3-13).

First, the 6820 needs +5V power. Some busses have this voltage available, others do not. Those that do not will generally have an 8-volt unregulated line. The addition of a 7805 5-volt regulator chip and two 0.1 microfarad capacitors as shown will take care of the power requirements of the 6820. The 7805 can supply up to 1 ampere, and the 6820 uses only a few milliamperes.

SS-50

The SS-50 and SS-30 busses were originally de-

signed around the Motorola 6800 series of integrated circuits, so interfacing to these busses is a snap.

Figure 3-17 shows an interface for the SS-50 main bus. Address lines A2 through A15 need to be fully decoded, with A0 and A1 going to the register-select pins as usual. The chip-select input is the address decode, and the enable input is the logical AND of the VMA and 02 lines. All other lines (R/W, RESET) connect directly to their respective inputs on the PIA. The IRQA and IRQB outputs of the PIA can be connected to either the IRQ or NMI lines if interrupts are to be used. The only place where there is any difficulty is that the SS-50 data bus carries inverted data, while the PIA puts out normal data. The PIAs data inputs must be inverted in both directions between the bus and the PIA. A set of 8835 tri-state data buffer/inverters will handle this task very nicely.

SS-30

The SS-30 output bus must have been specifically designed with the 6820 in mind. All that is needed is to supply power and connect the PIA's interface lines to the bus, as shown in Fig. 3-18. The SELECT line has already done the address decoding of lines A2 through A15 and is connected directly to CS2. On most SS-50 systems, there are eight slots in which a 6820 PIA may be placed. These are arranged so that the PIA connected to a given slot will have a particular set of addresses. In the original SWTP 6800 machine using the MIK-BUG monitor. These slots corresponded to address locations $8000-$801F, with eight slots of four addresses each, in consecutive order. On the SS-30 bus, the data lines are not inverted, so no additional buffering is required. Again, the IRQA and IRQB lines may be connected to either IRQ or NMI for interrupts, if desired.

APPLE-II

There are many ways that the 6820 can be interfaced to the Apple-II output bus (see Fig. 3-19). It can be done as memory-mapped I/O, as an I/O port, either with full decoding or with partial address decoding. The Apple-II has eight expansion connectors at the rear of the main board, which we can use to connect our interface. These connectors already have been partially decoded with respect to address. Slot number N occupies the memory region from $CN00 through $CNFF, a whole 256 bytes of memory. To be frugal with memory, we should decode six more memory bits so that we occupy only the four bytes of memory that we need. If we were putting several interfaces on one card, we would be sure to do this. For only one interface, we only need the four memory locations. The card

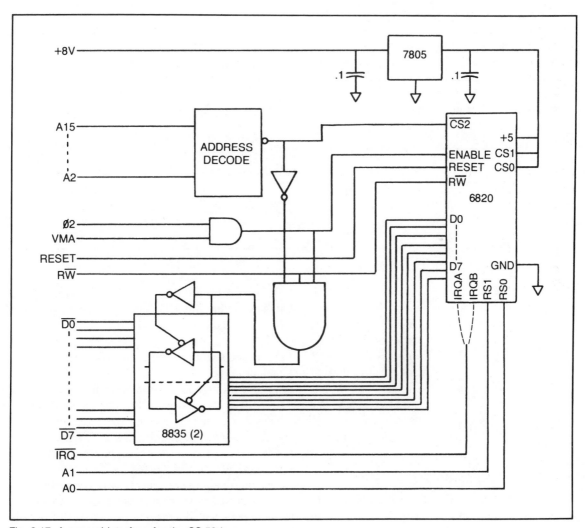

Fig. 3-17. A general interface for the SS-50 bus.

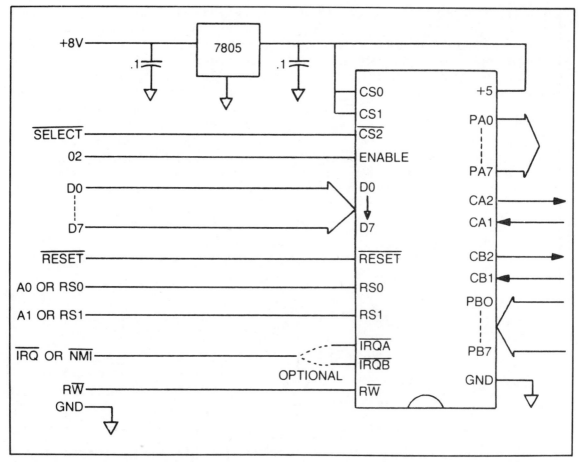

Fig. 3-18. An interface for the SS-30 bus.

will take up a whole slot anyway, so there is no need to decode all the address bits.

We will just use the I/O-SELECT line for the slot being used, and allow partial address decoding for the bits A2-A7. This means that the PIA will have address $CN00 for the A side data register. This register will also respond to $CN04, $CN08, $CN0C, etc. all the way to $CNFF. With this method, almost no hardware is needed to interface the 6820 to the Apple-II output bus.

TANDY COLOR COMPUTER

A standard parallel interface for the COCO ROM slot is shown in Fig. 3-20. There are 16 data lines, 14 of which must be decoded to use the PIA.

Otherwise, no additional circuitry is needed. If you will be calling the PIA from BASIC, the PIA will have to be addressed at $7FFF or below, since BASIC cannot address the area above that address. All I/O in the COCO, or with any 6809 processor, is memory-mapped.

Depending on your application, the switch grounding the line SLENB may or may not be needed. This signal is generated by logic connected to the ROM cartridge port. Taking this line low disables the internal address decoder in the COCO and turns off all internal devices.

Some address decoding may be dispensed with if you are content to have the PIA reside somewhere between addresses $C000 to $DFFF, which is the usual address of the 8K ROM cartridge. If

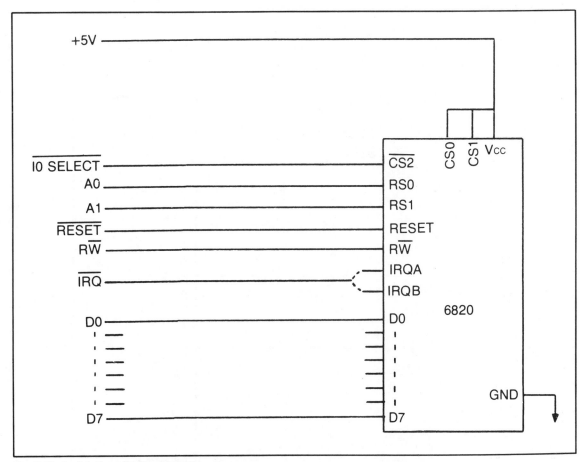

Fig. 3-19. An interface for the Apple-II bus.

this is acceptable, use the CTS line, through an inverter, instead of the E line for input to the chip enable lines of the 6820. The CTS line goes low whenever any address in the range $C000-$DFFF is accessed. If this is used, A13-A15 do not have to be decoded.

IBM PERSONAL
COMPUTER, PC-XT, AND PC-AT

A schematic of an I/O mapped output port for parallel processing is shown in Fig. 3-21. The 6820 is connected to the data lines much the same way as it is connected in all the other interfaces shown here. The major differences are that the address decode must lie in the range from 0200 to 03FF hexadecimal. Also, the PC uses I/O-mapped input

and output ports to conserve memory address space. Up to 65,536 I/O ports can be used on the PC, but internal decoding is turned off for all addresses above $03FF, and addresses below $01FF are reserved for system use, meaning that only addresses between $0200 and $03FF can be used of I/O. Some of these addresses are used already. See Table 3-6 for a list of addresses used by the IBM system in this range. No other I/O address should use these addresses. The interface to the I/O system is quite simple, consisting of just half a 7400 quad NAND gate.

COMMODORE 64

Let's construct a parallel interface using the expansion port of the C-64. Once we have the data

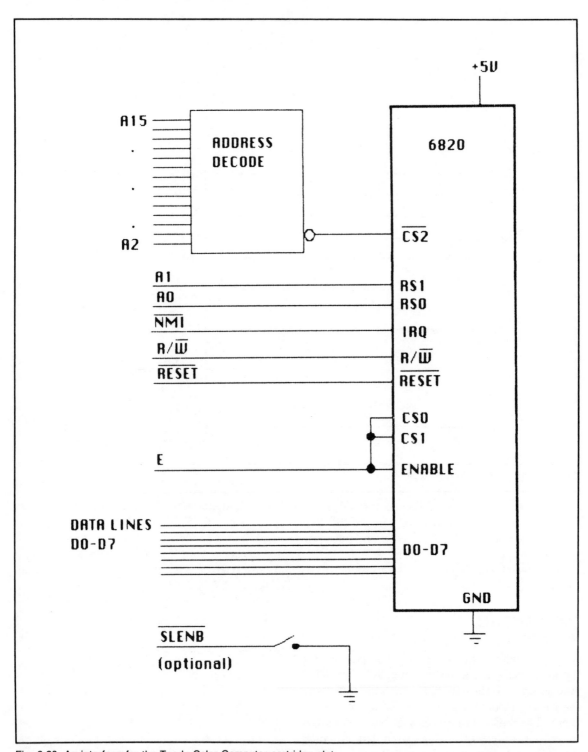

Fig. 3-20. An interface for the Tandy Color Computer cartridge slot.

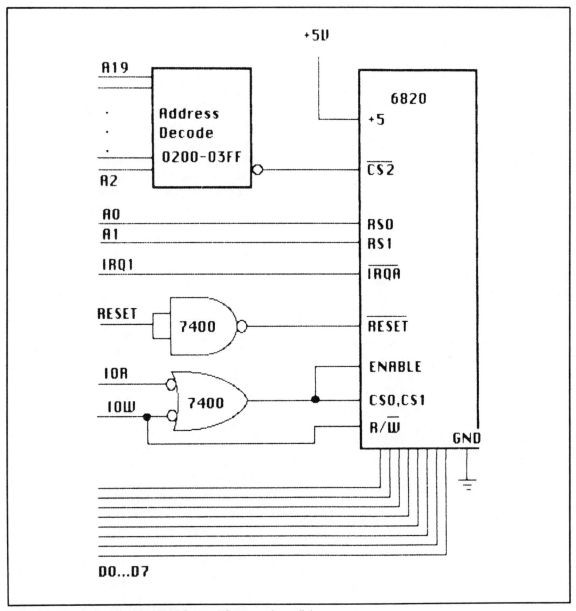

Fig. 3-21. An interface for the IBM-PC; and I/O-mapped parallel port.

lines to where we can get them, we ignore many of them as being unnecessary for our purposes, and simply connect the proper lines to the PIA as shown in Fig. 3-22. Most Motorola processor products will interface to the Motorola 6820 with little additional circuitry. In this case, almost no circuitry beyond the address decoder is necessary. The C-64 uses

memory-mapped I/O, and the port may be placed in memory anywhere it is out of the way. The I/O of the C-64 itself is located between $DEOO and $DFFF in all configurations of the machine. If you want to use I/O in this address range, part of the address decoding may possibly be replaced by the 1/01 or 1/02 signals. Use of addresses between

Table 3-6. IBM Memory Addresses $0200 thru $03FF.

Port Address	Usage in IBM-PC
0201	Game Control Adapter
0278-027F	Second Parallel Port Adapter
02F8-02FF	Second Serial Port Adapter
0378-937F	Parallel Port Adapter
03B0-03BF	Monochrome Adapter Card
03B0-03DF	Color Graphics Adapter card
03F0-03F7	Floppy Disk Controller
03F8-03FF	Serial Port Adapter

$D000 and $DDFF is recommended.

IEEE-488

I originally set out to provide an interface for the IEEE-488 bus that would be standardized to the 6820 outputs. That way, you could have used the IEEE bus as an additional bus for the construction of peripherals to be interfaced to the computer, which the bus was originally designed to do. After thorough examination of the bus for the purposes of designing an interface involving the 6820, I concluded that such an interface would be extraordinarily complex. Such an interface would involve use of the data bus as both two-way data and address. Each interface would take up eight of the 64 available addresses, and the decoding for "my talk address" and "my listen address" for each of the four register addresses in the 6820 would be quite difficult. If you are interested in the IEEE-488 bus, you should read the fine set of articles by Gregory Yob in the July, August, and September, 1980, issues of *Kilobaud Microcomputing* magazine. Also, Hewlett-Packard has patented the handshaking protocol, and a license is needed to use it.

Using the 6820 Interface

Examples of the use of the 6820 interface are shown in Figs. 3-23, 3-24, and 3-25. In each of these examples, it is presumed that the data is presented in one of the standard Centronics parallel formats—that is, eight bits of active-high data, with two-way active-low handshaking.

The first, Fig. 3-23, is a block diagram of the

initialization procedure. The program is given in block form for maximum generality. Again, to keep the standard, we will assume that side A is the input and side B is the output. The first step is to clear the two control registers, allowing us to access the data-direction registers. The A-side data-direction register is filled with zeroes, while the B-side data direction register is filled with ones. For Centronics-style handshaking, CA1 and CB1 will be inputs, while CA2 and CB2 will be outputs. On side A, the input side, we will want IRQA1 set when CA1 goes low, and not interrupt the processor. Let us initially set CA2 to be high. In which case, we will put 00 111 100, or $3C into the A-side control register. On the B-side, we want CB2 to be a handshaking output which will go low when data is written to the data register and not return high until the data is acknowledged by a low signal on CB1. We want CB1 to set bit 7 of control register B but not to interrupt the processor, so we will have to use polling to make sure that the output is complete. This means that the B-side control register must contain 00 100 100, or $24. When all this is done, the PIA is initialized.

Figure 3-24 shows the block program for a data input to the A-side of the PIA. The line CA2 can be used either as a "send data" request or as a "data acknowledged" signal, depending on when it is sent, before or after the arrival of the data. Let's assume it is to be a "data-acknowledged" signal. The computer polls the control register of the A-side and looks for bit 7 to be set. The data will not be known to have arrived until CA1, acting as a "data-present" line, goes low. When the computer finds the bit set, it then reads the data from the data register, sets CA2 low for a cycle, and then returns it high.

Figure 3-25 is the chart for parallel data output from the B-side of the PIA. Data is written into the B-side data register, which causes the line CB2 to go low as well. Then the CPU polls the control register of side B until bit 7 becomes set, indicating that the CB1 line has gone low, showing that the data has been accepted. Note that the CPU can spend a lot of time in the polling loop waiting for the CB1 signal from the peripheral.

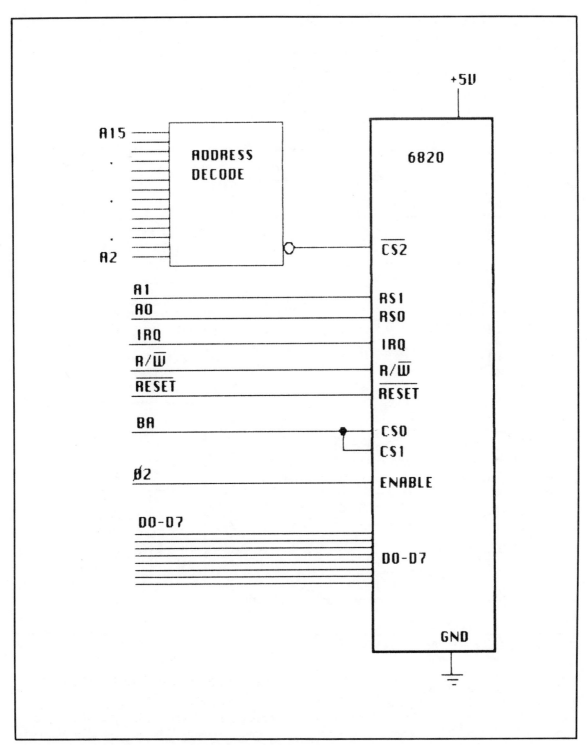

Fig. 3-22. An interface for the Commodore C-64 expansion port.

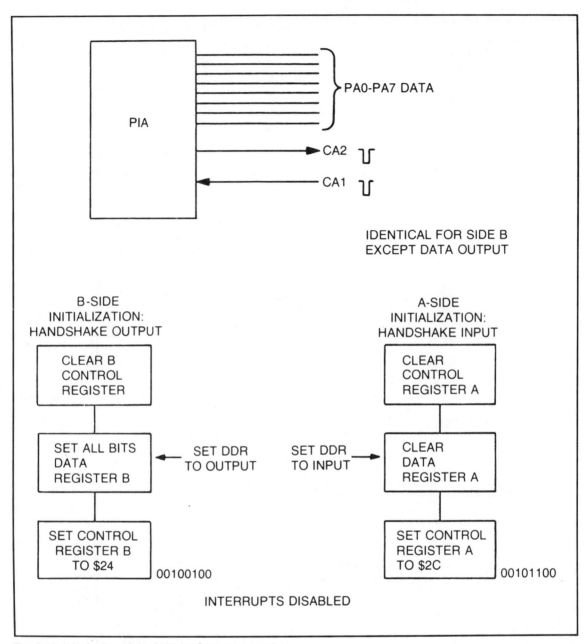

Fig. 3-23. Initialization of the 6820 for Centronics parallel.

In the input loop, the only difference if we were using interrupts would be to eliminate the bit-7 polling loop (just confirm that it was this PIA that caused the interrupt). The A-side control register would change from $34 to $35 to enable interrupts.

INTERFACING TO RS-232 SERIAL LINES

We've gone to a lot of trouble to develop a standardized parallel interface for a lot of different types of computer busses. What happens if the device we want to interface to is a serial device? Do we start

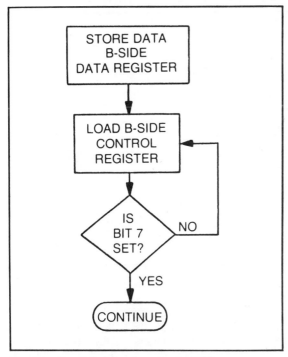

Fig. 3-24. Parallel-output program for 6820.

PIA (to be converted to RS-232), and the baud-rate clock (X16) is connected to CA1. The only additional hardware is the 1488 and 1489 converters to convert to and from TTL levels to RS-232 levels on the input and output. This configuration is called a software UART and is shown in Fig. 3-26.

Consider the output side first. After a proper initialization, the data register is cleared to provide a "0" at the PB0 output as a start bit. Then bit 7 of control register A is cleared (by reading it), and we wait for the baud-rate generator to reset it to a 1. Then it is cleared again, and again we wait for it to be reset to a 1. In fact, since we have a ×16 clock, we do it a total of 16 times, or *one bit time*. Then the data is loaded into the B-side data register, so that the least-significant bit will be put out over the PB0 data line. Again we wait 16 clock cycles, or one bit time. Next, the entire data byte in the B-side data register is shifted to the right by one bit, called a *rotate right*, and we wait another bit time. The process is continued until all eight data bits of the data byte have been shifted right

over? Do we develop a serial interface for each of the above busses?

Thank goodness, we do not have to go that far. All that is really necessary is to convert each of the standard parallel interfaces to a serial interface. There are three ways this may be done.

As usual, when there is more than one way of doing something, the way that takes the least hardware requires the most software. A PIA can be turned into a serial device with very little difficulty, requiring, in fact, no additional hardware. Only three bits of one side of the PIA are used for two-directional serial interfacing. To make the job slightly easier, all eight bits of both sides of the PIA, and one of the input control lines, can be used. The data register of the PIA becomes a temporary storage for the incoming information. Again, let's use the A side for input and the B side for output.

The only connections that need to be made are: the TTL serial inputs (from a RS-232 to TTL converter) are connected to the PA0 input of the PIA, the TTL serial outputs are connected to PB0 of the

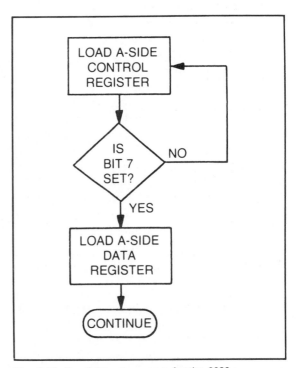

Fig. 3-25. Parallel-input program for the 6820.

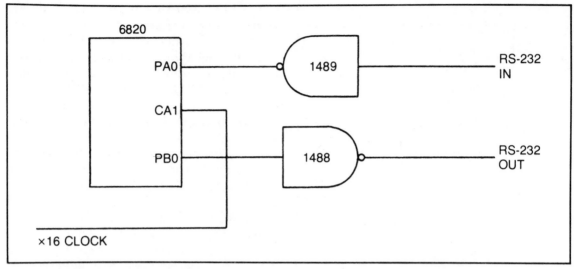

6820

PA0 ——o 1489 — RS-232 IN

CA1

PB0 —— 1488 o— RS-232 OUT

×16 CLOCK

Fig. 3-26. Hardware needed for the software UART.

into PB0, and each data bit has been in PB0 for one full bit time, or sixteen pulses of the X16 clock. Last, the data bit, PB0, is loaded with a "1" and we wait either one or two bit times, depending on whether one or two stop bits are required. Nothing more need to be done until we desire to send another data byte.

Figure 3-27 shows in more detail exactly what the process looks like from the point of view of the data register, and the output itself.

Data input is only slightly more complicated. We poll the data register and see if data bit PA0 goes to a 0. When it does, this is an indication that the start bit has been received. Again, we reset bit 7 of the A-side control register by reading it and wait for it to set itself eight times. Only eight because we want to catch the center of the start bit by waiting one half of one bit time. If the input PA0 is still a 0, then we can be sure that the input is a true start bit, and not just noise. We wait 16 more transitions of CA1, or one bit time, so that we are in the middle of the first data bit. Then the whole input register is rotated to the left, putting the data in bit 0 into bit 1. Wait another bit time, and now we should be in the exact middle of the second data bit. Rotate it left, as well. Now the first bit is in bit 2, the second in bit 1, and we are waiting to fill up bit 0 with the third bit. We continue this procedure

until all eight bits have been received. It is a good idea to check to make sure that the next bit is a proper stop bit after the eight data bits have been properly stored into memory. Look for a "1" at PA0 for a whole bit time. If your system requires two stops bits, better make sure that two have been received.

The feature of microprocessors that allows us to use a PIA for serial input and output is the fact that the microprocessor is so much faster than the serial data transmission. In only takes a few microseconds to keep track of the CA1 bit, or to rotate the data left or right, while it may take three milliseconds to receive one data bit at 300 baud.

Figures 3-28 and 3-29 are the flowcharts for the input and output via a software UART. Notice the use of the subroutine to count the timer.

One major disadvantage of using a software UART is that the processor is busy the whole time the data is being input or output. The processor is busy checking on the status of the X16 clock, rotating data left or right, and interacting with the memory for storage. The processor is dedicated solely to the use of putting data in or out. Since serial data transmission is generally slow, this slows down the computer capability of the computer as a whole.

The solution is, of course, more hardware. The more hardware we have, generally the less software we need. What we really need is a method of converting parallel data into serial data. The software method above will work, at a cost of a lot of processor overhead. If conversion from parallel to serial is such a common task, surely there must be a special chip to do it for us?

Of course there is! The chip is called a UART for universal asynchronous receiver-transmitter. There are dozens of different types, made by dozens of different manufacturers. The one that seems to enjoy the widest popularity, probably because it is so easily adaptable to many different situations, is the General Instruments AY-5-1013. It is so widely used that other manufacturers have come out with their own versions of this integrated circuit, and these other versions can be directly substituted for it, as they are pin-compatible. Even General Instruments has three different versions, all pin-compatible, called the 1014 and 1015 in addition to the 1013. Other versions are the Ameri-

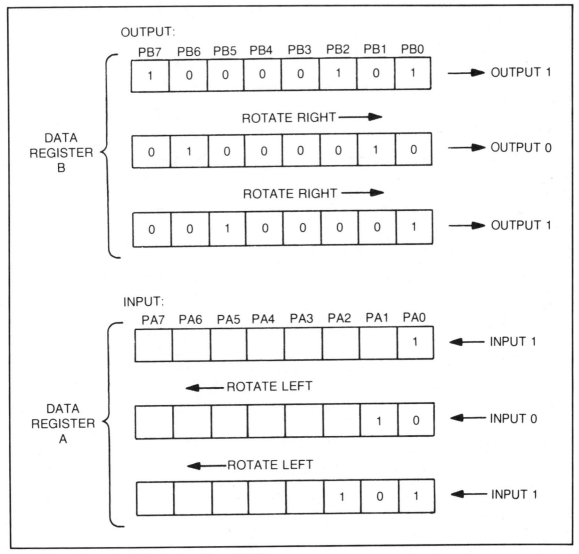

Fig. 3-27. Rotation of data bits in the software UART.

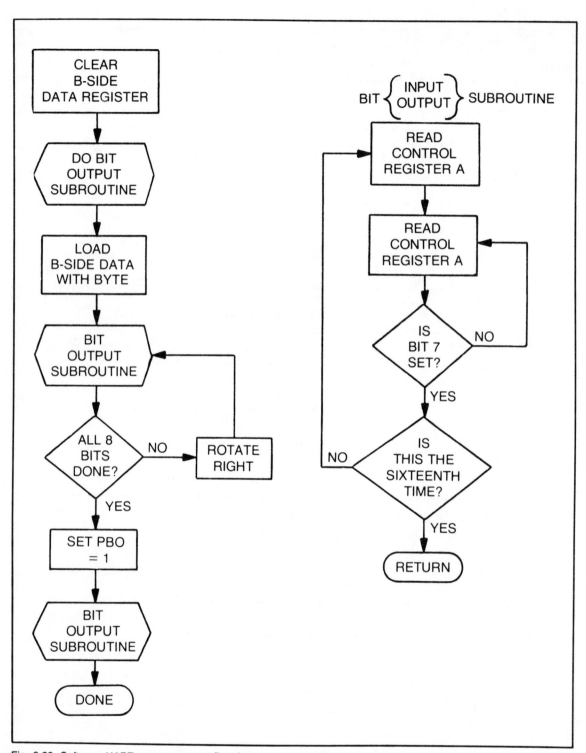

Fig. 3-28. Software UART output program flowchart.

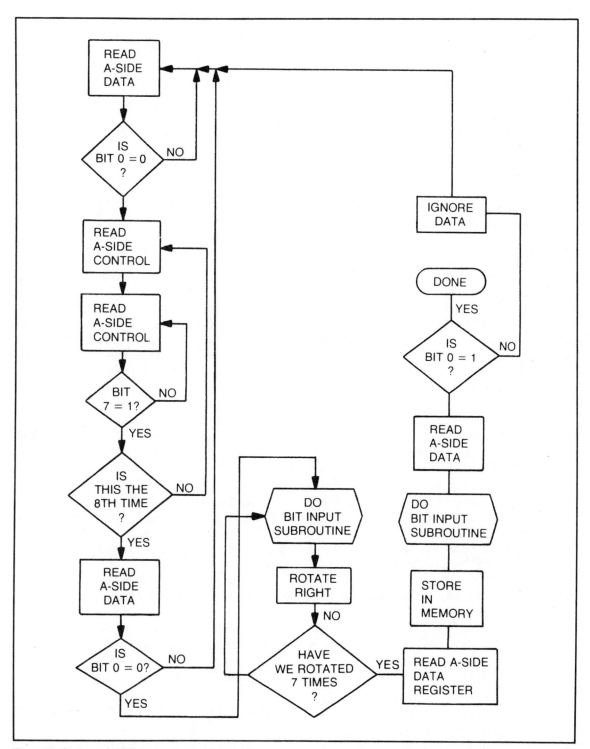

Fig. 3-29. Software UART input program flowchart.

can Microsystems S1883, the Signetics 2536, the Standard Microsystems COM 2502, the Texas Instruments TMS 6012, and the Western Digital TR1602.

The purpose of the UART is, quite simply, to convert serial to parallel and to convert parallel to serial. There are input pins which allow the UART to be "programmed" for specific conditions of number of data bytes, parity, number of stop bits, and the like. These chips are built for a × 16 clock and have outputs that can detect framing errors, receiver overrun, or parity errors.

The UART is connected to the PIA as shown in Fig. 3-29. The A side of the PIA is used as the input side from the UART, and the B side of the PIA is the output to the UART. The inputs and outputs of the UART are at TTL levels, and conversion to and from RS-232 levels must be made by the 1488 and 1489 chips. If desired, error detection can take place through CA2, used as an input, with the outputs from pins 13, 14, and 15 ANDed together to form a "error-in-received-data" signal. This error signal is active high.

To "program" the UART, simply make the appropriate connections to the input pins for the configuration you will be using. For example, pin 35, NP, is to be a logical 1 if the parity bit is to be eliminated from both the transmitted and received character. That is, no parity bit will be transmitted, and the parity-error flag will not operate in the receiver. Pin 36 selects the number of stop bits. A logic 0 will send or expect one stop bit, while a logic 1 will send or expect to receive two stop bits. Pins 37 and 38 specify the number of data bits that will be sent. The following explains these inputs:

Pin 37	Pin 38	Bits/Character
0	0	5
0	1	6
1	0	7
1	1	8

When sending ASCII, there are usually 7 bits, with bit 8 = 0. At any other time, send 8 bits. The use of 5 bits is reserved for the older Baudot-coded machines, such as the Teletype® model 15. Pin 39 selects the type of parity used, if parity is to be used: a 1 uses even parity; a 0 uses odd parity.

In addition to the programming, data I/O, and × 16 baud-rate clock, there are also three control lines which need to be tied in to the PIA control lines.

Pin	PIA Input	Active Level	Function
19	CA1	1	Indicates character is received
23	CB2	0	Send character
22	CB1	1	OK to send next character

There are also a number of other pins that must be held high or low in order for the UART to work in this configuration. These pins are noted on the diagram, Fig. 3-30.

The software for initializing the PIA, and for transmitting and receiving serial data through the UART, is given in flowchart form in Fig. 3-31, 3-32, and 3-33 respectively. The correct values for the control register are also given, assuming that interrupts will not be used. Essentially, the receive method is to wait until the control register indicates that a "data-received" pulse is present on the UART, and then get the data. The transmit method is to check to see that the transmitter is not busy, to wait until it is not (if it is), and then enter the data and send it.

Note that the receive part of the UART and PIA are set up so that the UART can receive the data and tell the PIA about it even if the CPU is busy doing something else. So long as the CPU checks the status of bit 7 of the A-side control register every ten milliseconds or so, no data will be lost. A better way would be to use interrupts. When a "data-received" pulse is found, the processor interrupts, and the received character is placed into a data buffer on a first-in, first-out basis. When the computer needs an input character, it simply looks in the buffer. This way, no data can be lost at all.

SERIAL TO PARALLEL DATA CONVERSION

We should discuss the reverse problem: Some computers, such as the Tandy Color Computer and

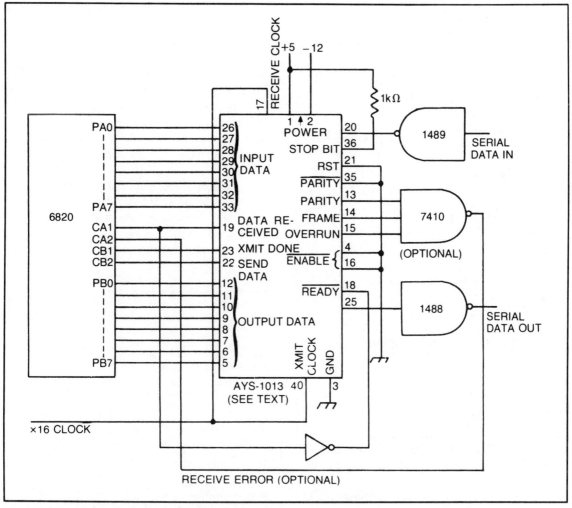

Fig. 3-30. PIA to UART connection: parallel to serial.

the Apple Macintosh do not have parallel ports *per se*. It may be desired to operate a parallel device directly from a serial port.

The circuit of Fig. 3-34 shows how to operate the A-Y-5-1013A UART chip in reverse so that an RS-232 serial port (to the left of the diagram) can operate a device which requires parallel data. Again, a ×16 serial clock from one of the circuits above is used for setting the data rate. Parallel data enters leaves the device in two separate ports on the right of the UART diagram, and serial data, after being converted to RS-232 by the 1488 and 1489 chips, enters to the left.

The only real difference between this port and a true parallel port is the handshaking lines. For parallel data output, pins 18 and 19 form a READY and DATA RECEIVED lines. The READY line is an active-low line telling the UART that there is data on the parallel output lines ready to be sent. The DATA RECEIVED line should be taken high by the parallel device to acknowledge the UART that the device got the parallel data and it can receive another serial character. Similarly, for parallel data input, a SEND DATA line, pin 22, when high tells the UART that there is parallel data on the input lines, and to begin conversion. The XMIT

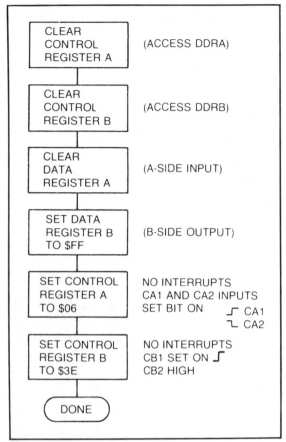

CLEAR CONTROL REGISTER A	(ACCESS DDRA)
CLEAR CONTROL REGISTER B	(ACCESS DDRB)
CLEAR DATA REGISTER A	(A-SIDE INPUT)
SET DATA REGISTER B TO $FF	(B-SIDE OUTPUT)
SET CONTROL REGISTER A TO $06	NO INTERRUPTS CA1 AND CA2 INPUTS SET BIT ON ⌐ CA1 ⌐ CA2
SET CONTROL REGISTER B TO $3E	NO INTERRUPTS CB1 SET ON ⌐ CB2 HIGH

DONE

Fig. 3-31. Flowchart for initializing the PIA for serial data with the UART.

DONE line will go low when the data has been sent, for a handshake to the parallel device.

Users should be careful, in that this circuit does not act to the computer or to the peripheral exactly like a PIA in all cases. For example, there is no interrupt processing for the computer: this device cannot cause an interrupt. Secondly, the handshake lines do not act the same as the handshake lines C1 and C2 for the PIA. Users who plan to use this circuit with some of the peripherals described in this book should make sure that the handshake signals are compatible with their needs.

An alternative to the PIA-UART marriage is to use a chip that combines both PIA and UART in one, without ever going to parallel output. Such a device is called an asynchronous communications

interface adapter, or ACIA. With this scheme, the PIA is completely replaced by the ACIA, whose input and output to the peripheral are both serial, not parallel. Our choice of the 6820 for the PIA was determined in part by the fact that we could do this subroutine with very little effort. In fact, the 6850 ACIA, also manufactured by Motorola, is, on the side connected to the computer's bus, almost pin-for-pin identical to the 6820. It is *almost* possible to unplug the 6820 from the socket and plug in the 6850.

In the first place, even though there are four registers in the 6850, the ACIA need only occupy two memory locations. Two of the registers are read-only, and two are write-only, so the read/write line serves to choose between two registers that oc-

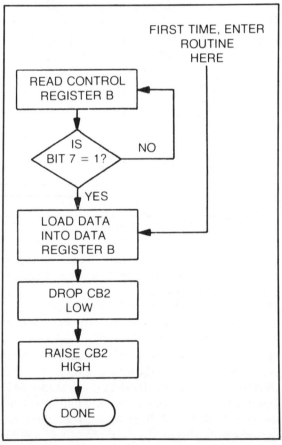

Fig. 3-32. Flowchart for sending data through the UART.

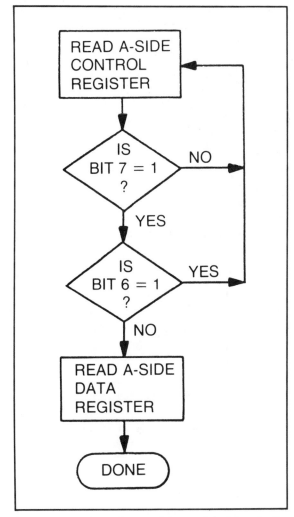

Fig. 3-33. Flowchart for receiving serial data via the UART.

insert an ACIA. If the ACIA's pin 1 is situated where the PIA's pin 6 would be, then all eight data lines and the enable line are in the same place. This places nine of the 12 pins on the CPU side of the ACIA in the same place as the pins of the PIA. The read/write pin, all three chip-select pins, address line A0, power, and ground must be moved. In addition, there is only one interrupt output. See Appendix A for details of the pin connections.

The ACIA has four registers. They are selected as shown in Table 3-7.

The control register is what "initializes" the ACIA. It tells the ACIA what the baud-clock rate is, how many stop bits are to be used, and the like. It is a write-only register.

Bits 0 and 1 of the control register select the rate of the baud rate clock, which in turn sets the baud rate. All the ACIA has to know is, "Is it a ×1, ×16, or ×64 clock?" That is set according to Table 3-8. Notice that there is no reset pin on the 6850. The reset function has to be performed through software.

Bits 2, 3, and 4 select how the word will be transmitted, as Table 3-9.

The ACIA is designed to be able to control a modem for connection to telephone lines. To facilitate control of the modem, bits 5 and 6 of the control register set the output called RTS (request-to-send) as shown in Table 3-10. The transmit-data register, when empty, will cause an interrupt when enabled.

Lastly, bit 7 controls whether the ACIA will cause an interrupt when the receiver part of the ACIA detects a received character. A 1 enables interrupts, which can be caused by either the receiver data register full bit of the status register going high, or a low-to-high transition on the data-carrier-detect signal line.

The status register can only be read by the CPU; it cannot be written into. The purpose of the status register is to inform the CPU that certain conditions have occurred in the ACIA, and may require attention.

When bit 0 is set to a logic 1, it indicates that the receiver data register is full. That is, data has been received. It also sets the IRQ bit (bit 7) which

cupy the same memory location. Line A1 is not needed. It can be added to the address decoding, or, as is often done, the A1 line can simply be disconnected, leaving the ACIA to occupy four memory locations, with the second two being an exact repeat of the first two, due to incomplete address decoding. This is the method used on the SS-30 bus, where each PIA and each ACIA occupy one slot on the output bus, each with four addresses.

Secondly, it was mentioned above that it is *almost* possible to unplug a PIA from a socket and

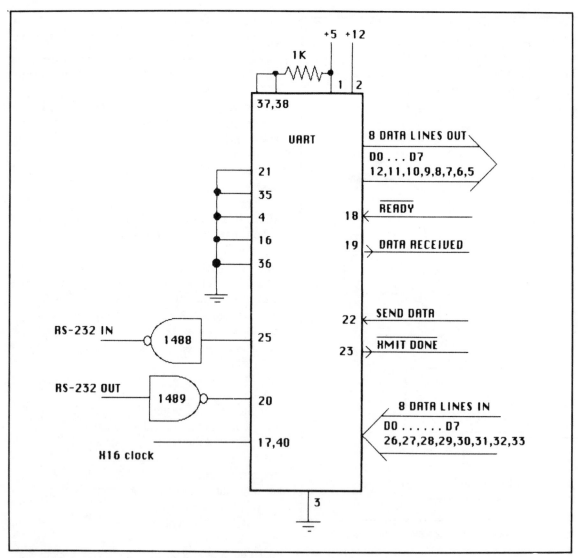

Fig. 3-34. Connecting a serial port to a parallel device using a UART.

Table 3-7. The Four Registers of the ACIA.

Address Line A0	Read/Write	Register	CPU Function
0	0	control	write only
0	1	status	read only
1	0	transmit data	write only
1	1	receive data	read only

Table 3-8. Baud-Rate Selection for the ACIA.

Bit 1	Bit 0	Function
0	0	X1 clock
0	1	X16 clock
1	0	X64 clock
1	1	resets ACIA

Table 3-9. Transmission-Mode Selection for the ACIA.

Bit 4	Bit 3	Bit 2	No. Data Bits	Parity	Stop Bits
0	0	0	7	even	2
0	0	1	7	odd	2
0	1	0	7	even	1
0	1	1	7	odd	1
1	0	0	8	none	2
1	0	1	8	none	1
1	1	0	8	even	1
1	1	1	8	odd	1

Table 3-10. RTS Selection for Control of a Modem.

Bit 6	Bit 5	RTS	Function
0	0	low	Transmitting-interrupt disable
0	1	low	Transmitting enabled
1	0	high	Transmitting-interrupt disable
1	1	low	Transmit-interrupt disabled also transmits break level on the transmit-data output.

remains set until the data is read into the CPU. When bit 0 is a 0, it means the received data has been read by the CPU, or that the contents of the data received register are not current.

When bit 1 is a 1, it means that the transmit data register is empty and new data may be transmitted. When it is a 0, the transmit data register is full, or the ACIA is still busy sending the last data byte.

Bit 2 is used with modems. When it is a 0, there is a carrier wave present on the modem. When it is a 1, there is no carrier. When bit 2 gets set to a 1, it also sets bit 7 which will remain set until the CPU reads both the status register and the receiver data register.

Bit 3 is information from the modem indicating that the modem is or is not ready to send. If bit 3 is a 0, the modem is ready for data.

Bit 4, when set, indicates that the received character is improperly framed by the start and stop bits, or that the first stop bit was absent. This error indicates a synchronization error or faulty transmission. This bit is only present during the time that the associated character is available. Of course, if the bit is a 0, the character is all right.

Bit 5, when set, indicates that one or more characters have been lost from the data stream. That is, a character or a number of characters were received, but were not read from the receiver data register by the CPU prior to subsequent data being received. The bit is cleared by reading the re-

ceiver data register. A 0 on this bit indicates that all data has been received properly.

Bit 6 indicates by being set that a parity error has occurred in the received data. That is, the parity-error flag indicates that the number of 1s in the character does not agree with the preselected odd or even parity. Odd parity is defined to be when the total number of 1s is odd. If no parity is selected, then both the transmitter and receiver parity checks are inhibited. A 0 means that no parity error has occurred.

Bit 7 is the interrupt indicator. If the IRQ line is connected to one of the interrupt lines on the CPU's control bus, when bit 7 makes the transition from a 0 to a 1, an interrupt condition will occur. Bit 7 is the ACIA's way of telling the CPU that "It was I that caused the interrupt" when the CPU starts polling all the peripherals. Remember that bit 7 can be set by bits 0, 1, and 2 of the status register, and is enabled by bit 7 of the control register.

Finally, we've gotten all of the "background" out of the way. Chapters 1, 2, and 3 have the purpose of giving us the information we need to be able to interface a peripheral to a computer. Now we can start on the real meat of this book and construct some peripherals. We have seen that connecting a peripheral to a computer is far more difficult than just connecting some wires. We need to have an interface circuit, and we need to have a software handler to get data from or to the interface.

Now all we need is the peripheral!

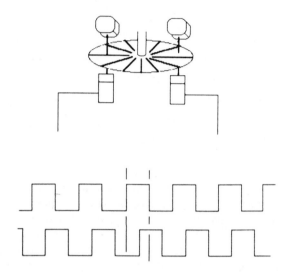

Chapter 4

Digital Peripherals with Parallel Input

Let's start with some devices that can be counted directly to the standard parallel interface. These will be digital peripherals in that the information will be in 1s and 0s with TTL logic levels.

SENSE SWITCHES

One of the simplest, and most useful, peripherals that can be connected to a computer is a set of sense switches. These are nothing more than a number of switches, connected to a parallel-input port, whose status may be checked by the CPU to determine if a course of action is to be taken or not. The CPU does not have to query the control terminal and wait for an answer, so the processor can run at full speed, without waiting on the pleasure of the operator.

Such a set of sense switches is easy to build, requiring only eight switches, eight 1000-ohm resistors, and a source of +5V power and ground. A diagram is shown in Fig. 4-1. The data line is held high by the pull-up resistors and is grounded low by the closing of the switch. The input to the inter-

face is just the condition of the switch.

While at first glance, a set of sense switches may seem to be a trivial addition to a computer system, it really can be an invaluable aid, especially to a system in which a lot of hardware and assembly-language software is being developed.

Consider the following uses of sense switches: many machine-language programs are written for the purpose of testing a piece of equipment, or a method of programming. Often, these programs involve an endless loop of instructions, so that the waveforms can be examined with an oscilloscope, or so that a particular piece of equipment can be tested thousands of times with the computer. Since the operator does not want to continually re-enter an instruction to perform the loop, he will often just let the loop run, and abort the process by hitting the reset switch. An alternative to this method, using the sense switches, would be to examine the status of one of the sense switches during every loop, and do the loop again if the switch is off, or terminate the process and return to the monitor if

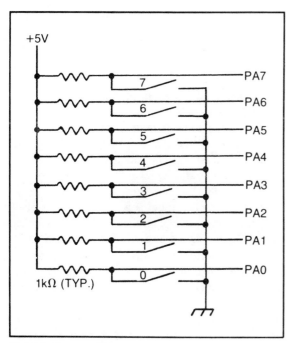

Fig. 4-1. Sense switches.

of the switches has just been changed, and that the CPU should read the switches. This is done by installing an additional button, a few gates, and connecting to the control-line inputs of that side of the PIA. Pushing the button could then cause an interrupt, and the CPU would then process the information immediately.

Figure 4-2 shows an arrangement which can be used along these lines. The button is used to take the input of one side of a set-reset flip-flop to ground, causing that output of the flip-flop to go low. Since that output is connected to the CA1 input of the PIA, bit 7 of the A-side control register will be set, and if interrupts are enabled, will cause an interrupt. The interrupt causes the CPU to read the switches, adjust its efforts accordingly, and then a low signal is sent out over CA2 to reset the flip-flop.

An arrangement such as this is used with the main data-acquisition computer at the University of California at Davis' Crocker Laboratory. The switches are used to control the analysis of a set of samples. If a switch is changed and the button pushed, the parameters of the analysis may be changed on the terminal, or a previous sample may be re-run, or any number of similar effects.

A HEXADECIMAL KEYBOARD

A hexadecimal keyboard can be a very useful addition to a microcomputer. It may be that your

it is on. If this is done, it will save having to re-enter the program, or re-initialize peripheral PIAs. Hitting the reset button on a computer will sometimes have adverse effects on the program you are running. It will, for example, clear the control registers of all PIAs used. It may cause the machine to re-initialize the disk drive. Sometimes it may even clear the memory, depending on your monitor. Alternatively, turning the switch on can have the computer stop the loop until the switch is turned back on.

Another use of the switches would be to direct the output to the proper peripheral. If a switch is off, the output would be directed to the terminal; if the switch is on, the output could be directed to the printer. The destination of the output could even be changed in mid-transmission!

The nice thing about sense switches is that they are always readable. The output of the sense switches is connected directly to the data register of the PIA, and a simple command to "read A-side data register" will give the position of the sense switches at any instant that the switches are read.

It is also possible to tell the computer that one

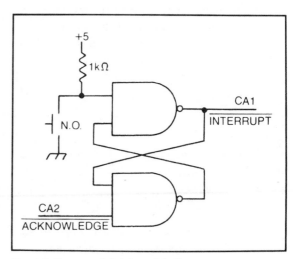

Fig. 4-2. Sense-switch interrupt button.

computer does not have a terminal—that you are forced by circumstances to enter programs or data through a series of switches on the front panel, or something like that. You may have a full terminal already, but find that its typewriter keyboard is very inconvenient in entering long lists of numbers because of the positioning of the numbers across the top of the alphabetic keyboard. The usual solution in cases like this is to add a numeric keypad. Indeed, most better-quality terminals offer not only the typewriter keyboard but also a numeric keypad for ease in entering numbers.

There are a large number of numeric keypads available on both the new and the surplus market. A replacement or experimenter's calculator keyboard may be had for only a few dollars. Even a full hexadecimal pad is not very expensive and will have all ten numbers, as well as the hexadecimal digits A, B, C, D, E, and F. For extensive work in machine language, this is a handy tool.

The keypad may be wired in one of two ways, either ASCII characters or the binary numbers themselves. The two are very similar. For an ASCII addition to an existing keyboard, all that is needed is to wire the terminals of the individual switches to the terminals of the same switches on your keyboard.

For a first-time keyboard, or to use a separate input, a little more electronics hardware is required. In hexadecimal, there are sixteen possible letters and numbers, including the zero. To represent the closing of sixteen switches as a binary number is the problem. We could construct a diode ROM encoder, or use one of the scanning keyboard encoders, but the expense is a little large for just sixteen keys. A TTL alternative is inexpensive and easy to construct.

As shown in Fig. 4-3, each button on the keyboard is used to ground an input which is normally held high by a pull-up resistor. The actual encoding is done by a pair of 74148 eight-line to three-line priority encoders. If buttons 0-7 are pressed, the NAND gate will enable the upper 74148, and the buttons 8-F will enable the lower one. The output of the two NAND gates will be ORed together to give a "keypressed" strobe. To make sure that

the correct code is sent to the computer, a 74157 will choose from the outputs of either of the 74148s depending on the state of its enable input, which will be the output of the NAND gate directing which button set was pushed. Note that bit 4 of the 74157 is either a 1 or a 0 depending on whether the upper or lower set of buttons is pushed.

This setup gives the output of the keyboard in binary. If ASCII is desired instead, the components in the dashed box may be added. Basically, the ASCII characters 0 through 9 are their binary equivalents with a 0011 added as most significant digits. But if the digits A through F are sent, then we need 0100 instead. This is complicated by the fact that two of the upper set of digits are numbers while the rest are letters. We simply add a gate to tell us if either the 8 or 9 has been pressed, and to go with the number configuration rather than the letter.

There are a few features of interest in the circuit. First, the inverters on PA4 through PA6 have to be open collector inverters because of the 3PST switch. This means they will need pull-up resistors on the outputs. All resistors on the circuit are pull-up resistors and are shown to be 1000-ohm nominal, but almost any value from 1000 to 10,000 ohms will do. When the switch is closed, PA4 through PA6 are grounded, regardless of the status of the other gates, making the output binary. With the switch open, output is the ASCII equivalent of the number. If you want ASCII all the time, eliminate the switch, and the 7405s may be replaced with 7404s and the pull-up resistors eliminated. If you want binary all the time the entire section in the dashed box may be dispensed with, and inputs PA4 through PA7 may be tied directly to ground. Or, if you will be using these other four inputs for some other purpose, at least AND the input with $0F through software to get a proper binary number.

Three of the four gates in the 7402 are used. The net result is to provide a "keypressed" strobe to the computer. This strobe is presented through CA1. The computer, upon reading that there is a key pressed, will read PA0 through PA7 to get the word as it is at the moment of reading. There is no key lockout—that is, pressing one key does not

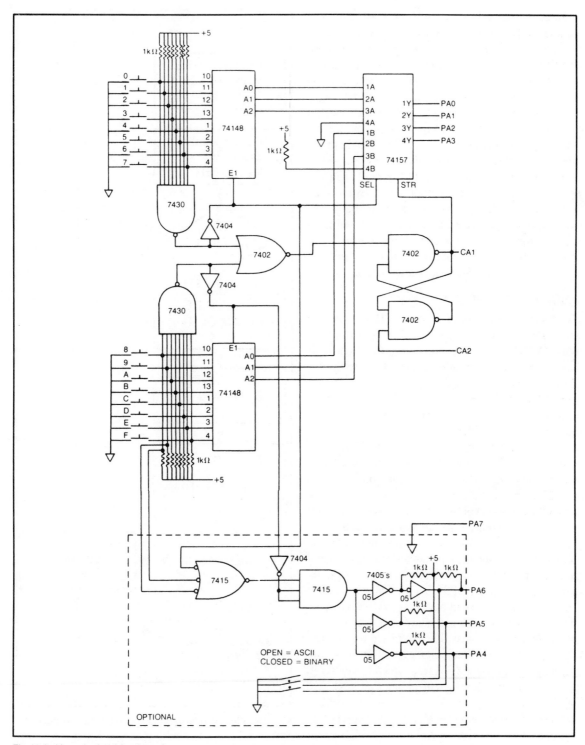

Fig. 4-3. Hexadecimal keyboard.

assure that no other key can be pressed. CA1 will be low until a low pulse is sent out over CA2 to reset the flip-flop. CA2 should be normally high, and immediately return to the high state after going low to reset the keyboard. Another way just as good would be to invert the output of the first 7402, which is acting as an OR gate, and use the inverted output to reset the flip-flop. This procedure assumes that the computer will read the data immediately upon receiving a CA1 low.

Figure 4-4 is a flowchart of the read program to inspect and to read the output of the hexadecimal keyboard device through the standard PIA interface. The program goes into a loop which examines bit 7 of the control register and keeps examining it until it finds a 1. When a 1 is found, it reads the data and sets CA2 low, then high again.

ASCII KEYBOARD

No one can dispute that an ASCII keyboard is an absolute necessity for the "compleat" computer. With a typewriter keyboard, full communication with the computer becomes a possibility. ASCII opens up the possibility of using BASIC and other higher languages, a text editor and assembler, a word processor, and many other full-feature aspects of a computer.

But why speak of adding a keyboard? Don't all computers have a typewriter-like keyboard these days? Well, yes, most do. Yet some do not. There are still plenty of "microprocessor trainers" around, as well as lots of hobby kits that have only front panel switch inputs or hexadecimal keypads. One of the most popular early computers was the KIM-1, which used only a hexadecimal keypad and hexadecimal displays, much the same as a calculator. The first version of the Tandy Color Computer had a keyboard more like a calculator than a typewriter. The Timex/Sinclair's keyboard was so small as to be difficult to use. The keyboard on the first models of the IBM PC-junior was felt to be inconvenient by many, and IBM was forced to modify it.

Here, then, is a means of adding that keyboard you've always wanted.

Even if your computer already has a keyboard, you may want another one. The IBM PC-JR and

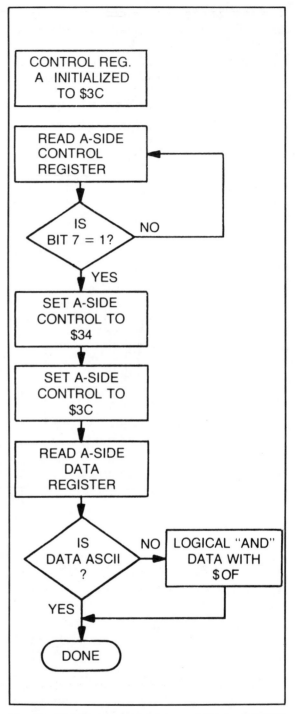

Fig. 4-4. Flowchart of program to read the hexadecimal keypad.

the early PETs from Commodore had a smaller version of the standard keyboard that was rather hard to use. Many games can be constructed to use a second keyboard for interaction between two players on two keyboards, making the game more fascinating. Maybe you'd like to have a party and have your guests play games on the computer, without the fuss of bringing the whole machine in to the living room, or having the whole party in one of the bedrooms you're using for your computer. All you will need is a cable to the second keyboard, and a video cable to the living room TV set (and a little creative programming). Even timesharing can be worked out on your machine, with the use of two keyboards (see Chapter 5).

As you can see, the uses for a second keyboard are manifold. A complete terminal can cost over a thousand dollars—some as much as two thousand dollars! A keyboard can cost less than fifty if you're willing to do the interfacing yourself. You can even buy ready-made keyboards, with complete encoding, ready to plug into a parallel port. They will cost anywhere from two hundred dollars for a new, top-of-the-line keyboard, to as little as seventy for a reconditioned surplus model.

Unencoded keyboards, that is, just the keyswitches on a printed circuit board, can cost as little as twenty dollars on the surplus market, or up to fifty brand new. By spending less than ten dollars on some integrated circuits and doing the wiring yourself, and with a little creative programming, you can have a fully encoded ASCII keyboard.

Coding a keyboard is easier than it sounds, thanks to modern LSI integrated circuits. There are twenty-six letters of the alphabet to code, ten numbers, and a whole host of punctuation symbols. Each of these letters, numbers, and symbols will have both an upper- and lowercase, so the shift key must be accounted for as well. In addition, there are a number of control codes, such as carriage return, line feed, and back space, which have to be programmed in. We will follow the standard terminal usage and add a "control" key, which works just like a shift key. Do a "shift J," and you get capital letter J. Do a control-J, and you get a carriage

return. If neither shift nor control are pressed, you should get just ordinary lowercase letter "J." Most display units and printers these days are capable of printing upper- and lowercase letters. However, there are still many display devices that don't have lowercase capability, so we must provide for an ALL-CAPS mode, as well.

Surplus keyboards may be 47-key, 56-key, 64-key, or even 80-keyboards. How in the world are we going to be able to code all 128 members of the ASCII set?

The magic of LSI circuitry strikes again. Naturally, with a task as frequently done as encoding a keyboard, there should be an integrated circuit devoted especially to the task. Indeed, there are several. The one that is perhaps easiest to use (and certainly the one in most common use among hobbyists) is the AY-5-2376 Keyboard Encoder. This integrated circuit is a scanning type of keyboard encoder. That is, it scans all 88 possible keys that it can interface, and when it finds one pressed, gives the ASCII code for that key at the outputs. The scanning rate is very fast—50,000 keys every second. It also has two-key rollover. That is, if a second key is depressed while the first key is still down, the encoder will hold the first until it is released, and *then* do the second. The encoder has inputs for shift, control, and provision for uppercase—only encoding. The switches are also *debounced.* Most mechanical switches, when first pressed, will "bounce" against the contacts several times. This could result in several keyings of the same key. That is, we press "a" and get "aaaaa" because of switch bounce. A small resistor-capacitor network connected to pin 19 of the integrated circuit will assure that no two keypresses occur within the specified period of time. Using a 470,000 ohm resistor and a 0.01 microfarad capacitor in parallel will set this period to about eight milliseconds. Most switch bounces are less than three milliseconds in duration. Yet eight milliseconds gives plenty of time between keys. (Just try to type a key every 8 milliseconds! That's equivalent to typing 1250 words per minute! Even the best secretaries don't type significantly more than 100 words per minute.)

The complete circuit for the keyboard and encoder is shown in Fig. 4-5. Note the way the encoder works: There is an 8 × 11 matrix of wires coming out of the encoder. The outputs are the pins marked X0 through X7. The inputs are the pins marked Y0 through Y10. The key connects one of the inputs to one of the outputs. For example, to get the capital letter "A," not only do we have to have the "shift" key depressed, but the button which connects X5 to Y8 must also be depressed. No other combination will result in the ASCII code for a capital"A." Notice that in our encoder, we do not use the first two rows of Xs, X0 and X1. In our case, they are redundant. If we were to have a key at X0, Y4, to get an EOT control code, that would just be a key that can't be used for anything else. If your surplus keyboard has an EOT key on it, fine. Use it. Most will not, however, We can get the EOT function by doing a control-D. That is, by holding down the control key and hitting the key that connects the wires X5 and Y6, which should be a "d.".

Note that the keyboard not only requires a source of +5V power, but also a source of −12 V power. The current requirements in either case are slight.

The network connecting pins 2, 3, and 40 is the clock network for the chip's internal scanner. With those components, a clock rate of about 50 kHz will be established.

The ASCII outputs are pins 8 through 15. Note that there are eight output pins for a seven-bit ASCII output. You have your choice of pins for bit 6: If you want upper- and lowercase, use pin 10 as the output for bit 6; if you want uppercase only on the letters (but upper- and lowercase with numbers and punctuation symbols) use pin 8 for bit 6. You can even install a switch, as shown, to select between them.

Pin 6 is the parity input. For even parity, ground pin 6. This will give a low parity bit when the number of zeroes in the output code is odd and a high bit when the number of zeroes in the seven output bits is even. For odd parity, do just the opposite; tie the pin 6 input to +5V. Pin 7 is the parity output. If the use of parity is not desired, simply do not connect pin 7 to anything. Otherwise, treat it like a bit 8.

Pin 16 is the "keypressed" strobe, indicating that a key is making contact between two matrix wires when it is high. Since most devices want an active-low keypress strobe, it has been inverted here. If your application requires an active-high keypress strobe, leave off the inverter. The keypress strobe (and the other outputs) can be counted on to drive one TTL load. It is important that no data be read from the keyboard unless the keypress strobe is active. When the integrated circuit is scanning, it looks at every matrix location in turn. While it is examining a matrix location, the ASCII equivalent of that key is being displayed on the outputs. Only when a key is pressed does the scanning stop and the outputs are held on one character. In most cases this will not be a problem. The key will go down, a keypress strobe will occur, which will set bit 7 of the PIA control register through the control line, and the computer, if it is in a polling loop waiting for an indication that a key has been pressed, will see it immediately, and read the data. All this should take less than a hundred microseconds, which is even faster than the eight milliseconds of debounce time mentioned earlier.

Not surprisingly, the software for the ASCII keyboard is virtually identical to the software for the hexadecimal keyboard in Fig. 4-4. The only real difference is that we no longer need the CA2 line to reset the keyboard. It will take care of itself, so that instruction is not needed. Delete from Fig. 4-4 any reference to CA2.

Please note that a shorted key or a short on the key matrix will make the scanner think that a key is pressed, and stop scanning. If the output of pin 16 is high, the chip thinks a key is pressed, and the code for that key is on the outputs. This situation is often the case when it appears that the chip has gone bad.

EVENT SENSORS

An event sensor is very much like a sense-switch input. All that is really needed is to sense whether the state of a bit is high or low. If we know that an event has not happened yet, and define the input with no event to be either a 0 or a 1, then any

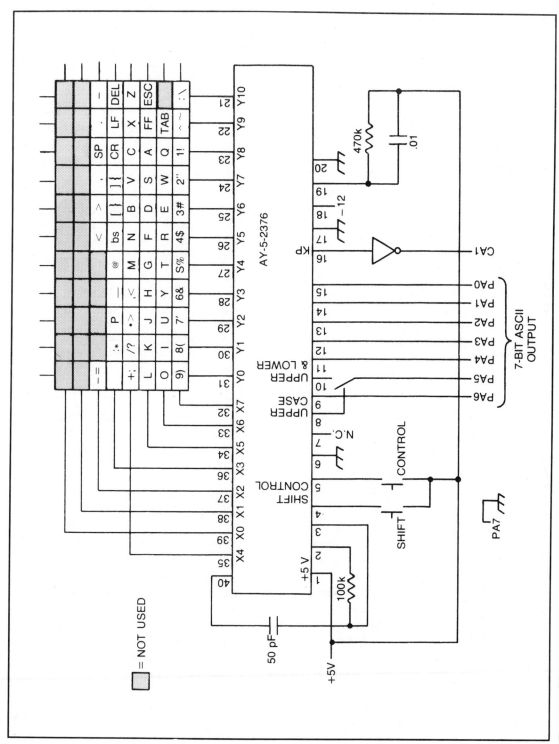

Fig. 4-5. ASCII-encoded keyboard.

111

change from that non-event state will be an indication that the event or condition has occurred.

As an example, let us consider the situation where a home computer is being used as part of the security system for a house. Let us furthermore say that we want the computer to sound an alarm (see later in this Chapter for devices controlled by the computer) if a window is opened. With the window closed, perhaps we have a switch that is kept closed, resulting in a low condition at one of the PIA input bits. When the window is opened, the switch is also opened, and a pull-up resistor could bring the bit high. If the computer were continually or periodically polling the bits of the input, it would detect that that bit had changed from a 0 to a 1 and undertake a sequence that would ring the alarm, or even dial the police on the telephone.

You see what has happened. This event or condition sensor is identical to the sense switch discribed earlier; the only difference is that the switches have been moved to where the condition being monitored is.

It would be nice if it were possible to have the event or condition cause an interrupt. With one line, this is no problem, just connect it to the CA1 input line. How about eight lines, though? The reason we would want to do this is simple: It's all right to be able to run a security program at night when the computer is not otherwise being used. The computer can be dedicated to that task when no other tasks are being done. But in the daytime the computer will be wanted for other problems, such as the use of the BASIC interpreter, or word processing. Should we have to give up (for example) home security for word processing? Not if we are willing to use interrupts.

To use interrupts, what is needed is a way of telling if a transition has occurred on any one of the eight data lines. Let's assume that all the data lines are active-low; that is, they are normally held high by a pull-up resistor. If any condition occurs which the processor should note, that line will go low.

The NAND gate of Fig. 4-6 will have its output normally low if all data lines are normally high. If any data line goes low, the output of the NAND gate will go high. If this output is connected to the

CA1 input of a PIA, and the PIA is configured to interrupt when CA1 goes from a low state to a high state, then we have our interrupt! All we need in addition to the input lines and their pull-up resistors is a 7430 NAND gate. The computer can be doing its normal job, unimpeded by the sensor system. Only when the sensor is activated does the computer stop what it's doing and begin the execution of an interrupt service routine to find out what caused the interrupt, and which one of the data lines is responsible.

There is only one problem with this "direct" input of a set of conditions or event sensors into a PIA, with interrupts. That problem is that we are limited to only eight possible inputs because there are only eight data lines. Naturally, we could add other ports.

A more elegant solution is to let one port sense events happening at more than eight locations. This is not impossible. There are only eight data lines, it is true, but those eight data lines have 256 possible combinations of 1s and 0s, so in theory, with the interrupt scheme described above, we could detect 256 events, and read the "address" of the event as a binary number.

Full encoding for 256 input lines would be quite horrendous in terms of the amount of circuitry needed to encode them. No circuitry or chips are readily available to the hobbyist to encode more than sixteen lines at a time, so at least sixteen chips, and more to select the proper encoder, would be needed to do this full encoding.

For only a few chips we can double the capacity of a PIA input port. Five integrated circuits— four if you are not interested in latching the output—are all that is needed. We gain a bonus, as well: the inputs are *prioritized*. That is, the inputs are arranged by priority, so that if two events happen at the same time, the one with the higher priority gets attention from the CPU first. There is also handshaking available to tell the event sensing (or producing) device that the CPU has things well in hand. The circuit is shown in Fig. 4-7.

Note that we are back to our old friend, the 74148. This is a most useful chip. Two OR gates detect that an input does exist to one of the '148s

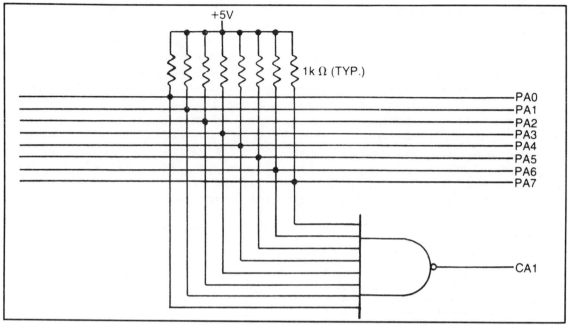

Fig. 4-6. An interrupt sensor.

by checking the GS and EO outputs. These serve as strobes for the CA1 line and also as a latching strobe for the 74100 8-bit latch. Only six bits of the eight are used as outputs. If we wished, we could add still another 74148. So long as we didn't use more than four of its inputs (preferably the lowest four) we can use two of the outputs as the last two bits of the data to the computer.

The latch is not really necessary. The 74148s will drive the PIA inputs just as well. The 74100 latch is added so that the device may be used as an event sensor with equipment that just gives a brief pulse to the outputs, rather than a continuous signal. If pulse inputs will not be used, the 74100 may be dispensed with.

The software to read the event/condition sensor is again identical to that used for the hexadecimal keyboard. Wait for a CA1 signal that indicates data is present, read it, and send a handshaking pulse via CA2. If no handshaking is needed; that is, if you don't feel the need to inform the device sending the event report that the computer has taken note of it, just delete the part of the software that handles CA2.

The only part of the software that may be tricky is figuring out what device sent the condition signal. The data to the computer is given as a "device number" in two three-bit forms. Each of the three bits forms a number between 0 and 7. If the lower three bits are all high, try the upper three bits. If both upper and lower are high, then one of the inputs is a zero. A seventh bit can be used to indicate which of the two sets of three is a zero. When bit 6 is a 0, then the lower of the three bits is active. When it is a 1, then the upper three bits are active. CA2 can also be used for this signal, if the other two bits are to be used for some other purpose.

EVENT COUNTER AND FREQUENCY COUNTER

Once the computer has the means of detecting that an event has occurred or a condition is met, then it is a very easy step from there to a counter for those events.

Counters have more uses than we have space to list them. They can count the number of customers that enter a store on a given day and count the number that go out, to make sure that a customer isn't left in the store when the store is locked for the night. A counter can be used on a production line to count the number of items manufactured in a day, or the number of times an air conditioner goes on and off every day. If the source of event pulses were to be designed to give exactly one pulse every second, the counter becomes a timer. As we will see later in this section, the counter can be used as a frequency counter, as well, to determine the exact frequency of a signal, or the rotation rate of a shaft. There probably isn't an application of computers in physical measurement that can't use a counter of some sort.

The simplest counter just uses the event sensor described above and a little clever software. All that needs to be done is to zero the counter before starting the count, and then every time an event is detected for that particular source, have the computer increment its internal count. The counting is done in memory in the computer itself. When the counting is done (due to some criterion inside the computer, or as a result of some other event being sensed), the computer already has the total count inside the machine safely tucked away in memory.

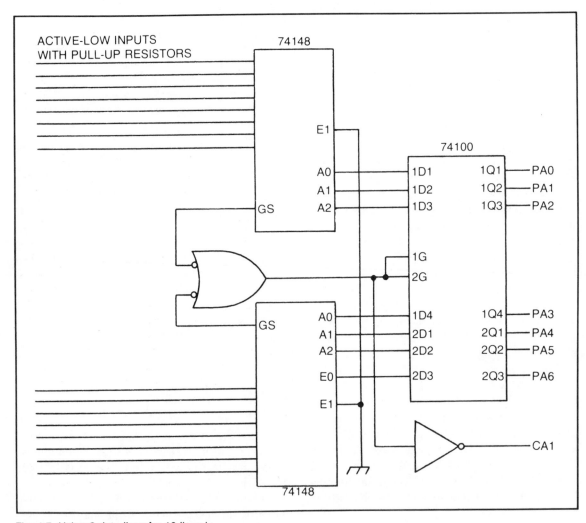

Fig. 4-7. Using 8 data lines for 16 lines in.

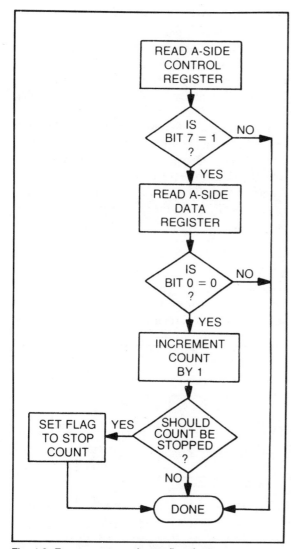

READ A-SIDE
CONTROL
REGISTER

IS
BIT 7 = 1
?

NO

YES

READ A-SIDE
DATA
REGISTER

IS
BIT 0 = 0
?

NO

YES

INCREMENT
COUNT
BY 1

SET FLAG
TO STOP
COUNT

YES

SHOULD
COUNT BE
STOPPED
?

NO

DONE

Fig. 4-8. Event counter software flowchart.

A flowchart of the software needed to conduct a count of the number of events that occur on data bit 0 of the A-side of a PIA is shown in Fig. 4-8. The program requires that a direct event sensor is used and an input to CA1 from a device as shown in Fig. 4-6. The CA1 input is used as an indication that an event has occurred, and bit 0 is checked to make sure that the proper event is being counted. You may supply your own reason for terminating the count.

By using CA1 in this manner, the counting

subroutine can be used as an interrupt-service routine, so as not to use up all the CPU time just waiting for an event to happen so it can be counted.

In either case, interrupts or not, a counter such as the one described requires a lot of processor overhead. As we've said before, to reduce the programming time, increase the hardware.

It is fairly easy to construct a counter out of TTL integrated circuits and get an output in binary. With eight bits input, the counter can only count up to 255, then it resets to zero. With the addition of a couple of multiplexers and some control circuitry, the counter can be made to go to 65,535 before resetting to zero.

Figure 4-9 shows the construction of just such a counter, with a capacity of 16 bits. They use the 74193 synchronous four-bit binary counter. To obtain 16 bits, four of these are needed to cascade. The carry output of the last counter can even be connected to the CA1 input of the PIA to give an "overflow" indication, effectively doubling the range of the counter. While some might call this a 17-bit counter, it is more proper to call it a 16 1/2-bit counter with this modification. No interrupts are needed because the data can be read at any time.

The problem is, only eight bits of the data may be read at any time. We need to have a way of reading two bytes of data through one eight-bit port. The solution is provided by the 74157 four-bit multiplexer, which we have used before in the hexadecimal keyboard. Two of these chips have sixteen inputs and eight outputs, and there is a select pin on each which allows us to choose between two bytes of data. The lower eight bits are read first, then a signal is sent to the multiplexer to select the upper eight bits, which is read in turn. Last, the overflow bit from the control register is read, if used.

There is a problem with using the 16 1/2-bit counter. Even though it only needs 8 bits of input for the data (plus CA1), it does need at least two outputs to control the counter. One control line is needed to switch between the lower eight bits and the upper eight bits of data. This is no problem because we can just use the CA2 line from the PIA.

But we also need to clear the counter to zero before starting the count. All of the 74193s have a clear input, which must be activated by an active-high pulse. Where do we get this pulse from? All eight bits of the input side of the PIA, plus the CA1 and CA2 lines, are in use. We shall simply have to get it from somewhere else. Perhaps we can find another PIA whose CA2 or CB2 line is not used and use that. Alternatively, later in this chapter we will describe a controller interface which can start or stop another device. One of the lines from this controller may be used for this purpose.

The software needed for the 16 1/2-bit counter is given in flowchart fashion in Fig. 4-10. It is represented as two separate parts of a program. The first part initializes the PIA and clears the counter to zero. The second part is a routine which accepts the count and stores it, according to the sequence outlined earlier.

Once a counter is in use, it can be expanded and modified to become a frequency counter. A frequency counter is one of the most useful instruments that a person working extensively in electronics can have. It can be used to determine the exact frequency that an oscillator is putting out, or the frequency that is being received by a radio, or the rate at which data is being converted by an analog-to-digital converter, or the speed of a rotating shaft, or many other such applications.

Basically, a frequency counter is a timer which allows pulses to enter the counter for a specific length of time. These pulses are counted, and the number is divided by the time to get the pulse rate. In addition to the counter, then, we need only a timer and a means of converting the input signal to pulses. For the latter, a simple amplifier will work very well. A couple of circuits that will accomplish this task are shown in Fig. 4-11. The output of these circuits is to be connected to the input of the counter, and their own inputs are the wave-

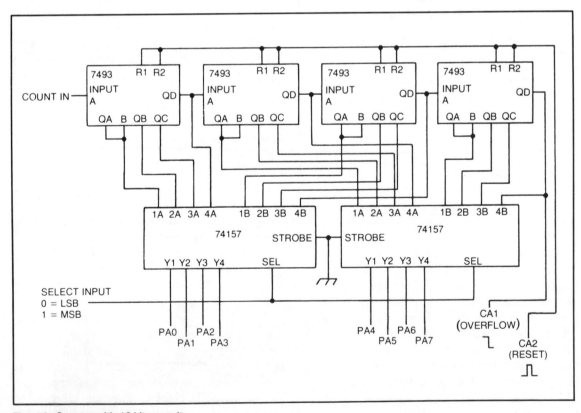

Fig. 4-9. Counter with 16-bit capacity.

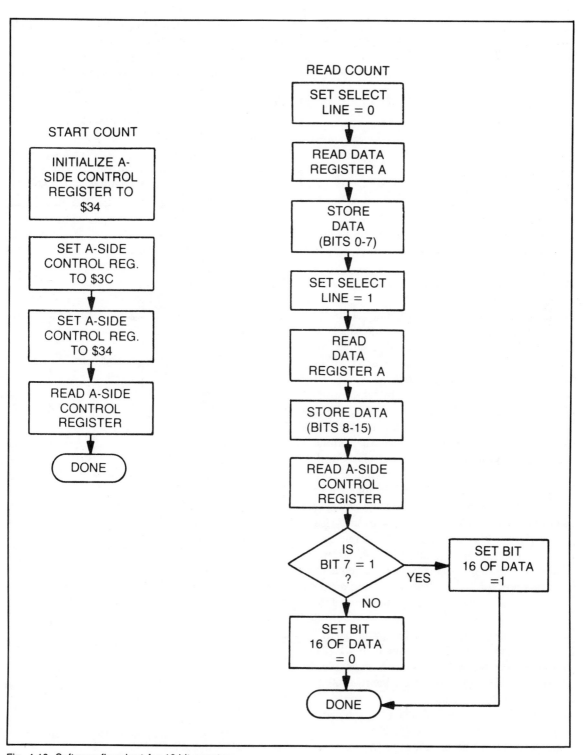

Fig. 4-10. Software flowchart for 16-bit counter.

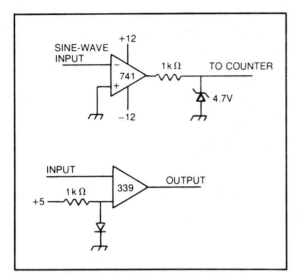

Fig. 4-11. Sine-wave to pulse converter.

form inputs for the frequency being counted.

The only other critical part is the timer. The subject of timers will be covered in detail in Chapter 5, and any of the timers described in that chapter will serve the purpose above.

Let us examine one method by which a timer may be used to make a frequency counter. The type of timer needed for this application is called an *interval timer*. Its purpose is to inform the computer that a present interval of time has elapsed. The amount of time may be set by the computer, or adjusted by external components. It is not necessary for the computer to be able to read the timer, only necessary that the computer be able to start it, and to know when the time interval is completed.

The simplest timer is, of course, all software. Computers work on system clocks. Somewhere in the computer, probably close to the microprocessor, is an oscillator which puts out pulses on a regular basis, frequently using a crystal-controlled oscillator. Depending on the computer used, the pulses will run from 875 kHz to about 18 MHz. The computer uses these clock pulses to schedule the instructions. Each microprocessor instruction takes a certain number of clock cycles to complete. This number is fixed and unyielding for a given instruction. By knowing the number of instructions that a process takes, and by knowing the number of

clock cycles each instruction takes and the length of a clock cycle, the amount of time it takes to complete a series of instructions can be determined very accurately. If a loop were to be set up, of known length and known time, and this loop were to be cycled a known number of times, then the loop could be used to time an event, such as counting the number of pulses that appear at the input of a counter.

A flowchart for such a software timing loop is given in Fig. 4-12. In this example, a register is

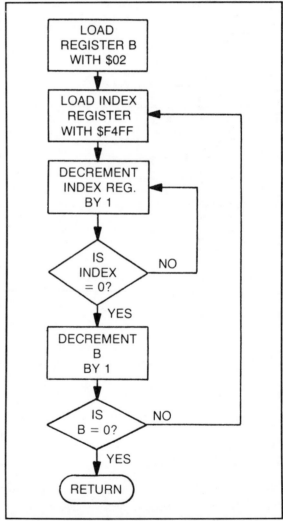

Fig. 4-12. One-second software timing loop for 6800 processor with 875 kHz clock.

118

loaded with the hexadecimal number $F4FF. Every time through the loop, this register is decremented by one. If the value in the register has dropped all the way down to zero, we exit the loop, If now, we run through the loop again. By completing this loop once, half a second is used up in decrementing and testing. Twice through the loop, including overhead for entry and return, uses up 2 microseconds less than one full second, resulting in an accuracy of 0.000002, or 0.0002 percent. Most crystals are accurate to more than 0.001 percent, so this timer has the accuracy of the crystal used in driving the system clock.

The above figures are based on a machine-language 6800 program used on a machine with an 875-kHz system clock. Times for other processors with other clocks will vary, of course. Generally, the only thing that will need to be changed is the value of $F4FF in the internal register. For faster clocks, or fewer cycles per instruction, the value must be raised. If the number of loops is to be reduced, the time for one loop must be increased with more instructions, or with instructions that take more time. One way to increase the time it takes to execute an instruction is to store the number $F4FF, or whatever number is appropriate for your machine, in memory rather than in an internal register. Memory fetch and storage takes much longer than simply decrementing a register.

The only problem with using this software timing loop is that while the timing is going on, the computer can do nothing else. Suppose you had chosen to use the software-based counter described above, rather than go to the expense and trouble of building a 16 1/2-bit counter. Then you would be depending on the computer's software to handle both the counting and the timing. Neither of these tasks may be interrupted if all data is to be kept, or if the timing is to be accurate. The point is, only *one* software-only task can be maintained in a computer at a given time when interfacing to hardware. This is one of the reasons that interrupts are so important. Even above, the counter could be run on interrupts while the timer is free-running, but the solution is unsatisfactory. Whenever the counter interrupts the timer to process a count,

those few microseconds that the counter is being processed are lost to the timer—the timer takes that much longer to count all of its cycles. Say you add 30 microseconds every time the counter is processed. If 3000 counts are processed in one second, the timer will take almost a full tenth of a second longer than the one second of the timer's usual span. The count will be off by 10 percent.

Alternatively, the counter/processor could decrement the register by a few digits every time a count was processed, but unless the decrement was exactly equal to the number of microseconds lost, errors will still creep in. When using a frequency counter, it is best that either the counter or the timer, preferably both, be a hardware device. For hardware timers, please refer to Chapter 5.

Remarks in this chapter have been confined to a discussion of devices that use TTL logic and a parallel input port. A treatment of parallel digital I/O devices is not complete without a discussion of output devices as well. The remainder of this chapter will be devoted to devices which connect to parallel output ports.

PRINTER INTERFACE

The user of a microcomputer will rapidly find that a hardcopy device such as a printer will be indispensable. Anyone who has tried to discover the ''bugs'' in a program of hundreds of lines of code knows too well the value of a program listing over debugging from the sixteen lines displayed on the screen at a time.

It is not our purpose here to design a printer. Printers are complex pieces of machinery and electronics and usually require considerable mechanical skill in making the final adjustments. It is to your advantage to part with some hard-earned cash and purchase a printer. Prices range from as little as two hundred dollars for a used dot-matrix printer to several thousand dollars for a new 132-column line-impact printer. The hobbyist will find new dot-matrix printers available for five or six hundred dollars; the same money will purchase a reconditioned letter-quality printer.

Whatever type of printer you purchase, it will need an interface to the computer. Some printers come with a built-in serial receiver for RS-232 communications. These will require only three or four wires to be connected. Others will need a parallel interface. It is this last that we now look at.

The standard parallel interface will serve admirably as an interface to most parallel designs. It will give eight bits of parallel data, as well as strobe and handshaking signals. It will not give signals such as "fault," "out of paper," and the like. However, in most cases these will not be needed.

We can't just dump text to the printer at processor speed; the printer is not able to handle characters that fast. Instead, we use the handshaking lines to tell the printer that a character is on the data lines to be printed and to tell the computer that the printer is still busy with the last character and not to send any more.

Individual programming of the output interface for each type of printer is not possible in a book of this size. It would require a whole volume all its own. The best advice is to consult the manual on your particular printer, and then (using the discussion of the 6820 PIA in Chapter 3) to design your own initialization routine and output handler.

PARALLEL INTERFACE FOR IBM SELECTRIC

One of the best-kept secrets is that it only takes eight solenoids and a little electronics and programming to turn an IBM Selectric mechanism into a printer for a computer. The Selectric mechanism was originally designed as a printer mechanism for computers and was easily adaptable to office use. The Selectric mechanism has been used on all manner of computers as an operator console and as terminals and printers.

If you have a typewriter with a Selectric-type mechanism, it is quite easy to attach a set of solenoids and solenoid drivers to the bail mechanisms and to drive the solenoids from a parallel output port. These solenoids are critical in their current draw, inductance, travel, and pulling force, as well as physical size, but is beyond the scope of this book to describe their construction.

Solenoids may be purchased from any number of suppliers, including IBM. Several manufacturers make a conversion kit which contains the solenoids and related electronics to attach to a typewriter to convert it to a printer. Datel Corporation, a division of Harris Communications, Inc., sells the bail solenoid assembly as Part No. M100081 and the operational magnet assembly as part No. M100078. They may also be ordered through any IBM repair facility. The solenoids should cost about $30.00 and will require instructions to install. The IBM conversational terminal manual, available through IBM repair facilities for about $25.00, tells how to install them. Properly installed, the solenoid and driver assembly will not void the IBM warranty.

If you do not own a typewriter with a Selectric-type mechanism, instead of purchasing a typewriter and a conversion kit, obtain a used and reconditioned terminal with the Selectric printing machinery. These terminals were first put into use about fifteen years ago on various mainframe computers and are just now being seen in large numbers on the used market, as they are being replaced. A look at the advertisements in several computer-oriented magazines such as BYTE and MICROCOMPUTING will yield several addresses of suppliers of reconditioned terminals. Costs will vary from about $300.00 for a machine that may or may not run, to $1200.00 for a fully reconditioned, guaranteed machine. They will work well as typewriters, too.

Depending on the state of reconditioning of the terminal, or the quantity of electronics that have come with the conversion kit, some additional electronics may be required.

To decide what electronics are needed, let us consider the action of a Selectric printer: A Selectric printing mechanism involves a golf-ball shaped print head which glides across the paper and impacts a letter of character onto the paper as it glides. The ball can be vertically shifted, rotated, or tilted to provide the various characters. A carriage under the ball positions the print head and advances that position one character width after the impact. There are also operational functions, completely separate from the print head mechanism, for backspace, carriage return, spacebar, and tab. Unlike ordinary typewriters, the paper is stationary and only the printhead moves.

To actuate the movement of the printhead or to print a character, there are a set of *bails* (see Fig. 4-13) which are depressed by the keys. There are seven bails besides the operational bails for the printing of characters. These bails control the tilt, rotation, and shift of the ball. The ball may be tilted none, one unit, or two units. It may be rotated none at all, one bit, two bits (two different ways) or five bits, or any combination of these total motions. In addition, there is a shift function which turns the ball completely around by 180°. Six of these bails control tilt and rotation. The seventh is an indicator that a key is depressed. The shift is on a completely separate part of the mechanism and requires no bail. The function of the keys is to depress one or more of these bails by hammers on the bottoms of the keylevers. When a bail is to be depressed, there is a hammer available to depress it. When the bail is not to be depressed, there is no hammer. The bails are coded T1 and T2, for tilt one and tilt two, respectively, and R1, R2, R2A, and R5 for the various rotations. There is also the shift mechanism, coded "S." With these seven functions, any letter of the alphabet or any punctuation character available on the keyboard may be selected.

The beauty of the Selectric is that the bails do not have to be depressed by the hammers on the keylevers. They can also be depressed by the action of a magnetic solenoid, which can be controlled electrically from a computer. Since there are seven bails, including the shift, it requires only seven data bits to actuate the bails. Add a "data-ready" signal to actuate the "keypressed" bail, and the computer will happily cause the printing mechanism to type anything desired.

This brings us to an important difference between Selectric-type printers and other types of printers. Most other printers use the ASCII code for characters. Selectric does not. It uses a special code of its own. Indeed, it may use any of three special codes of its own, depending on how old the model is. The code is, of course, just the set of ons and offs which make the bails depressing solenoids active. This may be the IBM BCD code, the IBM EBCDIC code, or the newer IBM Correspondence code. IBM Correspondence code is shown in Fig.

4-14, along with its relation to the rotate, shift, and tilt signals. Table 4-1 shows the relationship between ASCII and the BCD, EBCD, and Correspondence codes.

In order to be able to use the Selectric as a printer with a computer that expects its characters to be in ASCII, (most systems programs, such as disk operating systems, BASIC, editors, and assemblers expect to be able to print in ASCII), the printer handler has to be written to convert ASCII to Correspondence code, or whatever code is being used. The easiest way to do this is by a lookup table. A table is made of the Correspondence code for each of the letters to be used in the order of increasing hexadecimal values of the ASCII system, such as found in Table 4-1. When the handler receives the printable character from the sending program, it uses the ASCII value of the letter as the position in the table and gets that character to use instead. It then merely sends the new character to the printer and waits for a "done" signal from the printer before continuing. If the character does not exist on the printer, an acceptable substitute must be found, or a "null," or no character, sent.

The operational functions are similar to the printed letters, except that no bails are used. Each operational mechanism has its own actuator—a separate "bail," if you please. We can either use separate data lines for each of these functions, or code the correspondence code such that unused portions of the code are signals to actuate one of the operational functions is given below:

	R1	R2	R2A	R5	T1	T2
space	1	1	1	0	1	1
backspace	0	1	0	0	1	0
tab	1	1	0	0	0	0
carriage return	1	1	0	0	1	0

These special codes are decoded easily by a series of AND gates and inverters, to distinguish them from other characters. Naturally, the printing of these characters has to be disabled during their

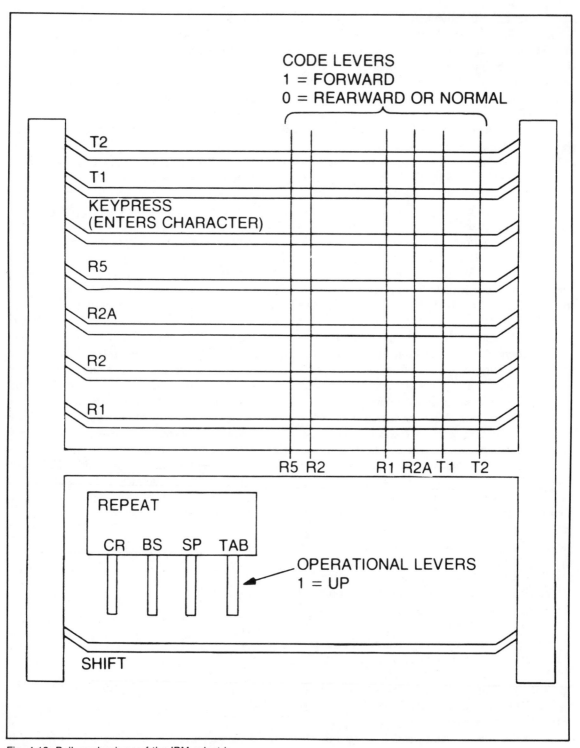

Fig. 4-13. Bail mechanisms of the IBM selectric.

				0	0	0	0	1	1	1	1	RS
				0	0	1	1	0	0	1	1	T1
				0	1	0	1	0	1	0	1	T2
SHIFT	R2A	R2	R1									
0	0	0	0	−	b	w	9					
0	0	0	1	y	h	s		/	|	o	4	
0	0	1	0							BS		
0	0	1	1	TAB			CR					
0	1	0	0	q	k	i	6	,	c	a	8	
0	1	0	1	p	e	'	5	;	d	r	7	
0	1	1	0	=	n	•	2	f	u	v	3	
0	1	1	1	j	t	½	z	g	x	m	1	
1	0	0	0	_	B	W	(					
1	0	0	1	Y	H	S	)	?	L	O	$	
1	0	1	0							BS		
1	0	1	1	TAB			CR					
1	1	0	0	Q	K	I	¢	,	C	A	*	
1	1	0	1	P	E	"	%	:	D	R	&	
1	1	1	0	+	N	•	@	F	U	V	#	
1	1	1	1	J	T	¼	Z	G	X	M	[	

Fig. 4-14. IBM Correspondence code.

operation: This is easily done by disabling the solenoid that actuates the "keypressed" during an operational sequence.

A few cautions about the Selectric: First, it can only receive as fast as 14.9 characters per second—no faster. The character time is exact because the whole mechanism is powered by a motor running at a constant rate, and each printed character takes one revolution of the cycle print shift. Second, whenever the shift is to be used—either up or down—the shifted character must be preceded by a code that does nothing but shift. Then the shifted character is printed. It is necessary to be firm on this point: To print a capital letter, print a shift-only first, then the capital letter with shift-bit set. You may print all the capital letters you want then, without shifting, so long as there are no lowercase letters printed in between. If you then need to print a lowercase letter, a signal must be sent to "shift down," and then all lowercase letters, with the shift-bit cleared, may be sent. Any time you change from a non-shifted letter to a shifted letter, or vice-versa, the shift command must precede it. Lastly, the carriage return takes considerable longer to execute than any other function or character. After sending a carriage return, the computer should wait the same length of time it takes to send eight letters. If you build in a delay loop of a full half second, you will not be far wrong.

Handshaking on the Selectric is very difficult. It can be done by tying into the cycle-clutch switch, but doing so will void the warranty and may cause

Table 4-1. Comparison of ASCII, Correspondence, BCD, and EBCDIC codes.

Character	ASCII	Correspondence	BCD	EBCDIC
Backspace	08	5D	5D	16
Line Feed	0A	6E	6E	25
Return	0D	6D	6D	0D
Space	20	40	40	40
!	21	01	75	5A
"	22	49	38	7F
#	23	70	34	7B
$	24	04	75	5B
%	25	08	68	6C
&	26	68	43	50
'	27	49	58	7D
(	28	34	64	4D
)	29	64	54	5D
*	2A	38	04	5C
+	2B	13	34	4E
,	2C	3B	76	2B
−	2D	37	01	60
.	2E	51	37	4B
/	2F	07	62	61
0	30	64	74	F0
1	31	46	20	F1
2	32	10	10	F2
3	33	70	70	F3
4	34	04	08	F4
5	35	08	68	F5
6	36	58	58	F6
7	37	68	38	F7
8	38	38	04	F8
9	39	34	64	F9
:	3A	6B	08	7A
;	3B	6B	70	5E
<	3C	*	*	4C
=	3D	13	20	7E
>	3E	*	*	6E
?	3F	07	62	6F
@	40	70	02	7C
A	41	79[†]	23	C1
B	42	76[†]	13	C2
C	43	77[†]	0A	C3
D	44	7A[†]	0B	C4
E	45	4A[†]	6B	C5
F	46	73[†]	5B	C6
G	47	23[†]	3B	C7
H	48	26[†]	07	C8
I	49	19[†]	67	C9
J	4A	43[†]	61	D1
K	4B	1A[†]	51	D2
L	4C	46[†]	31	D3
M	4D	61[†]	49	D4
N	4E	52[†]	29	D5
O	4F	45[†]	19	D6
P	50	0B[†]	79	D7
Q	51	5B[†]	45	D8
R	52	29[†]	25	D9
S	53	25[†]	52	E2
T	54	02[†]	32	E3

Character	ASCII	Correspondence	BCD	EBCDIC
U	55	32[†]	4A	E4
V	56	31[†]	2A	E5
W	57	75[†]	1A	E6
X	58	62[†]	7A	E7
Y	59	67[†]	46	E8
Z	5A	54[†]	26	E9
\	5C	*	*	E0
a	61	79[†]	*	81
b	62	76[†]	*	82
c	63	77[†]	*	83
d	64	7A[†]	*	84
e	65	4A[†]	*	85
f	66	73[†]	*	86
g	67	73[†]	*	87
h	68	23[†]	*	88
i	69	19[†]	*	89
j	6A	43[†]	*	91
k	6B	1A[†]	*	92
l	6C	46[†]	*	93
m	6D	61[†]	*	94
n	6E	52[†]	*	95
o	6F	45[†]	*	96
p	70	0B[†]	*	97
q	71	5B[†]	*	98
r	72	29[†]	*	99
s	73	25[†]	*	A2
t	74	02[†]	*	A3
u	75	32[†]	*	A4
v	76	31[†]	*	A5
w	77	75[†]	*	A6
x	78	62[†]	*	A7
y	79	67[†]	*	A8
z	7A	54[†]	*	A9

* Character does not exist in this code
† Correct case obtained by sending "shift" character first:
Shift up = 80, Shift down = 00

the machine to behave erratically. It would be better to time the output with a timer set to 68 milliseconds, so that one character is sent every 68 milliseconds. Alternatively, the typewriter could be connected via RS-232 serial communications at the expense of a UART and bit rate generator. In this letter case, a bit rate of 149 baud (using one stop bit) would be the fastest that the printer could operate. A carriage return could be accommodated by sending seven nulls after the command code.

We have discussed the solenoids and the Correspondence (or other) code needed to drive them. We still need to discuss the electrical drivers for the solenoids. The circuit shown in Fig. 4-15 will drive a solenoid magnet at 24V and up to 500 mA. The TTL input is active high, and current will flow through the solenoid when the input is high. It may be best to put the TTL inverters at the interface (computer) end of the data line and the rest, including the +24V power supply, in or near the typewriter. The solenoids can handle anywhere from 24 to 48 volts. Be sure to include the antispiking diode on the magnet driver, or inductive discharge may destroy the driver, the inverters, the interface, and the whole computer! The circuit shown is extremely similar to the one used in the Datel Selec-

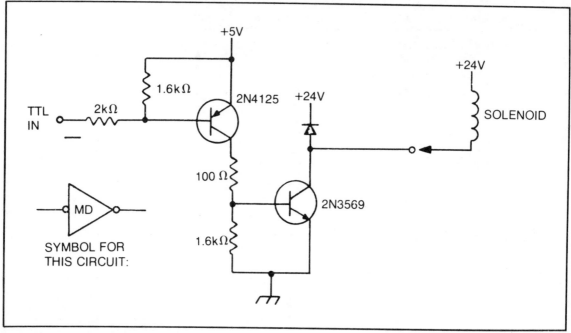

Fig. 4-15. TTL to Selectric magnet driver.

tric terminal. Each of the circuits shown above will drive *one* magnet, so as many as twelve may be needed, as shown in Fig. 4-16. This circuit shows the total wiring needed, less power supplies, to drive a Selectric magnet set from the standard parallel interface.

Nothing has been said about the conversion of a Selectric to an input device, using the keyboard. This conversion is much more complicated than that for the printer. It involves switches on the bails and a connection to the cycle-clutch switch. The addition of the operational functions further complicates the matter. Last, the unit has to be prevented from receiving while sending, and vice-versa, so a complex "half-duplex" communication system must be used, involving "ready" and "end of transmission" codes to be sent and received from the terminal.Conversion of a Selectric to a two-way terminal is vastly more involved than conversion to a printer and will not be covered here.

CONTROL-PORT OUTPUT

In addition to sending data to a peripheral de-

vice, you may need to control another device to the extent of turning it on and off. Or, it may be necessary to have an additional control signal available to assist with another peripheral. An example might be the counter just described, where a second output signal is needed to clear the counter before the count can begin.

Any situation where a single line is needed for control of an external device is called *single-bit control*. This type of computer control is one of the most common types of I/O used on a computer. There is always *something* that needs to be turned on or off, or which needs to be pulsed or cycled before it can be used. It is not unusual to find an entire I/O port devoted entirely to single-bit control of a number of devices.

With an entire I/O port side devoted to control, up to nine devices (eight bits plus CA2 or CB2) can be controlled directly. Each output becomes a control line, as well as one of the handshaking lines. To turn a device on, simply set the corresponding bit of the output PIA to a 1. To turn it off, simply set it to a 0.

Actually, it's a little more complicated than

126

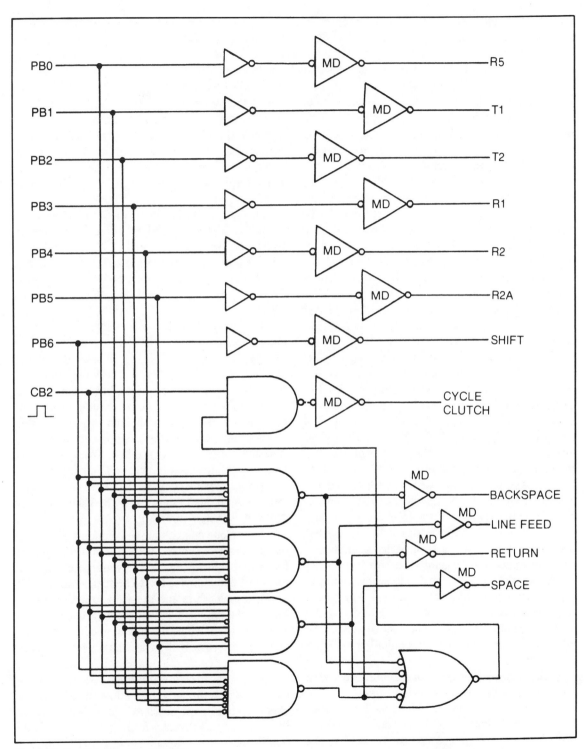

Fig. 4-16. Parallel driver for selectric.

127

that. There are no instructions on any microprocessor to set or clear a single bit of data in a byte. Fortunately, most microprocessors have, in addition to instructions that load and store and instructions that do arithmetic functions, a set of logical instructions for manipulating individual bits. In the context described in the previous paragraph, the AND and OR instructions will come in handy. Let's say we have a byte in which we wish to either clear or set bit 3. (Bit 7 is the most significant, bit 0 is the least significant.) We need to do this without disturbing the other bits in the byte. To set bit 3, we would OR the byte in memory with the byte 00001000, or $08 hexadecimal. 0 OR 0 is a 0, while 0 OR 1 is a 1. All other bits will remain unchanged, while bit 3 will be set if it is not already. To clear the bit, the byte is ANDed with 11110111, or $F7 hexadecimal. The 1s in the byte assure that any 1s in the memory location will remain 1s, while 0 AND 1 is a 0. To provide a pulse output, the memory location is first ORed, then ANDed.

This method works well and requires very little software or hardware. Its only drawback is that one side of a PIA will provide, at most, nine I/O or control lines. Control of a larger number of devices is simply not possible with only one PIA side using this method. There are two alternatives: use another PIA or expand the output of one PIA by multiplexing the outputs. Since the former method is obvious, let us examine the latter.

Eight output bits, in theory, can represent up to 256 combinations of 1s and 0s. Nine output bits can give us up to 512. Since we are only interested in on/off, the mere presence of device's "number" on the output would constitute activating it.

In practice, decoding even eight bits would require about twenty integrated circuits. For a fraction of this number of integrated circuits, the number of pulse outputs can be quadrupled, or the number of on/off outputs can be doubled. Figure 4-17 shows how.

Each "nybble," or group of four bits, is decoded independently by a 74154 4-to-16 decoder. The upper lines control the top 74154, and the bottom four lines control the bottom 74154. Only one of the "addresses" in each group of four can be used at one time.

The CB2 line of the PIA is used as an activator for the 74154s. It is routed through a 555 timer used as a one-shot to give a pulse several microseconds long. The components of the timer can be changed to give a longer pulse, if needed. The output of the 555 enables both of the 74154s at one time, so that any pattern of 1s and 0s at the address inputs of the 74154s appears on the corresponding output of the chip. These outputs are active low and will remain low as long as the enable inputs of the 74154s are low, as determined by the 555 output pulse.

In short, by giving each device to be controlled a number between 0 and 15, connecting its input to the corresponding output of a 74154, and placing that number in the upper or lower half of the PIA data register (depending on which 74154 was used) and cycling the CB2 line, the device is activated.

In theory, 32 such devices can be controlled simultaneously on one PIA. However, we lose one because we control both 74154s at once. If we place $04 into the data register, not only does output 4 of the lower decoder pulse low, but so does output 0 of the upper decoder! We get around this by connecting anything to be connected to output 0 of either 74154 to a gate which is low only when *both* 0 outputs of the 74154s are low. This means that two outputs are used to cycle one device, so only 31 devices may be controlled. To use device number 0, simply load $00 into the PIA data register and cycle CB2.

Thirty-one control pulses from only eight output bits sounds pretty good until you realize that the output is just a pulse of a few microseconds duration. When a device has to be turned on and left on for a long while and must do so under the influence of a single bit or control line, it doesn't seem so practical. It won't do us any good to have the device come on only to go off again a few microseconds later.

Two ways are shown in Fig. 4-18 and 4-19 to alleviate the problem. The solution is to use a set of RS flip-flops on the outputs of the 74154s. These flip-flops can be made from inexpensive 7400 NAND gates at two to a chip, or the 74129 has four complete RS flip-flops in each package. The former

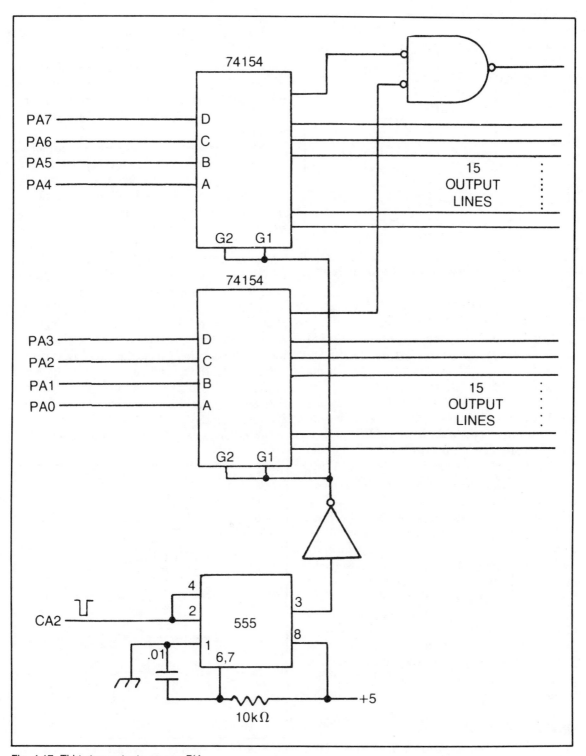

Fig. 4-17. Thirty-two outputs on one PIA.

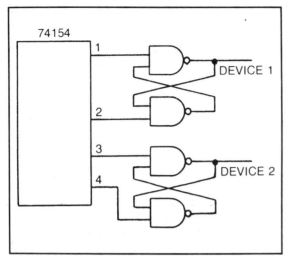

Fig. 4-18. RS flip-flop with 15 on/off outputs for Figure 4-17.

requires more wiring but is probably the less expensive way to assemble the device.

In Figure 4-18, one of the outputs of the 74154 drives one input of the RS flip-flop, turning the output on, and another 74154 output turns it off again. In this way, it takes two separate actions, one for each output of the 74154 to turn a device on and off. The 31 possible pulse outputs then reduce to only 15 on/off outputs with 15 pairs of RS flip-flops and one pulse line left over. This is still a better bargain than only eight on/off controls per PIA side.

Under certain circumstances, it may be possible to extend the number of on/off controllers to as many as 30. Figure 4-19 shows how: Each RS flip-flop is turned on by a single pulse from a 74154, as before, but now *all* are cleared simultaneously by a single off pulse. The $00 connection would be an ideal candidate for this purpose. The advantages are obvious—control of many more devices. The disadvantage is that when one device goes off, they all go off. It would be possible to turn all the desired devices back, of course, in only a few microseconds. The user will have to make the determination as to which of the schemes outlined above fits his needs best.

DEVICES TO CONTROL

It might be instructive to examine a few of the

possible uses that a control line could be put to.

Let's start with something simple first. Say you want to have a light come on for a moment when some condition is met. An example might be that we are using the computer to run a programmer for EPROMs, and we want to know when the programming is finished, while the computer then goes to some other task.

Small lights such as these are very useful on computers. For computer use, the light emitting diode (LED) is more appropriate than a regular incandescent bulb, because it uses less current and requires a lower voltage. Its response time is considerably faster, as well.

What is needed might be an LED that comes on for one second and then goes off again. It should be apparent that in order to simply turn a light on, all that is needed is to connect the LED (through a resistor) to high voltage and to an active-low, always-on control port, as in Fig. 4-20. The resistor is needed because the voltage drop across a forward-biased diode, including an LED, is generally 0.5 volts. If we put 5 volts across it, there has to be something to take up the other 4.5V. Not only that, but we must limit the amount of current that goes through the diode or risk burning it out.

In order to keep the LED on for a second or

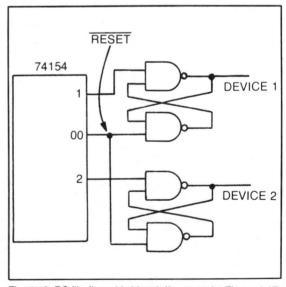

Fig. 4-19. RS flip-flop with 30 on/off outputs for Figure 4-17.

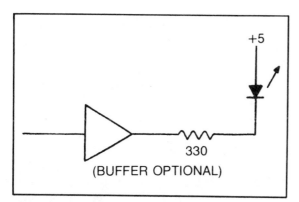

Fig. 4-20. LED on/off.

used to provide the audible sound or alarm. In order to find out if the terminal has a "bell," simply send the ASCII character $07, which is a control character to the terminal. In BASIC, the line

PRINT CHR$(7);

will have the same effect. If the terminal is equipped with a "bell" function, it will make some kind of noise.

If the terminal does not have a "bell" function, then the single-bit control post can be arranged to provide one. Figure 4-22 shows a way to modify the LED blinker to sound a small buzzer. Again, the 555 is triggered by a pulse output from the control port, and the components are arranged so as to keep the buzzer on for one full second. Almost any of the small buzzers will work; the 555 can supply up to 150 mA to operate it. There are several "hobby buzzers" on the market that are designed for 6 volts that will work fine on a 5-volt circuit. The only real difference between this circuit and the LED circuit is that the buzzer uses more current, so a 22-ohm resistor is used in place of the 330-ohm resistor used before.

A TTL output, as from a 7400 or a 74154 cannot "source" very much current—it is not designed to provide more than a few microamperes in the high state. In the low state, it can "sink" as much as 40 milliamperes. This means for a device that

so, the computer could turn the LED on and wait one second before turning it off. Or, a simple circuit with a 555 timer can be used (Fig. 4-21) to keep it on. This has the advantage that only a pulse is needed to start the sequence. The LED will go out automatically.

Often times it is desirable to have an audible output. If, for example, the user is loading a long cassette tape, one which takes several minutes to load, the user may not wish to stay close to the computer to watch the tape all the time it is loading. With an alarm or buzzer, the user could leave the machine to do other business, and come back to catch the tape when the alarm sounds.

Many terminals have a bell, beeper, or buzzer on them. The internal "bell" on a terminal may be

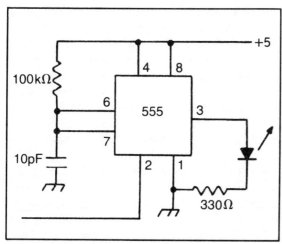

Fig. 4-21. LED one second on-time.

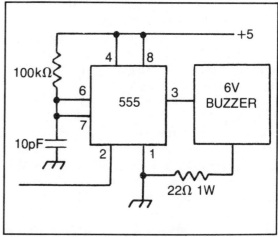

Fig. 4-22. Buzzer.

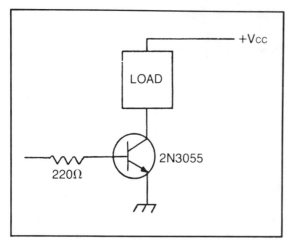

Fig. 4-23. Transistor current driver.

draws a lot of current to be "on," it has to be connected to the TTL outputs and to the supply voltage. When the device is to be on, the TTL output must be low, acting as the ground for the device.

Because a TTL circuit can only sink a few milliamperes, it is necessary to come up with some other methods for handling higher currents. The 555 method above will help, but it only goes to about 150 mA.

One such method is to add a high-current transistor on the output of the TTL device, and let the transistor drive the device, as shown in Fig. 4-23. The emitter of the transistor is grounded, and the base is connected to the TTL output through a resistor. When the TTL output is high, the transistor conducts, making the collector the same potential as the emitter, and allowing current to flow through the load device. Use of the transistor will also permit the use of higher voltages than TTL supply voltage for the load—up to a point.

Certainly, transistors are available with breakdown voltages over 300 volts, but that's not the point. There is some feedback of the collector potential into the base in any case. If the transistor should happen to become shorted, or open at the emitter-base junction, the base could reach a potential which is higher than normal TTL voltage. If, for example, the supply voltage for the load is at +60 V. If the transistor destroys itself in such a way as to cause conduction through the base, the

base, and therefore any TTL or MOS LSI circuitry attached to it, will feel the full +60 V! This high voltage will almost certainly destroy that chip, and may be passed on in such a way as to destroy others as well. I have accidentally shorted a +27 volt line to a TTL signal line and thus destroyed over $450.00 worth of integrated circuits and had the computer "down" for almost three months while replacements and repairs were being made.

It is important, therefore, to *isolate* the TTL and MOS logic from any high voltages that will be used in the circuit being controlled. This is especially true if the potentials being used are ac voltages rather than dc. In years past, such isolation would have automatically meant a mechanical relay. While relays are still used in many applications (indeed, there are specially built relays on the market today made just for interfacing with TTL and MOS circuitry), it must also be said that in most cases, there exists a solid-state device which will do the same job as well, if not better. A solid state device will generally have a faster switching time by a couple of orders of magnitude and not suffer from wear on the relay contacts over a period of years. Such devices are no more expensive than relays, either. Just to be on the safe side, though, relays *and* solid-state switching devices will be covered here.

Optocouplers

Let's start with the optically isolated coupler, which is called the *optoisolator* or *optocoupler* for short. This is an ingenious little device which combines two solid-state devices inside a single package with no electrical connection between them. See Fig. 4-24. The current in the load is controlled by the transistor in the same manner as before. Only, now notice that the transistor has no base! Instead of a base, carriers in the base region are generated, not by a base current, but by the photoelectric action of light on the base. When the LED is on—that is, glowing—light shines on the base and makes the transistor conduct. We cause light to come out of the LED by sending a current through it. In the example shown, a current will flow through the LED, and therefore through the tran-

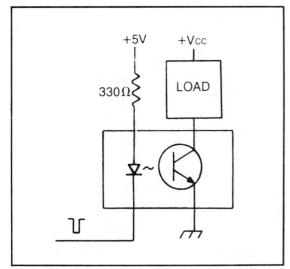

Fig. 4-24. An optocoupler.

sistor, when the computer output port is low.

The beauty of the optocoupler is that there is no electrical connection between the TTL part of the circuit and the circuit being controlled. The controlled circuit does not even have to be at the same potential as the logic.

There are several manufacturers of such devices at this time. One device that has found wide-spread use among hobbyists and engineers alike is the 4N33, which is shown diagrammed in Appendix A. Among the producers of optocouplers are Fairchild, Hewlett-Packard, Litronix, Monsanto, and Texas Instruments.

Most optocouplers are restricted to output currents of 100 mA or less, with phototransistor ratings of 30V or less. There are exceptions, like the Monsanto MCA2200, which will stand 200V. Generally, though, it means that an optocoupler will only handle a few watts at most.

This is not really a problem, because we can add a transistor to the output of the optocoupler and increase the current-carrying capacity of the device. Two such methods are shown in Figs. 4-25 and 4-26. In both cases, a "power" transistor of higher current capability is used to bypass the phototransistor. When the resistor in the collector of the phototransistor drops more than about 0.3V across it, the bypass transistor begins conducting. The pho-

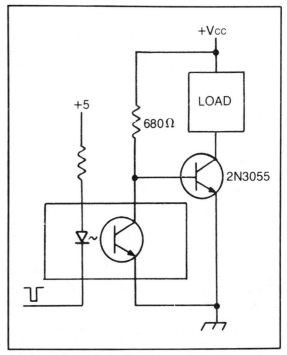

Fig. 4-25. Optocoupler with increased current-carrying capacity using an NPN transistor.

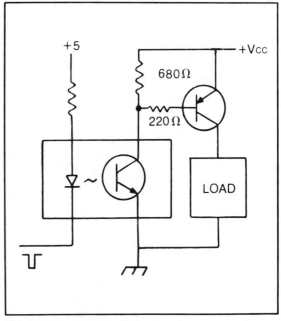

Fig. 4-26. Optocoupler with increased current-carrying capacity using a PNP transistor.

totransistor never even knows it is carrying more than a few tens of milliamperes, while controlling perhaps tens of amperes! There is no real difference between the circuits except that the load is at different potentials with respect to ground when not conducting.

Ac Control

A transistor will not be able to handle ac currents at all. Another method is required when ac is to be controlled. Ac control usually revolves around the use of some kind of thyristor.

In the case of controlling an incandescent light, or some device for which it is not critical that the voltages be full wave and bipolar, a silicon-controlled rectifier (SCR) is a very convenient way to handle ac. Figure 4-27 shows a way that, for example, a 100-watt incandescent light bulb could be controlled by a computer. (You can have the com-

puter turn on the lights in your house at a predetermined time, or subject to certain conditions, such as sensing that the front door has opened.) An SCR is just a diode that can have its forward conduction turned on and off by the presence of a pulse at its gate. Once the gate has gone positive with respect to the cathode, the diode conducts until the anode goes zero or negative with respect to the cathode. The gate draws very little current, and so may be turned on by the transistor in an optoisolator. If the transistor conducts all the time, then the SCR is retriggered every positive half cycle. The net result is that the SCR conducts every positive half cycle, and half wave rectified dc is supplied to the load.

For devices that need full-wave, bipolar ac, the SCR will not do. Such devices include most electronics, most ac motor-driven appliances, and the like. Only pure resistive devices such as lamps and

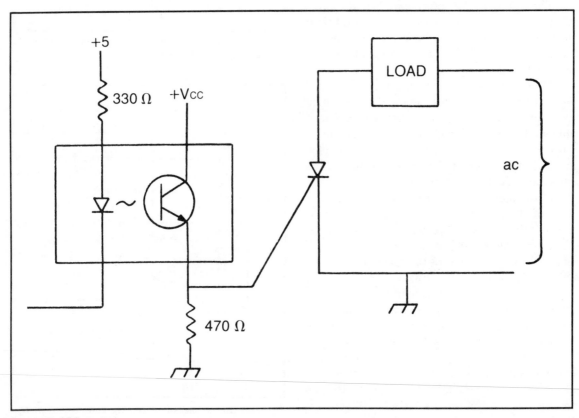

Fig. 4-27. SCR control.

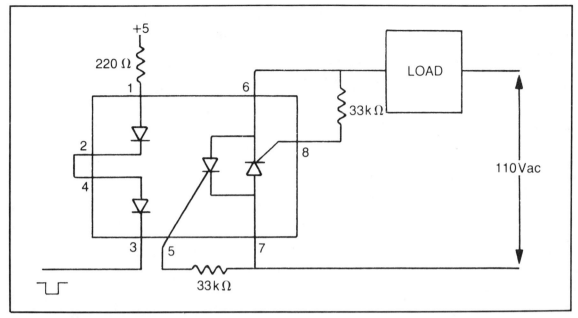

Fig. 4-28. Dual SCR optoisolator.

heaters can be controlled by an SCR.

For these other devices, a different type of controller is needed. We could use a triac, but it will require a zero-crossing trigger circuit to work with an optoisolator using a transistor. A better alternative is to use a dual SCR optocoupler, such as the Monsanto MCS6200 shown in 4-28. The coupling turns on the SCR in the correct direction, so that the device is always conducting in either direction. The SCR optocoupler acts just like an ac switch.

For really large currents, 10 amperes and more, nothing can beat a relay. Relays are slow, expensive, and tend to wear out over a few years, but they can sure handle current. Not only that, but the relay contacts don't care if the current is ac or dc.

Figure 4-29 gives a schematic for using an optocoupler with a relay. The relay is used as a load the same as in Fig. 4-24, and the transistor allows current to flow through the relay coil, which closes the contacts. The diode across the relay coil is an antispiking diode to protect the transistor from current surges when the current changes suddenly. Some might say that the optoisolator is not needed at all, but the presence of large current spikes from

the coil, even with the diode, makes it advisable to protect the computer.

Often times, one side of the relay contacts are connected to ac power, and the other to an ac service socket, while the other side of the ac power line is connected to the other side of the ac socket, to give a controllable source of 110Vac power, to turn on equipment, control devices, start the coffeepot in the morning, and the like. The user's imagination is the only limit. See Fig. 4-30 for details of the wiring.

With a series of such sockets, an entire household could be controlled via the computer. Add the input lines and a household security and control system can be easily constructed, although the programming will be quite involved.

As long as the discussion has turned around to optical-electrical devices, there are two such devices which make dandy peripherals. In many cases, those who use the peripherals wouldn't be without them.

PAPER-TAPE READER

A very popular medium for mass storage is pa-

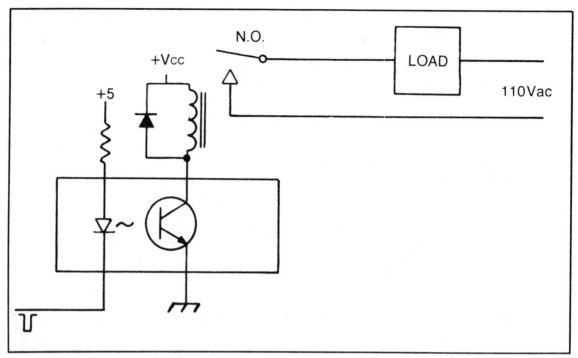

Fig. 4-29. Relay control.

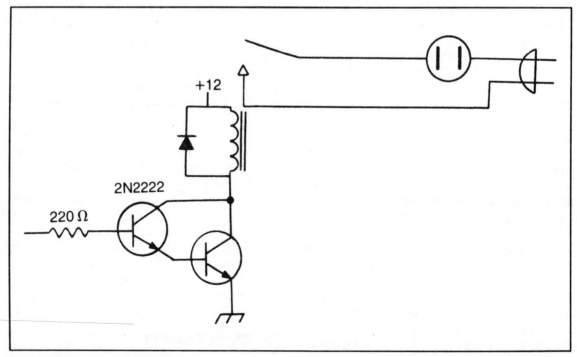

Fig. 4-30. Relay-controlled ac socket.

per tape. This medium is losing some popularity now with the advent of quality cassette drives and inexpensive disk drives, but due to the popularity of the ASR-33 Teletype®, which has a paper tape read/punch mechanism, it is still widely used. Reading a long program in on paper tape can be quite a chore, since the ASR-33 reads only ten characters a second. A program or set of data with 8K bytes would take hours to read.

A mechanical paper tape reader senses the holes in a piece of paper tape. Eight-level paper tape is one inch wide, and has nine holes punched along its width. Each hole means a logical 1 is present at that data bit in the byte. Eight holes or no holes can represent any possible data byte, then. See Fig. 4-31. In addition to the data holes, there are also sprocket holes.

Mechanical paper-tape readers work by sending little fingers up against the tape. If the finger goes through, there is a hole present. Mechanical readers are therefore both noisy and slow.

Electro-optical devices have made the reading of paper tape must faster. Recall that in the optoisolator, there was a phototransistor whose base was disconnected, and the transistor would only conduct if there was light falling on the base region. If a mechanical finger can go through a hole in tape, so can light! Figure 4-32 shows an array of nine phototransistors spaced exactly the proper distance apart to receive light that comes through a paper-tape hole. If there is no hole, the light gets blocked, and the transistor does not conduct.

Figure 4-32 also shows the complete circuit for reading the tape data and presenting it to a parallel input port. The emitters are all tied to ground, and all the collectors are held high by a pull-up resistor. When light hits the phototransistor, the collector goes to ground. NAND Schmitt-triggers are used to buffer and invert the signal. Schmitt triggers are used because they have a *hysteresis* characteristic and are less prone to edge-noise effects. One of these Schmitt triggers is used on the sprocket hole as well. The sprocket hole is made smaller than the data holes because, by the time the sprocket hole responds to the presence of light, all the other holes, if any, will have arrived at the phototransistor first, and the eight data bits will already have been set. So the reader first generates the data and then sets the data-ready signal. A 7474 latch is used to generate a data-ready pulse to the computer. The output of the 7413 is connected to the clock input of the latch, and the Q output is set when data is ready. An active-low, data-accepted signal is needed to clear the 7474 before the next sprocket hole comes along, so full handshaking is required.

With the mechanical reader on an ASR-33, as we said, only ten characters per second may be read. Using an optical reader with handshaking on a parallel port, up to 500 characters per second may be read—as fast as you can pull the tape through!

An aside: if you construct this reader, also construct a guide for the paper tape. Otherwise, the tape will be skewed on the reader and not read properly. Also, for optical use, the heavy black paper tape is better than the light oiled tape.

A flowchart for reading data from the paper tape reader is shown in Fig. 4-33.

RAECO Corporation sells the above device, or

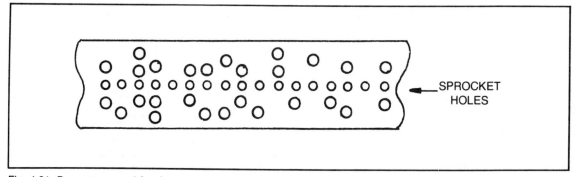

Fig. 4-31. Paper tape used for data storage.

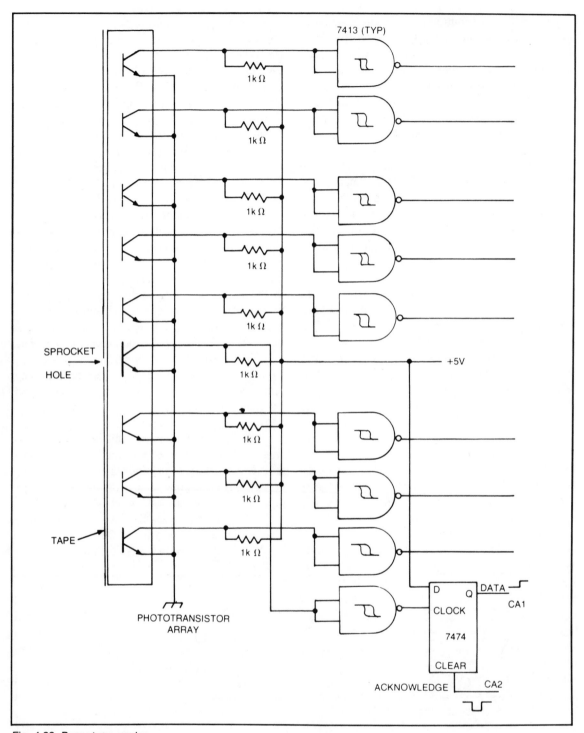

Fig. 4-32. Paper-tape reader.

one very similar to it, with all electronics and a paper-tape guide for only $35.00. Those interested in paper tape would do well to consider their product.

TOUCH-RESPONSE DISPLAY

Credit for this next idea has to go to Mr. Thomas Thornton, who built such a device for his own computer.

Entering responses to a computer's questions from the keyboard can sometimes be a great deal of trouble. The keyboard response time is slow, and it takes a few seconds to figure out which of several responses to make. Wouldn't it just be a lot easier to have the computer list the choices you have and then be able to *point* to the proper response?

There are light pens and "bit pads" on the market which allow you to do something similar to this, but they all have the same drawback: they need expensive equipment to be able to do it. A video-synchronized light pen, or a bit pad, can cost hundreds of dollars. Besides, it will take several seconds to find the "wand" and point it at the screen. Why not just use a finger?

If you will accept very low resolution, electro-optical technology can be used to create a "pointer." A parallel input port can be used to create a data-input system which tells the computer the screen position (roughly) of a finger pointing to a monitor screen.

Figure 4-34 divides a TV monitor screen up into a 8 × 8 grid. Along the bottom and side of this grid is placed a series of eight lights, one for each horizontal or vertical position in the grid. Along the top and other side are placed sixteen (eight horizontal and eight vertical) phototransistors, in small tubular housings to keep out unwanted light. Each phototransistor is to respond *only* to the light from the bulb immediately opposite the screen from it. When light falls on the transistor, it conducts. Otherwise, if light does not fall on it, as a result of having the light blocked by the presence of one's finger on the screen, the transistor does not conduct, and the collector of the transistor is held high by a pull-up resistor.

Notice that all collectors of the phototransistors are high *unless* the presence of a finger blocks the light coming from across the screen. In that case one and only one of the collectors in each of the vertical and horizontal arrays will be low. One vertical and one horizontal low bit in the byte is sufficient information to be able to tell *exactly* which of the 64 grid spots on the 8 × 8 grid is being pointed to.

Figure 4-35 shows the electronics that are needed to decode the eight phototransistors in each direction to enable the computer to use only one input port. The 74157 quad 2-line to 1-line multiplexers are used again, with the CA2 line from the PIA deciding whether the horizontal or the vertical array is being read. Two 7430 NAND gates suffice to determine if any of the sixteen phototransistor collectors has gone low, and will tell the PIA through the CA1 input.

A flowchart for the programming to be used with the touch-response display is given in Fig. 4-36. Essentially, the procedure is to wait until a "data ready" signal is received from CA1, then read first one array, then change the state of the CA2 line and read the other aray. A little additional software will be required to adapt the code for the vertical and horizontal positions to whatever purposes the user has in mind. The code will essentially be that all bits of the data byte will be 1s, except the bit corresponding to the finger position, which will be a zero.

The possibilities for the use of a touch-screen response system are endless. In games such as checkers, for example, (which uses an 8 × 8 grid) the player can simply point to the checker he wishes to move, and then point again to the new position of the checker. A little creativity will be required to display the pieces on the screen in positions where the touch-response will recognize them, but any good programmer should have no trouble formatting the screen in this manner.

In computer-assisted instruction in educational systems, instead of having a small child type in a response to a question, the computer can draw a picture to the response choices, and the child can point to the correct answer.

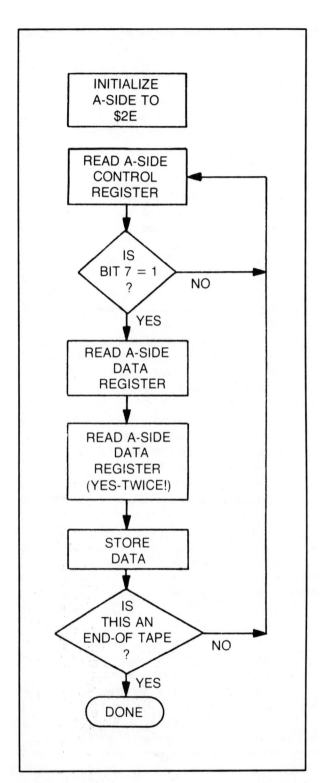

Fig. 4-33. Flowchart for program to read paper tape.

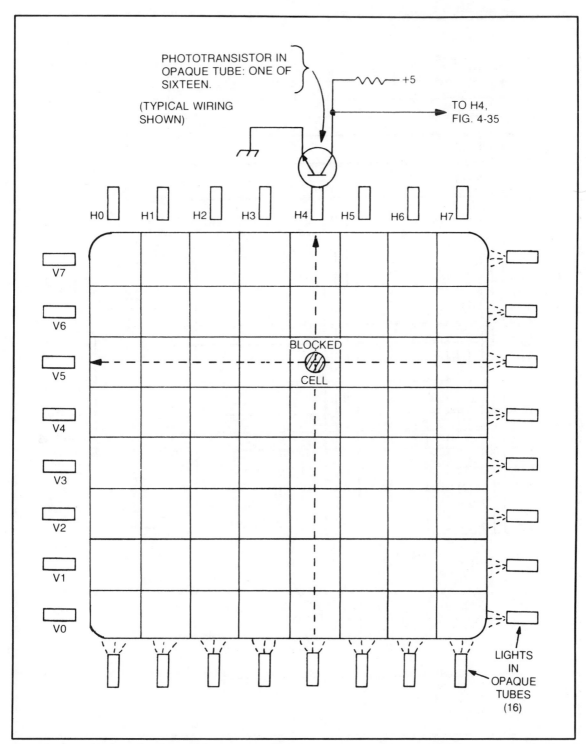

Fig. 4-34. A touch-screen data-input device.

141

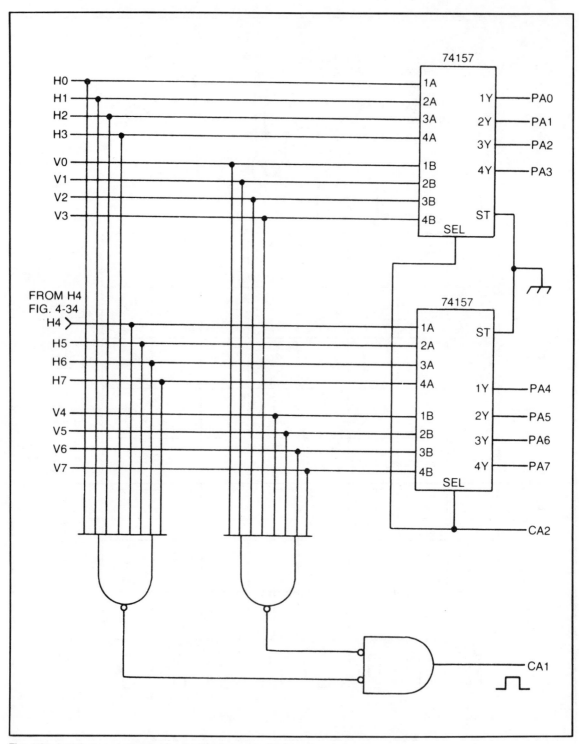

Fig. 4-35. Interfacing electronics for the touch-screen display.

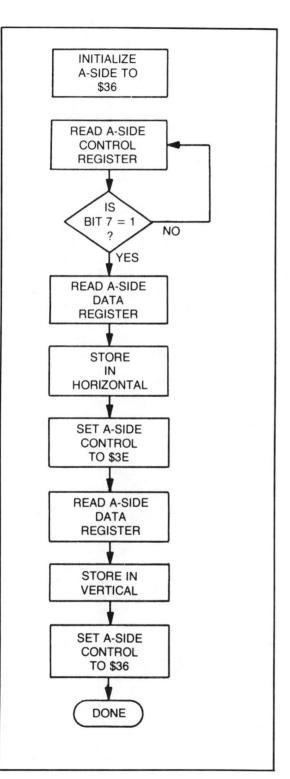

Fig. 4-36. Program flowchart to read the touch-screen display.

DC MOTOR CONTROL

As a last exercise in this chapter, let us consider the problems in controlling a small dc motor. There are available a large number of small hobby motors which run on anywhere from 1.5 to 6 V dc, and which have a large variety of uses. Such motors do not have a great amount of torque but can be useful in many applications anyway.

If all that was required was to turn the motor on and off, then only a single control bit would be needed, perhaps along with a relay or transistor to handle the current load. But dc motors have capabilities other than just on and off: the applied current sets the rotation rate of the motor, and the polarity of the voltage controls the direction of the motor's rotation.

Controlling the voltage level using a computer is an analog problem, and this type of problem will be covered in the next chapter. For the time being, consider the problem of simply controlling the direction of the motor's rotation.

Since, in order to control a motor's direction, all that is needed is to control the direction of current through it, what is really needed is a switching circuit which allows current to flow one way under one condition, and the other way under the opposite condition. Such a switching system is shown in Fig. 4-37.

Two computer control bits are used—one to turn the motor on and off, the other to control the motor's direction. A pair of NAND gates generates active-low forward and reverse signals. When the outputs of both of these gates are high, the motor does not turn. If either one is low, the motor will turn in the direction indicated. The forward and reverse signals are connected to four transistors in a totem-pole configuration. When the forward signal is low, transistors Q1 and Q4 are in the conducting state, while Q2 and Q3 do not conduct. In this case, current will flow from top to bottom in the circuit. When the reverse signal is low, Q1 and Q4 are off, and Q2 and Q3 conduct, causing current to flow from bottom to top. All that is controlled is the direction of the current.

The controller described above was used in a model-car racing set for display in a store window.

A few eyebrows went up when a car suddenly reversed direction.

Another possible use would be in controlling the motor in a cassette-tape recorder. One problem with cassettes as data storage devices is that they will only go in one direction for reading or writing. In order to do read and write simultaneously, two recorders are needed, one for each purpose. With the addition of this circuit in the tape transport mechanism, and two free control bits on the computer, the cassette can be made to back up slightly and re-read a missed piece of data, or to change a single bit or two. Considerable re-wiring of the cassette would be required for changing read/write modes, and the particular rewiring to be done depends on the recorder itself. Also, most cassette recorders free the supply reel so as to have no drag on the motor. In reverse, the supply reel will not function as a take-up reel without extensive mechanical modifications, so no more than a few inches can be reversed at a given time.

USE OF A "MOUSE" FOR RELATIVE POSITIONING

An input device called a "mouse" has been receiving a lot of attention in the various publications in recent years. It is rapidly becoming the preferable alternative to a joystick for positioning of a cursor or pointer on the terminal screen, mostly due to the fact that it is a device which translates motion of the hand directly into motion of the cursor or pointer, with immediate visible feedback to the user of the computer.

Most all manufacturers of computer systems have a mouse available as either standard or optional equipment. The most famous is, of course, that of the Apple Macintosh, whose whole operating system and user interface is totally and completely dependent upon the existence of the mouse. The IBM personal computer has a mouse as optional equipment, and there is a great deal of commercially available software which either requires the use of the mouse or is greatly enhanced by it, such as icon-based interfaces and graphics packages.

The idea of the mouse was originated by the

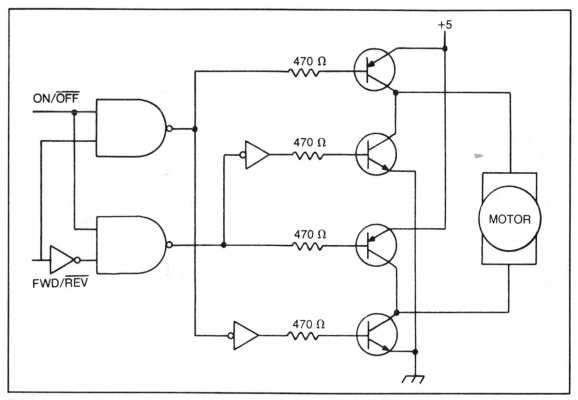

Fig. 4-37. Dc motor control.

Xerox corporation in the late 1970's and early 1980's for use in their STAR executive workstation and *Ethernet* local-area network. The Macintosh desktop and icon-based user interface were direct outgrowths of the Xerox effort.

The mouse is, physically, a box about the size of a tape cassette or pack of cigarettes connected to the computer by a single wire. When the mouse is moved across a flat surface such as a table, it senses the motion and its direction, and sends signals to the computer which cause the computer to interrupt its duties and move the screen pointer in a corresponding direction. There is also one, and as many as three, buttons on the mouse's top which can be pressed to cause an "event," or to point out that the current position of the pointer is the position of interest at the time. This could cause an icon to be selected, a point to be drawn upon the screen, or an action to be chosen from a menu, for example.

The construction and operation of a mouse are conceptually very simple. The mouse usually has a ball which rolls according to the direction of the mouse's motion. Pressing on this ball are two rollers at right angles to each other which rotate with the ball. Since they are at right angles, one will roll with motion in the X direction, and the other will roll with motion in the Y direction. Any combination of X and Y motion causes the rollers to move in proportional amounts. The rotation of the rollers causes a series of pulses to be sent to the computer, which interprets them as interrupts, and software takes care of the cursor positioning.

Other versions of the mouse dispense with the ball and just have a pair of wheels at right angles which contact that table surface directly, and rotate proportionally depending on the relative amounts of X and Y motion.

It must be pointed out that the mouse is a *relative* position indicator. It does not indicate the absolute position of the cursor, but, by its motion, only tells the computer to move the cursor so many units of distance in this direction *from its current location.* You can move a mouse, pick it up and return it to its starting point, and then move it an identical amount again, and the computer will register only the motion detected while it is in contact with the table surface.

An expanded diagram of a mouse, showing the inner workings of the circuit is shown in Fig. 4-38. The central object of prominence is the ball itself. Almost any kind of very hard rubber ball can be used, or, if the rollers in contact with the ball are themselves rubber, a clean plastic or even a steel ball bearing can be used, although a rubber ball will give better traction on a table surface. The ball should be housed in a semi-hemispherical container which just gives enough room for the ball to turn freely; about 1/8-inch clearance all around is about right. Pressing on this ball are three rollers, two of which are placed at right angles to each other, and the third being spring-loaded so that it presses the ball against the other two. These rollers need not be placed at the widest part of the ball; they can be placed near the bottom, near the table if desired. The weight of the ball will keep it near the table, and the light pressure of the third roller will keep the ball in contact with the other two rollers. It is important that the X and Y rollers be small compared to the ball's diameter. In this way, the rollers will turn many times for one revolution of the ball and cause many pulses to be generated. The third roller has no such restriction. Don't make the rollers too small, however, or you will be working against too large a mechanical advantage, and the rollers will be hard to turn.

At the opposite end of the shaft from the rollers is a wheel or disk. In the figure shown, the wheel is a mirrored wheel. It is this wheel that, with the assistance of a lamp or LED and a photodetector (such as a phototransistor, photodarlington, or photodiode), produces the series of pulses that control the positioning of the cursor or pointer on the screen. In the example shown, a beam of light from the lamp bounces off the polished surface of the wheel. Periodically around the wheel are dark lines made with paint. (The printed circuit marking pen

from Radio Shack is an ideal way of painting the black stripes.) When the light beam strikes a black line, there is no reflection, when it strikes the mirrored surface, it reflects into the photodetector. As the roller turns the wheel, the detector receives light on, off, on, off... It is not necessary for the wheel to have a very highly reflective surface, either. A disk 3/4 of an inch in diameter and 3/16 inch thick is about ideal. It should be sanded smooth with 600 grit wet-or-dry sandpaper and a little water. Then, use some automotive rubbing compound and a lot of elbow grease to polish it up. A felt polishing wheel will help a lot with the last step. Then paint the lines on, and mount it on the shaft. Two such roller-wheel combinations will be required, one for motion in the X direction, and one for motion in the Y direction.

You will notice from the diagram that there is an additional disk mounted on the shaft, about halfway along it. This is necessary because the rotation of the mirrored wheel states only that motion along that axis is taking place, but not what the *direction* of that motion is. These small disks, one for each shaft, are cut from thin sheet metal and shaped with a jeweler's saw. They are slip-fitted to the shaft with a fiber or nylon washer so that the friction of turning will turn them, but if they encounter an obstacle, such as the bar placed in the wedge-shaped slot, they will stop turning while the shaft and wheel continue to turn. The disk should be painted black to stop light. A small slot in the disk opposite to the side of the bar will admit light from the lamp to the photodetector if it is present, and the disk will stop light from the lamp if it is turned away. The operation of the disk is as follows: when the shaft turns, the disk turns with it until it reaches the bar, and stops. The shaft keeps on turning. When the shaft begins turning the other way, the disk turns in that direction until it reaches the stop bar again. In only one of the two extreme stopped positions will the slot allow light from the lamp to fall on the photodetector. When light is present at the photodetector, it indicates motion in one direction; when it is not present, it represents motion in the other direction. You have a simple 1 or 0 state indicating direction, and that state can

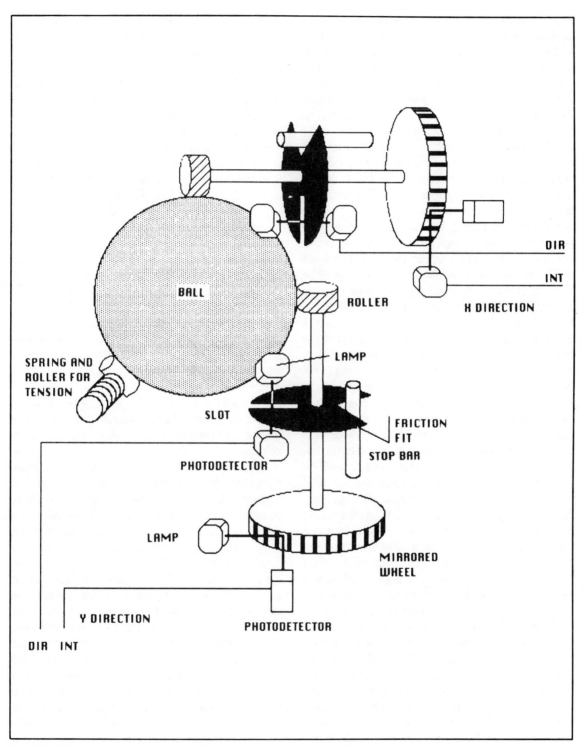

BALL

SPRING AND
ROLLER FOR
TENSION

ROLLER

LAMP

SLOT

PHOTODETECTOR

FRICTION
FIT

STOP BAR

DIR

INT

X DIRECTION

LAMP

MIRRORED
WHEEL

Y DIRECTION

DIR   INT

PHOTODETECTOR

Fig. 4-38. Expanded view of a ''mouse.''

be applied directly to the computer input port to be tested by the computer. There is a direction bit and a pulse bit for each of the two axes of travel.

Lastly, don't forget to add a button for event sensing. The "debounced" button of Fig. 2-14 is an excellent choice. This gives you a total of five lines, plus power and ground, to be connected to the mouse.

The pulse bit of each shaft should be applied to a parallel input bit, and it should also be connected to the interrupt input, as well. The pulses and the button should all cause an interrupt. It is up to the software to test the various input bits to determine which one of the three caused the interrupt. The mouse button is an indication that "something is to be done", while the pulses are an indication that the pointer on the screen should be moved. A good method of programming your mouse is to let one pulse from the mouse move the pointer by one "pixel", or one dot-width on the video screen. A set of electronics for applying the signals from the mouse to the computer PIA is shown in Fig. 4-39. Schmitt triggers are used to obtain a "clean" signal.

The mirrored wheel is not the only method that can be used to generate pulses from the rotating shaft. Figure 4-40 shows two other methods that can be used, as well. These may be easier to implement, depending on your level of expertise. The top method is just the mirrored wheel again. The method in the middle is a thin disk, with multiple slots cut into it with a jeweler's saw. As the wheel rotates, each slot in turn will admit light, then cut it off. A variation on this method is shown on the bottom of the figure, where the slots are replaced with a series of drilled holes. This last method will be easier to construct, but will require more precision in the placing of the lamp and detector.

For those who have exceptional talent and a shop full of machine tools, you might try the method used with the Macintosh. This method uses a slotted wheel as above, but the direction sensing method is quite different, using a technique called *quadrature*, which is used in many other electronic

applications, such as high-speed telephone modems. The method is illustrated in Fig. 4-41. Basically, it consists of a slotted wheel with not one, but two pulse sensors. The sensors are carefully placed that the waveforms produced are exactly 90 degrees out of phase. The interrupt wave has exactly the same shape whether the mouse is moving to the right or to the left, only then the wave itself, as shown, will move to the right or left. Likewise, the quadrature wave will also move to the right or left, with a 90-degree phase difference. The interrupt wave causes an interrupt on the receipt of the *rising edge only* of its waveform. The computer senses that an interrupt has occurred, and then interrogates the direction wave bit to see if it is a 1 or a 0. When moving to the left, a rising edge of the interrupt wave will have a 0 bit for quadrature, while when moving to the right, a rising edge of the interrupt wave will have a 1 bit for quadrature. The method is ingenious, but requires extremely precise positioning of the lamps and detectors. It is not recommended for amateurs.

TRACKBALL

A trackball is also a relative-positioning device similar to a mouse. It only determines the relative motion, not the absolute position of the cursor or pointer.

A mouse is better for situations which require immediate visual feedback of position. A trackball adds an element of excitement to games. Many commercial video games, such as *Centipede*, use a trackball, and they are for sale as add-ons or mouse replacements for almost all popular computers.

In fact, a trackball is really nothing more than a mouse turned upside down. Instead of moving the mouse housing over a surface so that friction with the surface will rotate the ball and turn the shafts, the fingers and hand of the user rotate the ball directly. The ball still rests on the three rollers, and its own weight keeps it there. The rollers still turn shafts which cause pulses and direction readings, and so on. If you can build a mouse, you can certainly turn it upside down and build a trackball.

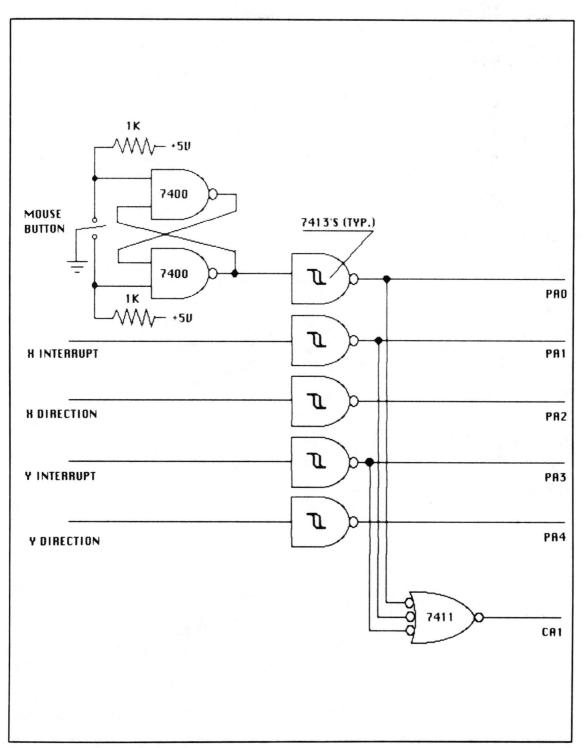

Fig. 4-39. Interfacing electronics for mouse.

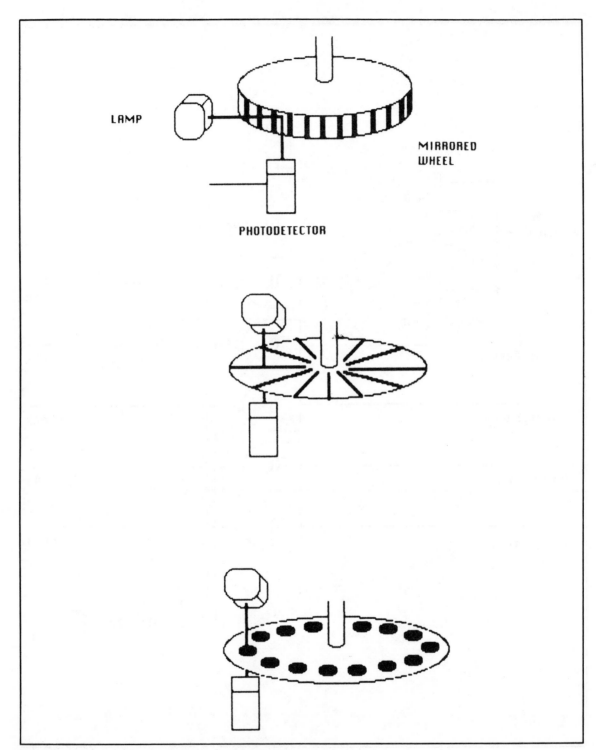

LAMP

MIRRORED
WHEEL

PHOTODETECTOR

Fig. 4-40. Several methods of causing interrupt pulses using a mouse.

150

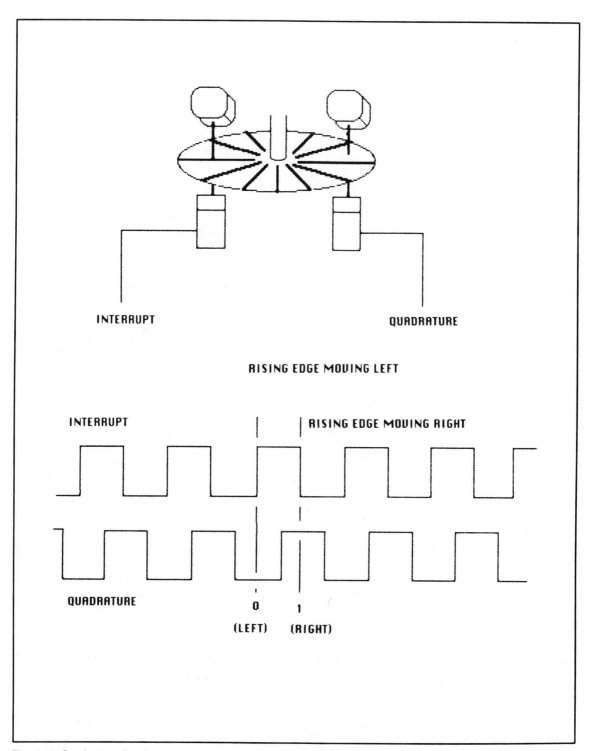

Fig. 4-41. Quadrature direction sensing in the mouse of the Apple Macintosh.

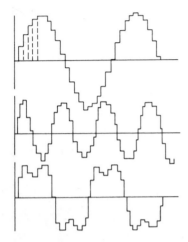

Chapter 5

Parallel Digital Ports and Analog Signals

Very few statements can be made about the physical world we live in that are either wholly true or wholly false. We can say things like, "It is raining," or "It is not raining," and we can even make statements like "The wind is blowing." But a wind of two mph is considerably different from a wind of 57 mph. In the former case, we might be tempted to say, "The wind is not blowing," when in fact it is—the air is moving!

In the case of the wind, it is much easier, and more specific to say that the wind is blowing a certain number of miles per hour, rather than making a blanket statement about whether the wind is blowing or not. This comparison illustrates the difference between digital and analog signals. The statement, "The wind is blowing" is akin to a digital signal—on or off. An analog signal would tell us that "The wind velocity is 14 mph."

A digital voltage is either on or off, high or low, 1 or 0. An analog voltage can have any value in the range of possibilities of the creator of the voltage. Instead of being +5V or ground, an analog volt-

age can be 2.23V, 4.91V, or anywhere within a defined range.

The level of the voltage means something, too. If an analog wind-velocity meter were to have an output of 1.4V, that might correspond to a wind velocity of 14 mph, where every tenth of a volt of output corresponded to one mile per hour of wind velocity.

Often times, we like to make measurements about some property of the physical world. Those measurements invariably end up in analog form.

A device which takes energy from the physical parameter being measured and converts it into electrical voltage or current is called *transducer*. Ideally, a transducer should produce an analog voltage which is proportional to the quantity being measured. Examples of transducers are light meters, microphones, pressure gauges, and thermocouples. Some transducers, such as a stereo speaker, can be run in reverse as well, with an electrical quantity being used to produce physical energy of some kind. It takes an electrical current and turns it into sound waves. The higher the amplitude of the current, the louder the sound. A speaker can be used in reverse to turn sound into ac electricity. When this is done, the speaker (transducer) is called a dynamic microphone.

An analog signal is not compatible with a digital signal. A digital signal tells us on or off—analog tells us how much. It is not possible to connect an analog signal line directly to a digital input or output port and have the computer understand the voltage levels involved. The computer expects the signal to be either 5V or 0V and will try to interpret anything else as one of these two, depending on internal thresholds.

For this reason, a whole science has developed around the conversion of analog signals to digital signals or vice-versa. Entire books have been written on the subject. Basically, the problem is to convert a *voltage level* into a bunch of digital *on-and-off bits* representing a binary number corresponding to the value of the analog voltage level. This process is called *analog-to-digital conversion*, and any device which does this is called an analog-to-digital converter, or ADC for short. The reverse process, converting from a set of digital bits to an analog voltage is, naturally, called *digital-to-analog conversion*, and the device which does it is called a DAC, for digital-to-analog converter.

There are many ways to do each of the conversion processes. Generally, the more complicated the method, the more accurate the conversion is. It is possible to do either analog-to-digital or digital-to-analog conversion using only a single operational amplifier and a few resistors, while letting the computer's software do most of the work. Naturally, the process is time-consuming and not very accurate with this method.

Both DACs and ADCs share a common problem: that of *resolution*. Figure 5-1 illustrates the difficulty. An analog signal can have virtually any value in its range. If eight data bits (for example) are used to represent an analog voltage, then the eight data bits can be a binary number anywhere from 0 to 255. The range of the analog voltage is divided into 256 equal ranges. For example, let's

say that an analog voltage can run from 0V to +10V. Then with eight digital bits, that 10 volt range is divided into 256 equal voltage ranges of about 0.04 volts each. Any analog voltage falling within ± 0.02 volts of the central value in the range is considered to have the same voltage as the central value. Put another way, if the binary number 10000000 represents 5.00 volts ± 0.02 volts, then the binary number 10000001 will represent a voltage of 5.04 volts, ± 0.02 volts. The binary number 10000001 can be used for 5.04 volts, 5.03 volts, 5.05 volts, even 5.059 volts! It is interesting to note that the same binary number represents both 5.021 volts and 5.059 volts. Both are within 0.02 volts of 5.04 volts.

The difference in increasing digital signals and increasing analog signals is the difference in going up a staircase or in going up a ramp.

The point is, we live in an analog world, but computers only understand digital.

As an aside, it should be pointed out that analog computers do exist. In fact, they existed before the programmable digital computer was invented. They are still used to some extent, particularly in engineering concerns, because they are a whiz at solving simultaneous partial differential equations in multiple variables. One example I saw was an analog computer set up to solve the set of differential equations which apply to the flight of a jet aircraft, subject to conditions such as throttle setting, weight, airfoil construction, and engine type. The various parameters were adjusted on the analog computer by changing the settings of potentiometers, and the design tested before even putting it on paper. The analog outputs were connected to meters to look just like the console of an aircraft flight deck. It was a marvelous selling point to be able to let buyers "fly" the plane on the computer before the plane was even off the drawing board!

In talking about the resolution of a DAC or ADC, it seems obvious at first glance that, in order to improve the resolution of a converter, all one has to do is increase the number of bits being converted. The more bits, the finer the steps between the individual voltage levels. In general, this is true, and the resolution of a DAC or ADC is generally measured in *bits*. A four-bit DAC can only divide the voltage range into 16 steps, while a 16-bit DAC can divide it into 65,536 steps. An 8-bit converter is about the smallest practical size, while converters of more than 12 bits become very expensive. An 8-bit ADC can cost as little as twenty dollars, while professional 13-bit ADCs cost more than two thousand.

One problem with increased resolution is that all parts in the converter have to meet the same precision as the overall converter, at least. An 8-bit converter will give a relation between analog and digital signals accurate to 0.4 percent. This means that every component within the converter must be precise in its value to 0.4 percent. Most converters will have an amplifier of some kind, whether it be an operational amplifier or a comparator, and will have a voltage reference, and the computation of the conversion will depend on the values of several components, such as resistors. The amplifier has to be linear in its response to better than 0.4 percent, the voltage reference must maintain an accurate and precise output voltage and not vary in its value more than 0.4 percent, and the values of all the individual components must be known accurately to within 0.4 percent. In the case of an 8-bit DAC, at least 24 resistors must all have the same value, plus or minus 0.2 percent. While 5 percent resistors are rather inexpensive—only a few cents each—a precision resistor with a value known to better than 1 percent can be as much a a dollar each. A 0.2 percent resistor becomes almost prohibitively expensive. In going to 12 bits resolution, all the 0.4 percent figures change to 0.025 percent, or one part in 4096. Needless to say, the more bits of resolution, the more components are needed, and the more expensive the individual components become. A precision voltage reference good to 0.025 percent is almost prohibitively expensive to buy (if you can find one), and nearly impossible to build without very high technology equipment.

DIGITAL-TO-ANALOG CONVERTERS

Let's start with outputs first. We want to take a digital binary number, and convert it to a volt-age proportional to the binary value of that number. How can this be done?

Recall that a binary number depends on the place value system in base two, where every bit has twice the value of the one immediately to its right. A "1" in bit-4 position means twice as much (8) as a "1" in bit 3 (4). Zeroes, of course, are just place holders and don't have any value.

What we really need is a means of *weighting* individual data bits so that bit 7 is worth 128 times as much as bit 0, bit 6 is worth 64 times as much as bit 0, and so on. Then we need a way of adding up all the individual weighted bits to give an analog voltage.

In operational amplifier applications, there is a circuit called a *summing amplifier*. The schematic of the circuit is given in Fig. 5-2. The example given uses a 741 operational amplifier and requires bipolar power supplies of $+15V$ and $-15V$, respectively.

A nice little mathematical trick called "virtual ground" allows us to compute the value of the output voltage of the amplifier in terms of the various input voltages. This output voltage is found to be:

$$\frac{V_{out}}{R_f} = \frac{V_0}{R_0} + \frac{V_1}{R_1} + \frac{V_2}{R_2} + \frac{V_3}{R_3}$$

$$+ \frac{V_4}{R_4} + \frac{V_5}{R_5} + \frac{V_6}{R_6} + \frac{V_7}{R_7}$$

The input voltages will be either $+5V$ or $0V$. If we want the output to be between $0V$ and $-10V$ ($0V$ when all inputs are 0s), we can re-write the equation into the form shown on page 138 to give us an idea of what values of resistance to use:

$$V_{out} = -5V \left(D0\ \frac{R_f}{R_0} + D1\ \frac{R_f}{R_1} + D2\ \frac{R_f}{R_2} \right.$$

$$\left. + D3\ \frac{R_f}{R_3} + D4\ \frac{R_f}{R_4} + D5\ \frac{R_f}{R_5} + \ldots \right)$$

Here, D0, D1, D2, are the values of the data bits

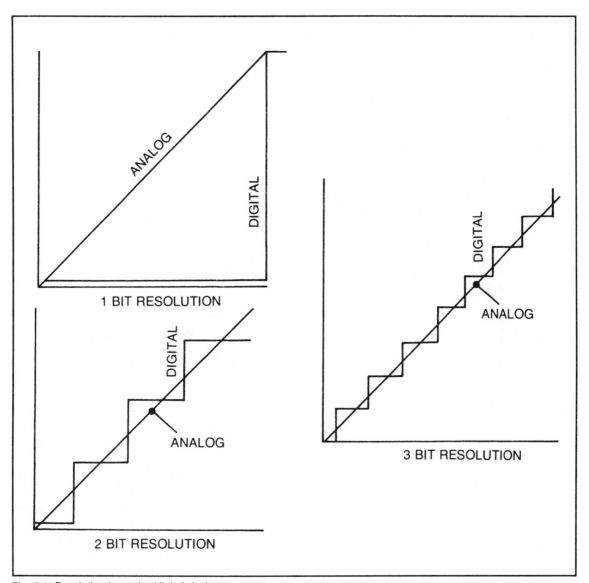

Fig. 5-1. Resolution in analog/digital devices.

0, 1, 2 . . . either 0 or 1. It is apparent that the output will be 0V when the input is 00000000. The output must be $-5V$ when the input is 10000000, so R_f/R_7 must be equal to 1, or $R_f = R_7$. Similarly, V_{out} must be $-2.5V$ when the input is 01000000, so $R_6 = 2 \times R_f$. If we make the value of R_f equal to 1000 ohms (a good general value to let the operational amplifier work properly), then we get the following:

R_0	$128 \times R_f$	128K ohms
R_1	$64 \times R_f$	64K ohms
R_2	$32 \times R_f$	32K ohms
R_3	$16 \times R_f$	16K ohms
R_4	$8 \times R_f$	8K ohms
R_5	$4 \times R_f$	4K ohms
R_6	$2 \times R_f$	2K ohms
R_7	R_f	1K ohms

155

An operational summing amplifier built according to the circuit of Fig. 5-2 and using exactly the above values will give an output voltage which is exactly proportional to the binary number represented by the inputs.

Notice that the output voltage is negative. For input bytes of 0 to 255, the output voltage varies between zero and −10 volts, respectively. To invert the input, an inverter amplifier can be attached to the output of the summing amplifier, as shown in Fig. 5-3. Another way, a little more risky depending on the application, is to switch the inputs to the amplifier so that the connection to the resistor sum-

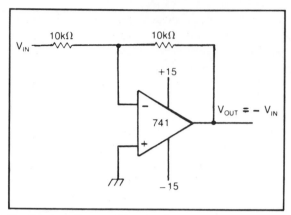

Fig. 5-3. Inverting amplifier circuit.

ming point is now to the noninverting input (+), and the inverting input (−) is grounded. This method does away with negative feedback, and with some applications the circuit may be prone to erratic behavior.

The binary weighted summing amplifier makes a good DAC—it is easily understood and quite easy to build. But it is not without problems, especially if more than 8 bits of resolution is desired. As an example, consider again the case when R_f is 1000 ohms, and the output is to be 10 volts. Then the current though resistor R_0 is only 12.8 microamperes. Very few operational amplifiers will respond to such a small current and still be linear in the output. This is about the lower end of the linearity scale of an inexpensive amplifier like the 741. More expensive amplifiers will, of course, work at lower currents. We could, of course, raise the amount of current through this resistor by lowering the value of R_f. But this approach is not without its attendant problems, too. To raise the current through R_0 up to about a milliampere (say, 1.28 milliamperes) then the current through R_7 goes up to a full ampere! The 741 amplifier will definitely not handle this kind of current, nor will very many operational amplifiers. (Unless, of course, the price goes up.)

There are other problems, as well. It suffers from the fact that a range of resistor values is needed. This imposes high-precision requirements upon the circuit, and this increases the cost significantly. Our example of the 8-bit DAC with preci-

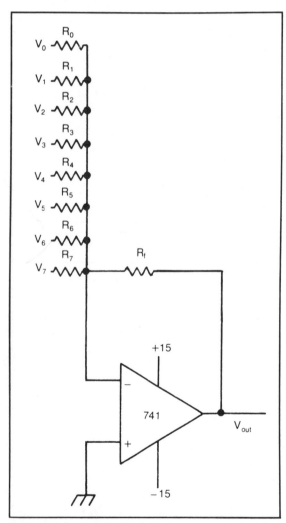

Fig. 5-2. Summing amplifier circuit.

sion of 0.4 percent means that resistors R_7 and R_f must be good to at least 0.4 percent. R_6 must be good to 0.2 percent, R_5 to 0.1 percent, and so on, until resistor R_0 must be good to .00625 percent. Such precision, when available at all, is not easy to find.

The R-2R ladder network largely overcomes the problems of the weighted resistor network. Only two resistor values are needed, one twice the value of the other, and, for an 8-bit DAC, only a precision of 0.2 percent. Integrated circuit manufacturing processes are such that this value can be achieved quite easily. The schematic for an R-2R ladder network is shown in Fig. 5-4.

The major problem with an R-2R system is that the inputs must be at 0V or the reference voltage. That is, the inputs must be able to source or to sink current and may require that the currents be substantial. TTL outputs can sink several milliamperes but can only source a few microamperes. Using an open-collector output is no help, either, because the collector requires a pull-up resistor, which makes the input look like a voltage divider with variable resistance for different states. One solution is shown where a totem-pole type of driver uses FETs.

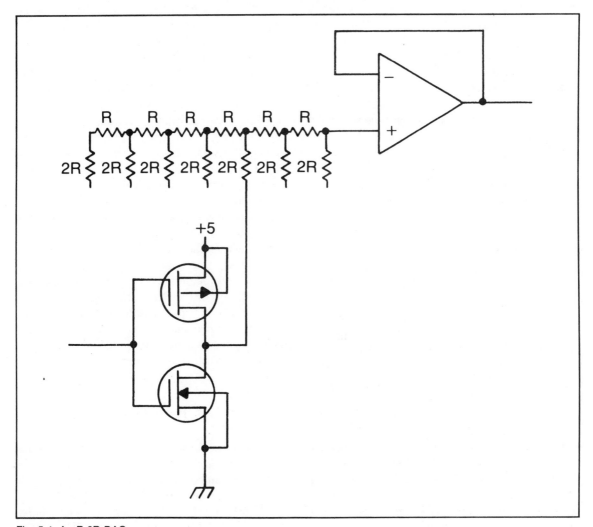

Fig. 5-4. An R-2R DAC.

Both the binary-weighted ladder and the R-2R ladder require a *voltage reference*. That is, the input to the operational amplifier is scaled to the value of a reference voltage somewhere in the circuit. Essentially, the output is some percentage of the reference voltage.

The use of a reference voltage is a common one in interfacing between analog and digital signals. Both DACs and ADCs will require one. The higher precision and more resolution the converter, the more precise the reference voltage has to be. Figure 5-5 shows some circuits that can be used to provide a stable reference voltage. All are essentially voltage regulators of one form or another, but they become progressively more precise and more expensive. Regulator A costs only a few cents and is good to about 2 percent; regulator D costs over ten dollars and is good to 0.001 volt! All the regulators suffer from the same difficulty—they can only provide currents in the milliampere range.

The use of the R-2R ladder and the reference voltage makes the circuit a "multiplying DAC," so called because the output is the product of a binary input number and a reference voltage. There are other types of DACs, such as the frequency-to-voltage converter, but they tend to be less precise, so we will not consider them here.

A PRACTICAL DAC

As we have seen before, any time there is a circuit that has several uses, there will be an integrated circuit which does most of the job of that circuit. This is again the case with the R-2R multiplying DAC. A large number of DAC circuits are available to the computer hobbyist. Analog Devices Corporation has an entire catalog full of just DACs and ADCs. However, one of the easiest to use from the point of view of the computer hobbyist is made by Motorola. It is the MC1408 and comes in three resolutions, the L6, L7, and L8 models for 6-, 7-, and 8-bit resolution respectively. The package contains an R-2R ladder, a series of current switches, and an operational amplifier. All that is needed to complete the circuit is a voltage reference and a current-to-voltage amplifier. Figure 5-6 shows how the MC1408L8 may be connected to a parallel output port with some additional circuitry to make an 8-bit multiplying DAC. The outputs connect directly to the parallel output port of a 6820 and use the 6820s latching characteristics to maintain the value of the output. The zener diode forms the reference voltage generator, and the operational amplifier does the current-to-voltage conversion. The output voltage is positive with respect to ground, and all-zeroes input will give a zero-voltage output. The output can be made bipolar by a simple change as shown in Fig. 5-6B. In this case, instead of varying between 0 and 5V, the output will vary between $-2.5V$ and $+2.5V$.

One advantage of this circuit is that almost no software is required for its operation. Once the PIA is set up for simple parallel output, there are no strobes, interrupts, or any need whatsoever for the handshaking lines. All that is needed is to put the data to be output to the DAC into the PIAs output data register, and the PIA does the rest. The parallel data is placed onto the output lines, and the DAC converts it to an analog voltage. The internal latching function of the PIA keeps the data on the output lines regardless of what else the processor is doing, until it is specifically changed by the processor.

In assembly language, the DAC handler (not including the PIA initialization routine) is nothing more than a simple "store the A-register into location XXXX," where the A register is the location of the data to be output to the DAC, and XXXX is the address of the PIA output data register.

This DAC can also be directly supported from BASIC. Most machines have the POKE command in their basic language. It means to take a number and put it into a specific address. For example, the command:

130   POKE (54,41024)

will take the decimal number 54 and place it in the decimal memory location 40124. The first number has to be a number which is an integer between 0 and 255, because only 8 bits are allowed to be POKEed at any time into an address. The second number is an address number. If your machine has

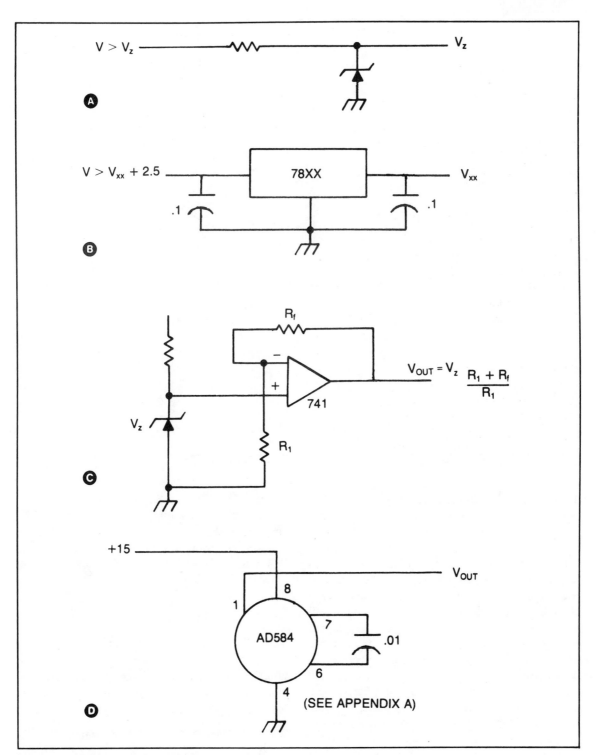

Fig. 5-5. Generating reference voltages.

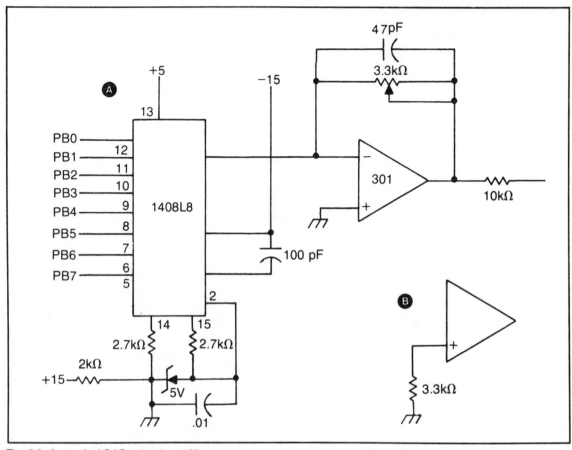

Fig. 5-6. A practical DAC using the 1408.

16 address lines, this number must be less than 65,536; if 20 lines, it must be less than 1,048,576. The largest number that can be put in this space is the largest address your computer can address. Each address corresponds to one byte of data. This is true even if your computer has a capability of processing more than 8 bytes at a time. Even though your computer may process 16 bits, it still has to get them one byte at a time. The decimal number 54 corresponds to a hexadecimal number of $36, and the number 41024 is hexadecimal address $A080.

Let A be a variable which contains the address of the data register of the PIA, and let X be a variable whose value is to be between 0 and 5, corresponding to an output voltage from the DAC between 0 and 5 volts. The actual output voltage

of the DAC is adjustable by the components independently of this number but let's say that the number and the voltage range correspond. Then the following program is needed in BASIC to drive the PIA and DAC within the specified voltage range:

```
100  LET A = 41024
110  LET Y = INT(X/5*255)
120  POKE(Y,A)
```

Naturally, this program assumes that the PIA has been initialized earlier, either within the BASIC program by a series of POKEs or with a machine language program done before the BASIC routine begins or calls from the BASIC routine.

PROGRAMMABLE VOLTAGE SOURCE

One almost trivial use of a DAC in this manner is as a programmable voltage source. It can take the place of a variable-voltage power supply in low-current situations. With a variable-voltage power supply, the desired voltage is dialed in from the front panel by tuning a potentiometer knob. If you don't have a variable-voltage power supply but do have a computer and a DAC output, the two can be substituted for the supply.

A program to read a voltage level from the keyboard, and output that voltage level from the DAC is given, in BASIC, as follows:

```
100   INPUT X
110   IF X>5 THEN END
120   IF X<0 THEN END
130   LET A=41024
140   LET Y=INT(X/5*255)
150   POKE(Y,A)
160   GOTO 100
```

The IF statements in the program set the range of the outputs. If a larger or smaller range is desired the 5s in statements 110 and 140 must be changed to fit the new range, and the DAC components adjusted to fit this range. Again, the PIA for the DAC is assumed to be at decimal location 41024 (hexadecimal $A080), and the PIA must be initialized before running the program.

There are a multitude of uses for a programmable voltage generator. The obvious is, of course, a quick source of rapidly changeable voltages. These voltages can be used to check out equipment just built or under repair, for construction projects, and the like. They can also be used as controlling voltages for any device whose function is controlled by a voltage level. For example, the level of light in a bulb can be controlled directly by a DAC by supplying the bulb with power from the DAC. The speed of a dc motor can be controlled directly by a DAC.

In most of these case, the DAC's output impedance is the limiting factor in the use of a DAC as a dc controller. Most DACs will only supply a few milliamperes of current. A low-output-impedance, unity-gain amplifier may be needed on the DAC output line if it will not otherwise supply

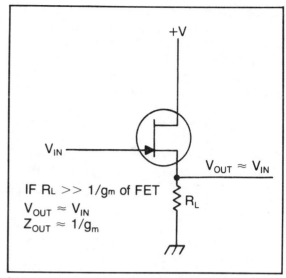

Fig. 5-7. Lowering the output impedance of a DAC.

sufficient current. An example is shown in Fig. 5-7, with a small electric motor being controlled by it as an example.

SERVO CONTROLLER

You may need to control the position of a mechanical device by a computer. Examples would be the arm on a plotter (more about plotters later), the position of an arm on an experimental robot, or the opening of a valve for the control of fluid flow, to name only a few. A transducer to convert from voltage value to mechanical position is called a *servo*.

The usual place to find a discussion of servos is in an electronics book covering feedback. Those who are of an academic bent or are exceptionally curious will do well to consult these texts. For our purposes, however, we don't need to know all the theory of a servo, just how to use it.

A type of servo well suited to the use of the computer hobbyist is the model-airplane servo. It is designed to work on 6 volts of power but does very well with only 5, so it may be easily interfaced to TTL integrated circuits. It generally draws very little current, is of light weight, has a surprising amount of torque or force—several ounces, in fact—and is surprisingly easy to connect to a circuit. Most of these model servos are of the *three-wire* type, used with proportional control systems in radio-controlled models. The position of the servo arm or shaft is controlled by the duty cycle of a series of pulses put into it. We can control this duty cycle with a voltage and two integrated circuits.

Figure 5-8 shows how two 555 timers can be connected as a pulse width modulator to drive a three-wire servo. The first 555 generates a series of pulses, and the second will modify their width according to the value of the voltage at the DAC

output. This has the effect of changing the duty cycle of the square waves.

The servo will have to be calibrated before it can be used. The usual method of doing this is called *centering* the servo. A manual included with the servo will give the information needed to center the device. While sending a 128 to the DAC from the computer, which will give just half of the maximum range of the DAC, the servo should be just halfway through its entire range. Send the 128 and perform the centering calibration. Then the

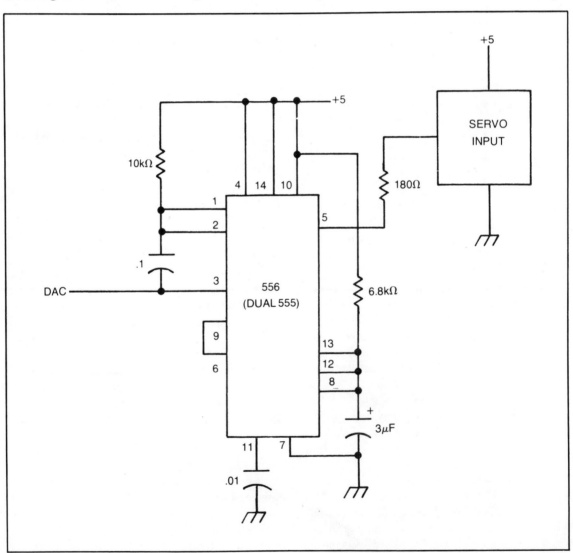

Fig. 5-8. Controlling a servo with a DAC.

162

Amplitude 0-10v
Duty cycle

servo will be ready to use.

PROGRAMMABLE FUNCTION GENERATOR

Oftentimes in the use of electronics, an input waveform is needed. Such waveforms may be used to run a sweep generator or a single-ramp ADC, as in a slowly rising voltage. Music may require a sine wave, computers may need a square wave, or some other function may need a series of pulses of a specific width at a specific frequency.

Generally, these waveforms are provided by a waveform generator, such as an audio oscillator. This device usually has both amplitude and frequency controls, and is capable of making sine waves, square waves, and triangle waves. If any other form of a wave is needed, it may be that a special generator will have to be constructed. What would you do if the waveform you needed was not sine waves, but full-wave rectified *half circles*? (See Fig. 5-9) for an example).

The DAC gives us a way of creating almost any waveform that can be imagined. Indeed, if the wave function can be described as "amplitude as a function of time" in a continuous function, or if it can be stated as entries in a table, the DAC can create that waveform with the computer's help. A waveform is nothing more than a voltage that varies with

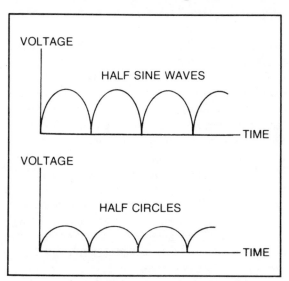

Fig. 5-9. Comparison of half-wave circles with half-wave sine waves.

time. It is possible to vary the output voltage of a DAC time by periodically changing the value of the DAC's output.

Consider the example stated above: a full wave rectified half circle. We can treat this waveform as an equation. Figure 5-10 shows a plot of X *vs* Y for the equation:

$$X^2 + Y^2 = R^2$$

Where R is the radius of the circle. It will be more convenient if, instead of having the center of the circle at the origin of coordinates, we place the circle so that the left edge is at the origin, as in Fig. 5-10B. Then the equation becomes:

$$(X - R)^2 + Y^2 = R^2$$

We can solve this equation for Y to get:

$$Y = ((X-R)^2 - R^2)^{1/2}$$

or

$$Y = (X^2 - 2XR)^{1/2}$$

(Now we let X be time, R be the period of the wave (where, in this particular example, the period must be numerically equal to the amplitude), and Y be the voltage value at any given time X.

In order to see this waveform at the output of the DAC, the computer is used as a timer and a DAC driver. The computer enters a loop where the value of the DAC's output is periodically changed according to the value of the equation. A program to accomplish this is shown below.

```
100   LET A = 41024
110   LET R = 100
120   LET X = 0
200   LET Y = X*X – 2*x*R
210   IF Y<0 THEN 120
220   LET Y = SQR(Y)
230   POKE(Y,A)
240   LET X = X+10
250   FOR I = 1 TO 50
260   NEXT I
270   GOTO 200
```

163

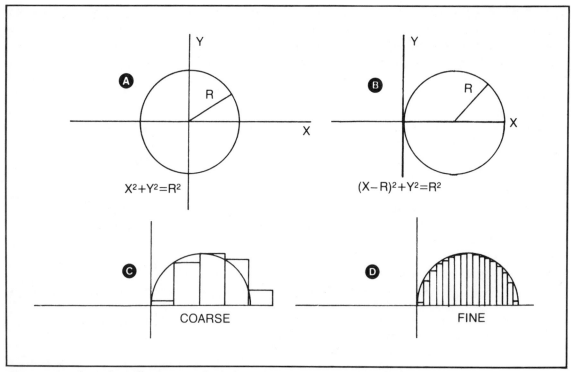

Fig. 5-10. (A) $X^2 + Y^2 = R^2$; (B) $(X + R)^2 + Y^2 = R^2$; (C) coarse plotting; (D) fine plotting.

In this program, the variable A gives the decimal address of the DAC's PIA. The value of R sets the amplitude of the signal but cannot be any larger than 255. The values in statements 240 and 250 (10 and 50) set the frequency of the waveform; that is how many times a second the waveform will repeat. To lower the frequency, the 50 in line 250 should be increased, as this will increase the delay between each successive change in the value of the DAC's output voltage. Alternatively, the value of 10 in line 240 could be decreased, because this sets the number of individual increases in the period of the waveform. The larger this number, the coarser the waveform will be, but the less time it will take to go through the cycle.

Lines 200, 210, and 220 control the actual function being plotted on the DAC. If any other function is desired, just replace those lines with lines describing the equation (in the form of Y *vs* X) to be used. For example, if a sine wave is to be put out on the DAC, replace these lines with

```
200   LET Y = SIN(X)

210   IF X > 2*PI THEN 120
```

(Note: some BASICs do not use the PI function. If yours does not, replace PI with 3.141592.)

One problem is that BASIC is very slow. This puts a limit on the maximum frequency that can be output from the DAC. The maximum frequency occurs when lines 250 and 260 are completely deleted, and the number in line 240 is the maximum possible. If the resulting frequency is still too slow, you may have to reprogram the sequence in machine language, which is typically about a thousand times faster than BASIC. Still, there will be a maximum frequency of waveforms which will be about one-twentieth of the machine's cycle rate. For frequencies above about 50 kHz or so, this DAC waveform generator is not effective.

A different way of generating waveforms is by table lookup. In the above example, the value of

164

the wave amplitude is to be calculated every time through the cycle. It would be faster to just make these calculations once, and then look up the values from the table. In many cases, a waveform cannot be calculated from an equation, but the function can be plotted on a graph and numbers picked from the graph and put into a table.

For example, the following program could be used to generate a table in Y:

```
1    DIM Y(100)
5    LET R = 100
10   FOR X = 1 TO 255 STEP 10
15   LET I = I + 1
20   LET Y = X*X - 2*X*R
30   IF Y 0 THEN 60
40   LET Y(I) = SQR(Y)
50   NEXT X
60   A = 41024
90   REM PLOT ROUTINE
100  FOR J = 1 TO I
110  POKE (Y(I);A)
120  NEXT J
130  GOTO 100
```

In this program, the values of the amplitude are put into an array Y(I) and called one at a time from a display loop, which is located from lines 100 to 130.

It may take some experimenting with these methods to get the desired waveform. Every machine is different, and each waveform will require different constants to obtain the right frequency and amplitude. Experience is the best teacher with this type of device.

MUSIC GENERATOR

A rather unique application of a waveform generator is the use of the computer and the DAC to produce music. After all, what is music but a series of audio waveforms of particular frequencies and durations? Ideally, the waveforms should be sine waves, but there can be variations on it to produce the effects of different instruments.

All that is needed is an amplifier and speaker hooked to the output of the DAC to produce sound,

and some creative programming to give sound waves of particular frequencies for the notes to be played, and some way of determining if the note has been played for a long enough time.

Later in this chapter, there will be a complete discussion of the ways of playing music with a computer. Let us postpone the discussion until then.

COMPUTER GRAPHICS

Graphics, when applied to a computer, is defined as either the art of letting computers draw pictures, or as the ability of the computer to recognize drawings done by others. The latter is more often called *pattern recognition*. Graphics, as discussed in this work, is defined as the ability of a computer to draw graphs, lines, pictures, or anything except what is contained just in the symbol generator (usually just letters, numbers, and special characters) of the display device.

Graphics is a very important part of a computer's task these days. Most of the "appliance" or "desktop" computers have some sort of graphics capability built in. One of the first personal computers to come with built-in graphics was the old TRS-80 Model 1. It could produce black-or-white, on-or-off graphics with a resolution of 48 vertical blocks by 160 horizontal blocks. The Apple-II increased this range, and added color, as well. The IBM-PC gives up to 15 colors, with a further increase in resolution. The Macintosh can display black-and white graphics up to 512 by 342 pixels on its screen, and the graphics editor *MacPaint* can process an 8 × 10 section 576 by 720 pixels at a time.

Graphics on TV screens is called raster-scan graphics , and uses the line-by-line scanning of the television's picture tube and circuitry. Raster-scan graphics is quite complicated, requiring as of this writing, about $300.00 worth of electronic components to make it work. It involves complex timing circuitry, as well as synchronization signals for both horizontal and vertical parts of the scan. Color adds a rather complex phasing to the signal, as well. Furthermore, the higher the screen resolution, the more complex and expensive the mechanism.

Fortunately, raster-scan is not the only method

of doing graphics with a computer. There is a type of graphics called *vectored graphics* which will work just as well, with surprisingly good resolution, and can even be applied to a hard-copy device for a permanent record of the diagram.

Vectored graphics is currently being used in many of the arcade video games currently on the market. It is primarily used for the faster-action ones, since it is generally quicker than raster-scan graphics.

The only problem with vectored graphics is that it cannot be applied to an ordinary TV monitor without considerable electronics. Special display equipment is needed. But, still, the display equipment can be built or bought used for under $100.00, including the graphics interface.

The display device required is either an oscilloscope with an "X-input" feature (one that disables the sweep circuitry and allows the user to input the value of the X-coordinate by means of a voltage) or an X-Y plotter, which translates the values of two voltages into a position of the plotting pen.

Oscilloscopes can be found advertised for anywhere from about two hundred dollars to several thousand dollars. There are some inexpensive kits or 'scopes on the market for as little as one hundred and fifty dollars. On the other hand, a military surplus shop in a large city may have a whole 'scope for as little as fifty dollars. A high school or junior college may have a collection of outdated 'scopes which they will gladly give to a member of the community who has a good use for it. You don't need to have the sweep circuits or the Z-axis working—just the vertical and horizontal amplifiers. We won't need the trigger circuits, either.

X-Y plotters tend to be a bit more expensive. A good research-quality plotter may cost several thousand dollars. There are plotters made which are developed specifically for computers for as little as three hundred dollars. Again, surplus houses or high schools and colleges may be able to help you out with it. Heathkit has both 'scopes and plotters available in kit form for reasonable prices. At the end of this Chapter, we will discuss how to make an X-Y plotter. The principles used in that case will not necessarily be of use here but can be applied to the same task with a little creative programming.

An oscilloscope, when used in the X-Y mode, places the spot on the screen in a place which corresponds to the value of the voltages put into the X and Y inputs. The higher the X voltage, the farther to the right the spot is. The higher the Y voltage, the farther upwards on the screen the spot stays. The HORIZONTAL and VERTICAL controls on the oscilloscope can be used to set the "zero mark," or position of the spot when the input is zero volts. Most oscilloscopes have an X-input with a sensitivity of 1 volt per centimeter. This means that a change of 1 volt on the input voltage makes the spot travel about 1 centimeter. Since the Y-axis sensitivity is adjustable, it should also be set to 1 volt per centimeter, so that squares look like squares and not rectangles, and circles don't look like ovals. This also means that the inputs should not exceed about 8 volts from zero, so that the pictures don't go beyond the screen. Some adjustment of the range of the voltage source is needed to ensure this.

Once you have a device, such as an oscilloscope, which uses a light spot or pen to indicate a position based on the voltage level of the X and Y inputs, all that is needed is a computer-controlled source of voltages to connect to the inputs.

Sound familiar?

It should—it's our old friend the DAC again, only this time, there is a DAC for each of the two axes. We merely divide the range of the display device into 256 increments in each direction, and assign a number from 0 to 255 to that segment. For example, as in Fig. 5-11, if the zero point for both X and Y is to be the lower, left-hand corner then the point (255,255) is the upper, right-hand, corner. Point (128,128) is the exact center of the display. The zero point is defined as (0,0). The numbers in parentheses indicate the X-coordinate first, then the Y-coordinate, as measured from the lower, left-hand corner. X is horizontal, as we have said, and Y is vertical.

Any point on the display, then, can be represented by a number. We say that, if 255 is the largest number that can be used and 0 is the smallest, the resolution of the display is 256 × 256.

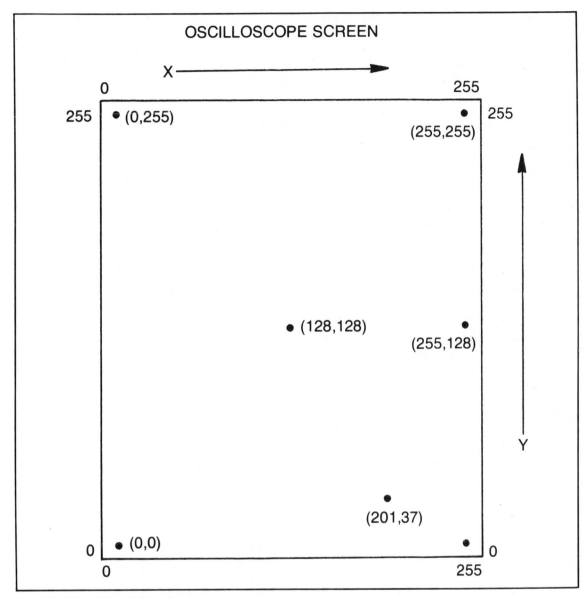

Fig. 5-11. X-Y graphics, 256 × 256.

Such a display is a very good one indeed. Compare this to the TRS-80 raster-scan display of 160 × 48. We can squeeze more points into the display.

There are disadvantages, though. Letters and numbers do not come immediately—they have to be drawn on one line at a time, so simultaneous graphics and data displays are difficult. Also, in the case of an oscilloscope, the display has to be *refreshed* several times a second, which limits the number of points that can be displayed.

In a modern computer, the refresh is taken care of by the video circuitry used for the character displays. In our vectored method, it must be done by the processor.

Nonetheless, a 256 × 256 graphics display is quite easy to build. It only takes two DAC systems, a pair of latches, and some triggering circuitry. The whole circuit is drawn out in Fig. 5-12. Two 74100s are used as 8-bit latches, and the DACs are the same as used before.

The latches are needed because the X and Y axis transitions need to be made at the same time. The way the device works is, the digital value of the position is presented to both DACs at the same time, and then while the new position is calculated

the trace stays in the position and gives off light. This appears as a single spot on the screen. It is the time between transitions that is seen on the screen. If this time were to go to zero, the trace would seem to be a set of continuous lines. We get around this by putting the X data into the X PIA data register, which is itself latched, and then the Y data into the Y PIA data register, which is also latched, and then entering the X and Y data simultaneously into the 74100 display latches by using the CA2 line as a strobe. Notice that both sides of

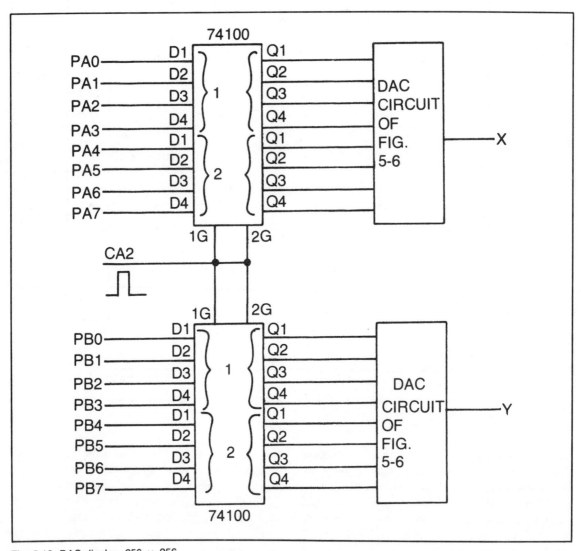

Fig. 5-12. DAC display, 256 × 256.

a PIA are needed, along with a handshake line, to affect a data transition. The DAC sends the data to the new position and displays it while the next point is being calculated.

Since the CA2 line is now needed, it is much more difficult to run the DACs directly from BASIC. Full control of the PIA is needed, as well as a more complex initialization, so it is better to drive the display unit directly from machine language.

One of the best ways to do this is to use a table lookup scheme in machine language, similar to the BASIC table lookup described above. Figure 5-13, presented in flowchart form, gives a program that will perform the table lookup and output the data to the display. The program works by keeping track of three numbers: the address of the start of the table, the number of entries in the table, and the number of the entry being displayed at the moment. The table is organized as a series of X-Y pairs, with the X coordinate first. The program takes the first pair, displays them, gets the second pair, displays them, and so on until the entire set is used; then it starts over. If a one-byte number is used for the number of pairs, up to 255 pairs can be displayed, and the pair number being worked on at the moment can be kept in an internal register. Since there are 256^2 possible pairs on the full display, or 65,536 pairs (more than twice what the whole computer will hold without any programming at all), only 1/256th of the total screen area can be covered. This is usually sufficient when doing line drawings, graphs, and simple charts. For more detailed drawings, a 16-bit arithmetic method must be used. Each data location on the display that is to be illuminated requires two data bytes in memory. As many points can be displayed as you have room for in memory.

While the PIA must be driven from machine language, the data locations from which the X-Y pairs are taken can be loaded from BASIC using the POKE statement, and then the display routine can be called from BASIC using a USER (or EXTERNAL or CALL, depending on your machine) statement to execute machine language.

An example of such a BASIC program, with plenty of remark statements to point out the addresses being used, is given in Table 5-1. I used

a system similar to this and found it to be very effective.

Figure 5-14 shows the example, which is a graph of radiation counts versus radiation energy in a nuclear physics experiment. These are given to show the mathematical plotting capabilities of the X-Y plotting system and the ability of the system to display charts of data. Many other applications are possible, as well, including games with pictures and the drawing of simple cartoons.

X-Y HARDCOPY

The only real difference between an oscilloscope and an X-Y plotter is the speed at which the plotting is to be done. The oscilloscope can easily plot 256 points 30 times a second, whereas the X-Y plotter depends on mechanical servos to position the pen. These servos have a settling time of about one-third second for any significant travel. All that is really needed is to slow the program down enough so that the servos can follow the data. Since most X-Y plotters have high-impedance inputs, a DAC operational amplifier output can easily drive the plotters. The electronics and programming is really no different for an X-Y plotter than for an oscilloscope.

Only two things need to be changed. The first is that the plotting speed must be slowed down. Note in the routine above that there is a provision to test the sense switch (see Chapter 4). If the sense switch is set, the program enters a delay loop which delays the display of the next data pair by a half second, to allow the servos to settle. Also, at the end of the routine, it prevents the whole display from being refreshed, so it won't plot it all over again. A simple sense switch allows the same program to be used for the oscilloscope and the X-Y plotter drivers.

The second problem is a little more subtle. A plotter, when plotting, draws a line from one point to another. The oscilloscope relys on its *not* plotting a line when going from one point to the next. With an oscilloscope, we are interested only in the resting points in between. When using a plotter, sometimes we will want the pen to be in contact with the paper when traveling from one point to the

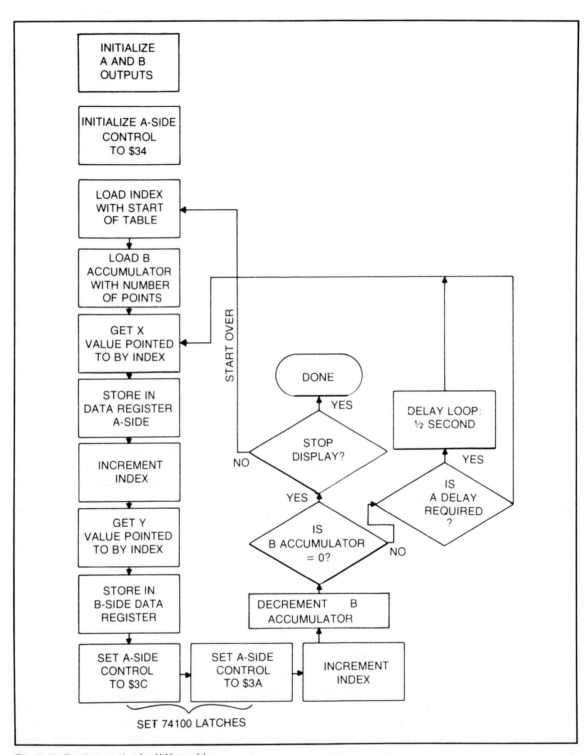

Fig. 5-13. Plotting routine for X-Y graphics.

Table 5-1. A BASIC Program to Run the X-Y Plotter.

```
5     REM PLOT4 X Y PLOTTER
10    DIM X(100), Y(100)
20    REM ASSUMES MACHINE LANGUAGE DRIVER SUBROUTINE
30    REM LOCATED AT $DFOO = 57088 DECIMAL
40    REM AND "USER" POINTER AT $0030 = 48 DECIMAL
50    REM N = NUMBER OF POINTS
60    REM STORED AT $DEO2 = 56834 DECIMAL
70    REM X AND Y MUST BE INTEGERS 0 TO 255
80    REM START OF TABLE POINTER STORED AT $DEOO = 56832 DECIMAL
90    REM TABLE ITSELF BEGINS AT $DDOO = 56576 DECIMAL

100   REM SET UP USER POINTER
110   REM 57088 = 256 × 223 + 0
120   POKE (223,48)
130   POKE (0,49)

140   REM SET UP START OF TABLE AND NUMBER OF POINTS COUNTERS
150   REM 56576 = 256 × 221 + 0
160   POKE (221,56832)
170   POKE (0,56833)
180   POKE (N,56834)

200   REM STORE POINTS IN TABLE
210   LET A = 56576
220   FOR I = 0 TO N-1
230   POKE (X(I),A+2*I)
240   POKE (Y(I),A+2*I+1)
250   NEXT I

300   DISPLAY POINTS
310   LET A = USER(A)
320   GOTO 310
```

next, and sometimes we will want the pen up. Most plotters have a pen-control input, which can be controlled by a signal voltage from one of the control devices described in Chapter 4. All that is needed is to add a third data point to each pair, called the Z axis, or the Z data, and if any bit in the Z data is set, keep the pen down. If all bits are 0s, lift the pen up off the paper. This way, each data point needs *three* data locations instead of two. The change in the programming is very insignificant. The new flowchart is given in Fig. 5-15.

Under certain circumstances, a stripchart recorder can be used in place of an X-Y recorder for the plotting of graphs. The stripchart recorder is a modification of the X-Y recorder where the X-axis is always time, and there is one, and only one, Y point for each X point or value. That is, if there are two values of Y corresponding to any value of X, this method cannot be used. Furthermore, there must always be a value of Y for each X, so that a continuous line is plotted.

If these rather restrictive conditions can be met, then the stripchart recorder, or X-T plotter can be used. Simply output the Y values in increasing order of X (sort the pairs by increasing X value) and do so one at a time, with the same time between each one. The stripchart recorder will happily plot Y *vs* X (as T) and draw a graph of the values.

PADDLE POSITION SENSOR AND JOYSTICKS

We have spoken above about inputs for control situations. The topic of sense switches and event sensors has been discussed at some length. But these are all digital types of inputs—the computer measures either an "on" or an "off."

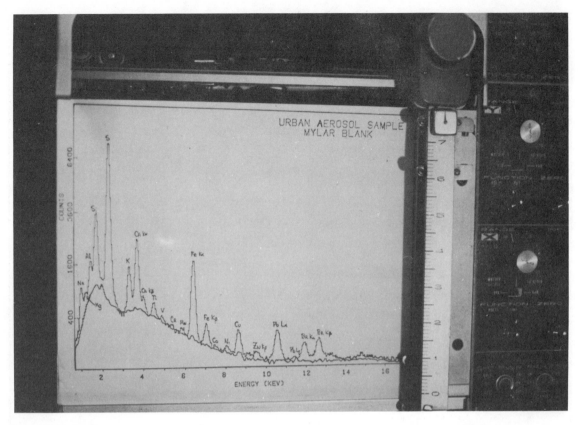

Fig. 5-14. Example plot.

In many situations, we really need to be able to more or less continuously adjust an input. We could, of course, enter values from the keyboard. Most games do, in fact, exactly this. Wouldn't it be a lot more convenient to be able to enter data by means of a potentiometer or joystick? Then we could see the results of the change immediately and adjust it more as needed. This type of situation is called *real-time interaction*. Video games in an arcade are examples of real-time interaction with a microprocessor and a graphics display.

There are two ways to measure the position of a paddle or joystick. Paddles and joysticks are generally just potentiometers in one form or another, and we can measure the resistance of the resistor, or we can measure the voltage at the paddle's center terminal. Measuring voltages is a little more complex than measuring resistances. We

will spend much of the remainder of this chapter on the topic.

For now, let's concentrate on the measurement of the paddle's resistance at its center terminal to ground. Resistance is a handy concept. All sorts of things can be controlled by a variable resistance. For example, we can control the frequency of an oscillator, or we can control the length of time that a timer is on.

Consider Fig. 5-16. There are two 555 timers. One is used as an astable multivibrator, for a source of pulses, and the other is used as a monostable multivibrator, or timer. The astable is running all the time. The monostable is started by a pulse from the CA2 line, and the length of time it is on is controlled by the setting of the paddle potentiometer. The two signals are gated together with an AND gate, to form a series of pulses into the computer

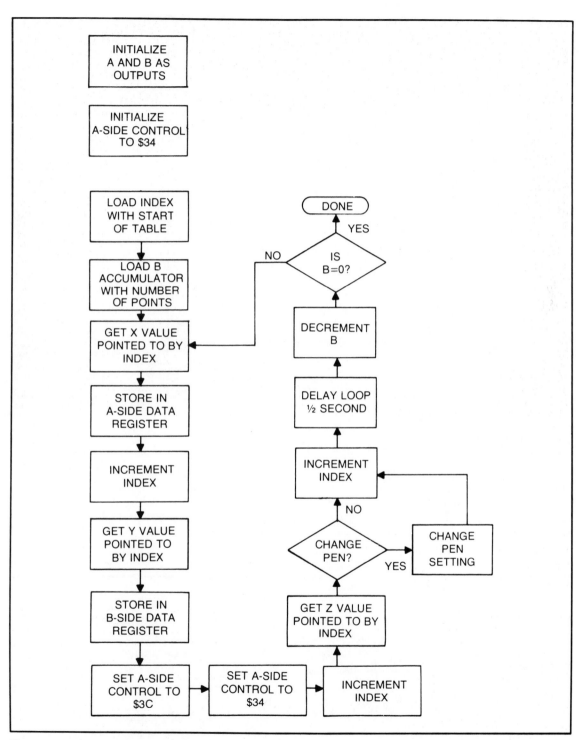

Fig. 5-15. Plotting routine with pen control.

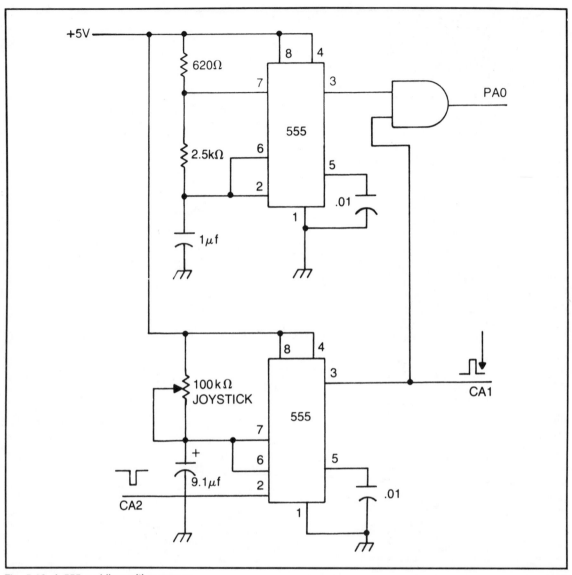

Fig. 5-16. A 555 paddle-position sensor.

put port. The computer counts the number of positive going transitions at the input port bit, and senses whether the timer has completed its cycle. The larger the resistance of the paddle, the longer the timer is active, and the more pulses will be counted. When the timer has completed its cycle, the CA1 line changes state, and the computer can sense that the timing is done and end the count.

The count left in the computer is a binary num-ber which represents the setting of the paddle. The paddle must be calibrated by adjusting the other variable resistor in the circuit so that, when the paddle is set at its maximum resistance, the computer will read just 254 counts, no more, no less. Actually, it might be easier to let the maximum be 250 counts. This is usually sufficient resolution. Check to make sure that the paddle gives a zero reading at the opposite end of the setting.

Only one 555 timer is shown. Since there are eight possible data inputs to a PIA port side, up to eight paddle sensors can be wired to a single port. All can be run off the same CA1 and CA2 lines, and all use the same astable multivibrator 555. All that is needed is a separate timer and AND gate for each. The program must mask out all the bits of the unwanted paddles and count only the one being used. Only one paddle can be read at a time this way, but several can be read in a row to get "simultaneous" reading on many paddles. Since it only takes a few milliseconds to read a paddle, all eight can be read several times a second.

Figure 5-17 is a flowchart of a program which will read one paddle. The program starts the timer by putting out a CA2 pulse and then counts the number of positive transitions on a data line until the CA1 line undergoes a transition, which tells the computer to stop counting. Note that the other bits are masked by the AND statement, so that only one line is read at a time. You will have to supply the code to do the proper ANDing. To read bit 0, the input data must be ANDed with $01; to read bit 7, AND the data with $80.

The above is not the only way to read the paddle. The paddle could control the frequency of the oscillator, and the length of time the timer is on could be fixed. This method is a little less accurate than the one given above, but it faster, because the length of time the timer is on is fixed and may be fixed at a very short time, if the frequency is high. The 555 timer will not work well over more than a voltage-range factor of 10 for one adjustment, due to internal resistances.

Lastly, for proper operation and stability, the voltages of the 555 supplies should remain very stable. Use as good quality voltage regulators as you can afford. The better the voltage stability, the better the stability of the data. The supply voltage should remain constant to at least 1.0 percent, and to 0.4 percent if possible. See Fig. 5-5 for some examples.

The use of paddles can add interest to many programs, make them more responsive,or make games more fun. Paddles can be connected to a computer with graphics capabilities, and the paddles can be used to draw pictures on the screen or

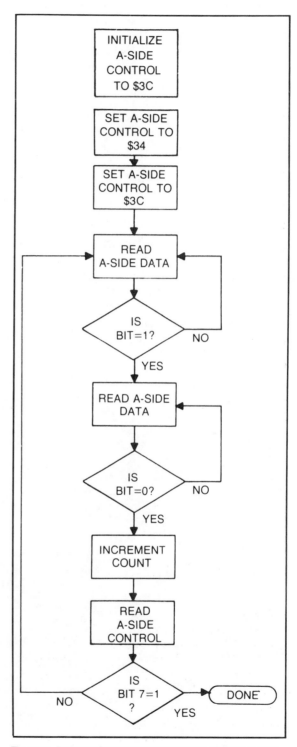

Fig. 5-17. Program flowchart to read paddle-position sensor.

to position a pointer. In games, a paddle can be a throttle for a machine, to speed it up or slow it down. They can be used as a real-time input to set the speed of a set of computations. For example, a paddle can be used to set a timer's delay time, or how many calculations of a given type are to be done during a loop. It can be used to adjust the number of times per second a pulse is put out over a control line, or adjust the data rate of serial communications.

Joysticks (Fig. 5-18) are two potentiometers tied together so that the position of the "wand" gives different resistances on each of the two pots. Generally, they are treated so that if the wand is all the way at the top, the joystick gives a maximum resistance on one pot, and minimum at the bottom. All the way to the right is a maximum on the other, and all the way to the left is a minimum. The position of the wand is then given as two "coordinates" in resistance, one in the X direction and one in the Y direction, which are then converted to binary numbers by the paddle position sensor.

A joystick can be used with graphics to be used as a pointer, or to draw pictures. It can be used to rotate a spacecraft or to fly a plane in a video game. They can be used to control devices that are being controlled by the computer. Imagine a robot being controlled by a computer, which is in turn controlled by the programmer. All sorts of real-time interaction possibilities exist.

Joysticks and paddles are also extremely effective when used with sense switches or event sensors. In a computer game, for example, the handle of the joystick can be used to position a spacecraft, while a pushbutton on an event sensor can be used to "fire the laser cannon." Alternatively, a paddle or joystick can be used to select a particular set of data in a graphics display, and the button used to tell the computer "examine and process this data," referring to the one pointed to by the pointer at that instant.

It is not even necessary to connect a sense switch or event sensor to use a pushbutton. If you have extra input bits that are not being used, just

Fig. 5-18. A joystick.

connect them up with a resistor that is fixed. When the button is pushed, have the button short the resistor to zero. This is just a paddle sensor with two positions—maximum resistance and zero resistance.

VOLTAGE MEASUREMENTS

Voltage measurement is called analog-to-digital conversion. Analog-to-digital converters, or ADCs, are among the most complex hardware and software tasks to be done on a computer. The very mention of the process has been known to strike terror in the hearts of many a computer hobbyist. Consider the fact that we must discuss resolution, conversion speed, stability and precision of the device, the comparator, and the power supply, sample and hold techniques, and clock frequencies. Add to this the fact that the better ADCs are connected to the computer by an interrupt processing, and the new hardware hacker can run from the room screaming.

It is true that there are a lot of factors to keep in mind when doing analog-to-digital conversion. It is true that the hardware and software are among the most difficult of all processes done on a computer. Yet analog-to-digital conversion need not be feared. The process can be involved, but it can also be simple if your needs are simple.

Conversion of voltages to digital information is one of the most useful of all computer processes. The ADC can be used as a paddle or joystick position sensor, as above, and it can also be used to take information directly from measurement devices and transducers. The ADC is a godsend to a scientist, for he can then program the computer to actually perform his experiment for him, take his data, analyze the results, and print or store them as necessary. ADCs are also used in speech recognition. Consider also the fact that a multichannel ADC could be used with a variety of instruments to measure data about the local weather (measuring air pressure, wind speed, direction, humidity, temperature, and total rainfall to date) and be able to come up with a prediction for the weather for the next 24 hours. An ADC can be used as an (albeit expensive) event sensor. ADCs have been used in character recognition, picture processing, radar pictures, image intensifying, nuclear physics, and many more tasks.

Analog-to-digital conversion is really taking a voltage level and converting the magnitude of that voltage into a binary digital number which represents that voltage on a one-to-one linear basis. A voltage which is twice as large as another should result in a binary number twice as large as the former.

There are several means of going about the conversion process. The dual 555 resistance measurement system described in the last section is a primitive type of ADC. The 555 counter illustrates the difference between DACs and ADCs. With a DAC, you just put binary into the inputs and analog comes out the other end within a few nanoseconds. With an ADC it isn't so simple—the conversion process takes time, and usually requires that something be counted or processed.

Let us spend a little time on a discussion of the various methods of analog to digital conversion, and the relative advantages and disadvantages of each. There are five basic methods.

Flash Encoding

The fastest method is called flash encoding. In this method, the input voltage to be converted is compared to a reference voltage, and the output is a 1 if the voltage is higher than the reference, and 0 if it is lower. Many such comparators are used, each with slightly different reference voltages. The place where 0s turn into 1s is the digital voltage, which is then converted into binary. Four-bit resolution requires 16 comparators; 8-bit resolution needs 256.

There are many problems with the flash encoder. It is far too complex to be used for any more than three-bit resolution. The slightly different voltage reference values are tricky to derive, and the binary conversion electronics are very complex. It is, however, very fast, with conversion times measured in fractions of a microsecond.

The flash encoder illustrates the basic purpose of an ADC. The whole idea is to convert an analog voltage to a digital number. We do this by dividing the range of the analog signal into lots of smaller ranges—usually some number which is a power of two—and assigning each of these smaller ranges to a particular binary number. Then, if a signal falls within the range of one of these small mini-ranges, we automatically assign the binary number to it.

Note that this process is very similar to the process used for the DAC signals above, only in reverse. For example, if the maximum range of the signal is 10V, and we are using an ADC with a resolution of 8 bits, then the 10 volts is divided into 2^8, or 256 mini-ranges, each approximately 0.04 volts wide. Binary number 00000000 corresponds to the range from 0 volts to 0.04 volts, the number 00000001 corresponds to 0.04 volts to 0.08 volts, and so on all the way to the number 11111111, corresponding for the range from 9.96 volts to 10.00 volts.

Again, as with DACs, the more bits of resolution, the higher the precision has to be maintained on all components. An ADC will usually have a comparator. The comparator has to be precise enough to distinguish between two voltages no farther apart than the precision of the ADC. In an 8-bit ADC with a 10-volt range, as above, the comparator must be able to distinguish between two voltages only 0.04 volts apart. Also, many ADCs have a clock in them. The frequency of the clock must be good to the same precision as the ADC. In the example above, the clock's frequency must be accurate to within 0.4 percent. Also, the higher the frequency of the clock, the faster the comparator must be. If a clock frequency of 50 MHz is used, a 741 operational amplifier cannot be used as either a comparator or an internal amplifier. The 741 is not reliable above 20 kHz. For frequencies above 1 MHz, the 301 operational amplifier is a good choice. There are also, in ramp-type ADCs, a source of linearly increasing voltage. This voltage must increase linearly with the precision of the whole device. Such linearity is very hard to achieve. It is generally done by using a constant voltage and integrating that constant voltage with an operational-amplifier integrator. The linearity of the output ramp is only as good as the quality of the components used to make it. A precision voltage

source is a must—simple Zener-diode references are not precise enough, nor are the usual voltage regulators. Fortunately, there are good precision reference sources available that work much like voltage regulators, for reasonable prices. There are also ADC's that use a type of DAC feedback, such as the successive-approximation type. These consist essentially of a DAC and a comparator, with some logic. Everything we've said about DACs earlier in this chapter applies to these types of devices.

Sampling

Precision and stability are not the only difficulties with ADCs. There are also a number of problems associated with sampling. For example, how often should the ADC do a conversion? In some cases, the answer is trivial. There are cases where we want to determine the height of a pulse that arrives at the ADC. In this case, the arrival of the pulse itself acts as a strobe to tell us that there is data to be analyzed. Or, a separate pulse can arrive to act as a strobe in the same way. This is called on-demand conversion, and is used in pulse height analysis. The computer may need to make a measurement of some parameter at a given time. An internal clock could, for example, cause an interrupt in the computer and allow it to perform a measurement of the outside air temperature every hour. In a dedication system used for security purposes, a switch on a window can be sampled as often as the computer can do so, just as a keyboard can be sampled for an input. This is just our old friend, polling, applied to data conversion. It's just another way to let the computer know when to do something. In this case, it tells the computer to go ahead and make a conversion.

These methods are all right if the input being sampled is a dc signal. The computer can sample the input at every point in a program loop, as in a video game. ("What's the setting of the throttle, captain?") Dc voltages, by definition, don't change. As we've said before, though, an analog-to-digital conversion takes time. It may take several microseconds in an advanced ADC, or in a simple ADC, even several milliseconds. What do you do if the voltage you're trying to measure changes while you're trying to measure it? How often do you have to measure it to get it right?

As an example, take speech recognition. Speech is a series of tones which appear as an ac signal in a microphone. To be effective in speech recognition, you have to know the amplitude, frequency, and duration of the various tones to be able to recognize a word. Speech recognition circuits and programs are very complex for this reason, and the process is still in the primitive stages.

The measurement of ac signals, however, is reasonably well advanced. Only two questions have to be answered in order to determine the frequency and amplitude of an ac signal. "How often do we need to sample the signal to determine its frequency?" and, "What do we do about the fact that the signal changes while it's being measured?"

The first is illustrated by Fig. 5-19. The binary number representing the signal is a value of that signal at one point in time, called a *sample*. Many such samples within a one-wave period will give us an excellent idea of the shape—and therefore the frequency—of the wave. On the other hand, fewer samples in a period will still give us an indication of the frequency, so long as the samples have the same frequency, more or less, as the wave. The question is, how few samples per period is enough to let us know that we have the correct frequency for the waveform?

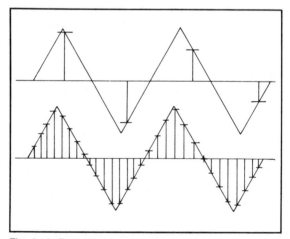

Fig. 5-19. Fast and slow sample rates.

The answer lies in the sampling theorem: *We must sample at least twice as fast as the fastest occurring signal in the system.* A rough rule of thumb is, in order to truly fit the sampled data to an equation representing the input waveform, we must sample ten times as fast as the fastest occurring signal in the system. Ten data values in one cycle will surely let us be able to determine both the frequency and amplitude.

The second problem is a little more complicated. To determine an ac frequency, we need only take data more often. What do we do about data that changes while we are trying to find out what it is? As an example, consider an ADC that has a conversion time of 5 milliseconds. Now try to determine the amplitude of a signal that is a sine wave of 100 Hz. The period of the signal is 10 milliseconds, so two samples can be taken in one period, meeting the needs as outlined in the previous paragraphs. But during that 5 milliseconds, the signal can go from zero to maximum and back to zero again!

We need a way to stop the changes of the signal so that we can look at what it was at a given instant. The analog input to a converter must be stable and constant for the entire length of time it takes to complete the conversion. This may be accomplished by using a *sample and hold* circuit. The usual method is to hold the voltage value in a high-quality capacitor for the few milliseconds or microseconds it takes to do the conversion, and then reset the capacitor. These circuits generally consist of a capacitor, a few diodes and transistors, and an operational amplifier for current buffering. Figure 5-20 shows two circuits that can be used as sample-and-hold amplifiers. Each has a data input and output and also a "sample" or "hold" logic input which allows the device to keep the output at the value of the input when the "hold" signal was first received. Most of these amplifiers are quite simple and will do an adequate job for most applications. They are generally used between the device whose voltage is to be measured and the ADC which does the measuring. A version of the sample and hold, called the *peak sensor* will be used later in this chapter.

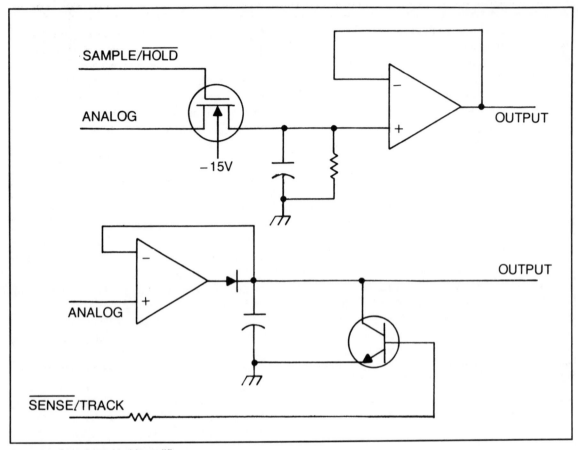

Fig. 5-20. Sample-and-hold amplifiers.

A SIMPLE, SINGLE-RAMP ADC

The single-ramp ADC, also known as the integrator ADC, is the easiest to build of all the ADCs, and gives reasonable, if slow,performance. Many of the functions which are normally done by hardware can be taken over by the microprocessor to save costs.

Figure 5-21 is a block diagram of a single-ramp ADC. The data signal comes into an amplifier which is used as a comparator, and the conversion process begins by starting a ramp generator. The start command can be the result of an on-demand strobe or a computer command. While the ramp voltage is less than the data signal, the gate allows pulses from a clock to pass through to a counter. When the ramp rises to a value equal to the data input, the comparator changes state and turns off

the gate, ending the count. The computer reads the count, which is the binary number corresponding to the number of clock pulses that have passed. The larger the input voltage, the more time it will take the linear ramp to rise to meet the input voltage, and the more pulses will be counted. Figure 5-22 shows the signals at the various points in the ADC. The ramp's rate of increase has to be adjusted so that at the maximum allowed input voltage, the number of pulses that are allowed to pass is the maximum number that can be counted by the counter.

It is extremely important in this type of ADC that the frequency of the clock be stable, the comparator be precise, and the ramp be linear. A crystal-controlled clock is best, and good quality comparators are relatively easy to come by. The

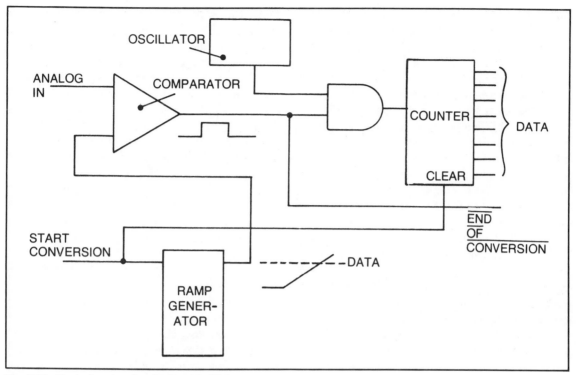

Fig. 5-21. Block diagram of a single-ramp ADC.

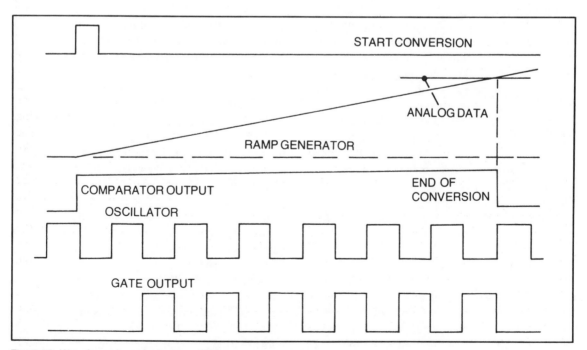

Fig. 5-22. Waveforms in a single-ramp ADC.

only real problem is the ramp generator. There are essentially two ways of doing a ramp generator. One is to charge a capacitor with a constant current, so that the charge that is placed on the capacitor is a linear function of time. The other way is to take a *constant* voltage (very precisely known) and integrate it with an operational amplifier integrator. The time-integral of a constant is a linearly increasing function of time, or a ramp! In either case, a transistor should be provided across the capacitor to allow the ramp generator to be reset by shorting (discharging) the capacitor.

The counter in this type of ADC can be a series of 7493 ripple counters or 74193 synchronous counters. Either one will give good performance and are relatively cheap. The outputs are in binary and are easily interfaced to a PIA. They are good to about 30 MHz, so fast clocks can be used. (A note about fast clocks—the faster the clock, the more precise the comparator must be.)

Another way of doing the counting is simply to let the computer count it and store it in an internal register, or even let the computer be both the counter *and* the clock! Such a procedure is perfectly acceptable as long as interrupts are not being used. The reason is that, in order for the computer to be used as a clock, the number of computer clock cycles in each of the timing loops must be *precisely* known. Interrupts take the computer out of the timing cycle, and the exact nature of the interrupt processor may not be known.

Two separate circuits are given here for the single-ramp ADC, one very simple, but accurate, circuit which can be made with a minimum parts count and will give satisfactory performance with dc signals. The other is essentially the same, but the counter and clock are external to the computer and may be used with other equipment that uses interrupts or may be handled with interrupts itself for on-demand conversions.

In the first case, in Fig. 5-23, the start-of-conversion signal is provided by the computer. It essentially just clears and starts the ramp generator. The computer then monitors the output of the comparator to see when a state change has taken place and keeps track of the number of times it has

polled the output of the comparator. This count of the times through the polling loop is the actual count of the ramp timing. When the comparator signals that the conversion is done, the count stops, and the number of times through the loop becomes the binary number which corresponds to the actual count or analog input.

Note that the same ramp generator can service several comparators.If you have eight input bits on a PIA side, the only additions to the circuit needed for an eight-input ADC is seven more comparators. The LM339 integrated circuit contains a very good general-purpose comparator, and there are four such comparators in a package. For an eight-input ADC, all you need is the ramp generator and two LM339s. Of course, only one PIA bit can be polled at a time, and, therefore, only one input can be converted at a time.

The conversion time on the ADC depends on the system clock rate of your particular computer and the number of instructions your machine must execute to perform the polling/timing loop. For a 6800 machine with a 875-kHz clock, a full-scale conversion will take a little less than seven milliseconds.

A flowchart diagram of the program used to do the conversion for the circuit is given in Fig. 5-24. Note the use of the data location called INTRUP. It is cleared at the beginning of the conversion and tested to see if it is zero at the end. On the surface, this seems ridiculous. However, its purpose is to determine if an interrupt has occurred during the timing cycle. If your system uses interrupts, the interrupt service routine should set any bit of the location INTRUP to a 1 before concluding its routine. Then the ADC service routine will know that an interrupt has occurred and start the conversion over again, because the count will be invalid.

A more hardware-intensive approach to the single-ramp ADC is shown in Fig. 5-25. Here, two 7493s are used as binary counters for a 1-MHz clock. The system clock of your computer could be used in place of the crystal-controlled clock shown. The conversion process is still started by the computer though CA2, but now all eight of the data inputs are used for binary data input. The computer

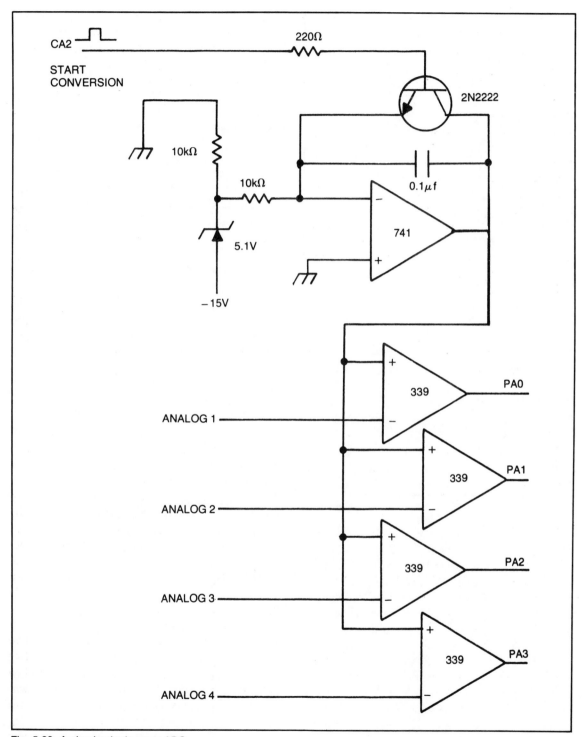

Fig. 5-23. A simple single-ramp ADC.

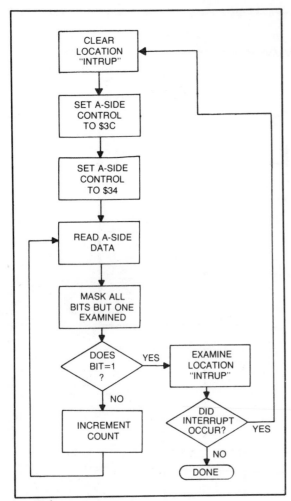

Fig. 5-24. Program flowchart for the simple single-ramp ADC.

just reads the binary count off the 7493s. The output of the comparator is converted to TTL levels and sent to the computer through the CA1 input as an end-of-conversion signal. Instead of polling the data bit, now the CA1 bit of the PIA's control register is polled. The start-of-conversion pulse (CA2) has to both start the ramp and clear the counter. The CA1 input can , if you wish, be configured to cause an interrupt, so that other processing can take place while waiting for the converter to finish its task.

The flowchart of the service program is given in Fig. 5-26. Essentially, it starts the process through CA2, then waits for CA1 to change state

and reads the data.

The single-ramp ADC can do anything that is desired of an ADC. It can be used as a paddle sensor, with a source of voltage so that the center terminal of the paddle gives a voltage that is proportional to the setting of the paddle and to the voltage source. It can be used for data acquisition. It can be used as a voltmeter for an electronics shop. It can be used to measure the outputs of any of the several types of transducers discussed earlier in this chapter, so long as the output of the transducer is a voltage within the range of the ADC. It cannot make direct measurements of resistance, capacitance, or inductance, but it can measure voltage changed as a result of changes in these quantities.

The major problem with the single-ramp ADC is that it is slow. The higher the voltage being measured, the slower it is. The ADC must laboriously count "one, two, three . . . done!" An ADC with a 10-bit resolution must count all the way to 512 just to get to a voltage which is *half* of its maximum value! Counting of large numbers, even with a fast clock, takes time.

A SIMPLE ADC USING A DVM CHIP

An improvement over the single-ramp ADC uses the double-ramp method. In this type of converter, the ramp is started the same as before, but now the ramp is allowed to continue until the counter reaches its maximum value. During this time, the input voltage charges a capacitor. The time it takes to overflow the counter is well known. The charge on the capacitor at the end of this time is a linear function of the input voltage. The higher the input voltage, the more charge on the capacitor. At this point, the overflow signal from the counter starts a discharge of the capacitor at a constant, known rate. The time it takes to discharge the capacitor all the way to zero is measured by resetting the counter and counting the number of clock pulses it takes before the charge goes to zero. The reason this is called dual-slope, or double-ramp, is obvious—the conversion takes a charge and a discharge of a capacitor.

The dual ramp method is somewhat more com-

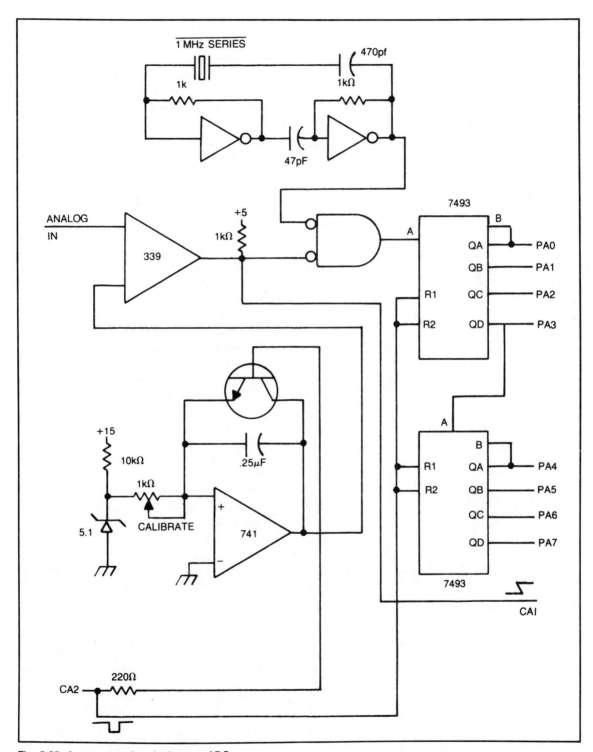

Fig. 5-25. A more complex single-ramp ADC.

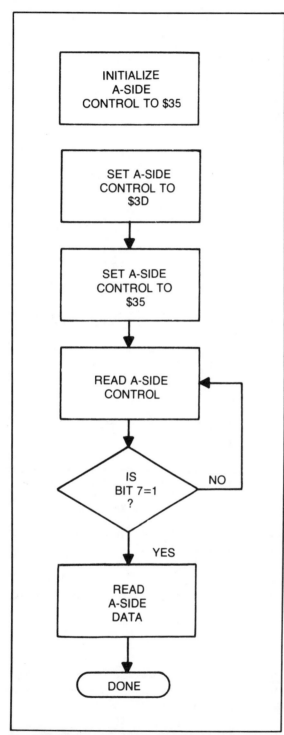

INITIALIZE
A-SIDE
CONTROL TO $35

SET A-SIDE
CONTROL TO
$3D

SET A-SIDE
CONTROL TO
$35

READ A-SIDE
CONTROL

IS
BIT 7=1
?

NO

YES

READ
A-SIDE
DATA

DONE

Fig. 5-26. Reading the ADC in Fig. 5-25.

plicated when viewed from a standpoint of discrete components, or even functional blocks. However, the dual-slope ADC is a popular method of determining voltages in digital voltmeter (DVM) circuits. So much so, that there are many DVM integrated circuits on the market that can be used directly as ADCs with a computer.

A good choice for a DVM chip to be used as an ADC with a computer is the Motorola MC14433. This is a 3 1/2-digit chip, roughly corresponding to a resolution of 12 bits. It uses a modified dual-slope conversion method and is very accurate in its conversion. As with most DVM chips, however, it tends to be rather slow. The number of conversions that can be performed every second is a function of the resistor connected between pins 11 and 12. A 68K resistor will cause about 25 conversions a second.

Figure 5-27 is a diagram of a circuit that uses the MC14433 as an ADC. A precision reference source is needed to supply a constant voltage to the device. Any of several chips can be used for this purpose, including the Motorola MC1403U or the AD584. The latter should be configured to provide 2.5V. The 1403 gives a voltage precise to within about 7 millivolts, and the 584 will be accurate to its programmed value within one millivolt. Neither one can supply more than about 10 mA of current and remain precise.

The analog input voltage is connected to pin 3 of the MC14433. The device has its own sample-and-hold amplifier inside. If the DVM is to be connected to the A-side of a PIA for input, the CA1 line is used as an end-of-conversion signal, and the CA2 line can be used as a start conversion output. These are connected to the DVM through a 7474 flip-flop for proper timing of the signals.

There are nine outputs from the DVM chip. One of these outputs, pin 15, is an overrange signal, to indicate that the signal to be converted is beyond the range of the DVM. It is not really needed if the device is to be used with voltages always within its range. If desired, it can be put into the computer through another input bit of another PIA. The other outputs are all TTL compatible, and will drive one TTL load. For proper operation,

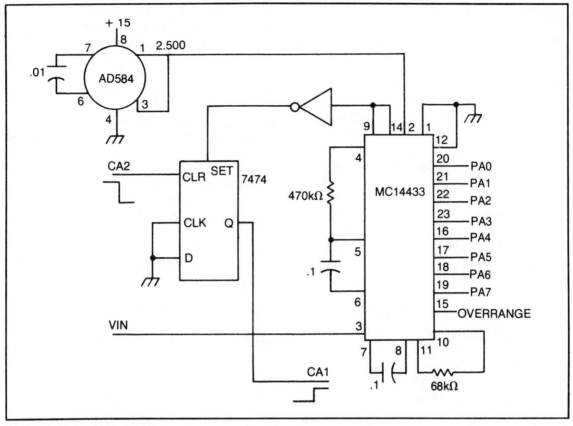

Fig. 5-27. A dual-slope DVM ADC.

they should be buffered through a 74LS04 inverter to the input port. The major problem with using this chip is that the outputs are *not* in binary. They are a mixture of serial and parallel data, in a BCD format. There are four digit select lines, and four data lines. The data lines are in BCD, giving the value of the particular digit being displayed at the time. The digit-select lines tell which digit is being "displayed" at the digit-data outputs.

Bit 7 contains the information for DS1, the most significant half-digit. It becomes available immediately after the end-of-conversion pulse becomes active. If Q3 is a 1, it indicates that the digit being displayed (the most significant digit) is a "1." Remember that this is a 3 1/2 digit DVM—it can measure from – 1.999 volts to + 1.999 volts. The most significant digit is really a half digit—it can only be a 0 or a 1, where the other three digits can

read from 0 to 9. Notice also that it is bipolar. If Q2 is high during the display of the most significant digit, it means that the input voltage is negative. After DS1 becomes inactive, it automatically moves to the next most significant digit, or DS2 (bit 6). The BCD code for the value of bit 6 is displayed on bits 0 through 3. Then the third digit, and the fourth, are displayed. The DVM is designed to interface to a time-multiplexed display, so the pattern will repeat if the computer misses it the first time.

A range of – 1.999 to + 1.999 volts is not always very useful. A voltage-divider circuit is provided on the input of the DVM chip to extend the range by a factor of 10. This has the effect of moving the decimal point over to the right by one digit, so that if the display reads 1137, it means 11.37 volts, not 1.137 volts.

Software is provided for the DVM chip in Fig. 5-28. The procedure is essentially, start the conversion by pulsing CA2, then poll the control register until it is seen that the conversion is complete on CA1. Then wait for each of the digit-select lines to become active, and read the BCD data from the data lines. Store the data, converting to binary form if desired, and go on. Many BASIC programs have BCD arithmetic, so it might be better if the DVM is to be used with BASIC just to leave it in BCD form. Machine-language programs are probably better off converting to binary.

Again, as with most ramp-type ADCs, the conversion process is slow. The circuit described will work well for dc measurements or, since it contains a sample-and-hold amplifier, for low-frequency ac measurements. Also, the dual-slope converter has more noise immunity than the single-ramp ADC.

SUCCESSIVE-APPROXIMATION ADC

To combat the lack of speed of the ramp-type or integrator-type ADC, the successive-approximation ADC was developed. This ingenious device can perform an 8-bit conversion in only 8 clock cycles, compared with as many as 256 (128 average) for a single-ramp device.

The successive-approximation ADC works, in general, as follows: Instead of dividing the voltage range into 2^n smaller mini-ranges, where n is the number of bits of resolution of the ADC, it divides it into only two. It then determines if the input voltage is above or below the dividing line of these two ranges and sets or clears a data bit accordingly. Then it takes the half-range the input voltage falls into and divides that into two pieces, and repeats the process for as many bits of resolution as is desired. Each "try" takes only one clock cycle. For 8 bits, this needs only 8 cycles. The successive approximation method always takes the same amount of time, no matter what the value of the input voltage.

If your computer already has a good-quality DAC, then it can be turned into a successive-approximation ADC by the addition of only a single comparator on a single bit of an input port. A specific example using the MC1408L8 DAC de-

vised earlier in this chapter is shown in Fig. 5-29. The analog input signal is directed into one input of a 339 comparator, and the output to a single input bit of a port. An output port is connected to an 8-bit DAC, whose analog output is the other input of the comparator. When a signal is received, a conversion must be made, the number 10000000 is placed into the DAC. If the output of the comparator shows that the input signal is greater than the DAC's output, the number is kept as a first approximation. If the input signal is less than the DAC's signal, the approximation is cleared to 00000000. Next, the "1" is moved to the right by one digit, and tried again. If the first approximation was 10000000, the second will try 11000000. If the first approximation was 00000000, the second will try 01000000. Again the comparator is consulted to see if the input signal is greater or less than the DAC's output. If greater, the 1 is kept, if less, the 1 is turned to a 0. Then the next bit is tried, going on and on through bits of less and less significance, until all 8 bits have been tried. This try-it-and-see process can be done by a chip called a successive-approximation register, or performed under software control. In any case, the DAC soon gives an output whose value is within one bit resolution of the input signal, and the last trial becomes the binary equivalent of the analog input. The output of the DAC "sneaks up" on the input signal in a manner very much like that shown in Fig. 5-30. The flowchart of the program is given in Fig. 5-31. It follows the procedure outlined above.

Successive approximation ADCs are quite fast. Instead of conversion times in milliseconds, as in ramp-type ADCs, conversion times can be as little as a few microseconds. For the above example, with software doing the work, the conversion time can be only a hundred microseconds with a typical microprocessor.

AN ADVANCED ADC
FOR MULTIPLE CONVERSIONS

Ideally, an ADC should not use any processing time other than to get the data from the ADC and store it in the location desired. In the example above, we have saved on hardware by using soft-

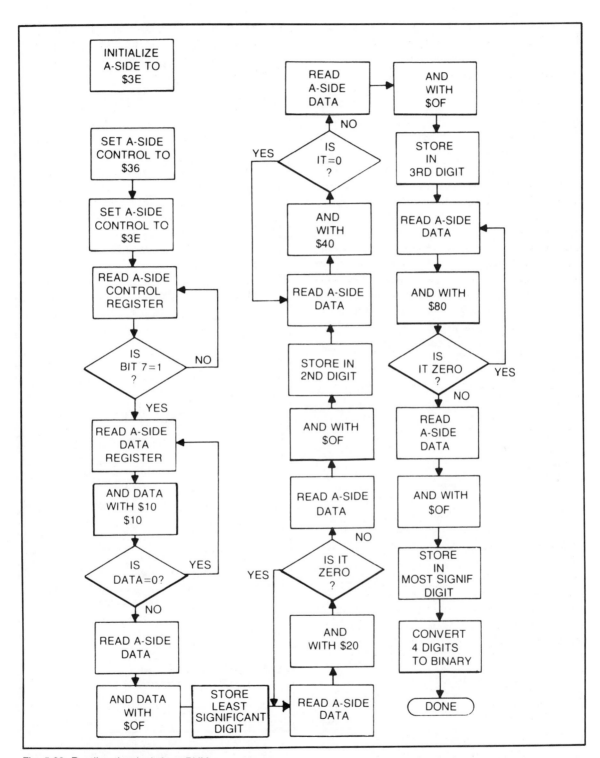

Fig. 5-28. Reading the dual-slope DVM.

189

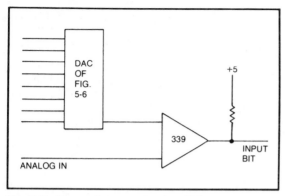

Fig. 5-29. Successive-approximation ADC.

ware to do most of the work. If our application is to be such that thousands of conversions are required every second, and the processor needs to be doing something else, like displaying the data on a graphics display, while it is not processing inputs, then we need an ADC whose functions are all done by hardware. Naturally, such an ADC requires a larger parts count.

As long as we have to spend a lot of time designing and building a more complex device, we might as well have it include all the features that we could want. Let's take a look at a "wish list" of some desirable features in an ADC.

1. At least eight bits of resolution
2. A conversion time less than 100 microseconds
3. Able to cause interrupts in the computer
4. Computer may start the conversion
5. External devices may start the conversion

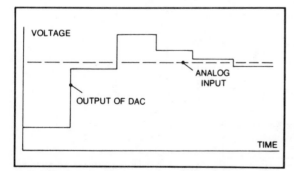

Fig. 5-30. Output of DAC vs time in Fig. 5-29.

6. More than one input, selectable by the computer or by the external devices
7. Sample-and-hold amplifier with peak sensing

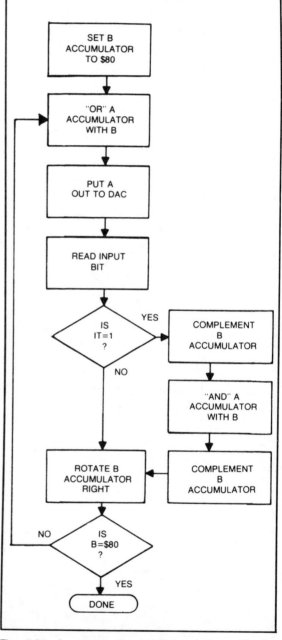

Fig. 5-31. A program for reading voltages with the successive-approximation ADC.

190

Integrated circuits containing analog-to-digital converters are quite common, some of them very good and very fast. Both Analog Devices and National Semiconductor have catalogs full of such devices.

One of the best general-purpose ADCs-on-a-chip is the ADC0817 Single Chip Data Acquisition System by National Semiconductor. This single chip combines a 16-line to 1-line addressable analog multiplexer, a comparator, a successive approximation register, and a three-state output latch. It is rather expensive, retailing for about $35.00, but for serious data acquisition, it is well worth the price. It requires only a source of precise voltage for reference and power and a clock from 600 to 1200 kHz to be able to work. Conversion time with a 1200-kHz clock is only 70 microseconds. The analog multiplexer may be used, or it can be left out of the wiring if only one analog input is desired. Up to 16 analog inputs may be used with the multiplexer.

Figure 5-32 shows a schematic using only 10 integrated circuits incorporating all of the features of the ADC0817 into a full-feature ADC, suitable for analysis of dc, ac, or fast pulses. The connections to the 6820 PIA are also shown for clarity. It requires both sides of the PIA for full use, as well as one handshake input line, CB1. Side B of the PIA is all input, while side A is half input and half output. The clock input, marked as $\emptyset 2$ on the diagram may be derived from the microprocessor bus, being anywhere from 0.6 MHz to 1.2 MHz. Or, it can be supplied by an oscillator specially for that purpose.

Fifteen of the sixteen analog inputs can be used. Seven of these are selectable by external strobes from an outside device for on-demand conversion. The strobes come in through transistors connected to IC1, a 74147. Any low output of the IC causes a start-conversion-cycle through IC2. Alternatively, the processor itself can request that a conversion take place by simply placing a conversion address from 0 through 14 on lines PA4 through PA7. Again, if the PA7 line is low, a conversion will start. Only when all four lines are high (line 15) does nothing happen. IC3 and IC4 tell the ADC and the computer which of the fifteen input

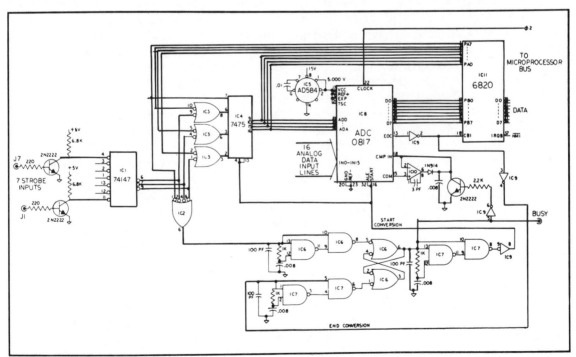

Fig. 5-32. A general-purpose ADC.

lines is being processed by feeding the information back to the computer through the lower four bits of the A-side of the PIA.

IC5 is very important. This AD584, which we have seen before, is a precision voltage regulator which supplies power to the ADC. Its output, as wired, is 5.000V ± .001 V. It cannot be used as a voltage regulator for the other chips because its maximum output is only 14 mA. The ADC0817 only requires 1 mA of supply current; most TTL circuits require at least 50 mA.

IC6 and IC7 form a series of flip-flops and one-shots that generate a start-of-conversion, busy, and end-of-conversion signal. The busy signal can be monitored by the computer or sent to the measuring devices so that no new information is sent to the ADC while previous information is being processed. When the ADC has finished processing the data, it sends an end-of-conversion signal to the PIA, which can set a status bit or cause an interrupt, signalling that the PIA needs to be serviced.

IC10, the 1N914 diode, capacitor, and 2N2222 transistor form a sample-and-hold and peak-sense amplifier on the output of the analog multiplexer, *before* the signal goes to the ADC. The amplifier is specifically designed for pulse-height analysis of fast pulses, but works moderately well with dc, or with ac signals up to 1000 Hz. If another type of sample-and-hold fits your applications better, these components may be replaced. If analysis of dc only is required, they may be dispensed with altogether, and a wire run from pin 15 to pin 18 of the ADC. Pin 15 is the output of the multiplexer, and pin 18 is the input of the ADC. If the multiplexer is not desired at all, the analog input can be routed directly to pin 18.

This circuit is described in full detail, with machine-language application programs for the 6800 microprocessing in the December, 1981, issue of *Microcomputor* magazine.

Programming for the circuit is quite simple. The hardware does most of the work. All that is really needed is to start the conversion if it is not being done by hardware. Then, when an interrupt occurs, or when the computer determines that the conversion is complete, simply read the data and

the input channel number, and store the data accordingly. Up to 14,000 conversions a second may be made with the circuit shown here, using a 1.2-MHz clock. A block diagram of the program is given in Fig. 5-33.

The circuit was originally designed as a pulse-height analyzer for physical-science applications. A word or two is in order regarding pulse-height analysis. In this type of work, a piece of equipment generates a data signal which is analog in nature, but may only last a few microseconds. A typical example would be a detector for gamma rays, such as that used in medical radiation scans. The height of the pulse in volts is proportional to the energy of the gamma ray, which in turn depends on the density of the tissue that the ray has gone through. Unfortunately, the gamma ray does not carry much energy in everyday terms, and only deposits a little in the detector. This means that the pulse output from the detector, indicating that a gamma ray has been seen, is very short—in fact only about 2 microseconds long. It is necessary to catch this pulse, find the maximum value of it, and *hold* that maximum so that an ADC can determine how big it was, thus determining the density of the tissues it went through. The peak sensor accomplishes this. In Fig. 5-32, IC10 amplifies the signal and provides current to charge up the capacitor through the diode. The current cannot leak off the capacitor back into the amplifier because the diode blocks it. The current cannot go forward because the input impedance of the ADC is very high. So the capacitor maintains the highest value of voltage placed on it simply because there is no place for it to go. If the voltage increases, eletrons flow through the diode to charge the capacitor further. So the capacitor always reads the highest value of voltage seen on it. The ADC reads this voltage, then causes the transistor to short the capacitor, clearing it for the next measurement.

COMPUTER-GENERATED MUSIC

It is surprising to many people to find out that a computer, in addition to doing games, calculations, storage and retrieval, control, and measure-

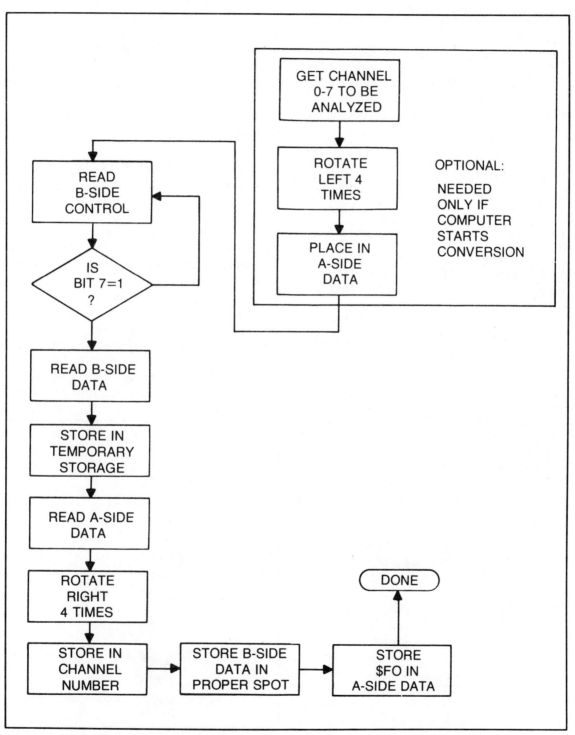

Fig. 5-33. Reading the general-purpose ADC.

ment, can also make noise. The noise itself can be controlled to make music.

The idea of music immediately conjures up all kinds of uses: The mind reels with thoughts of fancy musical doorbells, of writing whole symphonies, using a computer to interpret music from sheet form to sound, and of adding audio to computer games.

Music is just sound. It is sound with specific patterns to it, and it has an almost mathematical beauty to it. Music is characterized by tones and durations. The tone, or frequency, of a musical sound gives the pitch, which can be used to define the melody or harmony. The duration of each of the sounds gives rise to the rhythm and syncopations of the music.

The tones are divided into *notes*, and there are twelve notes in an octave. This is called the equally tempered scale. An octave is any range of frequencies with a factor of two in the start and finish. A tone of 200 Hz is an octave above a tone of 100 Hz; a tone of 512 Hz is an octave above a tone of 256 Hz. If a note is an octave above another, they have the same note name: An "A" note could be 220 Hz, 440 Hz, or 880 Hz. The twelve notes in the chromatic, or equally-tempered, scale are A, A sharp, B, C, C sharp, D, E flat, E, F, F sharp, G, and A flat. Each is a factor of the twelfth root of two higher in frequency than the last.

The tones are divided into durations which are notes and fractions of a note. A quarter note lasts twice as long as an eighth note, and half as long as a half note.

A sound which corresponds to a sine-wave vibration of air is called a *pure tone*. Such a vibration sounds rather bland and nondescript. A square-wave type of vibration, on the other hand, sounds much harsher, but will have the same basic note if the fundamental frequencies are the same. Variation in the *shape* of the wave gives the characteristics of the different instruments. For example, both a guitar and a banjo use strings: They both have a B string which is 27 1/4 inches long, made of phosphor-bronze steel, is exactly eleven-thousandths of an inch in diameter, and both are under the same tension, and both give a b note

when plucked. But they have different vibration characteristics, giving different waveforms, so that a guitar and a banjo don't sound the same.

When a computer generates music, all it has to do is produce an electrical waveform which has the proper frequency, duration, and tone characteristics, and then feed that voltage into a speaker to produce sound.

A SINGLE-BIT SQUARE-WAVE GENERATOR

The simplest music generator on a computer just uses a single output bit, much like a control interface. All that is really needed is a simple current amplifier to provide enough current to drive a small speaker, and the rest of the work is done by software. Such an arrangement is shown in Fig. 5-34. The transistor works as an emitter follower with the speaker being the load in the emitter circuit. The transistor is driven directly by an output bit of the computer. When the output bit is high, the transistor conducts, and when it is low, no current flows through the speaker. If the bit is alternately turned on and off, the speaker alternately has current flowing or not flowing through it. If this

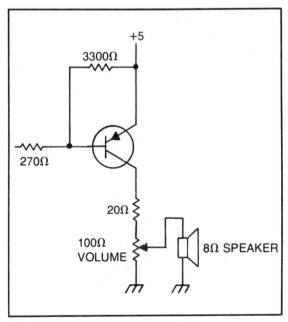

Fig. 5-34. A single-bit music generator.

happens at an audible frequency, we will hear sound of a square-wave nature. For example, if the bit is turned on and off 440 times a second, we will hear a rather harsh A-440.

The whole secret to using this type of music generator is knowing how quickly to turn the data bit on and off. For this, we need a table of frequencies, periods, and clock cycle times for the various notes of the scale, such as provided in Table 5-2. The last column gives the number of clock cycles at 1 MHz to provide a duration equal to the period of the note. If your computer has a different clock frequency, just divide the value by the frequency in MHz. A computer instruction in machine language takes an integer number of clock cycles. To provide a square wave of the desired frequency, just form a loop of machine-language instructions that take half the number of clock cycles stated, turn the bit on for that number of cycles, and then turn it off for that number of cycles. Repeated often enough, this process will give a square wave of the frequency of the note.

For example, a concert-pitch A note in the middle of the human vocal range has a frequency of 440 cycles per second. Therefore, its period is 2.273 milliseconds. A computer with a 1-MHz clock will take 2273 clock cycles for one period. Just turn the output bit on for 1136 cycles, and turn it off for 1137. (Actually it will not really matter if it is on for 1136 and off for 1137. The difference will not be noticeable.) Suppose you have a delay loop which takes 16 clock cycles to complete. Then 71 times through that loop will take 1136 cycles.

In addition to keeping track of the period of the wave for the frequency of the note, the duration of the note must also be accounted for. Otherwise, you get only that note. Music is a series of notes, all in the proper order, with the proper duration. The duration depends on the size of the note. A whole note lasts so long, a half note lasts half as long as a whole note, a quarter note lasts half of that, and so on. A *dotted note* gets half again its normal value. The duration of a whole note depends on the *tempo*. Usually a quarter note gets one "beat." A beat can last varying lengths of time. Slow tempo can be only 60 beats to the minute, while rapid tempo can be as fast as 180 beats to the minute. Tempo can have any value in between, too. So we need a means of providing for tempo and note duration.

All of this can be provided for in counting the number of times a given note has gone through one complete cycle. For example, at 60 beats per minute (one per second), a half note of A-440 takes 880 complete cycles. A quarter note takes 440 complete cycles, and so on. At 120 beats to the minute, these values are cut in half.

Another way of doing the timing is to do a note until a timer has elapsed. (Timers are discussed later in this chapter.) The timer can cause an interrupt, or the computer can just poll the timer at the end of every note cycle to see if it is done yet. With two timers, one can be used for the note duration, and the other can be used for the duration of one cycle.

Table 5-2. Notes, Frequencies, and Periods of the Music Scale.

Note	Frequency	Period (ms)	No. Cycles @ 1 MHz
Middle C	261.6 Hz	3.823	3823
C#	277.2	3.607	3607
D	293.6	3.406	3406
Eb	311.1	3.214	3214
E	329.6	3.034	3034
F	349.2	2.864	2864
F#	370.0	2.703	2703
G	392.0	2.551	2551
Ab	415.3	2.408	2408
A	440.0	2.273	2273
Bb	466.2	2.145	2145
B	493.9	2.025	2025
Octave C	523.2	1.911	1911

A flowchart for the production of music using the single-bit generator is given in Fig. 5-35. The routine presumes that some other routine has placed a set of codings for each note's value and duration somewhere in memory. The routine then computes the frequency and number of cycles the note should last and drives the output bit accordingly. Then it gets the next note and starts the whole process over again. There should be a special code for "end of the song" included so the computer will know to stop. The flowchart is done in very general terms. Individual computers and programming styles will differ, so the process is just outlined. The user will have to supply many of the details of the programming in this case.

SINE WAVES AND OTHER WAVEFORMS WITH A DAC MUSIC GENERATOR

The major disadvantage to the system described above is that only one tone is available. The tone is a square wave, which many people find harsh to the ears. True, it is simple, but just a little more hardware and software gets us a music generator which can, theoretically at least, reproduce the sounds of any instrument. This is a great device to experiment with. All sorts of waveforms can be produced, from an oboe to the ringing of a bell.

We have already discussed the major portion of the needed hardware—earlier in this chapter we described the DAC and its wiring. We are beginning to find out that this little circuit, simple as it is to build and use, has a large variety of very useful applications. The only thing that may be needed in addition to the DAC itself is an amplifier, on the output of the DAC, which has a low enough output impedance to drive a speaker. Most electronics stores sell a small "amplifier module" costing only a few dollars which can drive a small speaker. Or, the DAC can be connected directly to the AUX input of a stereo amplifier through a capacitor. A value of 1 μF or so should be sufficient for this purpose. Don't use an electrolytic capacitor—a nonpolarized one will do the job well. Also, electrolytic capacitors can explode if you don't observe the proper polarity. You may even find that the opera-

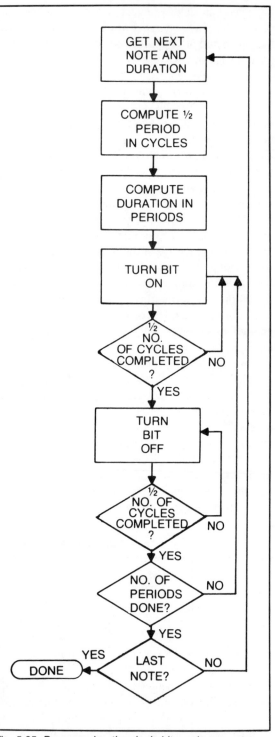

Fig. 5-35. Programming the single-bit music generator.

tional amplifier used as the current-to-voltage converter has a low enough impedance and a high enough current capability to drive the speaker directly through a capacitor and 50-ohm resistor. A lot will depend on the speaker you are using. A very low-power speaker may work well this way.

Once the hardware is in place, all that is needed is software to turn the DAC into a function generator as described earlier. Now, you must know the shape of the waveform you are trying to achieve, how to translate that into a series of values for the DAC, and place those values onto the DAC in the right order at the right intervals of time.

Perhaps the easiest way to do this is to generate a table, using BASIC, of the waveforms. That is, assume you will be placing a value into the DAC every so many microseconds.Let's say it takes 50 microseconds to place a value from a table into the DAC and then go get the next value from the table. Then you should have a value in the table for the amplitude of the way every 50 microseconds. This means that the table will be longer for notes whose period is longer, or whose frequency is less. A different table will be needed for every note that is to be used. Then all the program has to do is decide which table should be used, and start loading the values in every 50 microseconds, and continually check for the end of the note's duration. Figure 5-36 will help to explain this whole concept. Parts A and B show two sine waves of different frequency and how the values are added to give the proper wave. Part C shows how it might be extended to waveforms other than sine waves.

Another part of the "character" of a musical sound is its "attack" and "sustain." Attack is the rate at which the waveform goes from zero to full force. An instrument will not just start making sound all at once. It takes a short period of time before the music builds up to a level. In most instruments, this is only a few milliseconds. More important is the sustain, or rate of decay of the note once it is formed. Wind and brass instruments can sustain the note at full volume as long as the player has wind. Strings and percussion instruments, on the other hand, start quickly, then decay down to nothing in a few seconds at most. A guitar has a

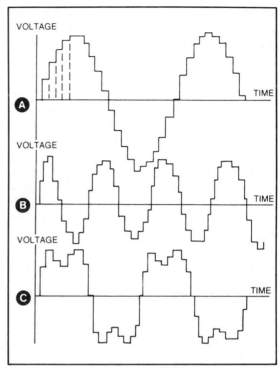

Fig. 5-36. Generating tones with a DAC.

sustain time of a few seconds; a banjo, on the other hand, has a sustain time of less than one second. These times are rather long compared to the period of the note and can be calculated as a multiplying factor every ten cycles or so. The process is exponential in nature, shown by:

$$e^{-t/C}$$

where e is the number 2.71828, and C is a constant stant related to the decay time. For ease in calculation, the exponential function can be approximated by the series

$$1 - t/C + t^2/2C^2 - t^3/6C^3 + t^4/24C^4 \ldots$$

as far out as is needed for sufficient accuracy.

Also, another property that can be applied using a DAC as a music generator is the fact that one note does not generally run into another in "real music." With the single-bit generator, we had to let one bit run into another because there wasn't any way to distinguish between an "off" for a half cycle and an "off" for the end of a note, unless we just let the latter last a lot longer. In most instrumental music, there is a short delay time between one note and the next. It normally doesn't last long—only ten to twenty milliseconds. However, if we are trying to emulate the sound of an instrument, it should be included. It makes the music easier to listen to, as well. With a DAC generator, we can just drop the value of the note to zero about ten milliseconds before the note would otherwise end. At one hundred hertz, this is one cycle. At a thousand hertz, it is ten cycles. Just drop it to zero an integer number of cycles before the end of the note, and disregard any small errors.

Also remember that most music will be within one octave of middle C (261.6 Hz) so a range of more than 24 notes will not normally be required, unless you are trying for a full range of symphonic instruments. A low-bass viol can have a low frequency only 25 Hz. A piccolo can have harmonics extending beyond 18,000 Hz. For ordinary "singing" music, though, twenty-four note tables will likely be enough.

A flowchart for the production of music using a DAC generator and a note table is given in Fig. 5-37. Again, it is a generalized program, with little in the way of specifics. Provisions are made for note duration, attack, sustain, and a pause at the end of the note before the next one begins.

TOP-OCTAVE-DIVIDER MUSIC GENERATOR

Electronic generation of music has been with us for many years. The Theremin music generator was one of the first, followed quickly by the Moog Synthesizer generator. These instruments regulate wave shape, frequency, amplitude, attack, and sustain. They are quite complex and can have a full piano keyboard, or even two or three for different "voices," and can play several notes at once with each voice. They are heavily used in much of popular music today, mostly because of their versatility.

Needless to say, forming a frequency generator for each note of each voice is a chore. So, as we might expect, an integrated circuit has been

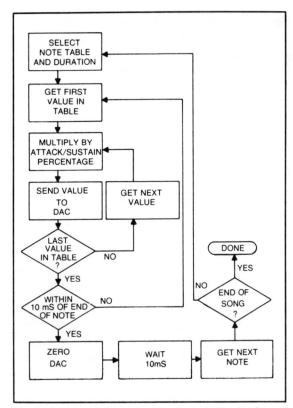

Fig. 5-37. Program for generating tones with a DAC.

made which will do this for the device. It is called a *top-octave-divider* and essentially is a circuit which takes a 2-MHz square wave, and divides and redivides it so that its twelve outputs are notes of the evenly tempered scale in the audible range. Then all that is needed is a selector for the particular note to be played, and perhaps a divider on the input to halve the frequency to get a lower octave.

Top-octave-dividers are not cheap, but they're not overly expensive, either. The one we will use in this work, the 50240 by American Microsystems, has been advertised from $15.00 to as little as $3.75. Add four or five more ICs, and you have a whole music generator.

The circuit begins with an oscillator to provide an output that will be divided down to form the actual tones. Two circuits to form the oscillator are shown in Fig. 5-38. Circuit A provides a precise output frequency due to the crystal controller. To be exactly on concert pitch, the crystal should be

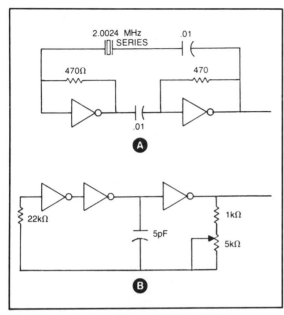

Fig. 5-38. Oscillators with a top-octave divider.

2.0024 MHz, but such crystals will be hard to find. An ordinary 2.000 MHz crystal is readily available and will give results that are less than a hundredth of a semitone off. If your computer has a 2-MHz clock, this clock can be used in place of the oscillator. Circuit B is an RC oscillator which can be *tuned* to adjust the frequency slightly. It is also less expensive to build.

Figure 5-39 is a schematic diagram of the completed music generator. In addition to the top octave-divider, a 4024 seven-stage ripple counter is used to select the proper octave to be sounded. The octave and the note which is to be played are selected by a 4512 eight-channel data selector or a 74150 16-bit multiplexer. With each of these chips, sixteen possible notes could be selected, but there are only twelve, so the other four will simply indicate silence, or a "rest." One chip uses only two of the address inputs to select one of four octaves to be sounded by selecting one output frequency

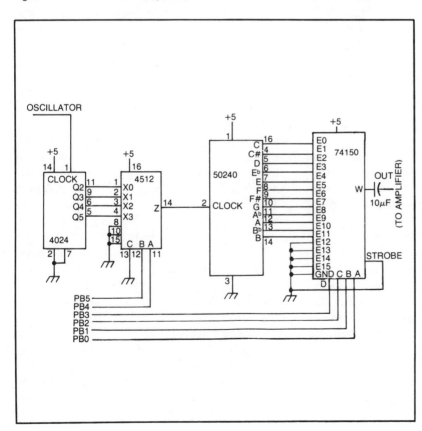

Fig. 5-39. The top-octave divider music generator.

199

D7	D6	D5	D4	D3	D2	D1	D0	
X	X	0	0					Octave 1
X	X	0	1					Octave 2
X	X	1	0					Octave 3
X	X	1	1					Octave 4
X	X			0	0	0	0	C
X	X			0	0	0	1	C #
X	X			0	0	1	0	D
X	X			0	0	1	1	E b
X	X			0	1	0	0	E
X	X			0	1	0	1	F
X	X			0	1	1	0	F #
X	X			0	1	1	1	G
X	X			1	0	0	0	A b
X	X			1	0	0	1	A
X	X			1	0	1	0	B #
X	X			1	0	1	1	B
X	X			1	1	0	0	Rest
X	X			1	1	0	1	Rest
X	X			1	1	1	0	Rest
X	X			1	1	1	1	Rest

Table 5-3. Note-Selection for the Music Generator.

of the oscillator/divider series. The other chip selects which output of the notes from the 50240 will actually be sounded. Only six output bits are required. The least-significant-four select the note, the next two select the octave. The generator has a four-octave range, which should be plenty for most applications. The device can be extended to an eight-octave range by adding another octave-selection bit at the output of the ripple counter in the 4512 or 74150.

Table 5-3 shows how to select the note to be played. The 6820 PIA resets to all 1s in the data output register on reset, so the arrangement shown will assure that there is no sound until the program starts.

There are two data bits left over. These can be used for additional decoding. For example, all that is necessary to use the music generator is to place the code for the note into the output register of the PIA that drives the device. The notes could be stored at the end of every sixteenth note, for example, so that an eighth note is just two identical notes, and a quarter note is just four identical notes, and so on. Bit 6 could be used as a signal that the tone is about to end and to cut the sound off a few milliseconds before the end of the note.

TWO OR MORE VOICES SIMULTANEOUSLY

All the music generators described thus far will play one and only one note at a time. Much, if not most, of today's music (and, for that matter, almost all music since Bach) relies on at least two notes being played simultaneously for harmony. In fact, the definition of a *chord* is three notes played simultaneously in certain defined patterns.

The top-octave-divider-circuit can be paired with another such circuit, with a mixer amplifier on the outputs, and use the unused bits of the inputs to select which of the two voices will be updated. They can both be driven by one PIA port if two 74100 data latches and some "data-ready" circuitry is added, as in Fig. 5-40. A nice part is that the same oscillator can be used for both.

In this circuit, the seventh bit is used as a channel selector. The channel-select bit, either normal or inverted, is ANDed with the CB2 data-ready strobe from the PIA, which then allows the data to flow into the proper latch, where it is stored. Then the same can be done with the other latch.

Programming for the two-voice music generator is rather simple. The easiest approach is to have another program take data from a keyboard and form a table of notes, every sixteenth note, for the

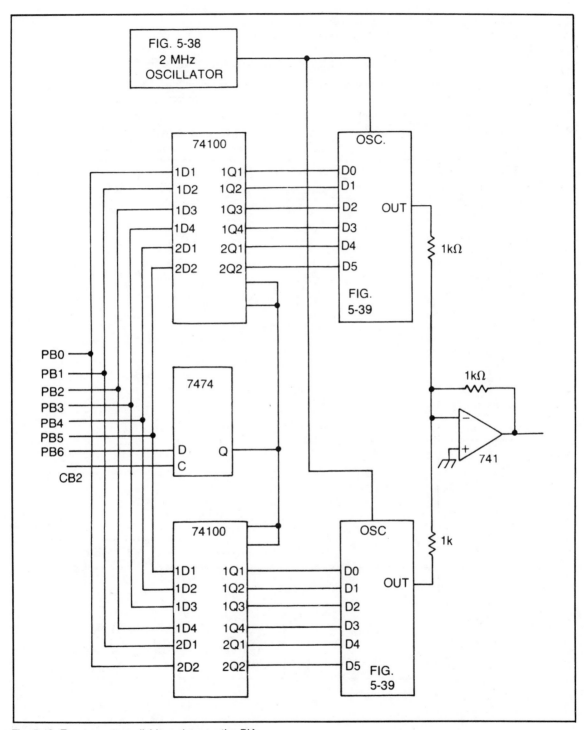

Fig. 5-40. Two top-octave divider voices on the PIA.

two voices. The output program then goes through a series of waiting loops, whose timing value is determined by the value of a tempo input, and at the end of every one of these loops, both data latches are updated. The whole program is presented in flowchart form in Fig. 5-41.

For a good discussion of music theory as it applies to the computer, see Bill Struve's excellent article, "A $19 Music Interface" in the December, 1977, issue of *BYTE*.

A MORE COMPLEX SOUND GENERATOR

Another possibility for the generation of music is the Texas Instruments 76489 Sound Generator chip. This device generates not only music, but also all sorts of different sounds. Many video games

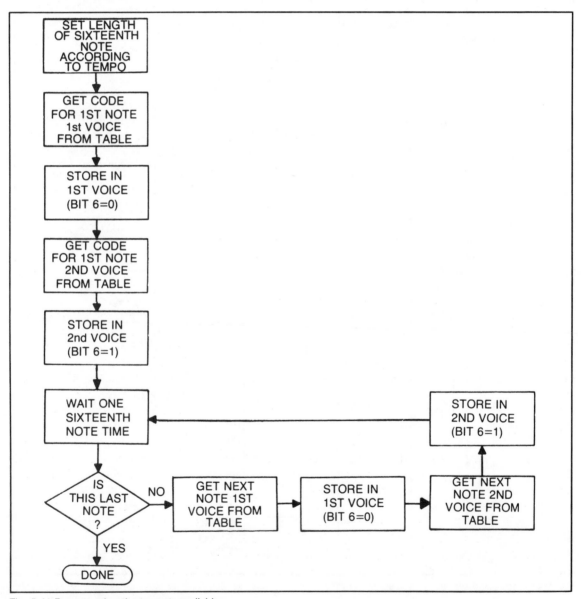

Fig. 5-41.Programming the top-octave divider.

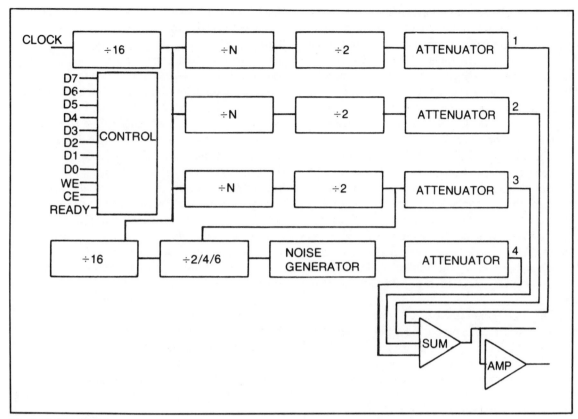

Fig. 5-42. The 76489.

use this chip for their sound effects. It is quite a complicated chip and somewhat expensive, but it has enormous capabilities. With the proper wiring and programming, it can reproduce virtually any sound the mind can conceive—up to four simultaneous sounds. I have seen it used to make the sounds of music, explosions, birds twittering, automobile engines, train whistles, and breaking crockery.

Another advantage to the use of this chip is that is very easy to program for several voices of music, or several notes at once. The chip contains not one, but four independently programmable sound generators. Instead of writing a program to count the delay in a square wave for the frequency, all that need be done, is to send a code for the note to be played. Two voices with a single-bit music generator becomes quite complicated but is very easy with this chip.

A look at the internal architecture of the 76489

is shown in Fig. 5-42. The device is essentially a series of downcounters which take a clock input, such as a 2-MHz clock from the computer bus, and divide it down by a specific integer, programmed by the user, to get a square wave of a particular frequency. Each tone generator also has a programmable attenuator to adjust the output level of that particular tone, in effect changing the "envelope" shape. Lastly, there is a summing amplifier which adds all the sounds together, to produce a signal which is compatible with the high-level, or "AUX," input of a tape recorder or stereo amplifier.

Number 4 tone generator is a little different from all the others. It still has a programmable tone generator, but it only has three divide frequencies. It has an attenuator just like the others, but it also has a "white noise" generator. This generator can be set by the fixed rates of the programmable divider, or controlled by tone generator number three. With these control possibilities, and the programmable attenuator, the chip can be made to produce a variety of sounds. The internal generator and divider work together to produce a frequency range. The attack and sustain created by the attenuator add to the possibilities. It can cover the range from a low-frequency explosion to a high-frequency gunshot. It can also be used to imitate a snare drum or cymbals.

The three "normal" dividers are ten-bit down counters whose counting ratio is programmable by the user. A ten-bit number is loaded by the processor to set the frequency provided by the chip. Every time the counter underflows, the "borrow" pulse is used to reload the counter and toggle the output, producing a square wave. It has a large enough range to cover the musical scale from two octaves below middle C to three octaves about middle C.

The noise generator has a 15-bit random sequence generator for producing white noise. The range can be set by its own internal counter or by the output from generator number three.

Each generator has an attenuator with a range from full volume to an attenuation of 28 dB. The attenuator is programmable in 2-dB steps. A setting of 30 dB turns the particular generator off. An attack/sustain envelope can be created by reprogramming the attenuator in the middle of the tone.

The device, except for the audio-output level, is essentially write-only. It is not possible to read any of the internal registers.

Connection of the 76489 to a computer is simplicity itself. All that is needed is eight-data bits from a PIA, a write-enable signal which is active low (can be provided by CB2), and a source of square waves in the 1- to 2-MHz range. A computer's system clock will do very well for this purpose. The PIA also acts to latch the data to the inputs while the data transfer is taking place.

The 76489 is rather slow in accepting data from the PIA. While most chips will accept data in a few nanoseconds, and rarely more than a microsecond, the 76489 takes a full 32 clock periods to accept data to its control registers. With a 2-MHz clock,

this takes 16 microseconds; with a 500-kHz clock, it takes 64 microseconds. The data has to be latched to the inputs of the 76489 for this whole period. Naturally, no other data can be input during this time, so that a delay loop has to be placed in the handler whenever data is written to the chip. Or, use handshake thru CB1. A diagram of the wiring of the 76489 to a PIA is shown in Fig. 5-43.

Since the hardware is so simple, the software is naturally complicated, but only because there are so many registers inside the chip. The 76489 only has eight input lines, thus it essentially looks like one memory location. With the control register and data register of the PIA controlling it, it will tend to look like two memory locations in the use described here. The data output of the PIA must contain all programming data and also information as to which of the internal registers must be accessed. A diagram of these registers is given in Fig. 5-44. There are eight registers, one for each frequency divider and one for each attenuator. It will take three bits to determine which of the registers is being addressed.

The programmable counters controlling the frequencies are each ten-bit devices, so it will take

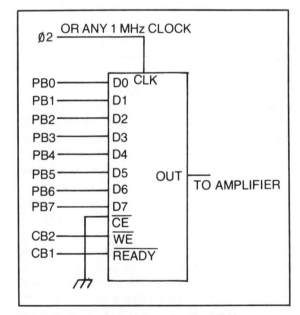

Fig. 5-43. A sound generator using the 76489.

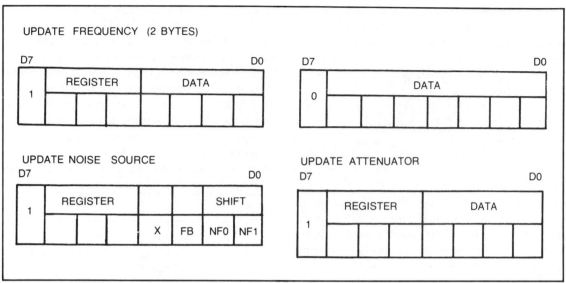

Fig. 5-44. Registers of the 76489.

more than one byte to make any change in the value of these counters. Changing any frequency register of the three normal sources requires a two-byte transfer. To tell the two bytes apart, the most significant bit of the first byte is set to a 1, and the most significant bit of the second byte is a zero. The second byte must immediately follow the first.

The first byte contains the register address, and also four bits of data for the counter—the most significant four bits of the frequency divider counter input. Again, the most significant byte must be a 1. The register addresses take up the next three most significant bits, and will cause the data to be placed in the appropriate register according to the following table:

D6	D5	D4	
0	0	0	Tone 1 frequency control
0	0	1	Tone 1 attenuation control
0	1	0	Tone 2 frequency control
0	1	1	Tone 2 attenuation control
1	0	0	Tone 3 frequency control
1	0	1	Tone 3 attenuation
1	1	0	noise control
1	1	1	noise attenuation

Anytime there is a 1 in bit 7 of the data, there must

be a register address in bits 4-6. To change one of the tone generator frequencies, the proper register is selected, with a 1 in bit 7, and the data in bits 0-3. When this transfer is complete, bit 7 is changed to a 0, and the least significant part of the data is loaded into bits 0-5.

Changing an attenuator setting requires only a single data byte. Bit 7 is again a 1, and the register address again occupies bits 4-6. For the remainder of the bits, these indicate the attenuation in dB. Bit 0 is 2 dB, bit 1 is 4 dB, bit 2 is 8 dB, and bit 3 is 16 dB. If any bit is set, the output is attenuated by that many dB. If more than one is set, the attenuation is the sum of all the attenuations. If all bits are set, instead of a 30 dB attenuation, the device is turned off, and no sound is produced from the generator.

The noise source acts very much like the other generators, except that the counter is only a two-bit counter, instead of a ten-bit counter. There is a feedback register, marked as the FB bit, which controls the feedback to the internal 15-bit shift register used to produce the noise. If you set the FB bit, you will get white noise. If this bit is a 0, then the feedback is disabled, and a square wave with a seven percent duty cycle is produced.

Bits 0 and 1 are the shift rate register control

to the clock on the shift register. It controls the rate at which the shift register cycles, according to the following table:

Bit 1	Bit 0	Shift rate
0	0	clock/512
0	1	clock/1024
1	0	clock/2048
1	1	output of tone generator three

As you can see, the rate can be varied from one of three fixed rates in each of three octaves, or can be controlled directly by tone generator three. Many unusual effects can be obtained by changing or ramping the frequency of this generator.

A handler program is shown in flowchart form for the 76489-PIA peripheral, see Fig. 5-45. The program is itself very simple, consisting only of a machine-language routine which will place data on the output lines of the PIA, actuate a "data-ready" pulse on CB2, and wait for a "ready" pulse on CB1. The actual mechanics of placing a particular tone on the amplifier outputs are contained in the register-structure information.

It is not our purpose here to describe the actual mechanisms for the production of specific sounds. The exact tones, are, in any case, dependent strongly on the frequency of the clock input, which in these descriptions is the computer's system clock. Such clock frequency will vary with the machine being used. Furthermore, since almost any sound may be reproduced, it would not be worthwhile to catalog a few. The application will vary from user to user. The reader would be better advised to study the description of the device above, and the function of each of the registers, and spend considerable time experimenting with the various sounds that can be made.

AN RC INTERRUPT TIMER

In the previous three sections of this chapter, we have seen the need for measuring or counting off a specific period of time. We needed, for example, to measure the length of time of the period of

a square wave for tone-creation purposes.

The specification of a length of time for a program's use is a common one. We nearly always will want to wait some period of time before continuing with some procedure, or will want to measure the amount of time between the two events.

Until now, we have used the software timing loop as the main-stay of our timing efforts. We have seen this software timing loop in Chapter 3, with the software UART, and with the single-bit music generator of Fig. 5-35. It is a very useful subrou-

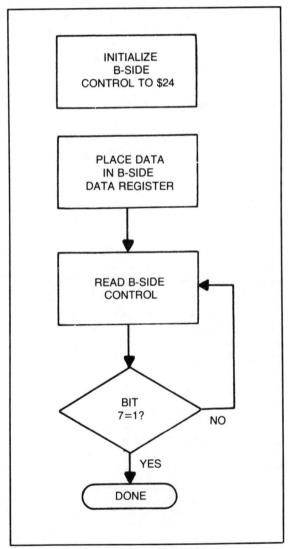

Fig. 5-45. Programming the 76489.

tine for any program. Again, the essential method of the loop is to loop through the series of commands, each of which takes a few microseconds a given number of times, until a known number of microseconds has elapsed. We have seen earlier that a routine to delay one second can be easily written. The software timing loop could also include a counter which would count the number of times that the program goes through the loop before an external event happens. In this way, the computer could measure the interval between two events. A flowchart of such a counter-timer loop is shown in Fig. 5-46. An example of its use might be this: An event is signalled over the CA1 line of a PIA. The timer then counts the number of one-second loops the computer goes through until another event comes in over CB1, and the total count gives the number of seconds between the events.

The loop could be divided into subloops of a hundredth of a second each. Then the computer can keep track of the time interval in hundredths of seconds. Don't forget to include in the timing the amount of time it takes to update the counter!

A better way, less dependent of the vagaries of the program and the ability to design a loop which is *exactly* one-hundredth of a second long, is a hardware timer. In a case like this, there will exist a hardware device that will either be polled or cause an interrupt every hundredth or thousandth of a second. The interrupt routine, or the polling decision, would then commence to update the counter. Since the time between interrupts is not dependent on software, but only on the components of the hardware, it is less likely to accumulate errors due to programming mistakes, or an inability of the programming to keep up with timing errors in the program loops.

The RC timer is perhaps the most easily built of these hardware devices. It consists of a single 555 timer wired as an astable oscillator, with components designed for a pulse every 1/100th of a second. As in Fig. 5-47, the output of the timer is connected to a handshake input, such as the CA1 input of a PIA. Everytime the timer goes low, the IRQ bit (bit 7) of the control register is set. If interrupts are enabled, an interrupt will be caused.

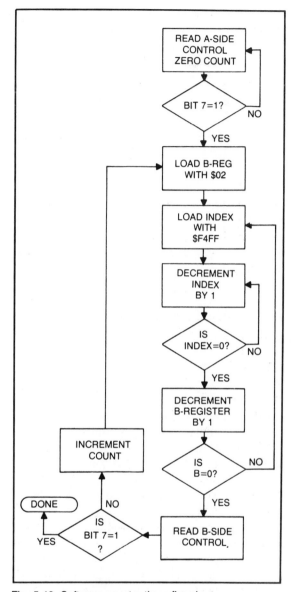

Fig. 5-46. Software counter-timer flowchart.

Otherwise, a polling loop simply looks for a set IRQ bit of this PIA. With interrupts, the computer can be going through other calculations or processes undisturbed, and still keep up the correct count of the timing. Figure 5-48 is the flowchart for this device to keep track of a specified interval between events.

The 555 timer can also be used for timing out a process. The timer can be set, interrupts allowed,

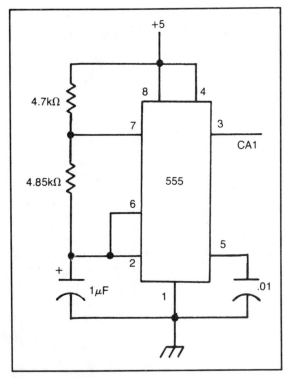

Fig. 5-47. A 555 timer.

and the process started. When so many counts have been received, the computer signals the process to stop. One example might be using the timer as a × 16 clock for a software UART.

The timer itself must be adjusted for the use to which it is to be put. For a "stopwatch" timer, the pulses will have to be every second, tenth of a second, hundredth of a second, or the like. For a software UART, the timer must be set to give a pulse every 1/300th of a second, or whatever the data rate or the × 16 data rate is. This is most easily accomplished by adjusting the resistance of the RC timing network by placing a variable resistor in the RC part of the circuit. The circuit must be calibrated by a long trial of the timer, and comparing it to a good watch. Alternately, a frequency counter of good accuracy and resolution may be used for the task.

A CRYSTAL-OSCILLATOR TIMER

The preceding circuit is quite cheap to build

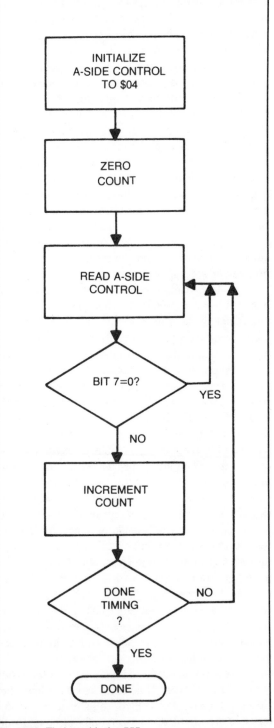

Fig. 5-48. Timing with the 555.

and easy to operate. It does suffer from one minor drawback, though. The RC timer is unduly sensitive to heat. The values of the resistor and capacitor tend to change dramatically with even small changes in temperature, and can be off as much as 5 percent with a 20-degree temperature change. Consequently, the timing will be off, as well.

A better way to go, assuming that the frequency of the oscillator is to remain constant, is to use a crystal-controlled oscillator in the place of the RC timer. The software is identical, but the frequency of the interrupts is governed by the crystal itself, within a fraction of a percent, rather than by the RC network. To choose or to change a frequency, the crystal must be changed. The only major drawback is that the values of crystal frequencies rarely get below 100 kHz, which is much too fast to use as a timer interrupt device. With a 1-MHz system clock, this means that an interrupt has to occur every 5 instructions, and the interrupt service routine, including the stack manipulation, cannot last longer than 10 microseconds—obviously impossible with present microprocessors.

A solution is to add a counter to the oscillator that will divide the frequency by 10 a specific number of times, to get to the 1/100th-second period. In addition, with the right choice of counter/dividers, the device can be programmed by the computer to give an interrupt every so often. Figure 5-49 gives a schematic for such a device with eight-bit resolution. A source of clock pulses is the start of the timing chain, with a crystal oscillator providing accuracy and stability. These are divided in turn by a series of 74900 or 74192 decade counters which divide the frequency by ten as many times as the user may desire. If the oscillator is a 1-MHz oscillator, and the desired output is to be a period of one second, then four such dividers in cascade will be needed. The dividing may be done by a 4024 seven-stage ripple counter, which can divide up to 7 stages, or as little as one. All that is needed is to take the output from the proper pin, as shown. The signal then enters two 74192s which form the programmable part of the timer. These two chips form a two-decade BCD down-counter. The signal

from the 4024 enters the "count down" input of the zero. When the counter reaches zero, the "borrow" output signals the next divider to count its value down by one. When the next one also reaches zero, the "borrows" output of it activates the CA1 input of the PIA, signaling the end of the timing period.

The 74192 is programmable in that a "start-count" pulse from CA1 clears the 4024, and loads the BCD number from the PA output into the "preset" inputs of the 74192s. This preset input becomes the number of counts (in BCD) which the last stage of the counter will count down to zero. In the example above, where a 0.1-MHz clock is used, and it is divided by four decades, the output of the 4024 will be one pulse every 1/100th of a second. If, then, the last two stages are loaded with 25 BCD, then 25/100ths of a second will pass until the CA1 input registers that the timing period has ended.

Another method uses the 74193 counter, which is pin-for-pin compatible with the 74192, except that the inputs will be in true binary instead of BCD. Eight bits BCD can go to 99, while eight bits binary will go to 255. In the above example, the 74192s can count up to 99/100ths of a second, while the 74193s can count to 255/100ths of a second with the same eight bits.

If the user wishes to count seconds rather than 1/100ths of a second, he need only add two more 74192s to the oscillator. If three more data bits are available, the octave range itself may be programmable through a 4512 eight-channel data selector, wired as used in the top-octave-divider music circuit, Fig. 5-39.

Three programs for the control of this device are given in Fig. 5-50. The first is a routine to set up the device so that an interrupt will occur at the end of a specified period. The PIA is initialized for interrupts, the number of periods to be counted loaded onto the data lines, and the "preset/clear" pulse sent through CA2. Upon the receipt of an interrupt by the computer, the second program is executed as an interrupt service routine, which disables the interrupts and performs the required program at the end of the timing period. The third program is for those who do not wish to use inter-

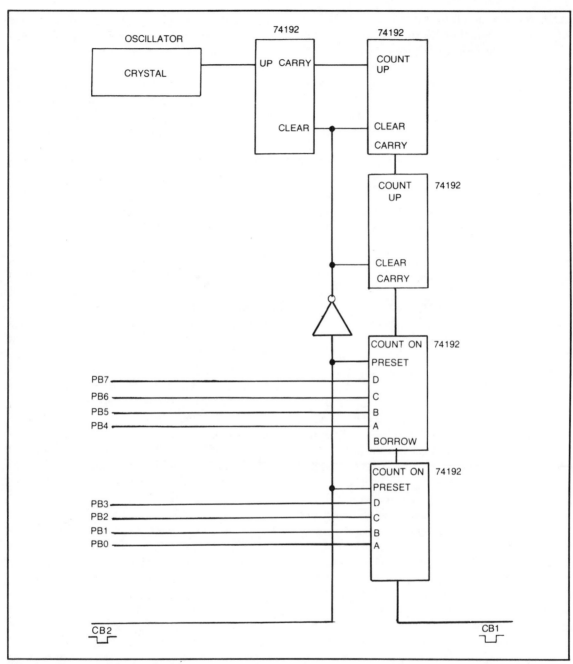

Fig. 5-49. Programmable-divider timer.

rupts in their machines, and merely combines the two programs, with a polling loop to detect the end of the timer's task.

Interval timing may be accomplished in the same way as described for the RC timer, or even with the software loop. All that is needed is a software counter to keep track of the number of timing intervals from one event to the next.

CLOCKS

It is often desirable to know the time of day that an ordinary clock would show (sometimes called "real time"). Such information is often included in a disk file to show the date and time the file was created, so that the user can keep track of which file is the newest, and delete all older versions of the same file. If the computer is used, for exam-ple, as part of a security system, the clock can give the time that a security violation occurred. The computer can, with appropriate programming, act as an alarm clock.

Creating a clock in a computer is simplicity it-self, from the hardware point of view. All that is really needed is an interrupt timer, such as the RC timer described earlier in this Chapter. The

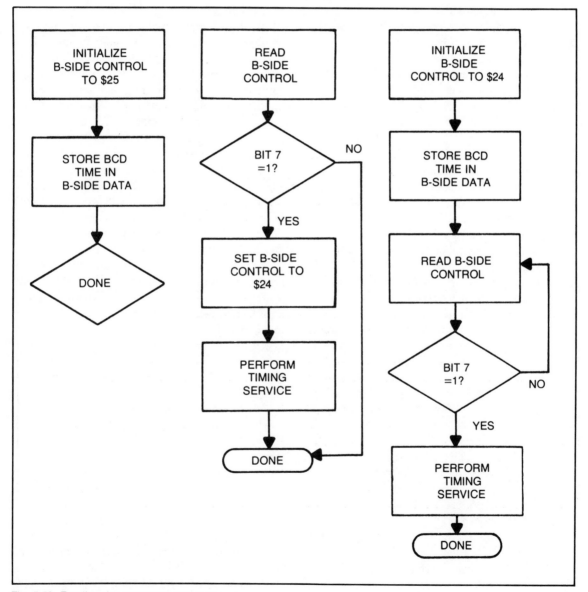

Fig. 5-50. Reading the programmable divider.

majority of the work is done by the software. All the timer does is produce a series of "ticks" that the clock can count.

The RC (or other) timer is nothing more than an oscillator with a fixed rate. Any known frequency can be used, so long as it is accurate. A crystal oscillator might be a better idea if great precision is desired. The period of the oscillator, like we say, is immaterial, as long as the computer "knows" what it is and adjusts the count accordingly. Let us use an example of an oscillator with a frequency of 1 Hz, or a period of one second.

It is absolutely necessary for the clock to interface with the computer by using interrupts. It can be done in the usual way, with the processor polling the PIA registers, but only in the case that the computer is doing nothing else at all. If the computer is doing other work, and only periodically polling the PIA, it may miss a clock "tick." Using interrupts, on the other hand, allows the computer to be performing virtually any function (so long as there are no critical software timing loops) and still not miss a single "tick."

Figure 5-51 shows a flowchart of a clock program using an interrupt oscillator with a period of one hertz. The flowchart is in the form of an interrupt-service routine. The first part is an initialization routine, which sets the time and initializes the PIA. The second is the actual interrupt-service routine, which updates an internal counter, graduated in hours, minutes, and seconds, every time an interrupt is received from this particular PIA. Provision is made for the display of the time on a screen, if desired. Note also the 12-o'clock to 1-o'clock changeover. With some creative programming, the clock can be either a 24-hour clock or a 12-hour clock. The day and date can also be input, as well, and updated by the computer at midnight.

The clock works only so long as the computer is on and the clock program loaded. When the computer's power is off, the clock will cease to keep time.

It doesn't matter if the clock frequency is different. Suppose the oscillator gives an interrupt every 1/100th of a second, instead of every second. Then the computer keeps track of each 1/100th of a second, and only updates the seconds counter storage when the hundredths counter reaches 100.

SYSTEMS CLOCKS AND MULTITASKING

Have you ever wished that your computer could do two things at once? Have you ever had a long BASIC program take forever to run, and wondered if it were working right? But you needed a listing of the program to tell, and didn't have one? Perhaps *multitasking* is for you.

Multitasking is a technique that is widely used on larger and more sophisticated computers. It is, very simply, a means whereby the computer can do two or more tasks at once. The hardware and software requirements for this technique are minimal, and only require care in that no two programs use the same memory locations or the same peripherals at the same time.

Let's consider a simple form of multitasking where two programs are to be run at a given time. This is commonly called *background-foreground* multitasking. For simplicity, we will assume that both tasks have equal *priority*, that is, neither is more important than the other, and we can switch back and forth between them with relative impunity.

What is needed is a means to allow one program to run for a while, then a signal to stop it, and switch to the other, so that it may run for a while, until it, too, gets a signal to stop and switch back to the first. The signal to stop and perform the other task is usually an interrupt, and a device which creates this interrupt on a regular basis is called the *system clock*. The program that services the interrupt and switches tasks so that two programs can be run together is called an *executive*.

Before considering the details of the executive, it is well to review the process that occurs in an interrupt. All machines have different ways of performing the interrupt, and the details will vary from computer to computer. But, the basic process is still the same.

When a computer receives an external interrupt signal, it will generally complete the instruction it is doing, and then will place all of its internal registers except for the stack pointer, into a special area of memory set aside for it called the *stack*.

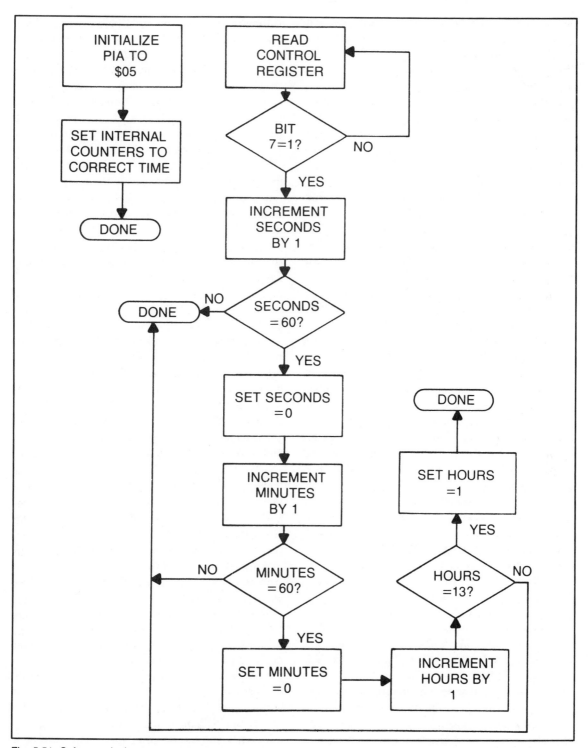

Fig. 5-51. Software clock.

This is a last-in, first-out memory used for temporary storage. When all internal registers of the CPU are placed on the stack in a particular and precise order (all done by the internal hardware of the CPU), the CPU looks in a special place in memory which has been set aside for it to get the *interrupt vector*, which is the address of the first instruction to execute in the interrupt service routine. It will then execute this program the same as any other program until another interrupt is received, or it comes to a *Return-From-Interrupt* instruction. At this point, it reloads all the registers from the stack, putting all the information back where it originally came from, *including* the program counter register, and takes up the right where it left off just as if nothing had happened. The interrupt-service routine must be careful not to unintentially change any temporary storage of the main program in memory, otherwise, the main program will work erratically when the computer returns to it.

In a multitask executive, the interrupt vector should point to the entry point of the executive itself. The executive must set aside space in memory to store the stack pointer of each of the two main programs, and also a space in memory to recall which of the two programs is being run at a given time. Other memory locations may be needed for other functions, as well, but these are just options which are not totally necessary to the operation of multi-tasking.

Therefore, let us now consider an executive for a background-foreground multitasking system. It will require the use of an interrupt timer which gives pulses every 1/10th to 1/100th of a second. If faster than this rate, most of the CPU's time will be taken up by overhead, processing for the executive; slower than this rate, and the computer will run erratically.

Let's follow the executive through the process of changing tasks. We will assume that there are two tasks, labelled 1 and 2, which reside in their own parts of memory, and that the executive has been set up so that when an interrupt occurs, the executive will be the program executed.

Task 1 is running. An interrupt is received, and the CPU takes all the registers internal to itself, and stores them in order to the location pointed to by the stack pointer, incrementing (or decrementing, depending on the CPU) the stack pointer each time. Then the CPU loads the interrupt vector and starts the executive. The first thing the executive does is to determine, by looking in the storage location it has set aside, which task has just been run. It looks, and finds that task 1 has just been finished. It then takes the stack pointer for task 1 out of the CPU and stores it in the location reserved for the task 1 pointer. Then the executive changes the program pointer to task 2, and loads, from the memory location set aside for it, the stack pointer for task 2. Note that each task has its own task stack pointer. When this is done, the executive turns control over to the second task by executing a return-from-interrupt. This loads all the registers for task 2 into the CPU, and the second task begins. When the next interrupt is received from the system clock, the process repeats, but continues task 1.

It is even possible to have a clock program as part of the executive, so that the executive takes care of updating the hours, minutes, and seconds of the clock.

An initialization program will be needed to start the executive, to install the correct beginning task stack pointers, to set the correct first task to run, and to initialize the interrupt PIA.

Multitasking need not be limited to a background-foreground system, either. As many tasks as you have room for in memory can be run with the right executive. There must be a location reserved in memory for each task's stack pointer. It is also possible to set aside another byte for each task which contains a priority number, so that tasks with the highest priority get done first, then are deleted from the task queue. You can specify time limits for a particular task, and turn a task on and off.

One application of multitasking is in the management of input and output through peripherals. Many peripherals take some time to process the data sent to them by the computer, or take time to send their date to the computer. By setting the I/O handlers as tasks with very high priority, they can be useful in speeding up I/O. For example, let's say we have a printer that takes 100 milliseconds to print a character. Normally, all the while the printer is printing the character, the CPU is looping, waiting for a handshake pulse saying that the printer is done. This is time that the CPU could use doing something else. With multitasking, we simply put the character into a temporary storage location called a FIFO memory, and turn on the "printer" task. Upon the next system interrupt, the printer task, which has the highest priority, will be executed first, and all characters in the FIFO memory will be printed. If the next interrupt occurs before the handshake is received, no worry, it will still be there next time the printer task comes up. Nothing else will be sent until the printer task has determined that the handshake has been received. If the printer empties the FIFO buffer, it simply turns its own task off, and the computer goes back to the main program.

One specific form of multitasking is timesharing. In the method, several terminals can use the same program at the same time. But instead of having each terminal active all the time, each terminal is only active for a few milliseconds of each second. A BASIC program being used by two terminals would have a separate location in memory for its program, and separate temporary storage. When a systems interrupt occurs, not only does the stack pointer change but also the pointer to the user's program, so that it seems as if both programs are running at once, but in reality are being switched back and forth a hundred times a second. Timesharing is a mainstay of most large mainframe computers.

DIRECT-READING
HARDWARE CALENDAR CLOCK

In addition to the software clock described above, there are a number of clock chips on the market which have been developed for so-called "digital alarm clocks." Most of these chips can be interfaced to a computer, and used to tell the time directly, without servicing interrupts from a systems clock. They draw very little current, and can be used with a battery to keep the time even when the power is turned off.

Most of these clock chips, however, have the drawback that they are designed for connection to a time-multiplexed seven-segment digital readout, and that makes them next to impossible to interface to a computer. Not only will we have to wait for the proper digit to show up, but when we read it, we must translate the information from seven-segment code to digital binary or BCD.

Fortunately, in recent months, a particular chip has become available specially for computers. It interfaces directly to a 6820 PIA with little trouble, and can be battery powered and crystal-controlled. It is the MSM5832 chip made by OKI semiconductor. The MSM5832 contains a full clock, with hour, minute, second, as well as a calendar with day, date, month, and year, with a leap-year register. It requires little hardware and software.

The connection scheme to a 6820 PIA is shown in Fig. 5-52. All that is needed is a few pull-up resistors, a crystal, and some capacitors. An optional regulator is shown for attaching three 1.25V Nickel-Cadmium batteries to keep the clock going while the computer's power is turned off. This way, the clock can still have the correct time even when the computer is not running, or even if the power should fail. The batteries will keep the clock running for more than a year all by themselves, and are slowly recharged every time the power comes on.

Twelve data lines are needed to interface to the clock chip, so two sides of the PIA are needed. Eight of the lines are write-only, and the other four are read and write. Four of the write-only lines are control lines, while the other four are address lines to allow the user to read from or write to the internal registers on the chip which contain the time and date data. Since the data lines coming out of a PIA are programmable as to direction, this is no real problem. The only difference between reading the clock and setting the clock is that in the former case the "read" control line is low and data flows from the chip to the PIA. In the latter, the "read" line is high and the "write" line is low, and data flows from the PIA to the chip.

There are thirteen registers, internal to the

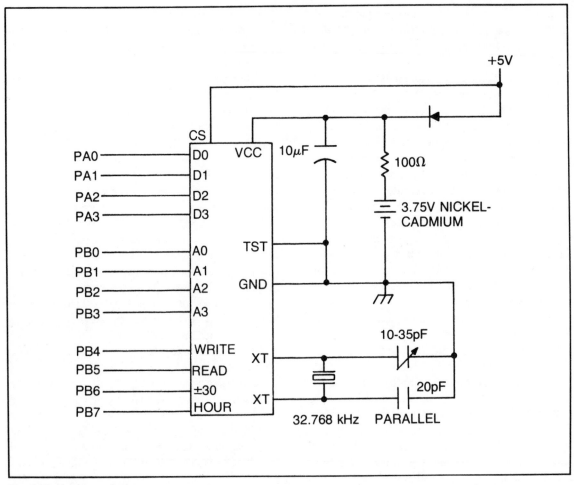

Fig. 5-52. Hardware clock.

chip, that can be read from or written to by the computer. These registers are the seconds, tens of seconds, minutes, tens of minutes, hours, tens of hours, day of the week (days from Sunday, with Sunday = 0), date, tens column for date, month, tens column for month, year, and tens of years. There is also a bit indicating leap year. Output from each of these registers is through the four data lines, and will be a single digit in BCD format. Table 5-4 gives the addressing and data formats. All that is required of the software for operation is to set the clock by putting into it, via a series of write cycles, the correct date and time, and then when the updated date and time is desired, simply execute a series of reads, getting the data in BCD.

PB4 and PB5 are the read and write enable lines. The respective lines should be low for the desired function.

The hold line, PB7, performs a special function. When the "hold" control input is low, and the read and all address lines are high, then the chip becomes in effect, a frequency divider. D0 is an oscillator with a frequency of 1024 Hz; D1, 1 Hz; D2 is 1/60th Hz, and D3 is 1/3600th Hz. If connected to a CA1 input, they can be used as an interrupt timer.

STEPPING MOTORS

Many times the computer hobbyist or design-

216

Table 5-4. Addressing and Data-Format for the Clock Chip.

A3 PB3	A2 PB2	A1 PB1	A0 PB0	D3 PA3	D2 PA2	D1 PA1	D0 PA0	Function
0	0	0	0	x	x	x	x	Seconds-units
0	0	0	1		x	x	x	Seconds-tens
0	0	1	0	x	x	x	x	Minutes-units
0	0	1	1		x	x	x	Minutes-tens
0	1	0	0	x	x	x	x	Hours-units
0	1	0	1	(+)	(+)	x	x	Hours-tens
0	1	1	0		x	x	x	Day of week
0	1	1	1	x	x	x	x	Date-units
1	0	0	0		(∗)	x	x	Date-tens
1	0	0	1	x	x	x	x	Month-units
1	0	1	0				x	Month-tens
1	0	1	1	x	x	x	x	Year-units
1	1	0	0	x	x	x	x	Year-tens

(∗) bit set if leap year
(+) bit 2 set if PM, cleared if AM
    bit 3 set if 24 hr. format, cleared if 12 hr. format

er would like to control the movement of some object or system by the computer. Earlier in this book we discussed the ideas of the servomotor and how it can be applied to mechanical control. But servomotors are either too complicated, or, more often, too expensive for widespread use, in which case the best alternative is to use a stepping motor.

A stepping motor is a motor that can rotate in either direction, stop, start again, and hold its position. These positions are well known, for the motor will only move in precise angular increments for each input excitation. An angular displacement is repeated only for each "step" command, and the shaft of the motor will only move this precise amount, to a known position. The position, velocity, distance and direction of the motor's shaft can therefore be controlled by a precise amount, generally within 5 percent of a step.

Stepper motors are available in 200 steps per revolution, and in 180, 144, 72, 24, and 12 steps per revolution, corresponding to an incremental shaft angle of 1.8, 2, 2.5, 5, 15 and 30 degree angle for each step. A stepping motor is the primary headpositioning device on a floppy disk drive, so it has to be accurate.

There are various types of stepper motors on the market, with winding for two, three, or four-phase operations. The most common is the bifilar four-phase motor, which has permanent-magnet motors with windings on the stator pole. It's main advantage is that it requires only one power supply, and is the type in widest use for this reason. These motors will have four separate windings, which we will label as 1, 2, 3, and 4, in order of their use. Consult the manual on the stepper motor you have to determine which winding is which. The usual method of internal connection is to have one wire from each winding be common to a single ground.

For the stepper motor to rotate, current needs to go through each of the windings. The power is supplied through the common wire to each of the windings, and each of the windings is activated in turn, in a particular sequence, to make the motor turn. An NPN transistor is connected to the winding, with the emitter grounded, and when the base goes high, current will flow through that winding. Indeed, we can connect these bases to the output of a PIA through a base resistor and drive the motor directly from the PIA, as shown in Fig. 5-53.

The pattern of activation of each of the PIA output bits is not simple, or immediately obvious. Two windings must be conducting at a given time, and these windings must shift when a step is to oc-

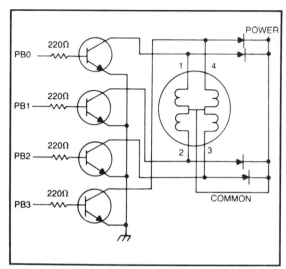

Fig. 5-53. Drivers for a stepper motor.

cur. Figure 5-54 shows the truth table and waveform for a series of rotations in the clockwise direction. The truth table shows that all that is needed is to rotate the two set bits to the right by one bit every time the motor is to be stepped clockwise one step. For rotation in the counterclockwise direction, simply do the bit shifting back the way you came, as shown. A flowchart of a program designed to perform the clockwise rotation of the stepper motor is shown in Fig. 5-55. The diodes shown are protection diodes on the motor windings.

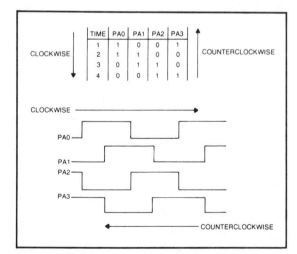

Fig. 5-54. Waveforms and truth table for a stepper motor.

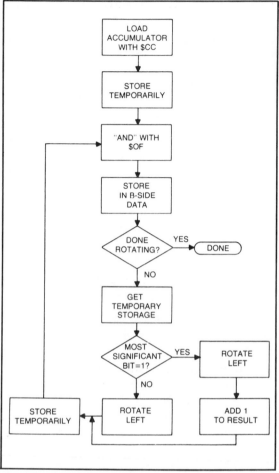

Fig. 5-55. Programming to drive a stepper motor.

It would be nice if it were possible to connect the stepper motor up to the control-bit PIA discussed in an earlier chapter. It can be, of course, connected directly, and the other bits used to control other devices. But with a little extra hardware—two more integrated circuits, to be exact—we can reduce the number of bits needed to control the stepper motor from four to two, one for direction, and one for a "step" signal. This circuit is shown in Fig. 5-56. When the direction input is high, the motor will turn clockwise; when low it will turn counterclockwise. A short pulse on the clock input will activate the motion.

This entire circuit is contained in an integrated circuit manufactured by North American Phil-

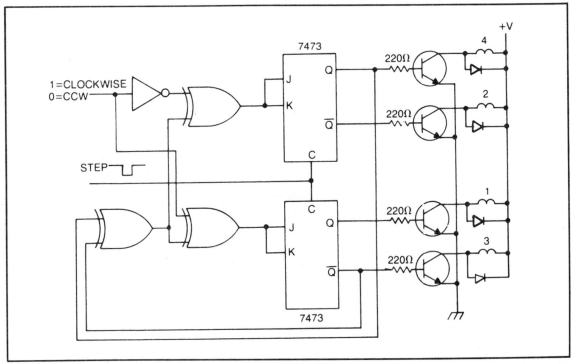

Fig. 5-56. Stepper motor controller-driver.

lips, called the SAA1027. It contains all the logic, the driver transistors, the protection diodes, and everything. A circuit using it is shown in Fig. 5-57. In addition to the direction and step inputs, it also has an initialize input, which sets the motor to a known position. Every time a 0-to-1 logic transition is seen on the step input, the motor will turn one step.

AN X-Y PLOTTER
USING STEPPING MOTORS

It should be apparent to the reader that a stepping motor is a good way to control any object whose position must be known exactly. All that is really needed to position an object is to connect it to a stepper motor and rotate the motor through a known number of steps.

One such computer peripheral that is commonly used, or at least commonly desired, is the X-Y plotter. In this device, both the X- and the Y-position of the pen must be known and repeatable. We will endeavor to show here how an X-Y plotter

may be used and constructed using only two stepper motors and one half of a PIA port.

Most X-Y plotters use servomotor mechanisms to position the pen. The associated electronics of a servo is quite complex, and X-Y plotters normally cost several hundreds of dollars. The plotter described here can probably be built for under a hundred dollars.

Stepper motors of small step-angle are recommended for this use, and may have to be geared down anyway. One motor affects motion along the X-axis, while the other positions the pen on the Y-axis. A solenoid and spring arrangement picks the pen up and sets it down. Almost any resolution that the user desires can be obtained, with the proviso that the higher the resolution, the slower the plotter will be. For example, a plotter with 1024 by 1024 resolution will be 64 times slower than a plotter with 128 by 128 resolution.

The overall mechanism is shown in Fig. 5-58. The stepper motors position the pen, and microswitches on the traveling arms tell the com-

219

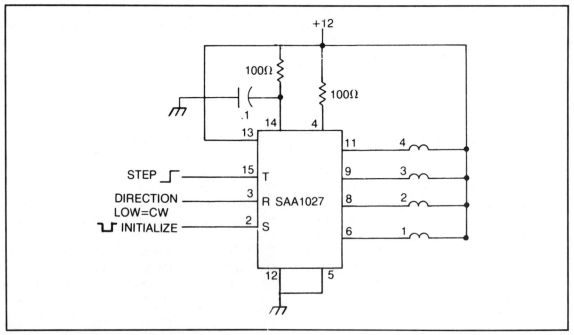

Fig. 5-57. Controller-driver using the SAA1027.

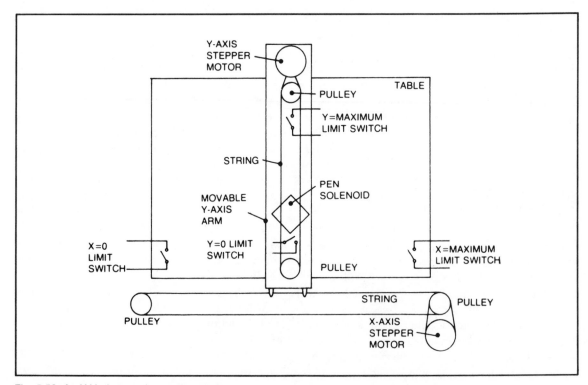

Fig. 5-58. An X-Y plotter using stepper motors.

220

puter when the pen is at the (0,0) position. A pulley arrangement translates the rotation of the stepper motor into liner traverse along the axes. Details of the pulley arrangement and the pen solenoid are shown in Fig. 5-59.

The programming for the plotter is somewhat involved. A flowchart of the program is provided in Fig. 5-60. Basically, the device initializes the system by initializing the PIA for proper input and output lines, as shown. No handshaking lines are needed, so all that needs to be done is assign the appropriate data lines to be either input or output. Then, before any plotting is done, the stepper motors move the pen until signals are received from the microswitches indicating that the pen is in the (0,0) position.

After initializing, to move the pen to a point (X,Y) the program first moves the pen along the X-axis. It asks, "which direction do I move the X-axis?—Clockwise or counterclockwise?" and then, "How many steps do I move it to get to that point?" Then it proceeds to move the stepper motor in that direction the required number of steps, looking after every step to see that the end-of-traverse switch has not been set. If it has, the point is beyond the range of the plotter, and an error condition occurs. Otherwise, the pen moves until the required number of steps have been moved. Then the same is done for the Y-axis. The pen is now at the point (X,Y).

A single bit is provided for the use of controlling the magnet of the pen solenoid. For pen up, the control bit must be 0. For pen down, the bit is a 1. The plotter can move the pen with the pen up, and draw a line, or with it down, and leave a space to begin drawing a line when it reaches its destination.

This plotter will plot as fancy or as a complicated a drawing as the programming will allow. A resolution of 256 by 256 is recommended. Complete line drawings, graphs, plots, even lettering in various scripts can be done with the plotter. The limits of this plotter are the limits of the programmer's imagination.

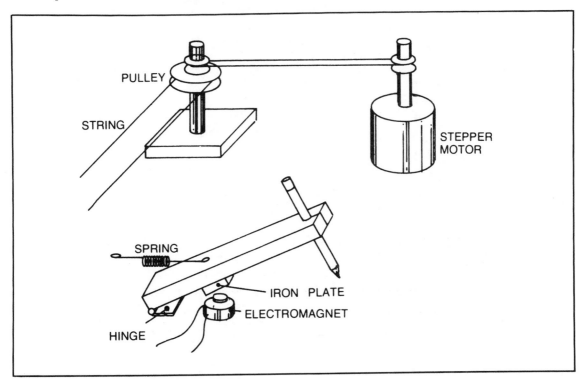

Fig. 5-59. Details of X-Y plotter.

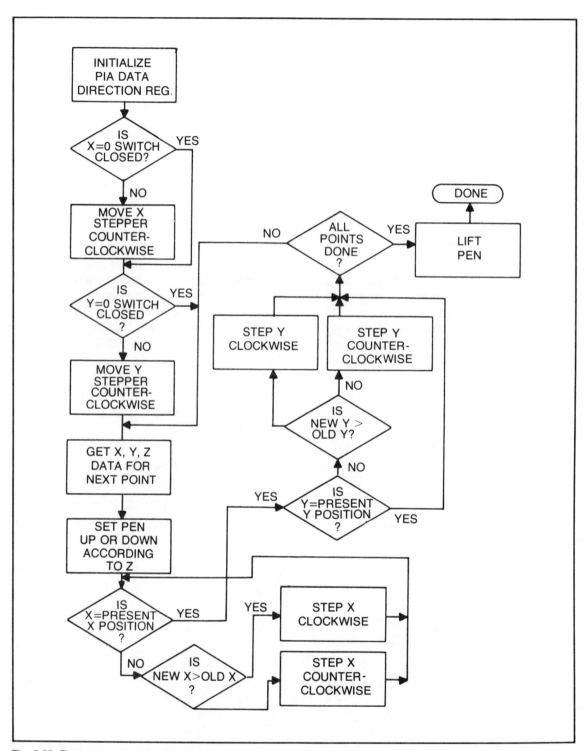

Fig. 5-60. Program to drive the X-Y plotter.

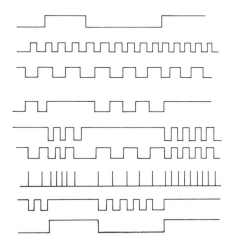

Chapter 6

Serial

Peripherals

All peripherals that we have discussed up to this point in the previous Chapters have been parallel peripherals. That is, either more than one data line has been required to activate the device, or, if only one data line, that line has had only an on/off control. When one data line is used with time multiplexing to send large amounts of information, it is called *serial data*. (Actually, the distinction between single-bit parallel and serial data is quite vague. Many of the devices described earlier could just have easily gone in this Chapter, but were kept where they were for organized purposes.)

Early in Chapter 3, we discussed the mechanics and electronics of serial data communications—the RS-232 convention, start and stop bits, synchronous and asynchronous communication, and baud rates. Now comes the time to apply these ideas to specific peripherals.

The usual purpose of serial data communication is for sending data from a computer to a terminal, or vice-versa. Depending on the particular application, all that is generally needed is a ground line, and a data line in each direction. Sometimes

clock lines in each direction and various "ready" and "accepted" lines will also be needed. The best course of action is to consult your terminal's user manual for the correct details of the connection.

SERIAL DATA STORAGE
AND RETRIEVAL (CASSETTE RECORDERS)

Other than the terminal, the most commonly used serial peripheral is the data recorder. *Mass storage* of programs is a necessity because most computers do not have enough memory to keep all the programs they might use in them at one time, and most are too long to re-enter via the keyboard each time they are to be used.

Serial recording is the slowest, but the least expensive way of storing data. It has the major advantage that the recording device can be an ordinary, inexpensive cassette recorder, available for from $20 to $50. The mechanical and electronic part of the construction is already done at a minimal cost. Compare this to a 5 1/4 inch disk drive at $300.00 for just the drive—this does not count the controller, formatter, or operating system, which can drive the price up to over $1,000.00! In contrast, a cassette storage system can be built, with all electronics, programming, and hardware for less than $75.00, including the recorder itself.

There are two drawbacks to using cassettes for mass storage. The first is speed. Maximum reliability is obtained at a data transfer rate of about 30 bytes per second. Even the high-speed "Tarbell" style of interfaces peak at about 1200 bytes per second. The transfer rate of a disk drive is over a million bytes per second! The second drawback is that a cassette recorder only moves in one direction. There is no real way that a cassette recorder can back up under computer control. If you are searching for a file that is already past on the tape, the only help for it is to manually rewind the tape and begin the search from the beginning, even if that file is the last file on the tape.

Why have a section in a book on peripherals for the computer on cassette recorders anyway? Most computers these days have a disk drive or two built in. Those that don't will have a cassette recorder interface. Some, such as the IBM-PC, will have both.

While it is true that disk drives are the preferred medium for permanent data storage, there are still two areas where cassette or tape storage may be the better medium. Those areas are backups and inter-machine compatibility. A great many personal computers these days have high-capacity "hard" disk drives attached to them. These drives handle 10 megabytes, 20 megabytes, or more of data, all on-line at once. A 10-megabyte hard disk on an IBM-PC will hold as much as 28 floppy disks. Anyone who has ever lost all the data on a disk realizes the dangers of running without backup copies of the data, so regular backups are an absolute necessity when doing any real work using hard disks. But backing up is a chore, especially when you have to manage 28 floppies. If each floppy take 2 minutes to load, the whole backup procedure on a small 10-meg hard disk will take a full hour! And you, the operator, have to be there the whole time to swap disks! A high-speed cassette tape will handle the entire 10 megabytes with ease

all in one chunk. There are vendors who offer high-speed "streaming" tape drives just for the purpose of backups.

Another major use of cassette tape is in sharing data between two different types of computers. Each manufacturer of computers uses his own format and protocol for recording data on a disk, so that a diskette produced by a TRS-80 model 4 will not load in an IBM-PC, and vice-versa. It would not be cost-effective to add a second disk drive and operating system just to be able to share data between computers. But if both computers used the same inexpensive cassette format, sharing becomes easy. The Kansas City Standard format was developed for just this purpose. Mainframe computers have been following these methods for decades, using 9-track tapes at 1600 bits per inch. It doesn't matter if the data comes from a Honeywell, a Univac, or an IBM—they all agree on the data format.

If you are about to construct a cassette storage-device from these instructions, a word or two of caution may be in order. Buy the best recorder you can afford, paying special attention to the frequency bandwidth and the amount of volume you can get out of the earphone jack of the recorder. The wider the frequency response and the higher the volume, the more reliable the data recordings will be. In addition, get the best quality tape you can afford. Off-brands may work well for a while, but will shortly begin dropping data bits. A high-quality audio tape, such as Maxell, TDK, BASF, or Scotch is a good buy, and if you want maximum reliability, purchase some high-density digital cassettes.

AN INEXPENSIVE
TARBELL BIPHASE INTERFACE

The Tarbell biphase recording method was one of the first, and remains one of the most popular methods of recording digital information onto an audio tape. The hardware is very simple and relatively inexpensive. Its speed is very high, but is rather intolerant as to minor variations in the speed of the recorder motor. It also may require a moderate amount of "tuning" to maintain fully reliable operation.

For RS-232 operation, only three active elements are required for the two-way interface, and two of those elements are just RS-232 to TTL translators. Figure 6-1 shows the full nature of the entire interface. Figure 6-1A shows the computer-to-tape portion of the interface, which is driven by the computer's RS-232 output port. The interface is designed to run at 2400 baud, including the start and stop bits. The transmitter portion of the interface is essentially nothing more than an impedance shifter and wave shaper so that the incoming waveform will be more compatible with being recorded on an audio cassette recorder. The output of this simple circuit is to be plugged into the "mic" or microphone input of the cassette recorder. If you use the "AUX" input of the tape recorder, the 470K and 100-ohm resistors may not be needed.

Figure 6-1B shows the tape-to-computer interface. Its purpose is to convert the audio signal from the recorder into a rectangular-shaped wave, to be converted to RS-232 levels. It is really little more than a high-pass network with a comparator. The operational amplifier requires balanced positive and negative power supply voltages for operation, but the input to the level shifter immediately following it must be TTL levels, so the resistor and diode network is added to ensure that the output of the operational amplifier does not go below ground voltage.

When using the device, all that is necessary to record data onto tape is to send the data out over the RS-232 serial port at 2400 baud with the tape recorder running on "record." To read it back into the computer, just run the playback into the RS-232 receive port and adjust the volume level on the recorder until proper data is received, then leave it at that setting. A sampling and storage program will be needed to take the data.

Examples of the types of programs needed to send and receive data from this interface are given in Fig. 6-2 in flowchart form. Since the cassette interface does not itself have a × 16 clock generator, the best course is to use the same clock for both

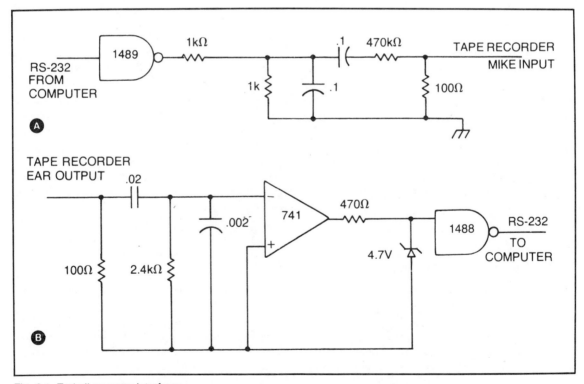

Fig. 6-1. Tarbell cassette interfaces.

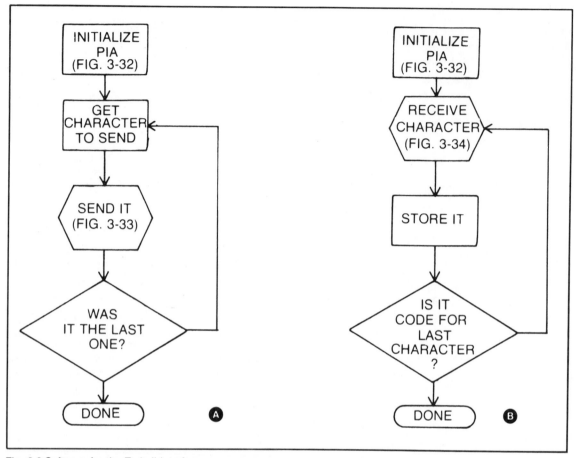

Fig. 6-2.Software for the Tarbell interface.

transmit and receive.

All the programs described in this chapter will make the assumption that the method of generating the RS-232 serial signals from the computer is that a UART is connected to a computer through a 6820 PIA. Accordingly, the PIA must be initialized.

KANSAS CITY CASSETTE INTERFACE

In November of 1975, a group of computer manufacturers and programmers met at a conference in Kansas City, Kansas, to discuss and determine a standard for the exchange of programs and data on cassettes by the computer hobbyists and more serious users. The idea was to determine a method whereby a person in one end of the coun-

try could exchange programs with a person on the other end of the country, even though the two persons may not have the same computer, or the same type of cassette recorder. The method that was proposed as a result of the meeting is a modified version of frequency-shift keying commonly used with telephone data transmission, and is similar to the coding technique described by Don Lancaster in several of his publications on homebuilt computers. Since that time, it has become known as the Kansas City Standard.

In this format, each 8-bit byte is written on tape in an asynchronous format at a data rate of 300 baud. Start and stop bits are included. A 1 is defined as eight cycles of a 2400-Hz square wave, and a 0 is four cycles of a 1200 Hz square wave. Both of these rates can be derived easily by flip-flop frequency division of a 4800-Hz, ×16 data clock of 300 baud data transmission, and therefore the data is limited to 300-baud transmission. These frequencies were chosen because it was felt that they represented the portion of a cassette recorder's frequency spectrum that was least noisy and least susceptible to fading or attenuation by frequency-dependent components in the electronics.

The major advantage to the standard is that, in addition to its suitability for virtually any inexpensive cassette recorder, the ×16 clock can be easily derived from the data recorded on the tape, and is therefore self-clocking. Any variation in speed from one recorder to the next, or within one recorder as the batteries age, is automatically cancelled out by the self-clocking feature.

The major disadvantage of the method is that it is slow. Data is recorded at 300 baud, or 30 bytes per second, compared to 2400 baud, or 240 bytes per second for the Tarbell format.

The Kansas City Standard has proven to be a good and reliable exchange standard and, even if slow, has wide acceptance in use. It will likely continue to be in use for many years.

Figure 6-3 is a pair of schematics for the modulator and demodulator from RS-232 serial to Kansas City Standard. Figure 6-3A connects the computer to the tape recorder for recording data. It consists of nothing more than a set of flip-flops and gates to divide the ×16 clock to the appropriate frequencies, depending on whether the data is a 0 or a 1. At the end is a simpler filter to prepare the square-wave data to be more like sine-wave data for better recording. The output of this circuit goes directly into the microphone input of the recorder.

Figure 6-3B is the receiver/demodulator, which takes the audio data off the tape and converts it to RS-232 levels, and at the same time generates the ×16 clock again. It starts with a filter to screen out any tape hiss, and features a voltage limiter to protect the LM339 comparator. The demodulator must detect whether the 1200-Hz or 2400-Hz data is present. There are many ways of doing this; however, a common one is to detect zero crossings of the input signal. This will end up generating either 2400 or 4800 pulses per second. A one-shot is used, tuned so that if it is not kept triggered at the 4800-Hz rate, it must therefore, by elimination, be the other rate. A simple gate on the output of this, coupled with another one-shot, provides the data directly and also generates the ×16 clock. An LM339 is used as a zero-crossing detector, and the propagation delay of three ×OR gates is used to form an edge detector on the output of the 311.

Figure 6-4 shows the waveforms at the various points of the modulator and demodulator, showing how the clock and data are transformed to audio tones, and how they can be transformed and recovered from the audio. The software needed for the cassette interface is identical to that needed for the Tarbell interface. The only difference is that separate transmit and receive clocks are used on the UART.

In both cases, the presence of the data on the tape does not guarantee that the reader will be able to decipher the contents of the data. Suppose you are sending a tape of a program to an associate of yours who has a computer identical to yours in every respect of the hardware, but whose programming style and monitors and operating systems are significantly different from yours. You tell him that there is a program on the tape. You have recorded the tapes so that you have placed the program byte for byte, in ascending order of addresses, onto the tape. You have included nothing else. But his loader program requires both a start-of-record and an end-of-record signal, and a checksum. He loads the tape with his loader, and gets an error. He concludes that the tape is bad, and sends it back to you. You receive it, try it on your machine, and get a perfect load. Now you are both confused.

The problem is that, even though you both agree on how the data is to be represented as a signal on the tape, you do not agree on the *format* for recording the data. He expects start, stop, and checksum bytes. You do not. If he were to send a program to you, you would interpret the start byte as a program step, load it, and try to execute the start byte—and probably bomb the program the first try!

A recommended format for the transmission,

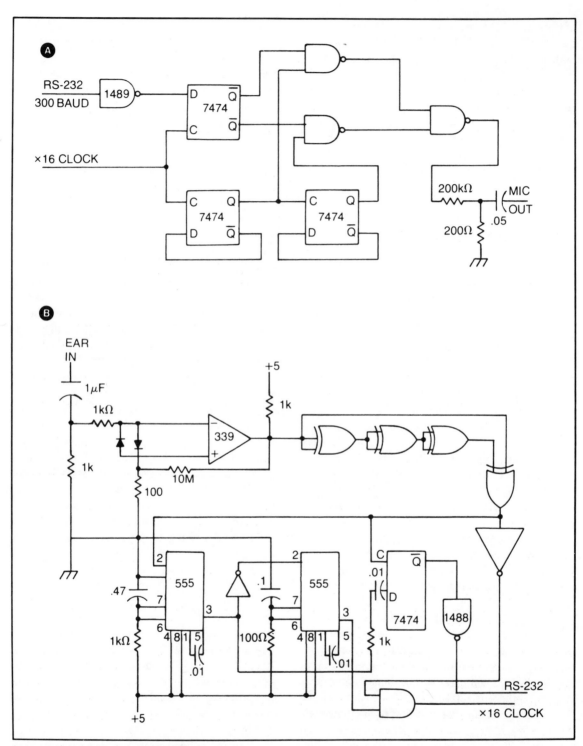

Fig. 6-3. Kansas City cassette interface.

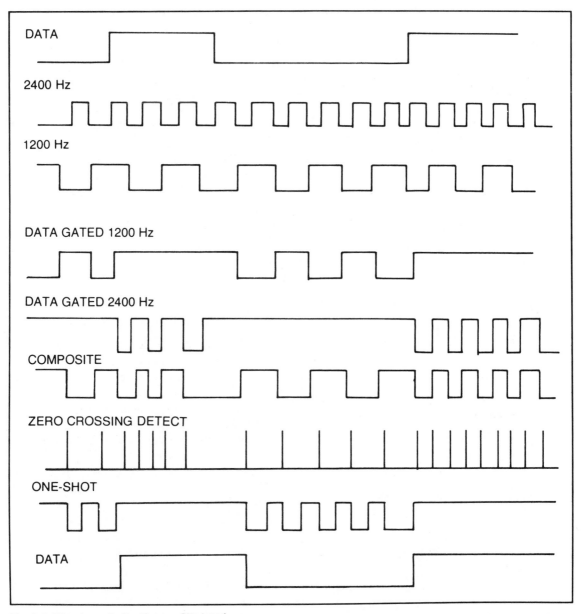

Fig. 6-4. Waveforms in the Kansas City interface.

recording, and exchange of data is the Motorola S1 format, commonly called the MIKBUG format after the name of Motorola's proprietary 6800 machine monitor which first brought the format to the attention of the general public. The format is described early in Chapter 3 in the section on serial interfacing standards, during the discussion of er-

ror detection and correction. This format tends to be a bit on the slow side, requiring 2.75 overhead bits of data transmission for each byte of data to be sent, but is also useful in discovering which of several data records within the transmission is at fault. A faulty data bit can be corrected usually by simply re-reading the data from the tape. It has

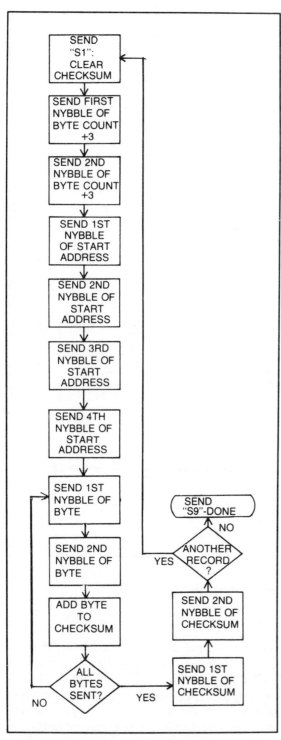

Fig. 6-5. Recording in the MIKBUG format.

been used for many years with 6800-based machines using the Kansas City Standard. Flowcharts for sending and receiving the format is shown in Figs. 6-5 and 6-6.

A final note on Kansas City Standard. There is a lot of redundancy built into the method. It is theoretically possible to record and recover data from tape using the same set of tones at up to 1200 baud. This will mean that a 0 on the tape is *one* cycle of 1200-Hz data, and a 1 is *two* cycles of 2400 Hz. It will take a very good electronic circuit to recover a 0 from only one cycle of audio, but it can be done, in principle. The exact details will not be covered here, and to my knowledge they have not been published yet. The user is encouraged to experiment if he is of that bent, and to publish his findings in one of the computer hobbyist magazines.

A HARDWARE RANDOM-NUMBER GENERATOR

Strictly speaking, random number generator is not by itself a serial device; but since the use we will put it to is a keyboard, and a keyboard is frequently connected to a computer through a serial channel, we can include it in this chapter.

Random numbers are an important asset to a computer's catalog of capabilities. Most people are familiar with random numbers on computers through various games. For example, in BASIC, the RND statement is used to provide a random number between 0 and 1 which is used to decide among various courses of action. If the random number is greater than 0.5, one set of actions is pursued, and if less than 0.5, an altogether different direction is taken.

Random numbers are also important to the sciences and to any branch of investigation that uses statistics. One application is the so-called *Monte-Carlo* modeling technique. In this method, every independent variable is represented by a random number within the range of possibilities, and thousands, even millions, of trials are made. The pattern of the outputs and the relative probabilities can be calculated from the ratio of the number of successful trials divided by the number of total trials.

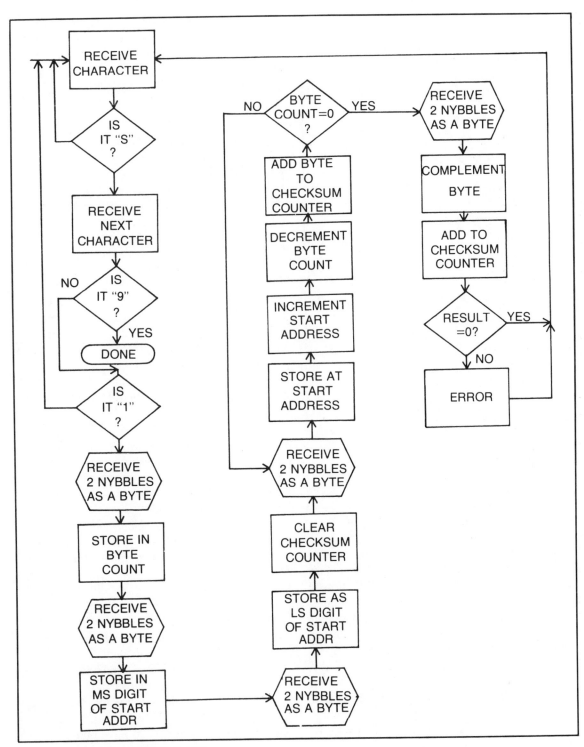

Fig. 6-6. Receiving the MIKBUG format.

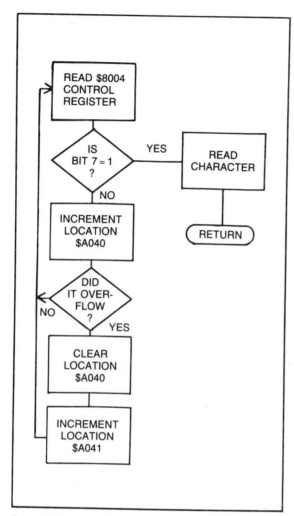

Fig. 6-7. Flowchart for a random number generator.

Seed	×899	Least 5	RND
1	899	899	.00899
899	808201	8201	.08201
8201	7372699	72699	.72699
72699	6535640	56401	.56401
56401	50704499	4499	.04499

Note that there are two keys to this method of generating random numbers: First, that the digit is allowed to *overflow*, so that we only take the least significant portion of the number, and secondly that the old overflow integer becomes the new seed. The method does not produce truly random numbers; the pattern will begin repeating after a certain (hopefully large) number of tries. But it will do well enough for most applications.

The RND function in most BASICs has a feature that it can be given an argument RND(X), so that the same random number is given every time for the same X. The above outline of the random generator process shows, that if the same seed is used every time, the same random number will result. If it were possible to find a value of X which is a truly random integer, then RND would give a truly random value.

We can accomplish this with a little programming. No person has a truly regular beat on the typewriter keyboard. There is always some variation on the rate at which the keys are hit. Also, the keyboard is usually interfaced to the computer through a PIA or an ACIA, and the interface is constantly scanned by a polling loop whenever a character is expected from the keyboard. If we insert a little counter that increments a memory location whenever the polling loop finds that there is *no* character present, and does nothing whenever it finds that there *is* a character to be read, then the fact that the polling loop is done so many thousand times a second will ensure that the numbers are truly random.

Figure 6-7 is a flowchart of an addition to the keyboard polling routine which will help to generate more random numbers. It assumes that the control register for the keyboard is at hex location $8004, and that a sixteen-bit random-number seed is to be kept in locations $A040 and $A041. These

In order for games to be fair, and for Monte-Carlo modeling to work, the random numbers must be truly random. The RND function in BASIC uses a pseudorandom number generator, which requires a *seed*. The usual method is to take a beginning number, and multiply it by some very large prime number, and then take the most significant digit or two and throw them away. For example, let the number 1 be the seed, and the prime number be 899. Then if we take only the least significant five digits, and move the decimal point so that the number is between 0 and 1, we get the following random numbers:

latter two addresses are the decimal addresses 41024 and 41025. Then, to get the BASIC random number, simply

```
10  DEF FNA(RND(PEEK(41024)
     *256 + PEEK(41025) + A))

    . . .

    1140 R = FNA
    1141 A = A + 899
```

The random number generator is defined as a function, and whenever the function is called, it produces a random number into the variable R. The variable A is used so that different random numbers will be used if a long time goes by without seeking an input from the keyboard, and thereby updating the random number seed.

A MORSE-CODE PRACTICE OSCILLATOR AND KEYER

There are many ways to code letters and numbers. We have discussed so far in this work the ASCII code, as well as the BCD, EBCDIC, Correspondence, and binary codes. We have not gone into the other methods of encoding, such as the Hollerith and Excess-3 codes. Even the *I Ching* is a form of binary code.

One of the earliest codes to be used was the Morse code, associated in most people's minds with the telegraph system of the late 1800s. It has also been used extensively with radiotelegraphy. In fact, to get an amateur radio license (the so-called "ham" license) an applicant still needs to be able to understand the International Morse Code.

The International Morse Code should not be confused with the American Morse Code—the two are quite different. Both, however, are similar in that they use a series of dots and dashes, or short tones and long tones, called *dits* and *dahs*, to code each letter of the alphabet, each digit of the numbers, and several punctuation marks. For example, the letter "e" is simply a short tone, or *dit*. While letter "r" is three tones in the pattern, *dit-dah-dit*, and the letter "v" is *dit-dit-dit-dah*. The code is shown in Table 6-1.

Table 6-1. The International Morse Code.

A	• —	T	—
B	— • • •	U	• • —
C	— • — •	V	• • • —
D	— • •	W	• — —
E	•	X	— • • —
F	• • — •	Y	— • — —
G	— — •	Z	— — • •
H	• • • •	1	• — — — —
I	• •	2	• • — — —
J	• — — —	3	• • • — —
K	— • —	4	• • • • —
L	• — • •	5	• • • • •
M	— —	6	— • • • •
N	— •	7	— — • • •
O	— — —	8	— — — • •
P	• — — •	9	— — — — •
Q	— — • —	0	— — — — —
R	• — •		
S	• • •		

Many who own computers also have a desire to become ham radio operators, and will want to learn the code well enough to pass the FCC code test. One method of learning is to listen to records, and another is to send the code with a key and oscillator so that they can recognize the code when they hear it. Also, there might be hams who already have their license who are looking for a way to send computer information via Morse code, or who will want to simply use the keyboard of their computer to send the code, instead of "pounding the key."

This section of this chapter will describe how to make a code-practice oscillator that will send letters to a speaker in Morse code, or which can substitute for the key of a transmitter.

Figure 6-8 shows the relatively simple circuit by which this may be accomplished. It requires only a single output bit from a computer parallel port. When the bit is high, the tone sounds from the oscillator, and when low, no tone is sounded. When

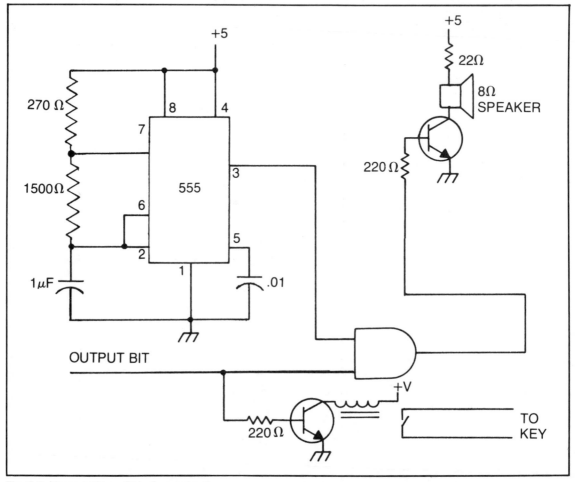

Fig. 6-8. Morse code oscillator/keyer circuit.

the tone is sounding, the keyswitch is closed, just as if the key had been pressed. The keyswitch should be wired in parallel with the key itself.

Since the hardware is so simple, it should be apparent that the software will be rather involved. The flowchart of the software is given in Fig. 6-9. This handler assumes that some other program, such as a text editor (which is a very common program, and easily available on virtually every machine for quite reasonable prices. No computer should be without one.) has placed the ASCII text which is to be sent through the keyer/oscillator into memory. We will also presume that we know the starting location in memory of the text, and that the hexadecimal number $04, which is the control

code for "end of text," finishes the text to be sent.

The code oscillator/keyer will also require the use of a timer or delay loop. We will use the convention that a *dit* is one unit of time long, a *dah* is three units of time long, that there is a space of one unit of time between each *dit* or *dah* within a letter, and three units of space between each letter.

Two bytes of code will be needed for the table of characters for each letter. One will tell how many individual *dits* and *dahs* there are in the letter, and the other will be a code for the pattern of longs and shorts. We will represent a long tone by a 1 in the byte, and a short tone by a 0. The byte will be read from least significant bit to most significant, until we have read all the bits listed by the count byte.

234

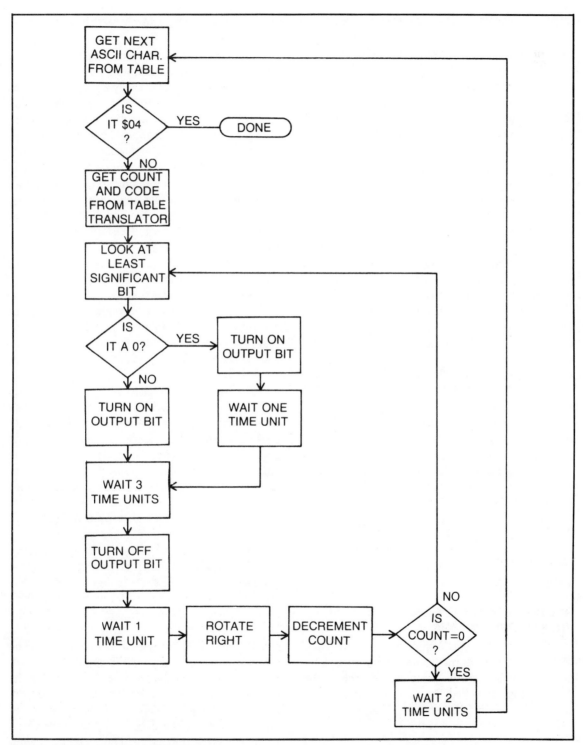

Fig. 6-9. Programming the oscillator/keyer.

This table will have to be built up by the programmer before the program can be used. For example, take the letter V again. When the computer sees that the letter V is to be sent, it looks in the table for the letter V, and finds from the first byte that the Morse code for that letter is four tones long. The second byte is hex $08, or binary 00001000. It will then read as follows:

Bit 0	0	dit
Bit 1	0	dit
Bit 2	0	dit
Bit 3	1	dah

At this point, a space of three units of time is left between the letters, and the next letter is obtained, to start the process over again. If there is no next letter, the cycle ends.

The rate at which words are sent can easily be adjusted by varying the length of time of one time unit on the timer or the delay loop. For fast rates, use a short time. Novices must be able to take code at five words per minute, while more advanced licenses require at least thirteen. A "word" is five characters. A good way to practice will be to read a page from a book into the computer, and have it sent through the keyer. Alternately, have a friend type into the keyboard while the computer sends the code for you to receive. The code rate could even be made adjustable while the computer displays the word rate on the screen.

The computer can be used to put together long messages, and then send them automatically using the keyer feature of this circuit, or the words can be stored in memory while typing on a first-in, first-out basis, and the keyboard can be used instead of a key.

HOUSEHOLD CONTROL
VIA ELECTRIC WIRING

If you want to control appliances in your house or business, it is normally necessary to run individual wires from the computer to each of the devices to be controlled. These look unsightly, and can trip passers-by. If the rates of control are not too large, that is to say, not too many control commands will be needed every second, the wiring of the house electricity can be used to affect these commands.

Ordinary household electricity is alternating current, 110 volts ac, rms, with a frequency of 60 Hz. These values are virtually constant. The rms voltage may vary from 105 to 125 volts depending on your location, but the the frequency never changes. (These values are only good in the United States. In Europe and Asia, other voltages and frequencies may be used.) Therefore, any low-voltage ac signal of a frequency significantly different from the 60 Hz will not affect appliances significantly, and can be easily separated and detected. All that is needed, then is a transmitter for these tones, and a receiver/detector for each device we want to control, which will include a set of logic to decode the control codes for that device.

We will use a 2-kHz tone for the data transmission. This frequency is a convenient one to use for control because it is easily separated from 60 Hz, easy to generate, and will not interfere with the normal operation of most appliances that attach to the house current.

The transmitter itself is very simple (see Fig. 6-10). All it does is accept serial RS-232 signals from a serial output port and converts all the 1s to a 2-kHz tone which is then superimposed on the ac lines. The current from the high-frequency tone is limited so that it will not get back in to the power lines and disrupt power service. A 555 oscillator and a gate is all that is needed to generate the tones, and a few diodes and a transformer will suffice to apply the signal to the ac lines.

The receiver is, by necessity, much more complex. Not only must the receiver detect the tones, but also convert those tones to digital bits, convert them to parallel, and have internal logic to decode the byte to see if it is a command code for that device. The detection is done with a simple filter, and a converted to digital with a low-pass filter. The receiver must contain a UART and its own baud-rate generator and power supply. The output of the UART is fed to one or more decoders, made from either 7430 8-input NAND gates and inverters, or if many codes will be decoded by this receiver, a 74154 will do the job nicely. The decoding of eight

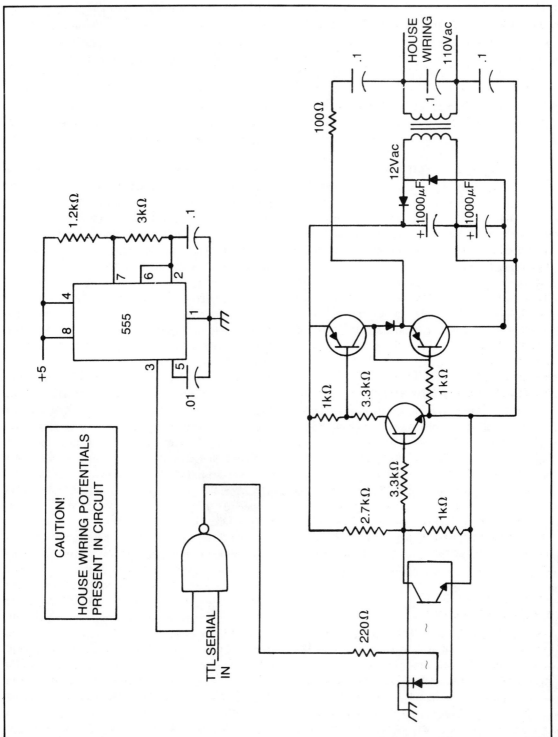

Fig. 6-10. Household control transmitter.

bits for a command code is just the same, only less complex than the decoding of 16 bits of address, as we did in Chapter 2. Figure 6-11 shows a circuit that will do the job.

The control codes activated by each receiver must be unique to that receiver. For every control function to be performed, there must be a unique control code to that function, and a receiver that contains that control code. To activate a specific function, say turning on the coffee pot when the computer alarm clock goes off, the computer sends the code $1F (for example) out over its serial interface that is connected to the ac transmitter. All receivers will receive the $1F, but only *one* (the one connected to the coffeepot) will give a "true" condition to the control decode, and start the coffeepot.

The reader would do well to re-examine the section on device control with the computer, Chapter 4. Many of the same ideas are used here for the control of devices. Especially the section on use of the outputs of a 74154 for control, and the use of RS flip-flops to turn devices on and off.

MODIFYING A TELEVISION SET TO ACT AS A MONITOR

Most small computers these days have a video display. That is, the information is displayed on a screen very much like a TV set. Many have the TV set or monitor included with the purchase price, while with others it is an extra-cost "option."

This section and the next will demonstrate two methods whereby an ordinary TV set can be converted to a video monitor for computer display purposes. The first is called direct video conversion, and requires a rather extensive knowledge of electronics, but provides far superior performance. In the next section, we will discuss an rf modulator which is an "add-on" circuit, with little effort or knowledge needed.

TV sets are readily available on the used market. Most TV repair shops have dozens around the shop that have been traded in on newer models, or not reclaimed when brought in for repairs. It is not unusual to be able to find a black-and-white TV set in good working condition for $25.00. If you can find a shop that has a TV with bad sound, a bad

tuner, or a bad rf front end, but the horizontal and vertical oscillators and the video amplifier and picture tubes still work, it can be easily used for this purpose, and the repairman will probably let you have them for nothing to get them out of his shop. My first two monitors cost me nothing.

Tube-type sets are the easiest to convert, but can't be depended on for more than a year or two. Inside the set is a tube guide, telling you what types of tubes there are in the set, what they do, and where they go. One of these tubes will be marked "video amplifier." You will need to identify this tube with the back cover off the set. Then go to a tube guide manual which lists tubes, and find out which pin of that tube corresponds to the "grid." If there is more than one grid, you will want the control grid. There may be more than one tube inside the envelope, so mark down both of them if you have to. Then, *carefully*, with the power on to both the set and the computer's video output, connect the video output to the grid through a 1 microfarad capacitor (see Fig. 6-12). Be extremely careful, as there are high voltages present in all TV sets. If you have the right pin on the tube, you should immediately see characters on the screen. You may need to adjust the horizontal and vertical hold. When you have determined which is the correct input pin, solder the capacitor into the set at that point, and set up a jack on the case to receive it. Then disconnect any other capacitor to the tube at that pin. Do not disconnect any resistors! These are needed for proper tube biasing. With transistor type sets, the problem is much more complex. First of all, you will need a schematic of the set. This can be ordered from your repairman, or purchased from a local electronics outlet as a "Sam's Photofact Sheet." You will need this schematic to be able to identify the transistor which is the input to the video amplifier. Most black-and-white transistor TV sets have a video amplifier that is connected to a dc bias source through a peaking coil. The reason that tube-type sets are easier to modify is that the video amplifier in a tube set is usually biased in the black, while a transistor set is biased so that the screen will be white when there is no signal. We have to keep the proper bias when con-

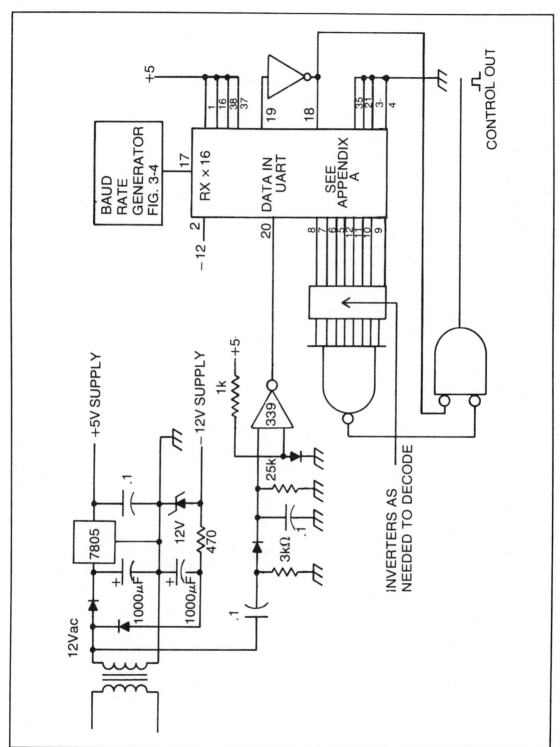

Fig. 6-11. Household control receiver.

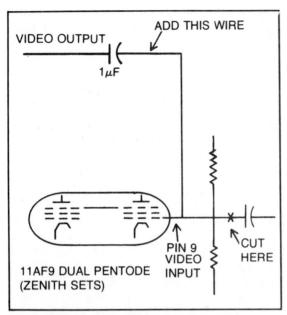

VIDEO OUTPUT

ADD THIS WIRE

1μF

11AF9 DUAL PENTODE
(ZENITH SETS)

PIN 9
VIDEO
INPUT

CUT
HERE

Fig. 6-12. Converting a tube-type TV to a monitor.

verting the set, in either case. See Fig. 6-13 for more information about the biasing of the video amplifier.

To make the modification, simply disconnect the existing input from the rf detector, *without disconnecting the bias source*, as shown, and add in the new source of video signal, again as shown. A switch can be used to switch back and forth between them if TV reception is still desired.

When doing a direct video connection like this, or indeed when making any electrical connection to a TV set, two things should be kept in mind: First, never work with the power on unless absolutely necessary! Secondly, even with the power off, there are capacitors inside the set that still store charge, and can give you a nasty shock!

Despite the cost of most TV sets, they do tend to be missing one essential item: a power transformer. Most sets are what is called "hot-chassis" sets. They get their power through direct connec-

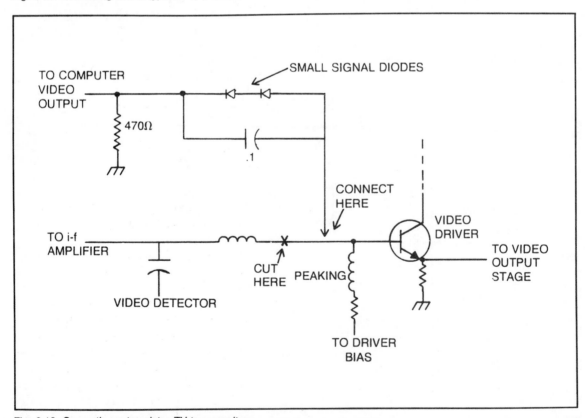

TO COMPUTER
VIDEO
OUTPUT

470Ω

SMALL SIGNAL DIODES

.1

CONNECT
HERE

VIDEO
DRIVER

TO i-f
AMPLIFIER

VIDEO DETECTOR

CUT
HERE

PEAKING

TO VIDEO
OUTPUT
STAGE

TO DRIVER
BIAS

Fig. 6-13. Converting a transistor TV to a monitor.

tion to the power lines, without going through a transformer. By themselves, when properly used, this does not constitute a hazard. But most TV sets are not designed with connection to low-voltage computer equipment in mind. Check the schematic of your set, or ask a repairman. Is there a power supply transformer (other than the high-voltage transformer) in the set? If not, you will have to purchase an *isolation transformer*. This is just an ordinary transformer that is neither step-up or step-down, but disconnects the set from direct connection to the power lines, so that the ground of the power supply "floats." That way, when you connect the ground of the computer to the ground of the set, they happily accept each other's definition of ground. Without the isolation transformer, not only are you running a shock hazard, but you may destroy chips! The transformer may be connected inside the set, and wired as part of the chassis, or there are plug-in types available, as well. If you have access to a "variac" type of adjustable transformer, in many cases these will work as well.

For more information on conversion of TV sets to direct video input, the *TV Typewriter Cookbook*, by Don Lancaster, available from any Radio Shack distributor, is highly recommended. See pages 185-197. The book is $3.95 in paper. It also gives much information on extending the bandwidth of a TV set so that a better display can be seen.

AN RF MODULATOR FOR TV-SET USE

The other method of connecting a video signal from a computer to a TV set does not involve any modification to the TV set at all. (Aside, of course, from the possible addition of an isolation transformer.) The way it works is this: The video signal is converted to an rf signal, and applied directly to the antenna terminals just the same as if it were a radio signal from the antenna. What you are doing is modulating the signal, and then demodulating it again with the TV's rf circuitry.

A device that adds the rf part of the signal to a signal carrying information is called a *modulator*. At this writing, there are many kits for rf modulators for TV use on the market—some for as little as $6.00. Two that can be recommended are the

"PIXE-VERTER" from ATV research, and the modulator by Pickles & Trout. Radio Shack also carries a small module for this purpose.

If you would like to try your hand at building a modulator yourself, they are quite easy to build, and will not cost very much. Don Lancaster has an excellent circuit mentioned in his book on page 202. It requires a modest parts count, and takes a little tuning, but is among the best available.

More recently, a circuit has been developed by the University of Waterloo in Ontario, Canada, which uses only one integrated circuit, one transistor, one capacitor, and three resistors. The schematic for it is shown in Fig. 6-14. The circuit uses a 7413 dual schmitt trigger as a free running oscillator. When this is running, the current through the 7413 is also oscillating at the same frequency—from power supply to ground! The second transistor just controls the amount of current that can flow, according to the video signal. The output of the 7413 is then an oscillator whose amplitude is controlled by the value of a voltage at the transistor's base. But this is just another definition for a modulator!

The device can be connected directly to the antenna leads of any TV set with a transformer or isolation transformer, as described above. Alternately, with the TV antenna disconnected, just run about 6 inches of 300 ohm twinlead out of the modulator, and tape it to the TV antenna leads. *Don't* leave the antenna connected to the lead-in (leave the lead-in connected to the set, though) or your neighbors will have something to say to you about their TV reception, and you may get a visit from the FCC! This method provides enough capacitive coupling to get a signal into the TV set.

With the values shown, the set should pick up the signal on channels 2, 3, or 4. Some adjustment of the variable resistor may be necessary.

The oscillator actually runs at about 19 MHz, with the values shown. But since the output of the modulator is a square wave, the third harmonic is 1/3 as strong in amplitude as the fundamental, and will give just about 1 volt of signal to the set, and the set's tuner will filter out the fundamental and all higher harmonics. At TV frequencies, the modulation is only about 20-30%, but should be sufficient

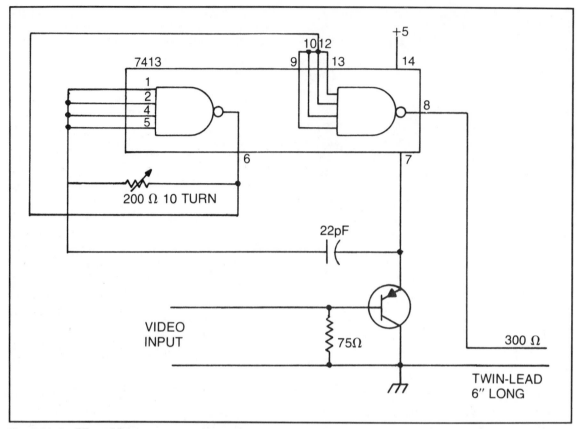

Fig. 6-14. An RF modulator.

to generate a good signal for the TV to pick up well.

LIGHT PENS FOR BAR CODE SCANNING

The use of the optical scanner for bar codes is increasing dramatically in past years. Uses for bar codes are multiple and manifold. Everyone is, of course, familiar with the optical scanners in supermarkets used for automated checkouts using the Universal Product Code (UPC), and we can all agree that this system makes the checkout faster. It is also an excellent method of inventory control for the supermarket itself, to know when to order more of a particular product. Smaller stores could also find this method useful, but the system is generally only available with larger computer systems.

The U.S. Postal Service is currently using an optical bar code scanner for certain types of mail. (Examine some of your bills: look for the bar codes on the bottoms of the envelopes.) One manufacturer of peripherals for the Macintosh has a bar code time and effort calculator for job tasking and accounting. Some software publishers are producing software in optically-readable format.

Construction of the optical scanner for reading bar codes is relatively simple. Even the electronics is not difficult, nor is the digitizing of the signals. The difficult part is interpreting the digitized signals because several codes are used.

First, let us examine the light pen itself. In reading bar code it is only necessary to detect the difference between light and dark at a particular point. There are a number of electronic sensors on the market that can do the job. We have already seen, in Chapter 4, the use of the phototransistor

242

and optiosolator. We shall show, however, that few of these devices meet the criteria for scanning bar codes.

Most bar codes have a "bit width" of around 1/100th of an inch. That is, the length of space that corresponds to a light or dark area is one, two, and sometimes three times the distance of 0.01 inch. A typical scanning rate for a light pen is about 20 inches per second. (Between 10 and 30, depending.) This means that in one second, a light pen scans 2000 "bit lengths," or about 500 microseconds per bit length. The software timing loop is unlikely to be less than about 30 microseconds in length, so we will need a detector with a rise time less than 30 microseconds. A phototransistor is just about this order of magnitude, or right on the edge of acceptability. A photodarlington, while having higher output power and more gain, is even worse, with a rise time on the order of 100 microseconds. A good photodiode has a rise time on the order of 0.01 to 0.1 microseconds, and is linear over a light level range of about 10 million, so it seems to be the answer.

The difficulty with a photodiode is that its light sensitivity is less than the transistor or photodarlington, and needs a higher light level. Also, its response is generally more toward the infrared than a phototransistor. We can overcome this by using a higher level incandescent light source, such as a 5 watt flashlight bulb, which is very heavy in the infrared, rather than a light emitting diode.

A rough diagram of a type of light pen is shown in Fig. 6-15. Light concentration and area selectivity is improved by adding some lenses for both the light source and light detector. The detector is housed in a small casing to allow only light from the work to fall upon it. The construction of the housing also allows the correct placement of the working surface with respect to the lenses. Edmund Scientific Corporation of Barrington, NJ, is nationally famous for carrying almost every type and focal length of lens that can be conceived at extremely reasonable prices. You will want a convex-type lens for light concentration.

The electronics for processing the signal is shown in Fig. 6-16. While it looks complex, it is actually quite simple when looked at as a set of mod-

ules. The RCA 3140 is the centerpiece of a current-to-voltage converter and amplifier. Adjustment of the 20K potentiometer adjusts the gain. The upper LM741 op amp is a peak-sensor, as described in Chapter 5. This circuit has a relaxation time of about 1 second, and senses the highest level of current (corresponding to the highest level of light, or a white spot on the paper.) The lower LM741 is a voltage follower which reproduces the voltage level. The output of each is put into the LM339 comparator, and any variation of the light level from its peak is seen as a "low" level of light, or a dark spot. The output here is put directly into two edge sensors, formed by two pairs of 7400 NAND gates, while one is inverted first. The net result is that the upper gates produce negative-going pulses on the falling edge of the signal, and the lower gates produce similar pulses on the rising edge of the pulses. The two signals are OR'ed together to get a pulse on the rising edge of each bar and another on the falling edge of the bar, or a pulse each time the light level changes. The waveforms are shown in Fig. 6-17.

We use these pulses to cause interrupts at the processor through the CA or CB input lines of the PIA. Then, using software, we will count the length of time between each pulse. The longer the length of time, the broader the light or dark band. A flowchart of an interrupt service program is shown in Fig. 6-18. It is necessary to use interrupts because we are using software timing here. In this type of program, the number of times through a loop is counted, and the result stored in a series of successive addresses at each interrupt. The count is proportional to the width of the light or dark band. The count is ended when a band is too wide to be counted, as when you get to the end of the dark bars and have only a long area of white left. It should be noted that this type of detector has a bias toward dark bands; that is, dark bands will be seen as longer than light bands of the same width. This should be accounted for in your software.

At this point you have the basic counts in your computer. Making sense of them is another matter, entirely. The process is complicated by the fact that there is no standardization in the various types of bar encoding. Figure 6-19 shows the three basic

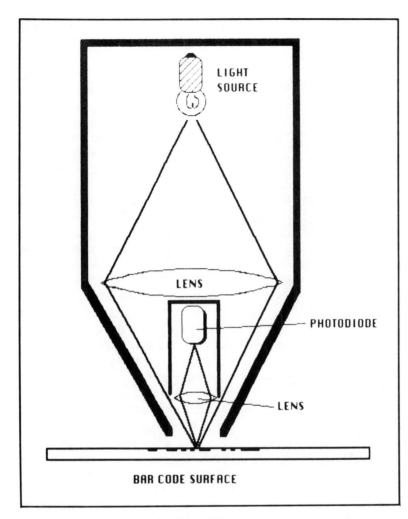

Fig. 6-15. Diagram of a light-pen bar-code reader.

methods of presenting bars. It must be realized that you will always have a light bar following a dark bar, and vice-versa. Two single-width dark bars following one upon the other would look simply like a single double-width dark bar. Therefore, the patterns of light and dark, and the width of those patterns, must contain the information in alternating light and dark bars.

Pattern type 1, as shown in the figure, is the most commonly used. This is the style of pattern that is used in the Universal Product Code. In it, each bar, whether light or dark, represents a 1, a 2, and sometimes a 3, depending simply upon the width of the bar. The figure shows any bar of width 1, whether light or dark, to be a "T1" bar, any bar

of width 2, whether light or dark, to be a "T2" bar, and so on.

Pattern type 2 is a different style altogether. Here, the width of a dark bar and the light bar immediately following it is a constant width of 3, represented by "TG." A dark bar of width T1 is always followed by a light bar of width T2, and a dark bar of width T2 is always followed by a light bar of width T1, with the proviso that T1 + T2 = TG always. In actual fact, the light bars are not needed for information. They are only needed to separate the dark bars, and to keep the total length of a bar interval constant. A variation on this method is the type 3 bar coding. Here, the white gap between dark bars is a constant width of T1, or Tg, while

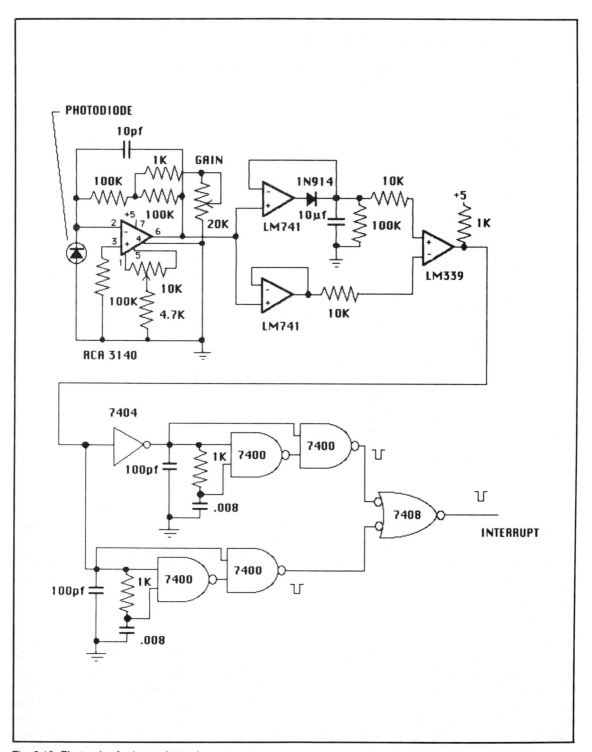

Fig. 6-16. Electronics for bar-code reader.

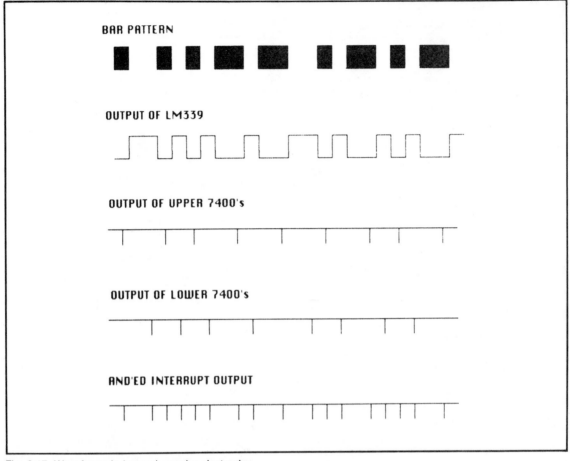

BAR PATTERN

OUTPUT OF LM339

OUTPUT OF UPPER 7400's

OUTPUT OF LOWER 7400's

AND'ED INTERRUPT OUTPUT

Fig. 6-17. Waveforms in bar-code reader electronics.

the dark bars themselves can be of width T1 or T2. All the information is carried in the dark bars, and the light bars are used only as separators.

Of the three methods discussed above, the Type 1 method carries the heaviest information density per length, because both light and dark bars carry information. That is probably why it is the most commonly used.

The flowchart discussed above only counts the relative widths of the light and dark bars. It does not directly tell whether the bar is of width 1, 2, or 3. Notice that this counting method is strongly dependent on the scanning speed of the light pen. Therefore, it is necessary to have some type of self-clocking feature which can decipher the width of a bar independent of the scanning speed.

The flowchart displayed in Fig. 6-20 is one method of decoding the bar scan. It makes two assumptions: First, that all white areas are ignored until the first dark bar is seen (the first dark bar is the start of the information); and second that the first dark bar encountered will be of width 1. This is the case in all examples seen by this author, including the UPC.

If the first dark bar seen is of width 1, it will have a certain number of counts involved with it. Using the figures for scanning speed and bar widths above, a count of 20 for a bar width of 1 is not unlikely. With variations in scanning speed across the complete printed code, we could reasonably expect that anything with a count between 15 and 25 would be considered to be a bar of width 1. Therefore,

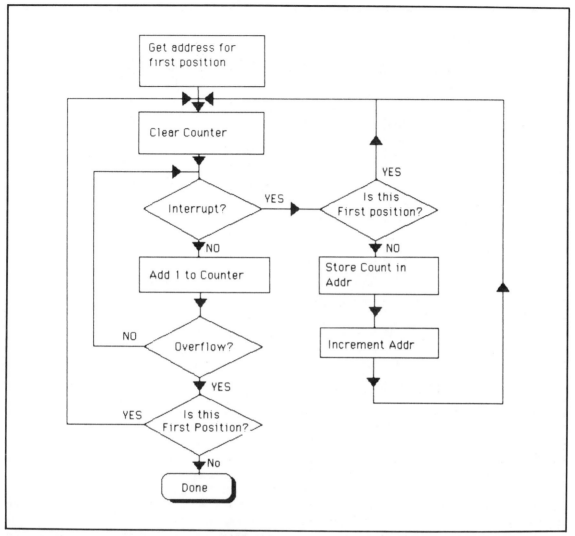

Fig. 6-18. Interrupt handler flowchart for bar-code reader.

let us use any count between 10 and 30 to be a 1, any count between 30 and 50 to be a 2, and any count between 50 and 70 to be a 3. We can get these numbers, scaled to the scanning speed by simply taking the width of the first bar and dividing it by two (easy to do in assembler—just shift the number to the right). This will be the lower limit of acceptability for a single-width bar. In our example, if the count of the first bar is 20, half of it will be 10. Then add the width of the first bar to the half just calculated, for the dividing line between a single and a double. In our example, $10 + 20 = 30$. Then add the first bar width again for the dividing line between double and triple, and again for the upper limit of the triple-wide bar. Anything over the width of a triple-wide bar is obviously an error or the end of the scan.

There is one consideration to be made in converting counts to bar-type. A zero-width bar may not be an error. It may be that there is a speck of dust or other foreign matter on the paper scanned, and it may cause an interrupt, especially if your

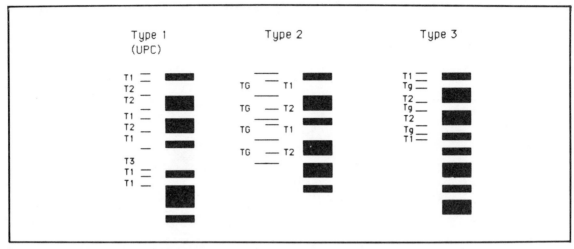

Fig. 6-19. Three types of bar-codes.

electronics is very fast. If you should find such a very short "bar," simply assume it is a false count, and add it to the next bar.

The actual decoding of the single, double, and triple width bars is even more complicated than simply deciding which of the three pattern types you will use, because each publisher of bar code has his own method of encoding numbers into the bars. A complete discussion of the various codes, even the common ones, would take more space than this book allows. You are referred to your local library for more information on these. Also, contact the manufacturer or publisher of the code for more specific information on the particular code you are interested in.

It will be briefly noted, however, that one common scheme is to print the bar codes simply as the RS-232 serial ASCII equivalent of the data is if it were going to be sent over a communications line. That is, let a digital 1 be represented by a double-width line, and a digital 0 be represented by a single-width line. Then, with start and stop bits, each character will take ten light and dark bars total.

The Universal Product Code uses a different method: The code starts with three bars of length 1 as a "start symbol," and then uses five bars to represent each number, as follows:

3 single-width bars to signal "start" (111)

5 bars for a number
5 bars for a number
5 bars for a number
5 bars for a number
5 bars for a number
3 single-width bars to signal "start" (111)
5 bars for a number
5 bars for a number
5 bars for a number
5 bars for a number
5 bars for a number
3 single-width bars to signal "stop" (111)
  a wide gap of white
2 single-width bars and a
  double-width bar (112)
5 bars for a number
5 bars for a number

Finally, there are a few hints to be observed about using a light pen. First of all, don't hold the pen exactly vertical. Most papers are quite reflective, and the reflected light will overwhelm the detector. Hold it at an angle of 10 to 30 degrees from the vertical. Secondly, most beginning users of light pens tend to scan too slowly. Remember, a good scanning speed is about 20 inches per second, or half a second for a full page width. Third and last, don't press too hard on the light pen. If you do, the paper will tend to catch, and the pen will skip, losing data.

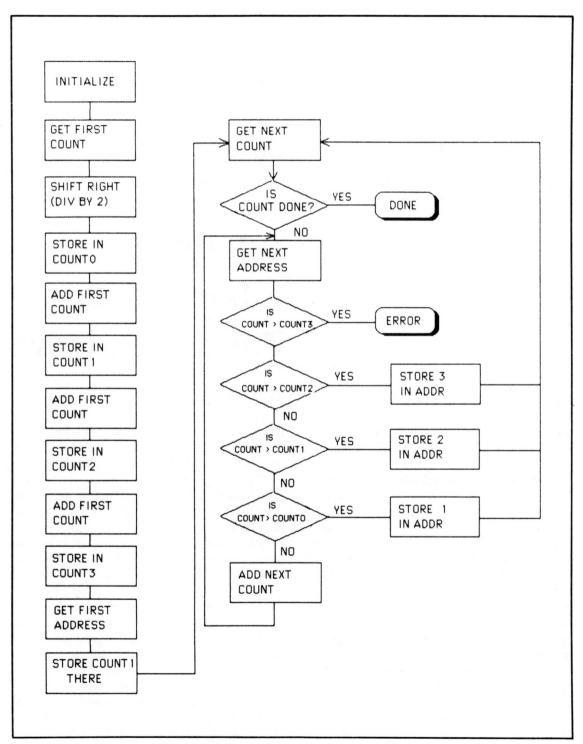

Fig. 6-20. Bar-code decoding software.

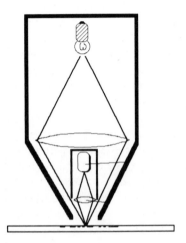

Chapter 7

Adding a Second or Third Disk Drive

Most computer systems these days come equipped with one or more floppy disk drives. Indeed, the direct-access storage device (DASD) has all but replaced the cassette drive as the main off line storage device for programs and data.

It does not take very long, however, for the computer user to realize that one floppy disk drive gives insufficient storage for the more demanding requirements. Usually, we find that the program itself must be loaded into the computer using one disk drive, but that there is insufficient room left on the diskette itself for all but the smallest of data files for a given application. What is usually done is to allow the program to reside on one disk, and the data on another. At the same time, single-drive systems are often faced with the dilemma that the program or system disk must remain in the drive for the entire time the program is being used. The addition of a second disk drive would greatly alleviate the problem.

Even users of a two-disk-drive system often find that programs must reside on one disk, and

both data files and temporary work files must share another disk drive. Large sorts, for example, often require a work file as large as the original file itself. Also, merging two files into a third is made much easier when three disk drives are used.

The creation of the first disk drive in a system which has no disk drives is a very complicated engineering feat. First of all, the disk controller unit has to be designed and integrated into the computer system. Secondly, the *disk operating system* must be written and tested, and, if software is to be purchased, it must be compatible with all existing software. A disk operating system is an extremely complex program. It must know how the data is organized on the disk, how the directory of all the files and their locations is kept, and must be able to transfer a file from disk into memory and from memory to disk, at the very least. Most disk operating systems also have a number of associated programs called *utilities* which provide additional support in the form of copying files from disk to disk, formatting the disk, printing a file or their directory, and so on.

Since the first disk drive is such a complex system, we will not concern ourselves with it here. It will be assumed that the user already has a computer that has a disk drive, and as such already has a disk controller and disk operating system written which is compatible with any software he may wish to purchase.

However, most disk controllers are capable of serving from four to eight disk drives at a time with no change in either hardware or software. Our discussion, then, will be about how to add a second or third disk drive to such a system. Adding a fourth disk drive is, for most controllers, slightly more complicated, and we will pass over it at this time.

Our discussion of disk drives and controllers will follow the structure of a system using one of the Western Digital disk controller chips, such as the WD1771 or WD1791, and a disk drive similar to the Shugart SA-400 5 1/4 inch floppy disk drive. Most disk drives in use are pin-for-pin replacements for this drive. (An exception is the external disk drive for the Apple Macintosh, which uses a different signal system.) We will also add some discussion of methods to be used to add additional drives

to a system using the Shugart SA-800 8-inch floppy disk drive.

The addition of a second or third drive can be a very cost-effective move to the person with a little electronics know-how. Such drives, when purchased from the computer manufacturers, can cost from $400.00 up. But the drive itself, when purchased direct from the manufacturer or from a discount electronics mail-order house, will cost in the neighborhood of $175.00-$225.00. Reconditioned and surplus drives can be had for as little as $60.00. The additional electronics and cabling needed to connect it can be obtained for about $50.00, or less if you have much of it lying around.

Up to three disk drives may be connected to a single controller through a technique called *daisy-chaining*. In this technique, all signals are presented identically to all disk drives, but only the drive being selected responds to the signals. All that is required is to extend the ribbon cable that connects the controller to the disk drive(s) with additional cable and additional connectors. See Fig. 7-1 for details on the connection method.

The Shugart SA-400 uses a 34-wire cable for data transfer, and has a card-edge connector using

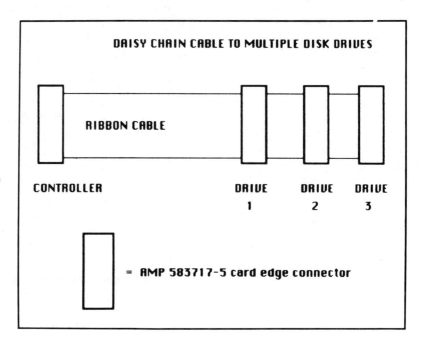

Fig. 7-1. Daisy-chaining multiple disk drives off one controller.

34 pins. This connector is the AMP P/N 583717-5 or the Scotchflex 3463-0001. You will need three of them for a two-drive system, and four for a three-drive system.

In addition to the cable, it is necessary to let the controller know which drive is which. On the disk drive itself is a circuit board. On the top left portion of the board is a dip socket marked "MX DS1 DS2 DS3," or something like that. There is also a resistor pack marked something like "760-3-R150." The dip socket contains a number of jumpers which are to be left conducting or cut as needed to identify the drive to the controller. If you have a single-drive system, you may also need to modify the jumpers in the existing drive. See Fig. 7-2 for a picture of the dip socket jumpers.

Drive	Jumpers to cut	Remove
1	MX,DS2,DS3	
2	MX,DS1,DS3	Resistor pack
3	MX,DS1,DS2	Resistor pack

In multiple-drive systems, the "MX" multiplexing indicator must always be cut, and only the jumper for the indicated drive must be left intact. The resistor pack is used as a cable terminator to suppress reflections in the cable, and should be re-moved from all disk drives *except* the one furthest from the controller itself. If your disk drive has a jumper marked "HM," first try the system with the jumper intact. If it does not work properly, try cutting the "HM" jumper in all drives.

The SA-800 8-inch drives has a 50-connector card-edge connector, and uses a 50-conductor ribbon cable. It, too, must be jumpered to select the proper drive. On the back of the printed circuit board near the cable edge connector is a set of four jumpers, which must be moved to the correct set of pins as shown below:

Drive	Move Jumper To
1	DS1
2	DS2
3	DS3
4	DS4

In addition to connecting the disk drive to the controller unit, the drive must be provided with power to run. Your existing power supply in your computer may have enough extra capacity to run the drive. IBM PC's do indeed have enough. Apple-II's definitely do not. In any case, it is always wise to make sure. The SA-400 requires 12 volts at 0.9 amps for sustaining the drive motor, and a surge

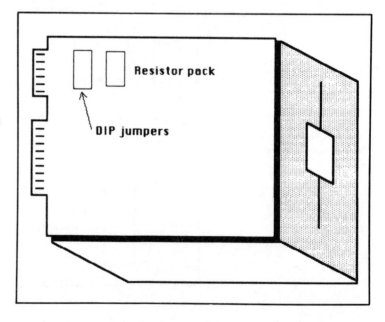

Fig. 7-2. Location of DIP jumpers and resistor pack on floppy-disk drive.

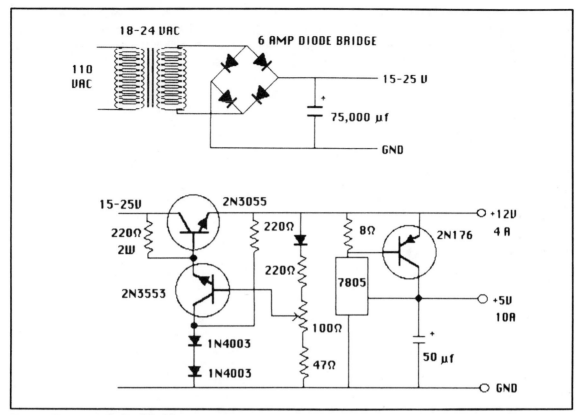

Fig. 7-3. Power supply for disk drives.

capacity of up to 1.7 amps when both the spindle and stepper motor are starting up. In addition, the electronics on the disk drive circuit board requires about 0.5 amps at 5 volts to run properly.

The circuit described in Fig. 7-3 will do for providing well-regulated electrical power for two disk drives. Any transformer capable of producing 6 amperes of ac at 18 to 24 volts should do well. All of the large transistors, as well as the 7805 regulator should be connected to a large heat sink, as they tend to get quite hot.

Connect the power to the drive using the J2 connector, which is mounted on the non-component side of the printed board on the disk drive. This is a 4-pin AMP Mate-N-Lock 350211-1. The mating connector you will need is an AMP 1-480424-0 using AMP 61473-1 pins. It is connected as shown in Fig. 7-4. It is also wise to ground the metal case of the disk drive itself using a piece of 18-gauge

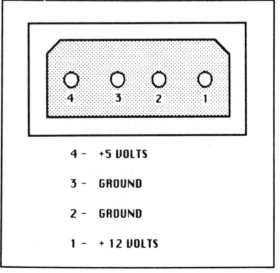

4 - +5 VOLTS

3 - GROUND

2 - GROUND

1 - + 12 VOLTS

Fig. 7-4. J2 power supply connector to SA-400 diskette drive.

twisted wire and a spade lug (AMP 60972-1).

There you have it! For a substantially smaller capital outlay than you would pay to the original manufacturer, you can add additional disk capacity to your system. The electronics and wiring involved are minimal. The only thing you won't get is a fancy case to match the one given you by the manufacturer.

Appendix A

Pinout Diagrams of the Integrated Circuits Used

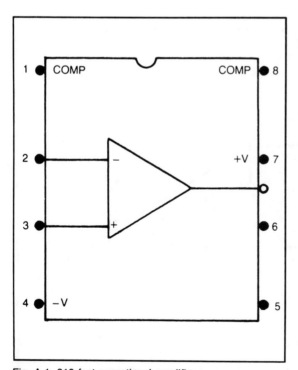

Fig. A-1. 310 fast operational amplifier.

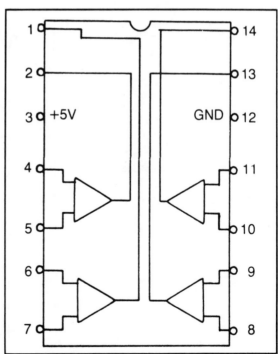

Fig. A-2. 339 quad comparator.

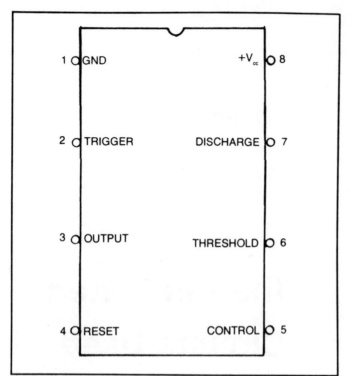

Fig. A-3. 555 timer (V_{cc} 3 to 30V).

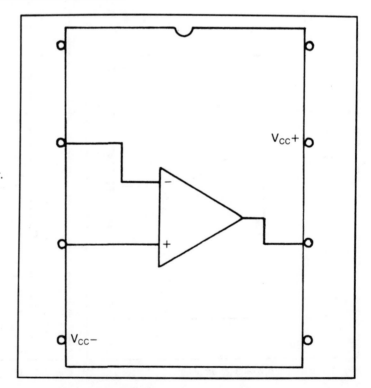

Fig. A-4. 741 operational amplifier.

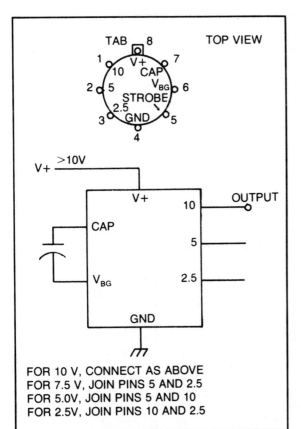

TOP VIEW

FOR 10 V, CONNECT AS ABOVE
FOR 7.5 V, JOIN PINS 5 AND 2.5
FOR 5.0 V, JOIN PINS 5 AND 10
FOR 2.5V, JOIN PINS 10 AND 2.5

Fig. A-5. AD 584 precision 10 mA voltage regulator (output ± 15 mV).

Fig. A-6. ADC 0817 data aquisition system.

Pin	Left	Right	Pin
1	IN3	IN2	40
2	IN4	IN1	39
3	IN5	IN0	38
4	IN6	EXPAND	37
5	IN7	ADDR A	36
6	IN8	ADDR B	35
7	IN9	ADDR C	34
8	IN10	ADDR D	33
9	IN11	ADDRESS ENABLE	32
10	IN12	D7	31
11	IN13	D6	30
12	IN14	D5	29
13	END CONVERSION	D4	28
14	IN15	D3	27
15	COMMON	D2	26
16	START	D1	25
17	+5	D0	24
18	COMPARATOR IN	GND	23
19	+5	CLOCK	22
20	GND	TRI-STATE	21

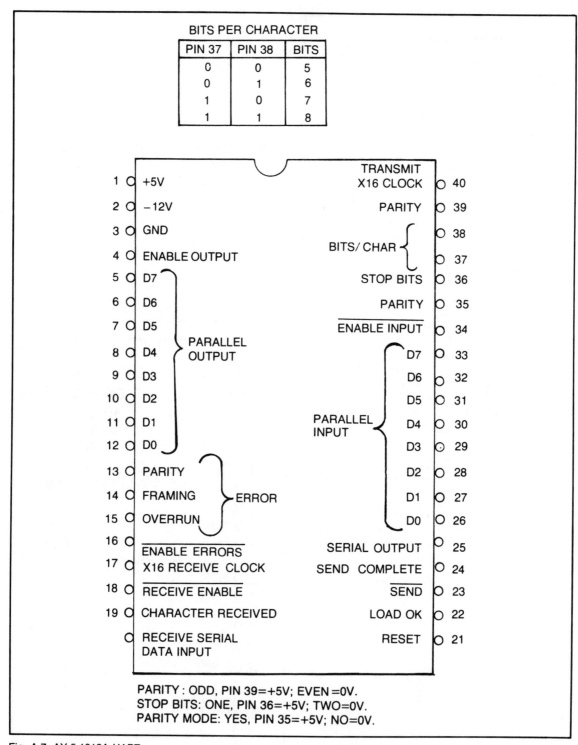

BITS PER CHARACTER

PIN 37	PIN 38	BITS
0	0	5
0	1	6
1	0	7
1	1	8

PARITY : ODD, PIN 39=+5V; EVEN =0V.
STOP BITS: ONE, PIN 36=+5V; TWO=0V.
PARITY MODE: YES, PIN 35=+5V; NO=0V.

Fig. A-7. AY-5-1013A UART.

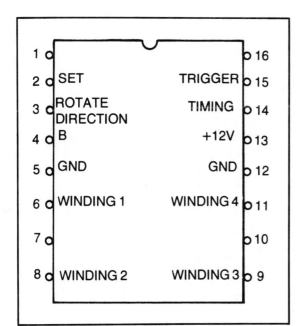

Fig. A-8. SAA 1027 stepper motor controller/driver.

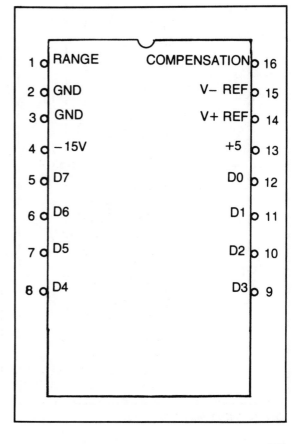

Fig. A-9. 1408 L8 8-bit digital to analog converter.

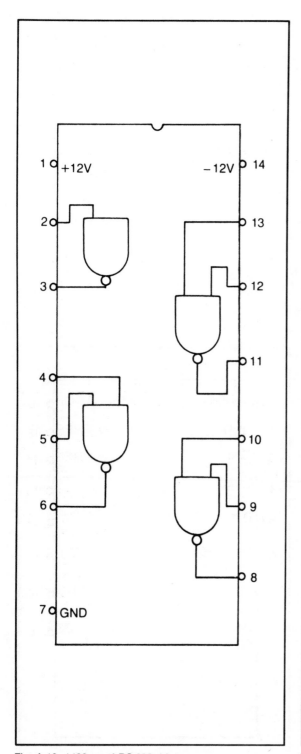

Fig. A-10. 1488 quad RS-232 driver.

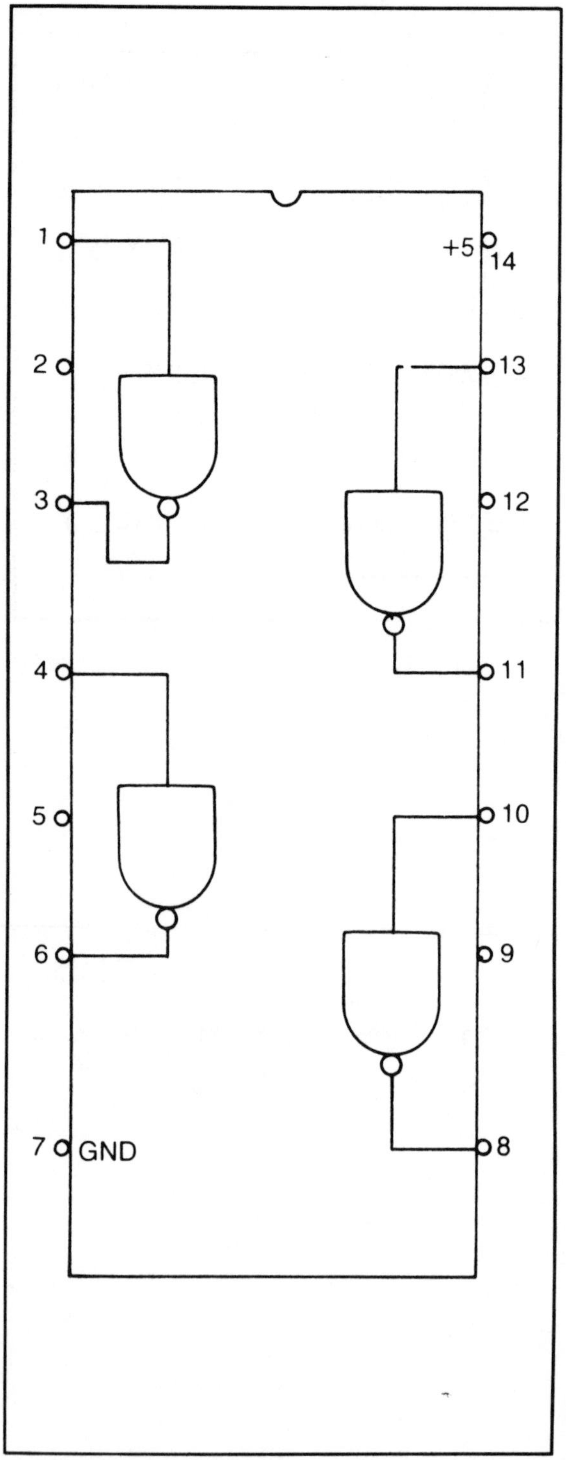

Fig. A-11. 1489 quad RS-232 receiver.

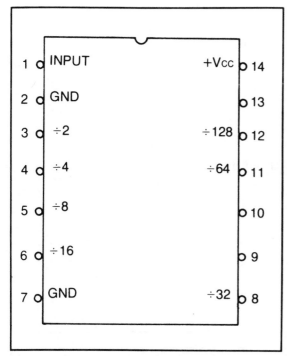

Fig. A-12. 4024 7-stage binary ripple divider.

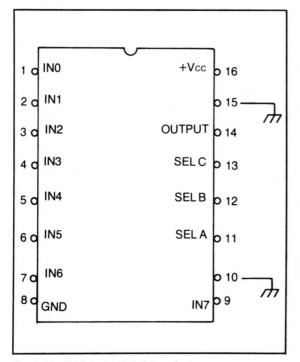

Fig. A-13. 4512 8-channel data selector.

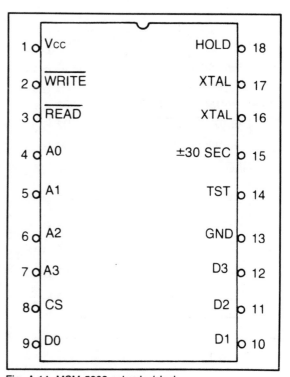

Fig. A-14. MSM 5832 calendar/clock.

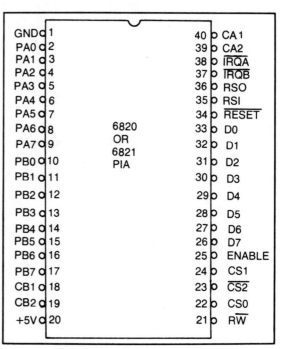

Fig. A-15. 6820 or 6821 PIA.

```
 1 ○ +5V                 CLEAR TO SEND ○ 24
 2 ○ RECEIVE DATA              DCD ○ 23
 3 ○ RECEIVE ×16 CLOCK          D0 ○ 22
 4 ○ TRANSMIT ×16 CLOCK         D1 ○ 21
 5 ○ READY TO SEND              D2 ○ 20
 6 ○ TRANSMIT DATA              D3 ○ 19
 7 ○ IRQ                        D4 ○ 18
 8 ○ CS0                        D5 ○ 17
 9 ○ CS2                        D6 ○ 16
10 ○ CS1                        D7 ○ 15
11 ○ RS                     ENABLE ○ 14
12 ○ GND                      R/W ○ 13
```

Fig. A-16. 6850 ACIA.

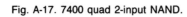

Fig. A-17. 7400 quad 2-input NAND.

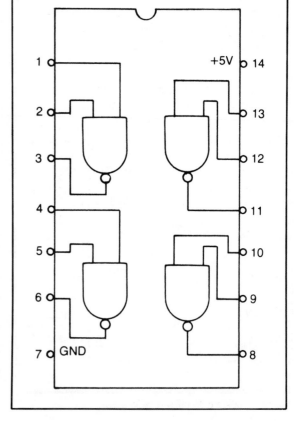

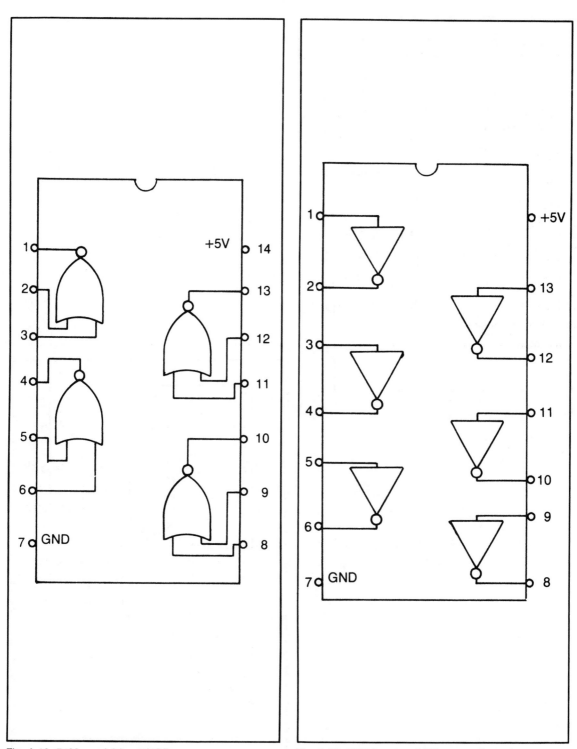

Fig. A-18. 7402 quad 2-input NOR.

Fig. A-19. 7404 inverter, 7405 open-collector inverter.

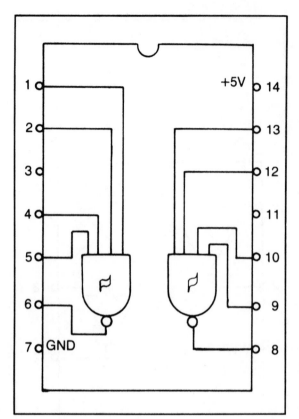

Fig. A-20. 7413 dual 4-input NAND Schmitt trigger.

Fig. A-21. 7415 triple 3-input AND.

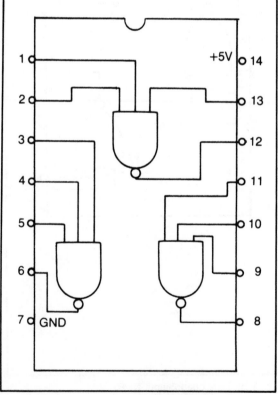

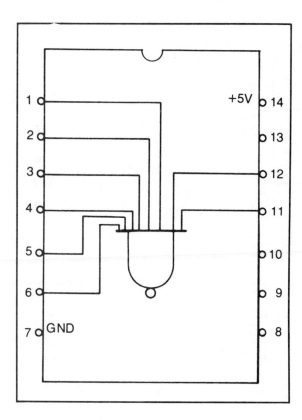

Fig. A-22. 7430 8-input NAND.

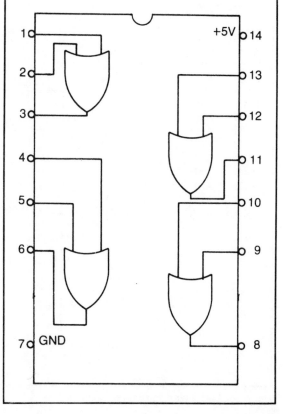

Fig. A-23. 7432 quad 2-input OR.

265

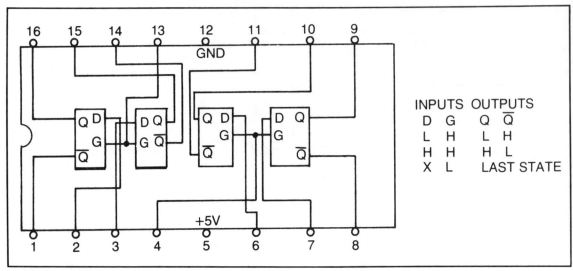

Fig. A-24. 7475 4-bit latch.

INPUTS		OUTPUTS	
D	G	Q	Q̄
L	H	L	H
H	H	H	L
X	L	LAST STATE	

TRUTH TABLE:

COMPARING INPUTS				CASCADING INPUTS			OUTPUTS		
A3,B3	A2,B2	A1,B1	A0,B0	A>B	A<B	A=B	A>B	A<B	A=B
A>B	x	x	x	x	x	x	1	0	0
A<B	x	x	x	x	x	x	0	1	0
A=B	A>B	x	x	x	x	x	1	0	0
A=B	A<B	x	x	x	x	x	0	1	0
A=B	A=B	A>B	x	x	x	x	1	0	0
A=B	A=B	A<B	x	x	x	x	0	1	0
A=B	A=B	A=B	A>B	x	x	x	1	0	0
A=B	A=B	A=B	A<B	x	x	x	0	1	0
A=B	A=B	A=B	A=B	1	0	0	1	0	0
A=B	A=B	A=B	A=B	0	1	0	0	1	0
A=B	A=B	A=B	A=B	0	0	1	0	0	1

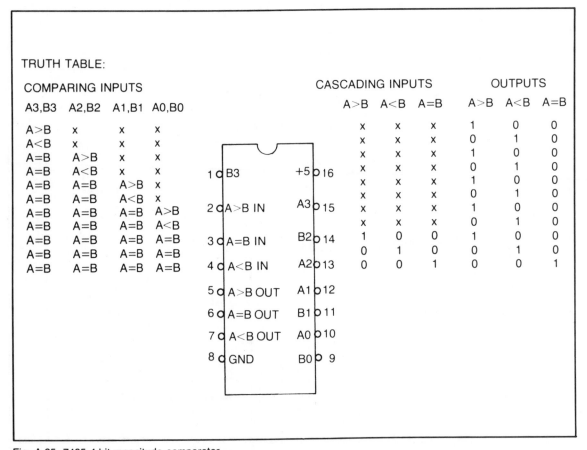

1	B3	+5	16
2	A>B IN	A3	15
3	A=B IN	B2	14
4	A<B IN	A2	13
5	A>B OUT	A1	12
6	A=B OUT	B1	11
7	A<B OUT	A0	10
8	GND	B0	9

Fig. A-25. 7485 4-bit magnitude comparator.

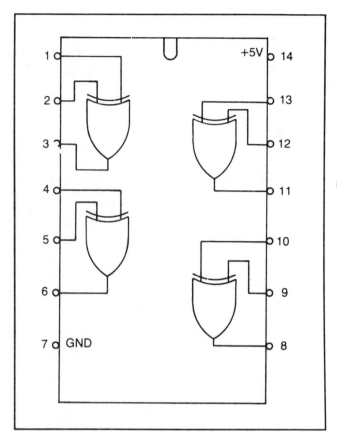

Fig. A-26. 7486 quad 2-input XOR.

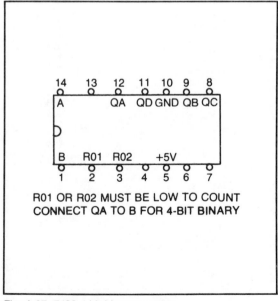

R01 OR R02 MUST BE LOW TO COUNT
CONNECT QA TO B FOR 4-BIT BINARY

Fig. A-27. 7493 4-bit binary counter.

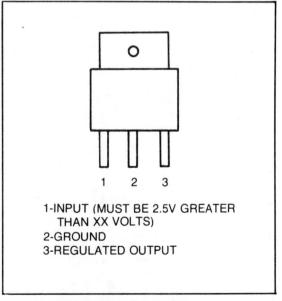

1-INPUT (MUST BE 2.5V GREATER
   THAN XX VOLTS)
2-GROUND
3-REGULATED OUTPUT

Fig. A-28. 78XX XX-volt 1 amp regulator.

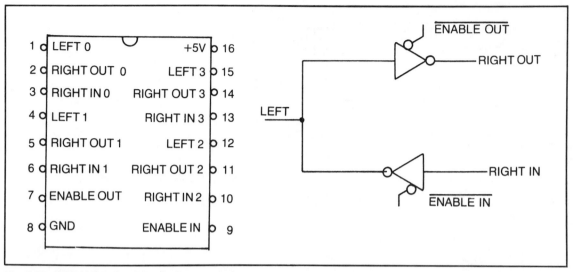

Fig. A-29. 8835 bidirectional 3-state bus transceiver.

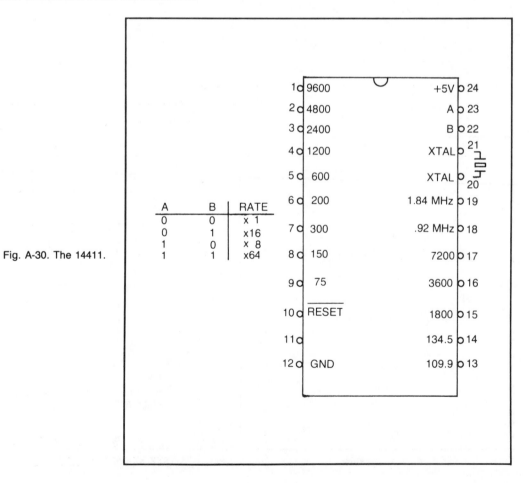

Fig. A-30. The 14411.

A	B	RATE
0	0	x 1
0	1	x16
1	0	x 8
1	1	x64

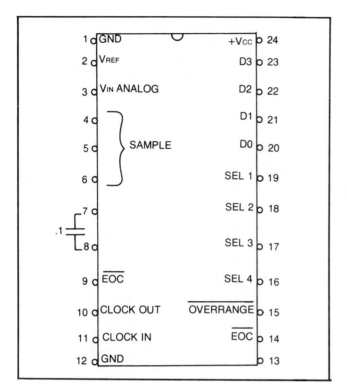

Fig. A-31. 14433 3 1/2 digit DVM.

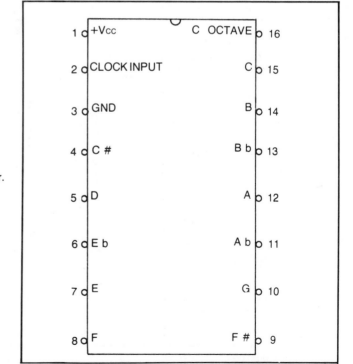

Fig. A-32. 50240 top-octave divider.

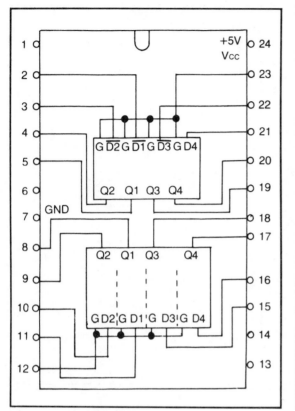

Fig. A-33. 74100 8-bit latch.

16	15	14	13	12	11	10	9
+5	Y0	Y1	Y2	Y3	Y4	Y5	Y6

A	B	C	G2A	G2B	G1	Y7	GND
1	2	3	4	5	6	7	8

SELECT — ENABLE

TRUTH TABLE:

G1	G2	C	B	A	Y0	Y1	Y2	Y3	Y4	Y5	Y6	Y7
x	1	x	x	x	1	1	1	1	1	1	1	1
0	x	x	x	x	1	1	1	1	1	1	1	1
1	0	0	0	0	0	1	1	1	1	1	1	1
1	0	0	0	1	1	0	1	1	1	1	1	1
1	0	0	1	0	1	1	0	1	1	1	1	1
1	0	0	1	1	1	1	1	0	1	1	1	1
1	0	1	0	0	1	1	1	1	0	1	1	1
1	0	1	0	1	1	1	1	1	1	0	1	1
1	0	1	1	0	1	1	1	1	1	1	0	1
1	0	1	1	1	1	1	1	1	1	1	1	0

Fig. A-34. 74LS138 3-line to 8-line decoder.

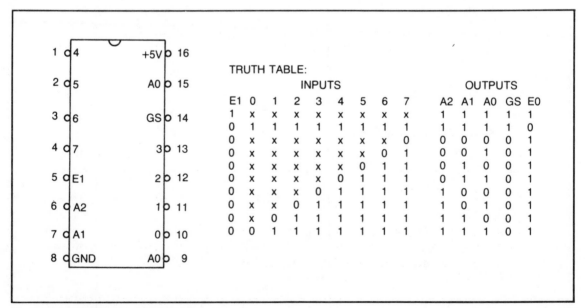

TRUTH TABLE:

E1	0	1	2	3	4	5	6	7	A2	A1	A0	GS	E0
1	x	x	x	x	x	x	x	x	1	1	1	1	1
0	1	1	1	1	1	1	1	1	1	1	1	1	0
0	x	x	x	x	x	x	x	0	0	0	0	0	1
0	x	x	x	x	x	x	0	1	0	0	1	0	1
0	x	x	x	x	x	0	1	1	0	1	0	0	1
0	x	x	x	x	0	1	1	1	0	1	1	0	1
0	x	x	x	0	1	1	1	1	1	0	0	0	1
0	x	x	0	1	1	1	1	1	1	0	1	0	1
0	x	0	1	1	1	1	1	1	1	1	0	0	1
0	0	1	1	1	1	1	1	1	1	1	1	0	1

Fig. A-35. 74148 8-line to 3-line encoder.

270

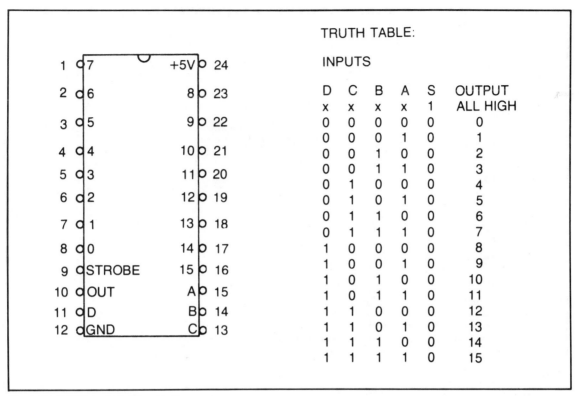

TRUTH TABLE:

INPUTS

D	C	B	A	S	OUTPUT
x	x	x	x	1	ALL HIGH
0	0	0	0	0	0
0	0	0	1	0	1
0	0	1	0	0	2
0	0	1	1	0	3
0	1	0	0	0	4
0	1	0	1	0	5
0	1	1	0	0	6
0	1	1	1	0	7
1	0	0	0	0	8
1	0	0	1	0	9
1	0	1	0	0	10
1	0	1	1	0	11
1	1	0	0	0	12
1	1	0	1	0	13
1	1	1	0	0	14
1	1	1	1	0	15

Fig. A-36. 74150 1-of-16 data selector.

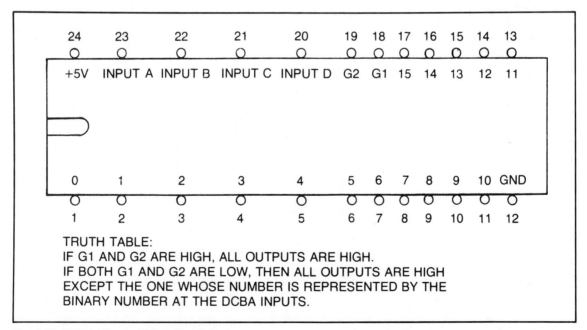

TRUTH TABLE:
IF G1 AND G2 ARE HIGH, ALL OUTPUTS ARE HIGH.
IF BOTH G1 AND G2 ARE LOW, THEN ALL OUTPUTS ARE HIGH
EXCEPT THE ONE WHOSE NUMBER IS REPRESENTED BY THE
BINARY NUMBER AT THE DCBA INPUTS.

Fig. A-37. 74154 4-line to 16-line decoder.

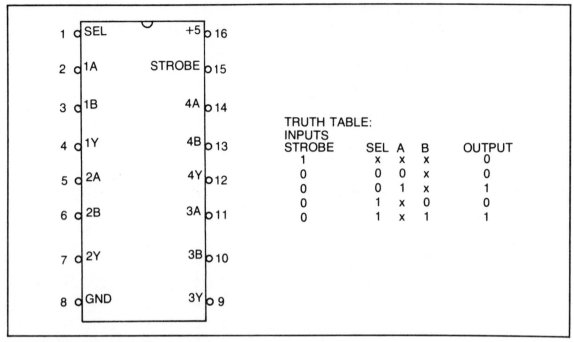

Fig. A-38. 74157 quad 2-line to 1-line selector.

TRUTH TABLE:
INPUTS

STROBE	SEL	A	B	OUTPUT
1	x	x	x	0
0	0	0	x	0
0	0	1	x	1
0	1	x	0	0
0	1	x	1	1

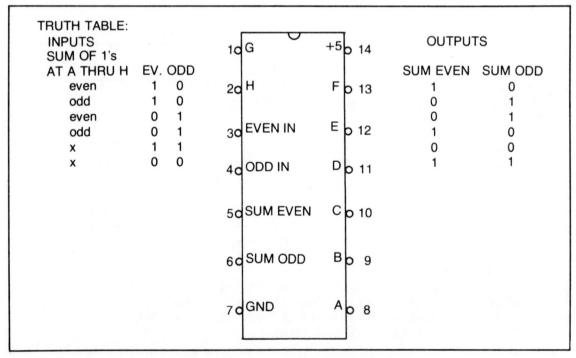

TRUTH TABLE:
INPUTS
SUM OF 1's

AT A THRU H	EV.	ODD
even	1	0
odd	1	0
even	0	1
odd	0	1
x	1	1
x	0	0

OUTPUTS

SUM EVEN	SUM ODD
1	0
0	1
0	1
1	0
0	0
1	1

Fig. A-39. 74180 9-bit parity generator/checker.

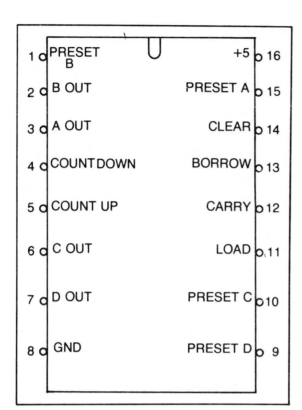

Fig. A-40. 74192 (BCD outputs) and 74193 (binary outputs) synchronous 4-bit counter.

Fig. A-41. 74367 (DM8097,8T97) 3-state buffer.

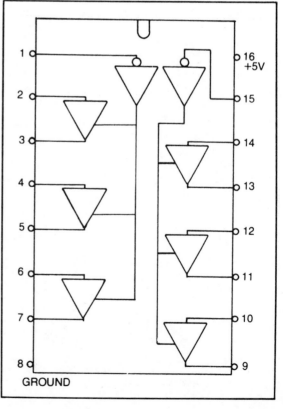

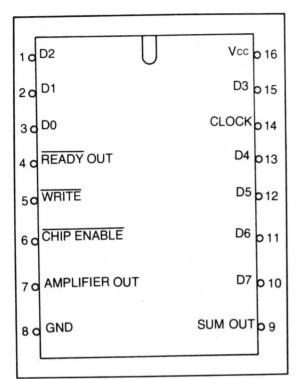

Fig. A-42. 76489 sound generator.

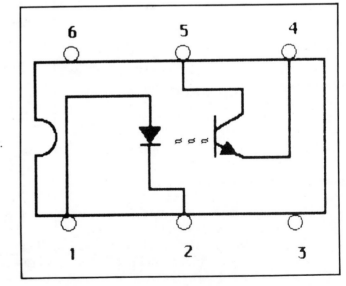

Fig. A-43. 4N33 opto-isolator.

274

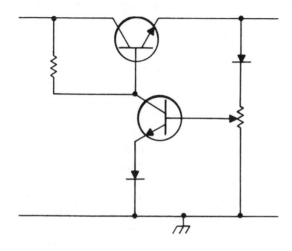

Appendix B

Construction Techniques and Hints

The majority of errors in the construction of electronic circuits made by the novice, aside from simple errors in wiring, are caused by improper soldering. The Heath Company of Benton Harbor, Michigan, reports that of the kits returned for repair, the vast majority of those kits were improperly soldered.

SOLDERING

Soldering is the most commonly used method of connecting two wires together for electronic purposes. It is simple, fast, easy, and forms a permanent bond with good electrical conductivity. With something as simple as soldering, it is surprising that there are so many ways to do it wrong.

Let us first consider the soldering iron. The type to be used depends on its purpose. Printed circuits don't need very much heat because they have little volume to heat up—a 25 watt to 35 watt iron will do very well for this purpose. For point-to-point soldering on the tabs of a terminal strip or the leads to a transformer or capacitor, an iron in the 75 watt

to 125-watt range is recommended. *DON'T* use a soldering gun, or a tinner's iron of 300 or more watts. These produce far too much heat, and can damage sensitive components. They are made for other, much heavier purposes than electronic work. A simple iron, with a narrow pencil tip 1/8 of an inch or less across, will be the best bet.

Secondly, use the right solder. Use *only* 60 percent lead, 40 percent tin *rosin-core* solder (sometimes called *resin*-core). Other alloys don't work as well. *Don't* use any kind of solder but rosin core solder. Specifically, avoid all acid-core solders! Work soldered with acid-core solder will corrode severely and destroy connections and electronic components. Kit manufacturers always put a disclaimer in their warranty which says that acid core solder voids the warranty. Also, try to choose thin solder. My personal recommendation is Ersin Multicore extra-fine solder.

Third, *keep the soldering iron's tip clean*! Clean it first by using some fine emery cloth on the tip while it is still cool. Get it down to bare metal. Then, while it is heating up for the first time, keep some solder handy. As soon as the tip will melt solder, spread a thin even layer of solder and flux all over the tip, and wipe as much off as you can get. This is called *tinning* the iron. When using the iron, you will find that the tip soon will become fouled. Keep a damp sponge close to the iron, and quickly wipe off the hot tip of the sponge. This will not cool the tip off very much, and it will heat up again in a few seconds. If you keep the tip clean and hot, it will transfer heat much better. Many people insist on cleaning the iron with a Sal Ammoniac block. This practice is a disaster in electronics—it will have the same effect as using acid-core solder. Don't use *any* kind of chemical cleaning block or soldering paste.

There is a definite sequence of events to be followed in soldering a wire to a terminal strip point. First, there should be a good mechanical connection made to the terminal. There is an old adage that he who depends on solder to hold his wires in place soon wonders why it doesn't work! The solder should do no more than maintain the electrical connection, not take the strain of the wires. Crimp the wires onto the terminals as well as is reasonable, using a pair of long-nose pliers. Only then will you be ready to apply the soldering iron to the work. Let the iron stay on the work for a few seconds until the *work* is hot enough to melt the solder. Never add the solder to the iron and expect it to flow onto the work—add the solder directly to the work. If the work isn't hot enough to melt solder, how do you expect it to hold? The solder should flow evenly onto the work and fill up all the tiny little holes and gaps. Don't worry about any large gaping holes—as long as the connection is mechanically sound and well soldered, it will do.

The solder should have a shiny appearance, and have flowed well onto all the work. If the solder has a pasty look about it, or if it has balled up on the iron or the work and refused to stick, the result is what is called a *cold solder joint*. The usual problem is that you haven't used enough heat. Try holding the iron onto the work for a longer period of time, or use a bigger iron. Cold solder joints are misnamed—they aren't joints at all, just places where there are wires and semi-melted solder.

There is no true connection between them. Your iron should have a high enough wattage to keep all the solder joint molten at one time.

A word about the flux is in order. The flux (the word comes from the latin word, "to flow") is a substance that melts at a slightly lower temperature than solder, and has a very low surface tension. Instead of balling up, it spreads quickly over all the work, and acts both as a wetting agent for the solder, to help it spread evenly, and as a protectant to the work, which is only hot metal after all, to keep it from oxidizing while the soldering process is taking place.

Soldering printed circuits is not much different from point-to-point wiring. Here, there is nothing to make a mechanical connection to, so no crimping is necessary. But the point of a mechanical connection is to prevent the wire from breaking loose. By simply putting the lead through the hole and bending it over slightly, the wire will be prevented from being pulled out, and the solder makes the electrical connection. Again, be careful of cold solder joints. The surface area of a circuit board trace is very small, and doesn't require a lot of heat to get it hot. Too much heat can cause the trace to peel up from the board. Not enough heat can cause a "cold" joint.

WIRE-WRAPPING

When using integrated circuits, point-to-point soldering is not the best method of interconnection. The leads of an integrated circuit are far too small to solder to, and certainly provide no point of purchase for a mechanical connection. Point-to-point wiring has been known to pull loose from IC leads frequently, and need frequent replacing. Sockets are no help either, because their leads are the same size as those on the IC.

For this reason, most commercially available devices that are sold with integrated circuits in them are made with printed circuit boards. A layer of copper is bonded to a glass fiber or phenolic board, and everything that isn't part of the wiring is etched away. Integrated circuits connect readily to printed circuit boards.

But printed circuit boards take time to design and to etch. If a thousand such circuits are to be made, it is easy to prepare a photographic negative and optically etch a thousand boards. For just one board, the effort may not be worth the trouble.

Recently, a third method, designed especially for prototype work has been developed. It has been touted as "just as reliable as point-to-point" and "easier than printed circuits." It is called *wire-wrapping*. It is much faster than either soldering or printed circuits. Indeed, it requires no soldering at all—the mechanical connections take care of all the electrical connections. The only real drawback is that it is considerably more expensive than either point-to-point or printed circuit because special sockets and wire are needed. The wire can be bought in bulk and cut and stripped by the user, but the effort makes it worth while to spend some extra money and buy the pre-cut, pre-stripped wire.

A special tool is needed for wire-wrapping. There are many different types on the market. Some have automatic wire feeding, cutting, and stripping, some are electrically powered. I recommend, for the beginner, the OK Machine Tool Company hand wire-wrapping tool. It costs less than five dollars. There are even beginner's kits under ten dollars that have the tool, a few hundred strands of pre-cut wire, some wire-wrap sockets, and a 0.100 Vectorboard® to mount the sockets on. I also recommend that you purchase lots of extra wire. A thousand short, precut and pre-stripped pieces will not last very long. This, and a tube of cyanoacrylate "Super Glue® " (or equivalent) are all you need. No solder, no wirecutters, not even electricity for the soldering iron.

The wire-wrap sockets look just like ordinary integrated circuit sockets, except that the leads on them are about an inch long and very stiff. They are also about three times as expensive as ordinary sockets. Mount the sockets onto the vector board by putting the leads through the holes and gluing them down to the surface. When the glue is dry, the ICs can be mounted into the sockets. Unused holes in the sockets can be used to mount extra components like resistors and transistors, or special carriers can be purchased to plug these com-

ponents into sockets.

The wire-wrapping process does just what its name implies. A piece of 30-gauge insulated wire, with the ends stripped, is wrapped onto the post connecting the socket leads to the chip. The wire is wrapped around the square post about seven times, and will therefore make about twenty-eight contacts with the post edges. In addition, the seven times wraparound gives the connection surprisingly good mechanical strength. Lastly, the operation is much faster than soldering.

Figures B-1 through B-4 show the wire wrapping sequence. The OK tool has a wrapping end and an unwrapping end, as well as a wire stripper in the middle. The wrapping end has two holes in it. One hole is a fairly large one, and is in the exact center of the tool end. This hole goes over the wrapping post. Off to the side is a very small hole. Put the stripped wire into this hole all the way up to the insulation. Then insert the tool onto the post, and *gently* twist it clockwise until the resistance of the wire is gone. Remove the tool, and you should have a perfectly wrapped joint.

Each and every connection between each and every pin has to be made with a separate wire. Connections to individual components can be made this way as well, if the leads are cut to about 3/4 of an inch.

For multiple connections on the same wire, the leads can be "daisy-chained" with a Vector Slit-N-

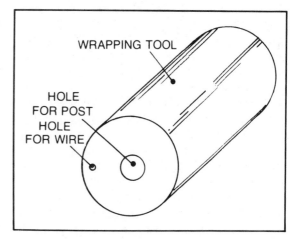

Fig. B-1. End of a wrapping tool.

Fig. B-2. Wire in tool before wrapping.

Wrap tool. This is a substantial improvement over the OK hand tool. No pre-stripped wire is needed, and multiple connections can be made with fewer moves. It has a substantial increase in price over the OK tool, as well.

HANDING MOS INTEGRATED CIRCUITS

With the advent of the integrated circuit came another problem—heat. The more devices you put onto a chip, the more heat they dissipate because the more current they use. The solution to the heat problem was to use semiconductors with a higher resistivity. This has led to development of a large number of devices that use MOS Field-Effect Transistors (MOSFET). A TTL chip is limited by its heat-dissipation capabilities to no more than a few hundred components on each chip. With MOSFETs, the number soars up to tens and even hundreds of thousands!

The very characteristics that make MOSFET or CMOS devices desirable (their very high gate impedance and moderately high breakdown voltage) also make them susceptible to damage by static charge. With junction transistors, when the spec sheet says the breakdown voltage is 30 volts, it means that 30 volts at the minimum current will either deplete the collector so that current won't flow, or 30 volts at saturation gives so much heat that the device is destroyed. With MOS, on the other hand, the impedance is so high that a 30 volt breakdown voltage means *any* source of 30 volts can destroy it—even static electricity. By shuffling across a nylon carpet, you can generate over

100,000 volts of static charge on your body. Simply by wearing a nylon shirt or a wool sweater, you can maintain over 100 volts through normal motion. The charge, if transferred to a MOS device, can break down the gate junction, causing an ion channel through the gate, which conducts electricity very well, shorting the gate. Since the impedance is so high, the ion channel does not re-stabilize, and the damage is permanent. You can kill an FET by simply rubbing your thumb across it!

The mortality rate of MOS chips is surprisingly high, especially in winter. Manufacturing processes have begun to protect the chip by putting Zener diodes on the input leads, but this has not reduced the failures due to improper handling.

There are a set of rules that the user should follow when working with MOS integrated circuits.

First of all, notice that the IC was shipped to you in conductive foam or wrapped in tinfoil. The purpose is to short all the leads together so that static potentials cannot build up. Conductive foam is usually black, but can be pink. Try an ohmmeter on the foam and confirm for yourself that it really does conduct. Leave the device in the foam until you are ready to put it into the circuit.

It is best to use sockets when working with MOS. Sometimes, despite all the best efforts to protect the IC, it will be damaged. But you won't know it until it's soldered into the circuit and put power to it for the first time! Have you ever tried to unsolder a 40-pin integrated circuit from a printed circuit board? It's not an easy task at all. Use the best sockets you can. Many problems with circuits are caused by poor connections within a socket, and

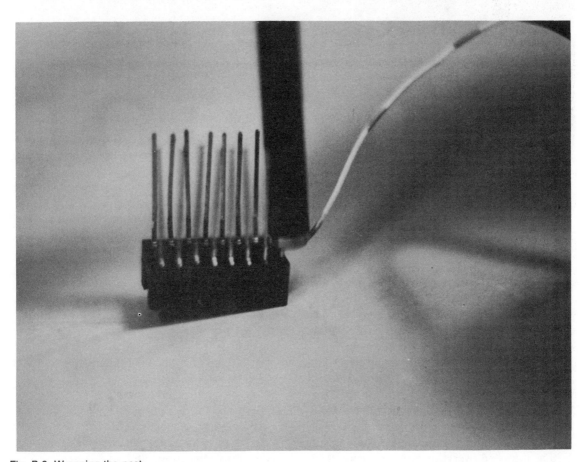

Fig. B-3. Wrapping the post.

Fig. B-4. Finished connection.

these are almost impossible to trace. At least one manufacturer of kits refuses to repair kits that have been constructed with sockets. I recommend using top-quality Texas Instruments gold-plated sockets.

Whether installing the IC into a socket, or simply soldering it to a circuit board, a few precautions are necessary. First, choose your day for it. Don't work on a day that is clear, crisp, and cold, with a strong wind blowing. Conditions then are perfect for static generation. Choose a day that is warm and muggy, or raining, if you can. Residents of the gulf coast will hardly ever have any problems with MOS, while residents of the states along the Canadian border will find the going very difficult. Secondly, don't wear nylon, silk, or wool clothing. Avoid polyesters. Use cotton if you can.

Then: ground everything! using a good thick wire—at least 14 gauge—connect one end of the wire to a good ground, such as a water pipe. This must be a solid earth ground. Drive a metal stake into the yard if you must. Connect the other end of the wire to a 1 meg-ohm resistor. All subsequent connections will be made to this resistor. The purpose of the resistor is to limit currents so that the electrical shock hazard is reduced. To the other end of the resistor, connect:

a) the ground plane of the circuit board
b) the conductive foam
c) the tip of your soldering iron
d) an 8 × 8 piece of sheet metal, which will be your working surface
e) your watchband or wedding ring, grounding yourself.

Alligator clips are a good way to make all these connections. Be very careful when removing the clip from the soldering iron! It will be hot!

Once everything is grounded, you can install the MOS ICs. Remove them from the package without touching the leads. If you are using sockets, the leads of the IC may be bent to shape by pressing the IC against the plate of sheet metal. Then insert the chip into the socket. If soldering directly, use the grounded tip of the iron to lightly solder each lead in place.

When you are done, handle the board as little as possible, since it now contains MOS devices. As soon as you can, install it into its permanent mount, and connect it up to the power supply leads, especially ground.

POWER SUPPLIES

In using this book, and in building a number of the peripherals described herein, you will find that your computer may not have enough power handling capability for these extras. Some computers, such as the S-100 and SS-50 types have large enough power supplies that a few more chips don't matter. But computers like the TRS-80 and PET are running almost as their limit right out of the box, and an additional supply may be needed.

TTL integrated circuits will need a source of +5V power. This can also be used by CMOS. Operational amplifiers need a balanced plus and minus supply, anywhere from 12 to 15 volts. CMOS and MOSFET sometimes need +12 and −12, as well as −5 volts. RS-232 transmitters will also need balanced plus and minus supplies, anywhere from +/−3 volts to +/−19 volts. The most commonly used value +/−12. The TTL supply will need to be the one with the most capability. You will need at least one ampere of current capability, and five will not be too much. SS-50 and S-100 supplies are capable of supplying up to 25 amperes of current at this voltage.

There are four parts to every power supply. In Fig. B-5, we see that there are the transformer, the

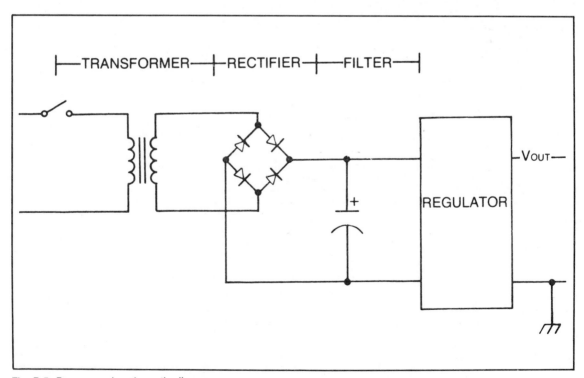

Fig. B-5. Power-supply schematic diagram.

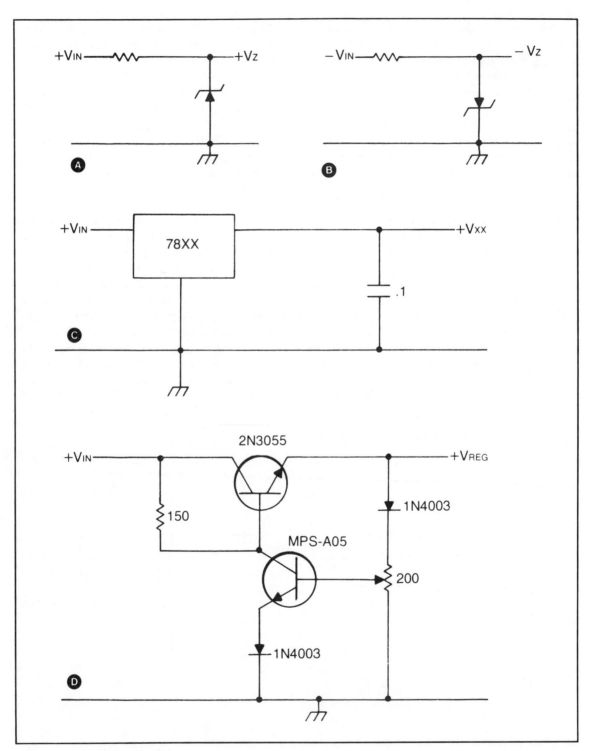

Fig. B-6. Some regulator circuits.

rectifier, the filter, and the regulator.

The transformer converts 110 Vac down to the desired voltage range. The output voltage is usually given in volts rms. For a desired output voltage (V_{out}), the transformer secondary should be at least

$$V_{rms} = 1.11 \ (V_{out} + 4.5) \text{ Volts.}$$

This formula takes into account the diode drops across a full wave bridge and the necessary drop across a 7805-type regulator IC. The formula allows the maximum possible current from the transformer. If you need 5 volts at 3 amperes, then you will need to purchase a transformer with an output voltage of at least 10 volts, with a current-carrying capability of 3 amperes.

Full-wave bridges are available in packages with all the diodes included, or they can be constructed from discrete diodes. Be sure that the diode can handle the current, and the *peak* voltage output of the transformer ($V_{peak} = 1.414 \ V_{rms}$).

The filter is generally nothing more than a large electrolytic capacitor. It will need a breakdown voltage as high or higher than the peak voltage of the transformer, and *be sure* that the negative lead is connected to the lower potential side of the power supply wires. For a positive supply, this is the ground lead. For a negative supply, this will be the power lead. The size of the capacitor is important. Always use at least a 1000 microfarad capacitor. A general rule of thumb is to take the voltage of the unregulated supply, multiply this by the current in amperes, and multiply by a thousand to get the number of microfarads of the filter capacitor.

At this point, you have an unregulated supply. This unregulated voltage is usually what is put out over the bus lines of the computer. The regulator, if one is needed at all, is generally placed right with the devices being powered. The reason for this is

that it is easier and cheaper to make a lot of small regulators than a single regulator for a large amount of current.

You may place any of several types of regulators on the individual cards. For integrated-circuit use, you will want the voltage to be very well regulated, indeed. The only place that will not need high-quality regulation will be the RS-232 supplies. The 7800 series of regulators, also sold under the LM340 series, makes a good set of positive regulators up to one ampere of current, which is sufficient for most applications. Negative supplies will need the 7900 series. The last two digits of the number indicate the regulated voltage of the device: A 7805 regulates to +5 volts, while a 7912 regulates to −12 volts, etc. For less critical applications, a simple Zener-diode and resistor combination will be sufficient. Be careful that the current through the Zener diode, multiplied by the Zener voltage, does not exceed the power rating of the diode.

A few diagrams of some simple regulators, including an adjustable regulator, are shown in Fig. B-6. All regulators need a few more volts to work with than their nominal (output) voltage. The 7800 series requires at least 2.5 volts more than the regulated voltage. For example, a 7805 will have an output of 5.0 volts, but only if the input is at least 7.5 volts, and not more than about 18 volts. The less current used, the higher the input voltage can be. All regulators work best when attached to a heat sink.

Lastly, bypass capacitors cut down on failures by providing an extra reserve of current. For every two ICs on a board, there should be one 0.1 μF capacitor connected directly between the power lead and the ground lead of one of the ICs. Be sure the leads connecting power and ground leads are as short as possible.

Glossary

ACIA—Asynchronous Communications Interface Adapter, a serial-communications interface.

ADC—Analog-to-Digital Converter.

address—A specific byte in a microcomputer's memory. The address points to that byte.

analog—A signal which carries information based upon its voltage level, which can be any value in a range.

AND—A logical state which requires both inputs to be 1s in order for the output to be a 1.

ASCII—American Standard Code for Information Interchange: a way of representing letters and numbers by digital bits.

asynchronous—Serial data communications that is not tied to a clock.

attack—In music, the rate at which the musical note starts.

base—In number theory, the number of digits you count before starting in the next place-value column.

baud rate—The number of digital bits sent per second in serial communications.

BCD—Binary Coded Decimal. A way of representing numbers.

binary—Numbers represented in base two. Also, representation by digital bits.

bit—A single digit or on/off state.

bus—The lines over which a processor communicates with memory and peripherals.

bus driver—Ciruits which improve the fanout capability of a microprocessor.

byte—Eight bits processed in parallel.

checksum—A byte which contains the complement of the lowest-order portion of the sum of a number of other bytes. Used for error detection.

CMOS—Complimentary Metal Oxide Semiconductor. A type of integrated circuitry using low-power field-effect transistors.

cold solder joint—A poor solder connection caused by insufficient heat from the soldering iron.

control codes-The ASCII characters $00 to $1F,

which are used to control devices and indicate conditions.

CPU—Central Processing Unit. The microprocessor.

cycle—The time it takes the computer to execute one instruction.

DAC—Digital-to-Analog Converter.

decimal—Numbers represented in base ten.

digital—Any electronic process which operates solely on the existence of on and off states.

DMA—Direct Memory Access. A way of transferring information to and from a computer without going through the processor.

D-type flip-flop—A data latch whose output is exactly equal to the input when the trigger is high, and will keep that last state when the output is low.

DVM—Digital Volt Meter.

EBCDIC—Extended Binary Coded Decimal International Code. An IBM encoding of letters and numbers.

EPROM—Erasable Programmable Read Only Memory.

Executive—A program in a computer that selects among several other programs to be run, based on an interrupt pulse.

expansion port—A place on a computer to attach additional peripherals.

fanout—The number of TTL chips that can be driven from a given chip.

flowchart—A general description of the programming of a process, drawn for ease in following the logic.

full duplex—Serial communications where data can travel in both directions at the same time.

gate—An electronic device which can perform a logical function.

graphics—The ability to draw pictures with a computer.

half duplex—Serial communications where data can only flow in one direction at a time.

handler—A short machine-language program which takes care of sending or receiving data from a peripheral.

handshaking—A series of signals which indicate that a peripheral is ready to receive data, has received data, has sent data, or is ready to send data.

harmonic—An integer multiple of a fundamental frequency. One of the Fourier components of a signal.

hexadecimal—A number represented in base sixteen.

high—A logical state represented by a "on" signal of +5V.

IC—Integrated Circuit.

IEEE-488—An instrument-communication databus developed by the Hewlett-Packard Company.

initialization—A process setting up parameters for a program or piece of hardware to work. Usually thought of in terms of a PIA or ACIA.

impedance—The ratio of voltage to current. Usually, a measure of a device's current-capability or requirements.

integrated circuit—A "chip" containing more than one electronic component. May contain thousands.

interface—A device connecting the computer's bus to a peripheral.

interrupt vector—The next instruction that a computer will execute upon receipt of an interrupt signal. Specifically, the address of that instruction.

interrupt—A signal that causes the processor to stop what it is doing and begin some special process, pointed to by the interrupt vector.

inverter—A logic device that changes the state of a bit.

I/O mapped—A form of input-output that uses special input-output commands and signals apart from ordinary memory processing.

JK flip-flop—A controllable, presettable device which changes state upon receipt of a trigger or clock pulse.

joystick—Two potentiometers mounted so that they can measure changes in the two-dimensional orientation of a paddle.

keyboard—A typewriter-like peripheral connected to a computer.

latch—A device which holds the input information after the input signal is gone.

least significant—In a place-value system, the rightmost digit.

low—A logical state defined by an "off" state of 0 V.

LSI—Large Scale Integration. Many components on a chip. Usually associated with CMOS circuitry having thousands of devices on a single package.

mass storage—Permanent storage of large amounts of data in a place other than the computer's main memory. Examples would be magnetic tape, paper tape, and disk.

memory map—A diagram of the available locations in a computer's main memory, and what those locations are used for.

memory-mapped I/O—Input/output that treats a peripheral as a set of memory locations and uses memory instructions to execute.

memory—Temporary, rapid-access storage of data bytes in a computer.

microcomputer—A calculating or processing machine which uses a microprocessor as the CPU. Usually restricted to 8 bits parallel.

microprocessor—An LSI integrated circuit whose function is programmable by the user. It is used as the primary logic device in a microcomputer.

microprocessor trainer—A circuit containing a microprocessor and a minimal amount of support circuitry which can function as a bare-bones computer.

minicomputer—A small computer having a capability of processing sixteen bits in parallel.

MIKBUG—Motorola's first operating system in ROM for the 6800.

modulator—A device that connects between a TV set and a video-display device which converts the TV signal to a TV-channel frequency.

monitor—A program, usually residing in ROM, which handles startup of the computer and terminal communications.

Morse code—An early code developed for electrical representation of letters and numbers. Developed for telegraph, but still used today in Amateur and military radio communications.

most significant—In a place-value number system, the leftmost number.

multiprocessing—A system whereby several processors share the same bus.

multitasking—A system whereby tasks are swapped by a processor according to an executive.

NAND—A logic state requiring two 1s at the input to insure a 0 at the output.

NOR—A logic state requiring at least one 1 at the input to ensure a 0 at the output.

nybble—Four bits; half a byte. Used to indicate BCD numbers.

octal—Numbers in base eight.

octave—An interval of frequencies corresponding to a factor-of-two difference between the highest and lowest.

optoisolator—A device that insulates one part of a circuit from another by optical means while still allowing information to pass.

OR—A logical state which requires any one of the inputs to be a 1 before the output can be a 1.

overhead—Incidental processing that must be done before the main task can be done.

paddle—A manual interface that can be varied and whose position can be read by the computer.

parallel—A communications system requiring a separate wire for each data bit to be sent.

parity—An error-checking process that counts the number of 1s in a byte, and compares it to the parity bit. If they are equal, the byte is correct.

peak-sensing—A sample-and-hold amplifier which stores the highest voltage applied to it.

peripheral—Any device connected to a computer

which is not part of the processor, bus, or memory. In most cases, the computer could function without it. Usually an input/output device.

PIA—Peripheral Interface Adaptor. An interface chip for parallel data.

polling loop—An endless loop which will continue to check to see if a signal is present, until that signal does appear.

port—A place to connect a peripheral to a computer.

positve logic—A system of logic where a 1 corresponds to a high state, and is the "true" or "active" form.

power supply—A source of dc current and voltage.

PROM—Programmable Read-Only Memory.

RAM—Random-Access Memory. More specifically, any memory which is capable of both read and write by the processor.

real-time—A function that happens as the computer does it; specifically, interaction between the computer and the user.

reference voltage—A precision voltage that is the basis of comparison in a DAC or ADC.

register—A byte or set of bytes internal to an integrated circuit that can be read by the processor.

regulator—An integrated circuit in the power supply that keeps the voltage within certain limits.

resolution—The measurement precision capability of an instrument, such as a DAC or ADC.

ROM—Read-Only Memory.

RS flip-flop—A data latch that has "set" and "clear" inputs only.

S-100—The data bus of the first home computer, consisting of 100 data lines modeled closely around the 8080 signals.

sample and hold—An analog circuit that will hold the last voltage presented at the input before a "stop" signal was presented to it.

SCR—Silicon-Controlled Rectifier. A diode that will not conduct in the forward direction until it gets a "conduct" signal at the gate.

Selectric—A printing mechanism developed by IBM corporation.

serial—A method of sending data over just one line by sending one bit at a time, in a precise order and frequency.

servo—A device that converts an electrical signal to a mechanical position.

software-The programming of a computer.

soldering—A method of connecting electrical wires together by covering them with a hot tin/lead alloy.

SS-50/SS-30—A data bus used commonly by the 6800 series of microprocessors which is known for its ease of interfacing.

stack—A set of locations in memory that is used by the processor for temporary storage of internal registers during interrupts and subroutines.

start bit—A signal of a serial data line that indicates that the transmission of a bit is beginning.

status register—A register that informs the computer of the condition of a peripheral.

stepping motor—An electric motor which can be controlled to turn only a fraction of a revolution at a time.

stop bit—A signal on a serial-data line that indicates that the byte transmitted is finished.

strobe—A signal sent along with a data bit or bits to indicate that the data is ready. Usually very short.

sustain—The rate at which a musical tone dies away.

synchronous—A serial-data transmission method which requires that a clock signal be sent with it. Data can occur only at specific times.

system clock—The main clock pulse generator of a microprocessor. Also the source of interrupts for a multitasking executive.

top-octave divider—A counter which divides a base frequency into musical tones.

three-state—Integrated circuits whose outputs have three possible states: On, off, and high impedance to act as if they are out of the circuit.

transition—The changing of any logic state.

truth table—The ordering table of the conditions of the outputs of a system of gates depending on the configurations of all the inputs.

TTL—Transistor-Transistor Logic. A family of integrated circuits in very common use in computers.

TTL load—The equivalent capacitance and input impedance of a typical TTL gate.

UART—Universal Asynchronous Receiver/Transmitter. A serial data communications chip. Converts serial to parallel and vice-versa.

volatile memory—Any computer memory that loses the information stored in it when the power goes off.

white noise—Signals of all frequencies. When referred to as a "white noise of a specific frequency range," it is often called a "pink noise."

wire-wrap—A method of electronic construction that does not use soldering, but is fast and suitable for prototype or single-unit production.

word—A collection of bytes whose size depends on the computer. With most microcomputers, a byte and word are the same thing. Technically, it is the number of bits the processor can process in parallel.

XOR—Exclusive OR. A logical process which requires that one and only one of the inputs be a 1 for the output to be a 1.

Bibliography

Horowitz and Hill. *The Art Of Electronics*. Cambridge: Cambridge, 1980.

Deifenderfer. *Principles of Electronic Instrumentation*. 2nd ed. Philadelphia: Saunders, 1979.

Texas Instruments, Inc. *The TTL Data Book for Design Engineers*. Dallas: Texas Instruments, 1976.

Carr. *Microcomputer Interfacing Handbook, A/D and D/A*. Blue Ridge Summit, PA: TAB BOOKS, 1980.

Artwick. *Microcomputer Interfacing*. Englewood Cliffs, New Jersey: Prentice-Hall, 1980.

Zaks and Lesea. *Microprocessor Interfacing Techniques*. Sybex, 1979.

Lancaster. *TV Typewriter Cookbook*. Indianapolis: Howard Sams, 1976.

Streitmatter and Fiore. *Microprocessors, Theory and Applications*. Reston, VA: Reston, 1979.

Cope Corporation. *Maintenance Manual, COPE 1030 Conversational Terminal*. Harris Communications, 1974.

Motorola. *M6800 Microcomputer System Design Data*. Phoenix: Motorola Inc., 1976.

South West Technical Products Corp. *SWTP 6800 Computer System User's Manual*. San Antonio: SWTP, 1976.

Bober, "Taking the First Step," *Byte*. February, 1978, p. 35.

Giacomo, "A Stepping Motor Primer," *Byte*. February, 1979, p. 90.

Banks, "The Waterloo RF Modulator," *Byte*. January, 1978, p. 94.

Parry, "Software Clock for the 6800," *Microcomputing*. January, 1980.

Foster, "Multifarous Cassette Interface," *Microcomputing*. June, 1980.

Winograd, "Try Computer Composition," *Kilobaud*. p. 102.

Marum, "Computer Music the Easy Way," *Microcomputing*. December, 1980. p. 72.

Barbier, "Colorful Baud-Rate Generator," *Microcomputing*. July, 1980, p. 182.

Derynick, "Bit Rate Clocks for Your Serial Interface," *Microcomputing*. October, 1979, p. 138.

Motorola. *Applications Note on MC1408L8*. Phoenix: Motorola Inc., 1975.

Sabot, "BASIC Control of Servomechanisms," *Kilobaud*. December, 1978, p. 88.

Struve, "A $19 Music Interface," *Byte*. December, 1977, p. 48.

Hallen, "TRS-80 Printer Interfaces; Serial and Parallel Designs," *Microcomputing*. January, 1980, p. 134.

Kitsz, "Build a TRS-80 to Synthesizer Interface," *Microcomputing*. December, 1980, p. 32.

Keener, "A Better Printer," *Microcomputing*. December, 1980, p.23.

Smith, "Build Your Own Interface," *Kilobaud*. June, 1977, p. 22.

National Semiconductor, *ADC0817 Single Chip Data Acquisition System Specification Sheet*. Santa Clara: National Semiconductor, 1977.

Analog Devices. *AD584 Pin Programmable Precision Voltage Reference Specification Sheet*. Norwood, MA: Analog Devices, 1977.

Ciarcia, "Try an 8-Channel DVM Cocktail!," *Byte*. December, 1977, p. 76.

Yob, "Get Your Pet on the IEEE-488 Bus," *Microcomputing*. July, 1980, p. 22, August, 1980, p. 134, and September, 1980, p. 44.

Yob. *PET User's Manual*. Palo Alto, CA: Mind's Eye Software.

Pytilk, "PET I/O Port Expander," *Microcomputing*. June, 1980, p. 58.

Ciarcia, "Tune In and Turn On!," *Byte*. April, 1978, p. 114, and May 1978, p. 77.

Lessley, "Computer-Controlled Triac Dimmer," *Microcomputing*. October, 1980, p. 92.

Olson, "Controlling the Real World," *Byte*. March, 1978, p. 174.

Walton, "Controlling DC Motors," *Byte*. July, 1978.

Rawson, "Clock/Calendar for the 6809," *Microcomputing*. July, 1981, p. 132.

William Barden, Jr. *TRS-80 Models I, III, & Color Computer Interfacing Projects*. Howard W. Sams, Indianapolis, 1983.

Micheal Angersham, *et al. The Anatomy of the Commodore*. Abacus, Grand Rapids, 1983.

Black Box Catalog of Data Communications and Computer Devices. Black Box, Pittsburgh, 1986.

Lewis Eggebrecht, *Interfacing to the IBM Personal Computer*. Howard W. Sams, Indianapolis, 1983.

Macintosh Software Supplement Guide. Apple Computer, Cupertino, CA 1985.

Apple Computer, *Inside Macintosh*. Addison Wesley, 1985.

OEM Manual, SA400 Minifloppy Diskette Storage Drive. Shugard associates, 1977.

Disk Systems, SSB disk system reference manual, Smoke signal Broadcasting, Westlake Village, CA 1980.

F. Merkowitz. "Signal Processing for Optical Bar Code Scanning", *Byte*, December, 1978, p. 77.

W. Banks, "Examples of Machine Readable Printed Software, *Byte*, December, 1978, p. 12.

K. Smith, "MODEM/XMODEM Protocol Explained," MAUG data library DL8, January, 1980.

G. Young. *The Selectric Interface, a Hands-on Approach*. Wayne Green Publications, Peterborough, NH, 1982.

M. Wesley, "Macintosh Plus, Packed with Power," *MacUser*, March, 1986.

Index

Other Bestsellers From TAB

Other Bestsellers From TAB